Studies in Modern History

General Editor: **J. C. D. Clark**, Joyce and Elizabeth Hall Distinguished Professor of British History, University of Kansas

Titles include:

Jonathan Clark and Howard Erskine-Hill (*editors*)
SAMUEL JOHNSON IN HISTORICAL CONTEXT

Bernard Cottret (*editors*)
BOLINGBROKE'S POLITICAL WRITINGS
The Conservative Enlightenment

Richard R. Follet
EVANGELICALISM, PENAL THEORY AND THE POLITICS OF CRIMINAL LAW REFORM IN ENGLAND, 1808–30

Andrew Godley
JEWISH IMMIGRANT ENTREPRENEURSHIP IN NEW YORK AND LONDON, 1880–1914

Phillip Hicks
NEOCLASSICAL HISTORY AND ENGLISH CULTURE
From Clarendon to Hume

Mary Keay
WILLIAM WORDSWORTH'S GOLDEN AGE THEORIES DURING THE INDUSTRIAL REVOLUTION IN ENGLAND, 1750–1850

William M. Kuhn
DEMOCRATIC ROYALISM
The Transformation of the British Monarchy, 1861–1950

Kim Lawes
PATERNALISM AND POLITICS
The Revival of Paternalism in Early Nineteenth-Century Britain

Marisa Linton
THE POLITICS OF VIRTUE IN ENLIGHTENMENT FRANCE

Nancy D. LoPatin
POLITICAL UNIONS, POPULAR POLITICS AND THE GREAT REFORM ACT OF 1832

Karin J. MacHardy
WAR, RELIGION AND COURT PATRONAGE IN HABSBURG AUSTRIA
The Social and Cultural Dimensions of Political Interaction, 1521–1622

Marjorie Morgan
NATIONAL IDENTITIES AND TRAVEL IN VICTORIAN BRITAIN

James Muldoon
EMPIRE AND ORDER
The Concept of Empire, 800–1800

W.D. Rubinstein and Hilary Rubinstein
PHILOSEMITISM
Admiration and Support for Jews in the English-Speaking World, 1840–1939

Julia Rudolph
WHIG POLITICAL THOUGHT AND THE GLORIOUS REVOLUTION
James Tyrell and the Theory of Resistance

Lisa Steffan
TREASON AND NATIONAL IDENTITY
Defining a British State, 1608–1820

Timothy J. Sinclair and Kenneth P. Thomas (*editors*)
STRUCTURE AND AGENCY IN INTERNATIONAL CAPITAL MOBILITY

Lynne Taylor
BETWEEN RESISTANCE AND COLLABORATION
Popular Protest in Northern France, 1940–45

Studies in Modern History
Series Standing Order ISBN 0–333–79328–5
(*outside North America only*)

You can receive future titles in this series as they are published by placing a standing order. Please contact your bookseller or, in case of difficulty, write to us at the address below with your name and address, the title of the series and the ISBN quoted above.

Customer Services Department, Macmillan Distribution Ltd, Houndmills, Basingstoke, Hampshire RG21 6XS, England

---

War, Religion and Court Patronage in Habsburg Austria

The Social and Cultural Dimensions of Political Interaction, 1521–1622

Karin J. MacHardy

palgrave
macmillan

First published 2003 by
PALGRAVE MACMILLAN
Houndmills, Basingstoke, Hampshire RG21 6XS and
175 Fifth Avenue, New York, N.Y. 10010
Companies and representatives throughout the world.

PALGRAVE MACMILLAN is the global academic imprint of the Palgrave Macmillan division of St Martin's Press, LLC and of Palgrave Macmillan Ltd. Macmillan® is a registered trademark in the United States, United Kingdom and other countries. Palgrave is a registered trademark in the European Union and other countries.

ISBN 0–333–57241–6

This book is printed on paper suitable for recycling and
made from fully managed and sustained forest sources.

A catalogue record for this book is available
from the British Library.

Library of Congress Cataloging-in-Publication Data
MacHardy, Karin Jutta.
War, religion and court patronage in Habsburg Austria: the social and cultural dimensions of political interaction, 1521–1622/Karin J. MacHardy.
p. cm. – (Studies in modern history)
Includes bibliographical references and index.
ISBN 0–333–57241–6
1. Austria – Politics and government – 16th century. 2. Austria – Politics and government – 17th century. 3. Habsburg, House of. 4. Patronage, Political – Austria – History – 16th century. 5. Patronage, Political – Austria – History – 17th century. 6. Austria – Military policy. 7. Courts and courtiers – Austria. 8. Church and state – Austria – History – 16th century. 9 Church and State – Austria – History – 17th century. 10. Austria – Kings and rulers. 11. Vienna (Austria) – Social life and customs. I. Title. II. Studies in modern history (Palgrave(Firm))
DB65 M26 2002
943.6'03-dc21 2001050806

10 9 8 7 6 5 4 3 2 1
12 11 10 09 08 07 06 05 04 03

Printed and bound in Great Britain by
Antony Rowe Ltd, Chippenham and Eastbourne

To Mike

Contents

List of Tables

List of Figures

Acknowledgements

'All good things take time', says a German proverb, but many friends and colleagues will be greatly relieved to see that this book is finally finished. They will find it a different and much broader study than initially anticipated and, I think, an improved one too. I would like to thank all my long-suffering mentors and teachers, especially Jan deVries, Gene Brucker and Gerald Feldman. This book would not have come to fruition without the unflagging moral support of all my friends during various stages of production, but particularly Stanley Berger, Bonnie Miles-Kamp, Lita Kurth, Judy and Paul Lansing, Albert Levy, Ulrich Nocken, Tip Ragan, Norma von Ragenfeld-Feldman and Isabel Tirado. My mother, Hilde Walzl, frequently provided the means to keep body and soul together, and Mausie and Muckie the calming purrs while writing. But my special thanks goes to Michael C. Howard, for his generosity and intellectual nourishment. His insights and suggestions contributed significantly to clarifying my arguments and my Austro-Germanic meanderings.

This is a cross-disciplinary study and I am indebted to the ideas of many other scholars, in particular to Charles Crothers, who led me to Bourdieu; to Jack A. Goldstone, who gave me a store of concepts to understand early modern rebellions; and to Sharon Kettering, who first introduced me to theories of patronage. I also would like to thank the members of the Interdisciplinary Reading Group at the University of Waterloo and Wilfrid Laurier University – Allan Cheyne, Lorne Dawson, Fraser Easton, Michael Howard, and Andrew and Harriet Lyons – who did much to keep alive my belief that interdisciplinary work is important. Commentators and audiences at conferences of the American Historical Association, the German Studies Association, Sixteenth Century Studies and the History of the Family Conference produced helpful questions and interventions, and I am particularly grateful to Jonathan Dewald for incisive critiques. I have also benefited from many conversations with historians at the University of Vienna, Austria, especially Peter Feldbauer, Gernot Heiss, and Herbert Knittler, who provided encouragement and an intellectual community during my years of isolated 'grubbing in the archives'. I also enjoyed brainstorming with Beatrix Bastl and Thomas Winkelbauer.

My research was productive to a large extent because of the help of many archivists and librarians, particularly at the Niederösterreichische Landesarchiv and the Niederöstereichische Landesbibliothek in Vienna, the Doe Library at the University of California at Berkeley, and the Dana Porter Library at the University of Waterloo. In addition, I would like to thank Gail Heideman, the former secretary of the History Department at the

University of Waterloo, for reformatting the tables, and all of my research assistants, especially Linden Hilson and Christine Brandt, who were most helpful in producing the charts.

I am very grateful for the generous support of the Social Sciences and Humanities Research Council of Canada, and for grants from the Ministry of Culture and Science of the Austrian government. Finally, I warmly thank Keith Povey and his colleagues for efficient copy-editing and index preparation.

KARIN J. MACHARDY

Versions of Tables 2.2 and 4.6 and Figures 4.6, 6.1–6.4 have appeared in MacHardy, 'The Rise of Absolutism and Noble Rebellion in Early Modern Habsburg Austria, 1570 to 1620', in *Comparative Studies in Society and History* 34/3 (July 1992), pp. 407–38; and versions of Figures 4.6, 4.7, 4.9 and Tables 4.1–4.6 in MacHardy, 'Social Mobility and Noble Rebellion in Early Modern Habsburg Austria', *History & Society in Central Europe* 2 (1994), pp. 97–39. A section of Chapter 5 appeared in MacHardy, 'Cultural Capital, Family Strategies and Noble Identity in Early Modern Habsburg Austria 1579–1620)', *Past & Present* 163 (May 1999), pp. 36–75, and large parts of Chapter 4 appeared in MacHardy, 'Social Mobility and Noble Rebellion in Early Modern Habsburg Austria', *History & Society in Central Europe* 2 (1994), pp. 97–139.

List of Abbreviations

Archives

HHStA	Haus-, Hof-, und Staatsarchiv, Vienna
Hs	Handschrift
HstA	Herrenstandsarchiv
NÖLA	Niederösterreichisches Landesarchiv
ÖNB	Österreichische National Bibliothek
RStA	Ritterstands Archiv
StA	Ständisches Archiv

Journals

Erg. Bd.	*Ergänzungsband* (special volume)
AÖG	*Archiv für Österreichische Geschichte*
JbGPÖ	*Jahrbuch für die Geschichte des Protestantismus in Österreich*
JbLkNÖ	*Jahrbuch für Landeskunde von Niederösterreich*
NF	*Neue Folge* (new series)
MIÖG	*Mitteilungen des Instituts für Österreichische Geschichtesforschung*
MOÖLA	*Mitteilungen des Oberösterreichischen Landesarchiv*

Places

NÖ	Niederösterreich (Lower Austria)
OÖ	Oberösterreich (Upper Austria)
VOMB	Viertel ober dem Manhartsberg (District above the Manharts Mountain
VUMB	Viertel unter dem Manhartsberg (District below the Manharts Mountain
VOWW	Viertel ober dem Wiener Wald (District above the Vienna Woods)
VUWW	Viertel unter dem Wiener Wald (District below the Vienna Woods)

Introduction

Historians usually consider the Bohemian Revolt of 1618–20 as the starting-point of the so-called Thirty Years' War. Whether they view the early stages of the war as the outcome of long-term rivalries among European powers, or as a Habsburg-centred, political-religious conflict, they have neglected to provide a systematic or comprehensive study of its origins. Most monographs in English that seek to include the Habsburgs' lands must rely on older research that concentrates on the Bohemian kingdom. Furthermore, Habsburg historians themselves have taken little interest in the developments which culminated in 1619 in a grand alliance of Protestant Estates from most of the dynasty's lands, even though they view the defeat of the Confederation as a crucial divide in Habsburg history. Hans Sturmberger's monograph of 1959 is still the standard work in German on the beginnings of the 'Bohemian' revolt that also pays attention to the involvement of the Austrian Estates.[1] The stronger interest that Czech scholars have traditionally shown in the Bohemian side of the uprising also waned after Polišenský's important contributions during the 1960s,[2] although Czech, Moravian and Silesian historians have recently renewed their concern with the pre-Confederation Estates.[3] It is not surprising, then, that Myron P. Gutmann, for example, concludes that 'the causes of the defenestration and the war which followed are easy to ascertain', and repeats the conventional interpretation of Habsburg historians, who have viewed the beginning of the war similarly 'as a conflict in central Europe between the Catholic Habsburg emperor and his Bohemian subjects over religion and imperial power'.[4] Like the conception of a unified Thirty Years' War, the notion that its starting point was a Bohemian affair has become something akin to a belief that endures solely because it is repeated so frequently.

This book analyzes the origins of the Civil War in the Habsburg lands by providing a case study of the much-neglected involvement of the Austrian Protestant nobility.[5] Although I do not ignore the role of European rivalries, I do focus on problems internal to the Habsburg territories and the Holy Roman Empire, which I consider to have been more important in transforming the complex relations between Catholic emperors and Protestant Estates into violent conflict. My study emphasizes social, economic and cultural dimensions of this interaction, but also gives considerable weight to how they are connected to political developments and differences. In order to explain why elites opposed centralizing monarchs, it is also necessary to determine when they co-operated with them.[6] The scope of this study therefore extends far beyond the Civil War to examine the relationship between Habsburgs and Estates during the entire century before 1618. In doing so it addresses crucial issues about the growth of the early modern state and the nature of power.

Because their domain was cobbled together rather late and remained a composite monarchy until the very end, the Habsburgs' state-building efforts can add both light and shade to the history of the early modern state. However, historians of their territories generally have not participated in recent discussions among theorists of state formation, such as Charles Tilly and Michael Mann, who have stressed the military impetus to European state growth and its connection to social and economic issues.[7] By contrast, historians of early modern Western Europe are re-examining the contribution of monarchs and subjects to the emergence of the modern nation-state and the nature of early modern rulership.[8] Probably one reason for this difference is that we still know surprisingly little about the nature and forces of Habsburg state-building during the early modern period. As Paula Sutter-Fichtner pointed out, 'for all of the useful and often distinguished work that has been done on the early modern Habsburg state ... we are still not really sure how it got to be what it became, not to mention what made it institutionally operational'.[9] As an attempt to fill this gap, my book contributes to a number of important recent and older historiographical controversies. One of these concerns the nature and extent of co-operation between centre and locality in state centralization; the others relate to the social, economic and cultural dimension of political interaction in early modern Europe, and to the nature of absolutism.

The study of the relationship between early modern rulers and Estates (*Stände*) has, itself, had a long history and used to be an important topic of Habsburg historiography. Traditionally, debates centred on the concept of the estatist state (*Ständestaat*), which denoted the dualistic rule of monarch and Estates. Searching for the long-term origins of the modern state, older constitutional historians were particularly concerned with the respective contribution of rulers and *Stände* in the state-building process, and the interplay of politics and religion in conflicts between them. During the early nineteenth century, conservative interpretations tended to view the relationship as a political struggle for hegemony, in which Habsburg monarchs were the heroes acting as a progressive force in state-building against the dark forces of the feudal nobility.[10] This changed with the emergence of nationalist and liberal historians during the late nineteenth century and the early part of the twentieth century, who began to stress the division of power between Estates and rulers from the Middle Ages until the seventeenth century. Most believed that this power balance between princes and elite was interrupted only occasionally by conflicts, and, supportive of a united Germany or a liberal democracy, viewed the role of the Estates in centralization and the forging of national unity in a more positive light.[11] German liberal historians, in fact, began to idealize the role of the *Stände*, considering them as a counter-force to absolute monarchy and even as precursors of modern representative institutions.[12] Anti-Habsburg, Czech nationalist historiography also turned the Bohemian Estates into the heroes of failed nation-building, and this reassessment allowed for a greater appreciation of the importance of religion because of the emphasis the Bohemians had placed on confessional concerns in their relations with the Habsburgs during the early modern period.[13]

Concentrating on the Austrian territories, Otto Brunner's important *Land und Herrschaft* (1939) gave this perspective of progressive state development a novel twist which, however, was an equally organicist argument. Resisting the notion of there being late medieval antecedents of the modern national state, Brunner considered the dualism between Estates and Habsburgs to be a logical continuation of early feudal practices and a peculiarly Germanic development. Its early modern version, he insisted, was new only in so far as it became institutionalized in a dualistic estatist state. He also suggested that, while the growth of the Estates' power developed in parallel with that of rulers, the latter strove to overcome the dualism and the ultimate victory belonged to 'princely absolutism'.[14] Although a few post-Second World War Western historians persisted in tracing modern representative institutions to the medieval and early modern Estates in order to explain the reasons for the failure of the German *Stände*,[15] others preferred increasingly to question the contribution of the nobility to parliamentary traditions and national unity, or abandoned altogether the search for the long-term origins of the modern state.[16]

German and Habsburg constitutional historians none the less continued to maintain the framework of dualism and to stress the rulers' initiative in overcoming the dualistic *Ständestaat*. And, when analysing the role of the 'Bohemian' conflict of 1618–20 in this process, Habsburg historians in the West, such as Hans Sturmberger, began to emphasize that religious and political motives were closely intertwined, concluding that the 'Thirty Years' War began primarily as a confessional war'.[17] While a few scholars continued to stress political over religious motives, most Austrian historians agreed that the Habsburg defeat of the Protestant nobility in 1620 was the key to implementing absolutist policies in the Bohemian and Austrian territories.[18] Among non-Marxist Austrian historians, this has remained the dominant interpretation of the causes and consequences of the 'Bohemian' rebellion.

Highlighting the autonomous interests of the state and the contributions of the Estates to state-building have proved to be lasting contributions of the older constitutional histories. But a major problem with their adherence to the dualism model was the treatment of the Estates as a homogenous group, and neglect of internal conflicts and divisions, especially within the nobility. Moreover, claiming the emergence of a Habsburg absolutist state in the early seventeenth century has remained largely unsupported by evidence, and, despite the focus on political authority, the dualism school failed to address crucial issues about the nature of power and how it connected to social, economic and cultural life.

This study views the growth of the Habsburg state as the product of continous bargaining beween rulers and subjects, but at the same time cautions against stressing unduly collaboration at the expense of contentious politics, especially during the sixteenth and early seventeenth centuries. In fact, I consider opposition to Habsburg authority to be integral to the interactive political process. As Part I demonstrates, elites and common subjects participated actively in extending the ruler's power to regulate social relations, and to build central institutions and larger armies. The conjuncture of religious Reformation, war with the Ottomans, and demographic change in particular fostered the interdependence between the centre and regions, making bargaining between them an ongoing requirement. At the same time, this created potential sources for conflict, especially when problems arose over the allocation of resources. Negotiations between claims and counterclaims thus contributed to state formation, but the outcome of this bargaining varied considerably, and depended on the nature and availability of resources, on the rules and conventions that had been established for negotations, and the sanctions that were put in place to enforce agreements.

Examining this growing interpenetration between Habsburgs and elites, and the conditions for the success and failure of bargaining during the century before 1620 is another aim of this book. Understandably, the co-operation of the nobility with the emperors depended above all on how useful it found political consolidation, and whether the latter upheld existing social and power relations. I therefore analyze the incentives the Habsburgs devised for gaining elite co-operation and integrating the nobility into a state-bounded role, and how this affected the bargaining process between them. The two major strategies they relied on during the late sixteenth and early seventeenth centuries were those of enforcing ideological conformity and centralizing the patronage system at the Imperial Court (comprising household and administration).[19] Nobles shared certain objectives with the Habsburg rulers and developed an interest in the benefits they could derive from enlarging the resources and co-ordinating the activity of the state, but they also pursued distinct goals. Similarily, the various groups within the nobility had different interests, both in terms of endowments and with respect to religion and politics. Determining the interests of nobles and monarchs is a central objective of this study.

Part I argues that it was not long-term constitutional problems as such that caused opposition to Habsburg rule, but the conjuncture of confessional problems with security concerns at a time when emperors began to distribute resources selectively among the elite. The Protestant majority was not a homogenous group, and substantial social and economic differences existed between them, which also fluctuated over time. But neither inequalities in wealth nor financial difficulties determined the various political strategies Protestant nobles pursued in 1618–20. What the opposition shared was a similar experience in the distribution of Habsburg patronage, and I demonstrate the importance of this. The subjective evidence also reveals that material interests were fused inseparably with spiritual and political interests, which inhibited a peaceful resolution of disputes. The first section further shows the existence of deep-seated political and cultural differences within the elite of the Bohemian and Austrian lands, which provided the necessary conditions for generating a grand alliance of largely Protestant nobles against the Habsburgs. But they were not sufficient. As I show in more detail in Part II, these religious and political divisions crystallized as discontent because they were fuelled through a combination of long-term and short-term problems arising from the distribution of Imperial patronage.

Among historians of Western Europe, 'absolutism' has become a highly controversial concept, and most circumscribe their use of the term, recognizing that absolutist government did not correspond to the ideal proposed by seventeenth-century theorists. In contrast, Habsburg historians have continued to view absolutism as a distinct stage of state formation rather than questioning the use of the concept. Thus, Robert Bireley, has argued that the emperor Ferdinand II ended 'the *Ständestaat* in the Habsburg lands' and that his 'was a practical rather than a theoretical form of absolutism'. At the same time, he also agreed with Robert J. W. Evans that the Habsburg monarchy after 1620 was 'based on a system of co-operation among dynasty, aristocracy or estates', which also creates tensions with his other arguments that Habsburg absolutism was characterized by 'an element of centralization, princely predominance over the estates, and the advancement of Catholicism'.[20] In fact, Evans' stress that enforcing ideological consensus led to compromise, shared objectives, and continued co-operation between Crown and aristocracy after 1620 only throws further doubt on absolutism as a useful category for Habsburg state-building. If religious ideology provided the basis for seventeenth-century absolutism that was characterized by co-operation between ruler and nobles, the question arises of why the re-Catholicization of Poland did not have comparable results, and whether we should not also define England and Sweden as absolutist governments.[21]

This book demonstrates in Part I that there is no evidence warranting the absolutist designation to Habsburg rule during the sixteenth or seventeenth centuries. Habsburg historians have tended to assume, rather than justify by research, that absolutism, or 'confessional absolutism', was indeed a distinct stage in the growth of the state. Utilizing Michael Mann's conception of the state as organized networks of power, I develop an alternative model of early modern rulership to that of absolutism, one that is based on the capacity to co-ordinate subjects. It emphasizes the crucial importance of distinguishing clearly between the growth of 'infrastructural' and 'autocratic' state power, because early modern rulers extended their infrastructure and radius of central co-ordination while their *control over* society remained relatively weak. It was the simultaneous growth of infrastructural power on the part of ruler and Estates that intensified their interdependence and the conflicts between them. The concept of the 'co-ordinating state' allows me to distinguish analytically between the early modern and the medieval forms of rule, while taking into consideration the continuity between them, and to relinquish the many other ambiguous terms currently in use to describe early modern states. Furthermore, it makes it possible to view constitutional and statist regimes as belonging to the same type of state, one weak in autocratic control, but gaining in infrastructural power. Explaining the variations between absolutist or constitutional regimes has been particularly controversial among historians, perhaps because the dichotomy itself is problematic.[22]

It should be stressed, however, that few historians have viewed absolutism as a despotic, or purely bureaucratic, form of government , as some critics claim.[23] In fact, most would concur with Rudolf Vierhaus that if 'absolutism means the unlimited exercise of authority at will by a sovereign territorial lord, then absolutism did not exist in legal terms within the imperial community. But it also did not exist practically either, because the unlimited exercise of authority was restrained by local and estatist rights and by an inadequate administrative apparatus.' Although Vierhaus regards absolutism as little more than 'a system of rule in which the sovereign acted as legislator and supreme judge and possessed military and supreme administrative authority', he insists that in 'this system the sovereign exercised authority *without* the consent of other institutions or groups, but he did observe the rights of his subjects [italics added]'.[24]

Critics of the concept of absolutism, in contrast, have begun to stress instead that most early modern monarchs exercised authority *with* the consent of their elites, but, in doing so, have obscured the distinction between medieval and early modern rulers. As these critics have pointed out, the claims of early modern monarchs to being the sole source of the law and ruling by divine right was 'as old as the institution [of monarchy] itself', as was their continued dependence on local authorities, especially the nobility, in implementing their policies. However, the arguments of the critics, such as Nicholas Henshall, that there was not much difference between the medieval and early modern state, is much less convincing.[25]

Unfortunately, the debates over the concept of absolutism among West European historians have become connected with politically charged issues associated with the newer approaches in historiography.[26] They also have lacked clarification because most of those who object strongly to the use of 'absolutism' to describe the political regimes of seventeenth-century Europe continue applying the concept, rather than provide an alternative conceptual framework that would enable us to compare and distinguish early modern government from medieval and modern states.[27] Other scholars who underscore the importance of legislative activity in early modern state-building have suggested the notion of a 'well-ordered police state' that aimed to expand and regulate the welfare of taxpaying subjects. Although this highlights an important aspect, the term 'police state' exaggerates, as does the concept of 'absolutism', the domestic control of early modern monarchs over their subjects, and few historians have opted to use it.[28]

Marxist historiography has made its own contribution to both the debate over absolutism and the 'Bohemian' Civil War. But, even though I stress the importance of material interests and socioeconomic differences, my focus differs sharply from Marxian approaches that emphasize class struggles between nobles and bourgeoisie, and argue that they 'grew out of the complicated economic and social situation that prevailed in the period of transition from feudalism to capitalism'.[29] Instead, I stress that the conflict was within the nobility, and I view the Civil War as the outcome of a multifaceted process in which political, cultural, demographic and social problems arose within a context of rivalry over resources, pitting a section of the Protestant nobility against a small Catholic state elite. Although the Protestant opposition tended to include older nobles, while Catholic and non-Catholic royalists attracted newcomers, the confessional difference was more important than social status. Thus, while my study does not support the idea of a class struggle between a declining nobility and a rising middle class, it does conclude that competition over social and other forms of capital within the nobility, and especially between Catholics and Protestants, contributed to the formation of political opposition to the Habsburgs.

Although most Czech Marxists refused to emplot the events of 1618–20 as a bourgeois revolution, they emphasized the economic and social tensions created by the transformation from feudalism to capitalism. During the early 1970s, Polišenský and Snider stressed the economic decline of the lesser Bohemian nobility, but also claimed that restricted opportunities for wealthier landowners 'led to the political radicalization' of the nobility. So, from the end of the sixteenth century they 'were pushed into opposition to the regime, whose feudal-Catholic program conflicted with the Hussite and Reformed-Humanist tradition of the country'.[30] Since the Bohemian opposition party was composed largely of small and medium property owners, this suggested to them a causal connection between economic deterioration and political activism. It remains unclear, however, why the moderately wealthy, whose economic losses (measured by the size of their landholdings) were clearly minimal, were politically the most active group, and why the leadership was in the hands of the richest lords.[31] And Polišenský's and Snider's data leaves us in the dark as to what proportion of landholders from each property category joined the rebels, and what percentages remained loyal or neutral in the conflict.

My own analysis of the Lower Austrian nobility shows that the decline of landholdings among the lesser nobility was connected to the decrease in the number of families belonging to the Estate of Knights, and this was due to biological extinction and to upward social mobility. Although the social advancement was a consequence of Habsburg strategies in the distribution of patronage, and therefore contributed to the deterioration of relations with Protestants, the size of landholdings and differences of wealth did not determine whether or not Protestant nobles joined the opposition party, nor is there evidence that rebels suffered from declining agrarian incomes. Again, this does not deny that material factors played a role. On the contrary. But they were of a different type. My study shows that the exclusion of Protestants from court patronage, at a time when noble families grew in size, threatened their dynastic reproduction, and this was a major contributing factor to the deterioration of relations with Habsburgs and Catholics.

Since the 1970s, Western historians have cast serious doubt on whether the European nobility experienced economic difficulties, competition from a rising bourgeoisie, and, subsequently, a crisis of identity characterized by loss of purpose and self-confidence.[32] Most recent research shows that, as a group, the nobility managed to overcome financial problems, and to retain its powers at the local level, in the army and in central government. While the previous emphasis on economic decline had led historians of Western Europe to exaggerate the opposition of nobles to centralizing monarchs, some revisionist historians now largely reject the role of material motivations altogether, and overstress the symbiosis between rulers and nobles, and the collaboration of the Estates in state-building. This has detracted from our understanding of why nobles put up widespread opposition to monarchs across Europe in the late sixteenth and early seventeenth centuries.

British Marxist historians and other Marxists have made important contributions to the debate concerning material interests and the social basis of absolutism, but they falsely characterized the issues as they arose in the Habsburg case. Initially, they stressed, like Friedrich Engels, the autonomous power of absolutist rulers, which they believed rested on balancing the interests of the nobility and the rising bourgeoisie.[33] This equilibrium theory was contradicted, both by the persistent feudal characteristics of Habsburg society and economy, and the absence of a strong urban class. It also failed to explain why the country with the strongest bourgeoisie, England, did not produce more autonomous rulers. Perry Anderson therefore argued differently, portraying absolutism as '*a redeployed and recharged apparatus of feudal domination, ...* the new political carapace of a threatened nobility', which was 'determined by the spread of commodity production and exchange'. He tried to resolve the paradox of why nobles revolted against absolutist rulers, who were the instruments of the maintenance of their domination, but in fact restated it when claiming that the noble class 'had to be broken into the harsh and unawaited discipline of its own conditions of government'. Once defeated, it 'slowly transformed itself to fit the new, unwanted exigencies of its own State power.' Anderson insisted simultaneously that, while the political consolidation of the state created noble discontent, this never turned into a 'united aristocratic onslaught on the monarchy, for the two were tied together by an umbilical class cord'.[34] Despite the obvious tensions in the argument, Marxian historians of the Habsburg lands also insisted that the absolutist state became an instrument of the dominant noble class,[35] and a number of non-Marxist historians followed suit in arguing for the closeness of interests between crown and ruling class.

A major drawback of these dominant-class theories is the neglect of the possibility, stressed by traditional constitutional historians and early Marxists, that rulers might have pursued interests independent of the dominant class.[36] Recognizing the importance of this, as my study does, seems essential in order to explain why rulers acted against noble interests, and why nobles sometimes revolted. For the most part, Marxian historians of the Habsburg lands have also ignored the political and socioeconomic divisions within the nobility, and how these affected relations with the crown. In particular, they overlooked how early modern monarchs distributed patronage in the form of offices, titles and other endowments to gain elite cooperation, and how this created competition and dissatisfaction within the dominant class, a neglect they share with non-Marxist Austrian historians.

Nevertheless, the enduring contribution of Marxist historiography has been in drawing attention to the social bases of princely power, and to divisions between Estates or classes. Moreover, the British Marxist historians influenced the emergence of a social-science-orientated social history, which received additional impetus from the French *Annales* school, and drew on pre-1945 Central European historiographical traditions.[37] Together with shifts in the social and political environment, this has left its mark on early modern history writing in Germany and Austria. During the 1970s, a number of Austrian scholars, especially those connected with the Institute of Economic and Social History in Vienna, began to take a keen interest in the social and economic history of the nobility. Initially focusing on the study of the emergence and social structure of Estates during the Middle Ages, since the 1980s they have turned to analyzing noble landholding, lifestyle, and court culture.[38] Nevertheless, they have shown relatively little interest in the social and cultural dimensions of Habsburg state-building, or the interaction between rulers and nobles, on which I concentrate in this book.

Since the late 1980s Czech, Slovak and Moravian scholars have not only abandoned Marxian perspectives, but have generally moved away from socioeconomic interpretations of the relations between Habsburgs and the nobility towards treating political and religious issues as autonomous.[39] Consequently, their interpretation of the relations between rulers and nobles has come to resemble conventional views of non-Marxian Habsburg historians, who have continued to view the 'Bohemian' rebellion as the first stage of the Thirty Years' War, and as the product of a long-standing constitutional dualism between emperors and the princes, or Estates, which became submerged in the religious dualism that emerged with the Protestant Reformation.[40]

New approaches in social history have also prompted German historians to pay greater attention to social and economic aspects of the Reformation. Adapting the concepts of social science to political history, they began to view 'confessionalization' as the motor of early modern state formation. Building on Ernst Walter Zeeden's work dealing with the impact of the Reformation on German society, and Gerhard Oestreich's linkage of the origin of absolutism to religion and social disciplining, Wolfgang Reinhard advanced the idea that the various Protestant Reformations all developed similar strategies and institutional structures to enforce confessional conformity. This cultural homogenization of society helped to enforce social control over subjects and thereby served territorial consolidation.[41] The emphasis of this 'confessional school' on the connection of religion and social disciplining in state-building dovetails with the stress placed by constitutional historians on the interlocking motives of religion and politics.

Along similar lines, a number of Habsburg historians have focused on social disciplining and confessionalization.[42] Nevertheless, others, such as Robert Bireley, who adopted the concept of 'confessional absolutism' to the re-Catholization attempts of the emperors, have continued to neglect the social and economic aspects of confessionalization.[43] The most recent work that evaluated the Estates of the Bohemian territories during the century before the 1618–20 uprising on the basis of primary documents, has very little to say about the social and economic forces behind state integration, or how they shaped relations between rulers and Estates. This signifies the continued fascination with political and religious problems. Even Ronald Asch's (1997) synthesis on the Thirty Years' War, which is generally more sensitive to socioeconomic history, does not question this conventional view of the causes of the 'Bohemian' War.[44]

Although I use the general framework of confessionalization, I pay far more attention to the social and cultural aspects of centralization, and put less stress on the process of social disciplining imposed from above. As I mentioned earlier, I emphasize particularly the interaction between social, economic, cultural and political issues. But because I do not privilege Habsburg rulers as the dominant agent in state formation, I also maintain that the ability of the early modern state in exercising power in localities rested on both the expansion of infrastructural reach and the capacity to secure the co-operation of brokers of power in local communities. And, in order to explain the role of patronage in early modern state formation, Part II of this book focuses on the social, economic and cultural interests and backgrounds of nobles, and pays attention to the distribution of various forms of resources at the Habsburg court during the half century preceding 1620.

Depite the fact that the history of patronage at the English and French courts has received considerable attention from scholars of various disciplines, we know little about either the methods of administrative recruitment and social advancement employed by the Habsburgs, or how the flow of their patronage affected elites and the bargaining process with them. In analyzing the much-neglected case of Habsburg patronage, I address several crucial issues in the history of the royal court and clientage in Western Europe. One of these concerns the question of whether or not the ruler's court was a force for social change. The sociologist Norbert Elias was instrumental in transforming court history from a subject that concentrated on describing display and ceremony into a topic of social and political importance.[45] He maintained that the royal court was an instrument to discipline nobles, but since the 1980s French historians in particular have opposed this and argued instead that the court's influence on noble behaviour was insignificant.[46] As with the 'court and country' controversy, part of the problem was that this challenge depended too much on literary evidence, and the revisionists focused overly on limited aspects of cultural behaviour, such as manners and etiquette.

The second half of this study therefore shifts attention to examining how social and economic change, stimulated by both the actions of state-building rulers and structural factors, transformed the cultural habits of nobles in the areas of socialization, education, manners and taste. I argue that these alterations were not simply a response to an overt disciplining process on the part of the state, but were also the outcomes of a voluntary adjustment on the part of the nobility, who found it was in their own interest to realign its strategies of social and dynastic reproduction to fit new conditions. It was this process of adaptation, fostered enthusiastically by the elite, as well as induced by monarchs and circumstance, that created new standards of noble behaviour, cultural distinction and taste. In other words, early modern European rulers modified noble behaviour through both co-option and coercion. And nobles were rarely passive recipients of royal favours, or fully pliable subjects. Although they had an interest in co-operating with rulers who distributed offices, privileges and honours in a way that maintained the identity of their class and benefited their families, the bargaining process with monarchs could turn into violent confrontations if they did not.

Elias's somewhat exaggerated thesis that the court was a tool by which rulers domesticated the nobility has been greatly enriched and modified under the impact of research on clientelism by social scientists. French and English historians now tend to argue that court patronage became the principal technique of governing and gaining elite co-operation in the state-building process.[47] However, others have questioned the importance royal patronage had for the elite. Kristen Neuschel, for example, believes that historians overestimate the power rulers had over noble clientage networks, because nobles could continue to rely on 'the existence of other material and ideological sources of power'.[48] Certainly, during the sixteenth century, clientage relations were still not completely connected to the state, despite concerted efforts by early modern rulers to centre the flow of resources at court. Victor Morgan has therefore quite aptly defined the early modern clientage system of political organization as 'patrimonial patronage'. Like its feudal ancestor, early modern patron–client relations involved personal attachments and interactions; they were asymmetric and depended on marked social differences, and they were reciprocal. However, the early modern clientage system also differed from the medieval patron–client society. Instead of depending on the allocation of land for military service, the significance of land dwindled in early modern relationships. And as rulers began to extend their activity and intervention into new areas, the role of the royal court was enhanced and gradually became the most important locale of patronage. This centralization allowed for the emergence of the broker, or mediator, within the court, and between it and clients outside, who regulated access to 'the fount of executive action in the person of the King'.[49]

Although it is important not to overrate the extent of the prince's power over early modern clientage networks, it is also unwise to devalue the force of court patronage. As Part II of this study shows, by the late sixteenth and early seventeenth centuries the withdrawal of Habsburg patronage threatened the social and material basis of a substantial section of the nobility. In particular, the exclusion from status and career promotion had an adverse effect on the interests, identity and position of Protestant nobles. Status mobility, offices, commands and other forms of social and symbolic reward were not only public proof of noble honour but also closely tied to the material survival of noble families. Despite the fact that individual nobles could often count on the support and resources of kin and peers if they were unable to draw on the prince's patronage, many Protestant nobles felt their exclusion threatened them with loss of honour and downward mobility, and this provided a powerful incentive to form a grand alliance against Habsburg rule and oppose the dynasty's leadership in centralizing their domains.

Another debate which the second part of this book addresses concerns the issue of whether the patronage system retarded or contributed to long-term political cohesion. Because it primarily satisfied special interests, critics have argued that clientelism fostered fragmentation and inefficiency in the distribution of state resources. On the positive side, scholars have stressed that it was an adaptable system which integrated diverse elites by tying them to the prince's interests. Both are valid points: as Sharon Kettering pointed out, this debate reflects the paradoxical nature of clientelism, which had both divisive and integrative features.[50]

Certainly, since early modern patron–client relations were not enforceable legally, they were inherently insecure. However, efforts were made to cement them by fostering solidarity and instituting moral sanctions. While remaining somewhat ambivalent, solidarity was therefore connected closely to perceptions of honour and obligation, and expressed in terms of interpersonal loyalty.[51] This partly explains the importance attributed to honour in early modern aristocratic society. Since patron–client relations were based largely on unwritten agreements, honour served as a moral bond: if one did not meet one's obligations, the only social and moral sanction that could be imposed was the loss of one's reputation. Thus, notions of honour, obligation and other personal sentiments helped to secure and legitimize patron–broker–client relations. Although kinship and corporate solidarity provided some bonding, alone they were frequently too weak to allow for the formation of broad alliances for political action, which is why early modern factions additionally tried to strengthen such loyalties through spiritual attachments, and define themselves by adhering to similar religious convictions.This study therefore views the vertical ties of patron–client relations at court in their connections with horizontal bonds, such as corporate identity, kinship and religion.

It is also clear, however, that the early modern patronage system was a potentially disintegrative force, creating a competitive and suspicious atmosphere. Political stability depended to a large extent on the ability of rulers, or their principal advisers, to balance factions, which were always potentially dangerous to them. It is exactly because patron–broker client relations were organized not only vertically, but also horizontally through spiritual, corporate and personal solidarity, that factions were able to mobilize grand alliances against a monarch. Despite such dangers, in a composite monarchy, governed through a small central administration, as in the Habsburgs' territories, both recruitment and social advance continued to depend strongly on patronage. Concentrating patronage at the court, however, offered rulers with weak central institutions advantages in better co-ordinating their elites. And even though noble clientage relations were not yet entirely connnected to the court, early attempts to centralize patronage allowed for the selective integration of those who counted – the state elite.

This book disagrees both with the recent overemphasis on the mutual-aid aspects of clientelism, because it tends to obscure the divisive impact that selective court patronage had on the elite, and with the tendency to underplay the role of deep-seated divisions and the long-term causes behind the numerous noble rebellions in the late sixteenth and early seventeenth centuries. The new emphasis during the 1980s on the economic resilience of nobles began to signal dissatisfaction with the social interpretation of rebellions and revolutions. The new orthodoxy that has emerged since then among revisionist historians of Western Europe rejects absolutism as a useful category, challenges long-term social and economic causes of political conflicts, and focuses on the collaboration between rulers and nobles. Thus, many historians of the English Civil War now oppose the claim that subversive constitutional and religious beliefs were simply the ideological weapons of a rising gentry and bourgeoisie struggling against a declining feudal aristocracy and backward monarchy. According to these historians, sufficiently pronounced social distinctions between members of the elite simply did not exist. Moreover, by eliminating the sixteenth and seventeenth centuries as distinctive stages in state-building, they can focus on interpreting the Civil War in terms of short-run causes rather than as a conflict arising from long-term constitutional and socio-economic change. It also allows revisionists to argue that the causes of the Civil War arose from misinformed factions pursuing narrow private interests, Charles I's misguided actions, the pressures of war, rebellion in Ireland, and subsequent financial stress, all of which suddenly converged to open the way for disruptive divisions over religion and politics.[52] A remarkably similar shift away from socio-economic frameworks has occurred in the historiography of the French Revolution.[53]

Without doubt, these historians have made an important contribution in pointing out that previous scholars have exaggerated social, economic and cultural divisions between elites, or between the court and the country. However, the failure of older social interpretations does not mean that seventeenth-century state-building and contentious politics were without any social foundations whatsoever. Revisionists tend to ignore 'that the aim of the traditional social interpretation was initially to provide a social basis, a social logic, for what was already a broadly accepted account of seventeenth-century conflicts in terms of differences over constitutional and religious principles'.[54] And, if we treat early modern elite rebellions as little more than large-scale historical accidents, how then do we explain their multiplicity and bunching throughout the late sixteenth and seventeenth centuries?[55]

Addressing problems in the conceptionalization of noble interest and exchange in patron–broker–client relations further helps to resolve some of the tensions between the argument that the relationship between rulers and elites was characterized by co-operation in state-building and the pervasiveness of divisive factionalism and elite opposition to central authority. Scholars of clientelism frequently stress the market-like exchange of economic resources in patron-client relations at the expense of what some social scientists define as generalized exchange. The production of social distinctions and cultural goods, or the symbolic exchange of gifts, are often overlooked, or viewed as being distinct from the exchange of material endowments.[56] Historians, too, have construed noble interests in modern terms, as measurable material gains, which were in opposition to emotive notions of trust, fidelity, prestige and honour. Thus, some assert that 'honour was more important to nobility than the accumulation of wealth', or that the 'prestige of serving a sovereign of the emperor's dignity and status outweighed such prudent [material] considerations'. And even Elias felt that 'motivation by rank, honour and prestige is more important than motivation by economic "interest"'.[57] I argue that it is inappropriate to view material interests as a binary opposite of affective and positional dimensions of noble relations, and that it is impossible to equate the goals of the elite with material interests alone.

Pierre Bourdieu's conceptual framework proves itself particularly useful in this context because it enlarges upon the conventional definition of capital as an exclusively economic resource by including non-monetary investments. And, while acknowledging the importance of economic concerns, it avoids a simplistic equation of family strategies with the conscious pursuit of material interests.[58] This allows us to recognize, on the one hand, that, while nobles were rarely uninterested in maintaining or improving the position and resources of their families, their strategies were not necessarily the product of fully-conscious, well-defined plans to maximize their resources. On the other hand, they cannot be regarded as reflex or mechanical reactions of individual nobles indoctrinated by a similar upbringing. Instead, reproductive strategies were infused with various traditions that evolved continually through practical activity.[59]

As Part II of this book demonstrates, maintaining and enhancing the position of individual families was tied closely to reproducing the social order, since this assured the dominance of the nobility at the apex of the social structure and in political life, which, in turn, safeguarded its economic and other privileges. Although economic capital in the form of landed wealth and other monetary investments were crucial to dynastic reproduction, in early modern conditions the power of economic capital became fully effective only when it was associated with immaterial resources, especially social capital (for example, noble titles, patronage networks) and symbolic capital (honour, reputation). Both the successful propagation of the social order and family enhancement depended to a large extent on the assimilation of cultural capital (for example, knowledge, education and skills) into the habitus of young nobles. And, by the late sixteenth century, access to Habsburg patronage had become essential for acquiring and enhancing the social, symbolic and cultural capital of noble families.

Thus the exclusion of Protestant nobles from court appointments meant that they no longer had access to its patronage system and to certain forms of what can be summarized as statist capital[60] (including the means to protect the Protestant religion). And this threatened both the cultural and material reproduction of their families. The majority of Protestants among the Lower and Upper Austrian nobles refused to adjust through conversion because, by the early seventeenth century, their networks and identity were fully confessionalized and their religion had become an inseparable part of their habitus, which infused the definition of their interests. Instead, they decided in 1619–20 to join the Bohemian Estates in opposing Ferdinand II's rule.

I conclude this Introduction by making more explicit some of my basic assumptions. Although I stress the importance of underlying structural problems, I also recognize that the past has been shaped by contingency and human agency. This reflects my belief that humans can, to some extent, modify their environment and, within limits, transform their identities. I also think that it is possible to determine to some degree the factors that motivate human action, and what degree of autonomy exists, and that this should continue to be a central project of the human sciences. While I offer no specific formula for analyzing causes and motivation, I have applied several organizing principles from sociology and cultural theory that helped me to understand past actions and experiences. In addition, while I provide statistics repeatedly for an entire provincial nobility, I do not claim that this data is complete. I consider my data and analyses as approximating actual conditions, and my conclusions as tentative and open to scholarly debate. I hope this book establishes a basis for further research and prompts other scholars to search for different source material on the nobility, such as diaries, private correspondence and records of estate management, much of which is still buried in private archives.

In my use of concepts from social and cultural theory I was guided by an awareness that scholarly frameworks are always in danger of totalizing, of imposing too much order on events, and deciding other people's aims and motivations for them. I realize that the concepts I use are the constructions of the analyst (that is, etic categories, or ordering principles), which are distinct from a 'native's own point of view' (that is, emic ascription). However, where possible, I search for alignment. My study does consider the voices of the past as an important guide to subjective beliefs, to how people made sense of their goals and actions, how they legitimized them to others and to themselves, and therefore how analytical concepts need to be formulated. But reasons or intentions of actions are not necessarily identical with the causes or the outcome of human action. Therefore, explicit 'discourses of reason', already sifted and organized by the authors of historical documents, cannot be the only, or even the dominant, guide to understanding the past. When I pay more attention to structural analysis and statistical methods than to the voices of the past, it is not because I believe in the inherent superiority of the analysts' viewpoint, but because systematic treatment does enlighten, especially when the sources available to me on the perspectives of Habsburg rulers and nobles were so restricted.

Because I anticipated that readers have different interests in the material covered in this book, I tried deliberately, as far as possible, to make each chapter stand alone as well as being part of an integrated whole. The first two chapters offer my own narrative account of the relations between the Habsburgs and the Estates of most of their territories. Chapter 1 provides a conceptual framework and chronology of Habsburg state-building, approximately up to the beginning of Maximilian II's reign in 1564, while Chapter 2 analyzes the impact of the Protestant Reformation, and the interactions between rulers and Estates until 1620. Chapter 3 then reconstructs the public discourse between Protestants and Catholics between 1618 and 1620, presenting key accounts of how the Protestant leadership in Bohemia and the Austrian duchies perceived the division of power and explained its motives for opposing the Habsburgs. Chapter 3 also examines, in turn, how emperors and the Catholic state elite legitimized the power of the prince, and their reaction to the Protestant opposition. Part II proceeds to test the Protestants' subjective account of the reasons for rebellion on the basis of other primary documents and statistical analysis. Although their perspective dovetails to a surprising extent with the outcome of my research, significant differences of focus do exist. Obviously, the politics of the moment dictated what could be, and could not be, said in these documents, and contemporaries did not always have the capacity or opportunity to assess every causal connection, including their own motives. The same, of course, could be said about historians. Nevertheless, together, etic and emic points of view do provide for a fuller explanation of past action and motives.

Although the second part of this book focuses more than the first on the hereditary lands, and especially on Lower Austria, it extends its scope repeatedly to the nobilities of the other Habsburg territories at the Imperial Court. Chapter 4 analyzes the social evolution of an entire provincial nobility during the late sixteenth and early seventeenth centuries, establishing its size, internal divisions, and methods of recruitment. Drawing attention to the important power of rulers over social classification, and how the Habsburgs used it to centralize patronage at the Imperial Court, I assess the significance of social and symbolic capital in noble society in order to determine the influence social mobility and the restructuring of the nobility had on the relations between Habsburgs and the Protestant Estates.

The last two chapters of the book, Chapters 5 and 6, analyze the social structure of the Habsburg Court during the half century before 1619–20, and the significance that Habsburg patronage held for provincial nobles, especially in terms of appointments to offices. Chapter 5 examines the flow of patronage at the Imperial Court among different noble groups from various Habsburg territories, and the importance it had for them. Besides showing the complextity of converting cultural, social and symbolic capital into economic resources, it explains how noble families adjusted their strategies of social and dynastic reproduction to the social advance of educated commoners, and refashioned the meaning of virtue and social distinctions. This facilitates, in the final chapter, an evaluation of the impact the redefinition of merit and virtue of the Habsburg rulers in favour of a new Catholic state elite had on Protestant nobles. Focusing on the changing confessional composition of the Imperial Court, this chapter assesses how inequities in the distribution of Habsburg patronage influenced the political activism of Protestant nobles between 1618 and 1620.

Part I

Co-ordinating State, Reformation and Elites

1
Political Culture, Political Space

Most Habsburg historians agree that the medieval or feudal political order had been transformed by the late fifteenth century. Maximilian I (1493–1519), whom they view either as the last representative of medieval knights, or the first among 'new monarchs', was succeeded by rulers whose main aim it was to expand and consolidate the Habsburg dominions, centralize the administration and improve their military capacity. Although political culture retained many feudal elements in the following two and a half centuries, they are usually considered to be part of a stage in modern state-building; and this process, while slower and on a smaller scale, resembled the road to absolutism in other European countries. Historians have also followed RJW Evans' lead in viewing the Counter-Reformation as a cornerstone in the formation of a symbiosis between the Habsburg rulers, the Church and the nobles. He believes that, although the 'decisive years for [the monarchy's] formation lay in the seventeenth century', and 'rested essentially on a series of bilateral agreements between the rulers and their mightier subjects', the beginnings of the 'aristocratic-clerical commonwealth' must be sought in the later part of the previous century.[1]

Yet we still know surprisingly little about the growth of the Habsburg state, what moved it forward, how it worked, or how the accommodation between nobles and rulers was in fact facilitated in the century before 1620. This has lead Paula Sutter-Fichtner to question 'the historical place of the Habsburg Empire in the early modern era, not to mention its internal history as a whole. Did anything indeed happen in those lands during the century or so prior to the Thirty Years' War that significantly adds to our understanding of the polity that historians agree emerged after that conflict?'[2] Indeed, the Habsburg lands remained a composite state of autonomous territories, a modern bureaucracy developed only during the eighteenth century, and re-Catholicization did not progress substantially until the mid-seventeenth century. This throws doubt on the idea that the sixteenth-century Counter-Reformation and military defeat of the Estates in 1620 were decisive in forging a symbiosis between Habsburgs and elites that fostered growth in state power. Moreover, older research by the Dualism school suggests that, from its beginnings, Habsburg state formation was dependent on compromise between rulers and Estates, and Marxian scholars have agreed, viewing this as complicity between state and dominant class in the consolidation of an absolutist state.[3]

The major problems with Habsburg historiography are in fact symptomatic of difficulties in Western historiography on state-building at large. It shares the tendency to regard the expansion of the army, bureaucracy and legislative activity as the hallmark of absolutism. This becomes particularly inappropriate when considering early modern constitutional regimes – for example, that in England – which also experienced an expansion of these infrastructures. Moreover, the idea that the seventeenth century, the so-called Age of Absolutism, was a distinctive stage in state formation has led historians to view the enhancement of the state's infrastructural power, in terms of bureaucracy, army, and law-making, as necessarily leading to a substantial increase in the autocratic power of rulers over society. But infrastructural power and despotic power are very different capacities. In addition, the renewed stress on elite co-operation in state-building has made it difficult to understand the reasons for widespread opposition to rulers throughout Europe, and ultimately inhibited the accurate characterization of the relations between monarchs and nobility, and the socioeconomic basis of state growth.

In this chapter, I suggest an alternative formulation, and outline the concept of 'co-ordinating state' to define the early modern Habsburg monarchy, which allows me to distinguish analytically the early modern from the medieval state while taking into consideration the continuity between them. It also makes it possible to relinquish the series of ambiguous terms currently in use to describe early modern monarchies, such as Renaissance monarchy, new, administrative or legislative monarchy, early and confessional absolutism, patrimonial and constitutional absolutism, and so on. Focusing on developments in the Habsburgs' Austrian core (or 'hereditary') lands, I provide a chronological overview of the transformation of political culture, and identify the major geopolitical and institutional features of state formation prior to their becoming fused more strongly with religious issues after the mid-sixteenth century. This facilitates the re-examination of co-operation and opposition on part of the regional elites in the centralizing process, which is also essential for understanding the long-term 'constitutional' causes behind the Austro-Bohemian rebellion of 1618–20, and for determining whether and in what way state growth played a major role in this conflict.

The rise of co-ordinating states

In defining the early modern state, it is crucial to differentiate between 'infrastructural' and 'autocratic' power.[4] Although these two forms of power are connected practically, separating them analytically is essential, particularly when analysing the growth of state power in early modern times, because their development was not always coextensive. Autocratic power denotes a capacity that gives the state elite (those who command the highest levels of institutions, including the monarch) full autonomy to have control, without having to negotiate, over civil society. In the extreme case, no one can escape the reach and authoritative command structure of a state with strong autocratic power.[5] Infrastructural power provides state elites with the institutional capacity to co-ordinate civil society and implement, usually through negotiations with elites, norms or rules to regulate social life, especially conflicts between groups and individuals, and the distribution of resources. This co-ordinating power of the state is greatly enhanced by regular taxation, a permanent, central administration staffed with dependent servants, as well as a monopoly over the military (especially a standing army) and over making and enforcing the law. Moreover, logistical techniques, such as the improvement of communications, literacy (to transmit messages and codify laws), and the means for exchanging commodities (for example, coinage and weights), help to further the central co-ordination capacity of the state elite.[6] While it is obvious that infrastructural growth has the potential to increase the autocratic power capacity of the state elite, the latter is not necessarily an outcome of the development of the former. Thus modern democratic states have strong infrastructural power, but weak autocratic control. Moreover, the growth of infrastructural reach has been relatively continuous since late medieval times, while the development of state autocratic power in the Western world has oscillated.

Medieval governments in Europe were characterized by 'intensive' or local power networks, and rulers lacked monopolistic control over these networks, since they did not have the territorial centrality that would have provided them with the potential for mobilizing sufficient and independent resources to use against these multiple and competing power groups in society. The decentralized, composite monarchies of Europe were usually governed by compromises between rulers, the Church and a variety of local elites, who had considerable autonomous powers. Although medieval monarchs also had a degree of autonomy in terms of extracting resources from crown lands and from dependent groups, such as Jewish and foreign merchants, they had weak autocratic power over society and feeble infrastructural reach. Centred around a small and moving court, the state was puny, its public functions very small and focused on warfare, and dynasties viewed it as their private patrimony.

Some of the basic characteristics of medieval monarchies did not change drastically in the early modern period. The main activity of the state remained military and, while expanding, its public functions continued to be relatively small. Rulers' organizational autonomy remained restricted, partly because they lacked good and rapid communication networks and extensive resources. Not surprisingly, the state continued to govern largely through bargaining and compromise with local elites, who still had extensive jurisdiction over their subjects. In fact, the interdependence between ruler and the various Estates or parliaments grew, rather than declined. However, what differentiated the early modern from the medieval state was the enhancement of the rulers' infrastructural power, which provided the basis for developing greater territorial unity.

As in other European monarchies, the impetus to infrastructural growth in the Habsburg lands arose in response to military and geopolitical pressures, and the co-ordination of early modern civil society derived from the geopolitical role of the state. Thus preparation for large-scale war forced the state elite to extract more resources from the subject population. The need for capital-intensive military supplies and a centralized administration helped to concentrate the extraction of resources and centralize them in the hands of the ruler. These military-fiscal boosts to state power coincided with the growth of economic production and of urban centres.[7] As local production and trade increased, the dominant groups in society needed better legal norms by which to regulate disputes and property rights and to foster the exchange of commodities over longer distances.

As I will show, the elites largely accepted the development of Habsburg power in co-ordinating certain social activities, especially the adjudication of conflicts, and contributed to the growth of territorially centralized institutions by entrusting more resources to the state elite. While this fostered the growing interdependence between rulers and the dominant groups in society, it allowed rulers to extend the infrastructure and radius of central co-ordination. By the late fifteenth century this capacity was sufficiently extensive in most regions of Western and Central Europe to enable rulers to begin organizing elites and other groups over a larger terrain than they had done previously, and we can define this as the beginning of co-ordinating states. The difference between the medieval and early modern state, then, was primarily a matter of degree in extending infrastructural power, while autocratic power, or control *over* society, remained comparatively weak in both cases.[8]

Applying the concept of co-ordinating state to the period from the late fifteenth to the late seventeenth century allows us to treat constitutional and statist regimes as belonging to the same type of state, one that was weak in control *over* society, but nevertheless having developed relatively strong infrastructural power. I suggest, however, that the various co-ordinating states of Europe should then be differentiated according to divergent paths in organizing political sovereignty (such as segmented, layered or territorial sovereignties) as suggested by Wayne TeBrake.[9] The eventual outcome of most co-ordinating monarchies were unified 'territorial states', or what other scholars also define as 'nation-states', organic or 'modern states', terms that assume the existence of a nation identifying with its state.[10] Although the Habsburgs failed ultimately to unite their dominions in a nation-state, this should not detract from their prolonged efforts in state-building, and their successes and failures are particularly instructive for comparative purposes.

The following sections re-examine how geopolitics, warfare and economic change forced the Habsburgs continually to seek expedients to deal with fiscal problems and how, beginning in the early sixteenth century, this furthered consultation and bargaining with local elites. It exemplifies how the growth of the state's infrastructural power intensified the co-operation and interdependence between nobles and rulers, while at the same time increasing the potential for conflict and the rise of factionalism within the elite. As I demonstrate, co-operation with and opposition to political authority arose to a large extent from the same process, namely the intensified interdependence between the court and elites, which made bargaining between them an ongoing requirement. As the interpenetration between them grew, so did the potential sources of conflict, especially during periods that coincided with problems in the distribution of resources.

In short, I view early modern state-building as the product of a continuous bargaining process between rulers and subjects. This does not devalue the challenges to the claims for centred authority. In fact, I consider opposition and revolts to be integral parts of the interactive political process. Successful negotiations between claims and counterclaims contributed to state formation and could eliminate or prevent resistance to governments. However, as we shall see, the outcome of such bargaining varied with the political culture and depended on the rules and conventions that had been established for negotiations and the sanctions that were put in place to enforce agreements. It also depended on the nature and availability of resources, and whether there was sufficient flexibility and substitutability in the issues over which parties bargained.

Geopolitics and territorial consolidation

Apart from the general factors outlined above, there was no typical or normal path of early modern European state-building. The eastern Habsburg territories are a portentous reminder of this, although scholars of state-building pay little attention to them. One reason for this is that most state theorists focus on determining the commonalities of state-building and prefer to exclude the complexities and deviations that are presented by the Austrian Habsburgs' domains, which are seen as obstacles to, rather than the causes of, territorial consolidation. Yet, as I will show, by studying the disincentives to state-building we can in fact gain much insight about the causes and mechanisms of political development. The character and outcome of state formation depended on a great variety of factors. Particularly important for the divergent paths were the variations in geopolitical positioning, the dimensions of political space, the different range of resources, and varying traditions in resource-extractive strategies available to specific political regimes. The pattern of infrastructural development was further shaped by the timing, the structure, and the extent of elite authority within the Estates' or parliamentary institutions.

The drive of the Habsburgs eastward during the thirteenth century, and, later, the fortuitous matchmaking of Frederick III (1440–93) and his son Maximilian I (1493–1519) was facilitated largely by geopolitical factors, especially the concern of European rulers over the threat posed by eastern dynasties (initially in Bohemia and Hungary), and by their desire to keep in check the kings of France. The Habsburgs were able to regain the Imperial title, and between 1525–1527, claim succession to the crowns of Hungary–Croatia and Bohemia that lay next to their Austrian core lands, largely because, at the time, the other German princes considered the Austrian dynasty less of a geopolitical threat than others, yet sufficiently prominent and strong to muster resources for checking the expanding Ottoman empire in the East. In comparison to Western European dynasties, the Austrian Habsburgs were thus assembling the largest part of their Eastern possessions rather late. These remained an unconsolidated patchwork of separate lands throughout the early modern period. In fact, by the time the Habsburgs had finalized the separation into a Spanish and Austrian line and divided their patrimony during the mid-sixteenth century, their Eastern domain had become larger, but also more, rather than less, fragmented.

Territorial consolidation and efforts to extend infrastructural reach were focused initially on the Habsburgs' core 'Austrian' territories, the *Erblande* or hereditary lands, which they had begun to assemble in the thirteenth century. Although Maximilian I united these diverse lands, comprising more than half a dozen distinct linguistic groups, into two administrative units, they were divided again into three entities by Ferdinand I (1521–64) in 1564. Until 1620, the two archduchies of Upper and Lower Austria were administered from Vienna, the three duchies of Styria, Carinthia and Carnolia, also known as Inner Austria, and the principalities of Istria, Gorizia and Trieste, were ruled from Graz, while, until 1665, the Tyrol and Outer Austria (*Vorlande*), including the diverse mixture of non-contiguous ancestral possessions in south-western Germany, were under the administration of an archducal line in Innsbruck. Moreover, these three regions remained fragmented internally, which explains why the Habsburgs considered it wise to first consolidate each region under the governorship of reliable and loyal relatives. Not only did each of the individual territories have its own laws, customs and Estates, they were also further subdivided into distinct units which often suffered from extreme localism, and contained numerous enclaves whose lords owed allegiance only to the emperor, or, in the case of the numerous Church lands, to foreign ecclesiastical overlords.

The kingdoms of Hungary–Croatia and Bohemia, which the Habsburgs acquired during the early sixteenth century, also comprised numerous political entities. The Bohemian kingdom consisted of five separate crown lands, held together by little more than the central Bohemian Court Chancery and the privilege of selecting a common king. Next to Bohemia, the margravates of Moravia, and Upper and Lower Lusatia, and the duchy of Silesia each had its own Diets or Estates – dominated by the nobility – with extensive legislative and administrative rights, which were carefully guarded. In addition, each of these Bohemian crown lands contained numerous enclaves and principalities that were almost completely independent of the Habsburgs.

Unlike Bohemia and the Austrian lands, Hungary was never part of the Holy Roman Empire, and by the mid-sixteenth century its division into three distinctive political entities was complete. The Habsburgs held only Upper Hungary (Slovakia, north-western Hungary, including western Transcarpathia), together with a small corridor along the eastern border of the Austrian lands, and the western third of Croatia–Slavonia, a kingdom that had been connected to Hungary since the twelfth century. Transylvania had become an Ottoman protectorate, while the remainder of Hungary was under the direct control of the Ottomans. The Croatian and Hungarian Estates had considerable autonomy, and the numerous local nobilities fiercely protected their extensive liberties, among them the right of royal election, which circumscribed Habsburg rule greatly.[11]

In the sixteenth century, most Europeans lived in states that were cobbled together in a similar fashion from several distinct and independent political entities and were, as Koenigsberger described them, composite states.[12] However, the Habsburg domains were not only more fragmented than others, but remained a multiple monarchy until the very end. Contemporaries, such as Niccolò Machiavelli, thought that princes could obtain closer union among their dominions because of contiguity and similarities in 'language, custom and institutions'.[13] However, the Austrian Habsburg experience proves that geopolitical location was more important than these factors in hindering territorial consolidation. Proximity and topography certainly played a role in state-building, since good communications were essential to increase the infrastructural reach of rulers. Most of the possessions of the Austrian Habsburgs were relatively contiguous, and the Danube and its tributaries connected a number of regions, even though the river's geographic pull was not unqualified, especially when it came to integrating Bohemia, and mountains hindered communications within and between various territories. Clearly, contiguity was necessary, but not sufficient in itself to further integration. Considering that the 6–7 million inhabitants living in the Habsburg lands spoke about a dozen distinct languages, linguistic differences did little to enhance communication and infrastructural reach. Nonetheless, since most of the elite spoke either German or Latin, linguistic diversity became an important centrifugal force only when it was combined with a strong regional and historical identity among the ruling elite, as was the case in Bohemia and Hungary. Ultimately, this reflects the fact that the Habsburgs were relatively late in assembling their dominions which, in comparison to monarchies like that in France, were still rather unconsolidated, so their elites had not had much opportunity to develop common historical and ideological ties with the Habsburgs or with each other.

Next to timing, the most significant factor delaying territorial unity was the geopolitical position of the Austrian Habsburg dominions. One of the main problems was that the Habsburgs attempted to consolidate not only their own lands but also to reform and unite the Holy Roman Empire. The status of Emperor had considerable importance for the dynasty, in part because its own territories were not held together by a single royal title or crown. As mere archdukes of Austria, the Habsburgs would have been indistinguishable from most other German princes. Plans of Maximilian I to establish an Austrian kingdom apparently failed in the face of opposition from German princes.[14] Although the Bohemian and Hungarian crowns were crucial they were still not a terribly secure possession during the sixteenth century because of the Ottoman threat, and because their Estates claimed that royal succession depended on their consent. In addition to these factors, connection with the inheritance of Imperial Rome, Byzantium and Charlemagne's empire conferred tremendous prestige to the emperorship, and thereby a symbolic capital that could be used for concrete purposes. The emperors were also entitled to important privileges which enabled them to dispense patronage in the form of honours, titles, fiefs and positions. Moreover, the Austrian dynasty hoped to derive taxes and other resources from a reformed Holy Roman Empire, which it needed to support its struggle with the Ottomans.

While the Habsburgs' desire to hold on to the Imperial crown was thus not unreasonable, their attempt to govern another diverse, disordered, and even more fragmented empire next to their own dominions strained their resources, especially since it involved them continually in wars with France and in Italian states. Although in more favourable circumstances they might have surmounted their problems at home and in the empire, the combined burden of the Protestant Reformation and war with the Ottomans depleted their resources and slowed attempts to reform the empire and consolidate their Eastern patrimony. However, it was a slowing down, not a complete halt, and both developments also opened opportunities for Habsburg state-building. As we shall see in the next chapter, the Counter Reformation offered avenues for extending their infrastructural reach over the Church and, by imposing greater social and moral discipline, over their subjects. And the dynasty could use religion as a regulative tool to bind the nobility more closely to the crown[15] and give voice to its ideology and culture. Moreover, the fear of Ottoman advance had made the Habsburgs kings of Hungary and Bohemia in the first place, and, having become the bulwark of Christendom, this prompted them to expand their infrastructure and made their elites more pliable towards enhancing resource extraction.

Coalescent infrastructures: military and financial administrations

Although he neglected to stress the significance of geopolitics, Machiavelli was, of course, quite correct in attaching great importance to similarity of 'custom and institutions' for consolidating composite monarchies, and all early modern rulers made efforts to enlarge and centralize the military, finances and justice, and to establish more uniform rules and practices. A number of princes were even able to establish substantial standing armies with which they could more easily coerce rebellious subjects, and enforce directives with punitive strikes. None the less, although subject to variation, their autocratic power necessarily remained relatively weak. Direct control over subjects and subordinate local elites would have required of the early modern state more highly organized powers of coercion. These depended on a revolution in land transport, and an increase in the yields of crops to generate more surplus, neither of which were forthcoming until the eighteenth century.[16] Prior to this, most states depended on the co-operation of urban and rural elites to manage military affairs, to enhance the extraction of resources, execute justice, and administer a number of other internal policies. The greater need for state finances required closer collaboration with the landed nobility, the Church and urban elites. The support of local power groups was also essential, because armies could still not march for more than nine days at a time, or about a hundred miles overland, without relying on local supplies or on plundering.[17]

To conclude, as does Paula Sutter-Fichtner, that one cannot identify clearly many factors that in fact 'advanced the cause of Habsburg state-building in the sixteenth century' neglects the interdependence between rulers and elite, and that geopolitical and military challenges enhanced the infrastructural power of the Estates, which increased the joint power of Estates and Habsburgs initially. And this interpenetration between central infrastructure and local, elite-dominated institutions provided the foundation upon which the Habsburgs extended their co-ordinating power, eventually enabling them to become financially and politically more autonomous. It was always the case, though, that states had to bargain with their elites (or sections thereof), and the significance of coercion often lay in turning the Estates into compliant partners in the creation of territorial states. The analysis of the Habsburg core lands provides a poignant example of the growing interdependence between local elites and crown, showing how this aided infrastructural growth, but also engendered conflict.

In the Austrian duchies, periodic assemblies of Estates, consisting of clergy, knights, lords and royal towns were common by the late fourteenth century. The legal basis for membership in the *Landstände* was immediate subject status (*Landesunmittelbarkeit*) *vis-à-vis* the sovereign, and the possession of land with legal authority attached to it (*Herrschaft,* or lordship), or, in the case of royal towns and markets, analogous communal property. *Unmittelbarkeit* was not merely derived from being directly subject to the ruler, but also from the reciprocal obligation of the sovereign on the one hand to secure protection (*Schutz und Schirm*), and of the subject on the other to assist with counsel and aid, a reciprocity that was linked implicitly to the principle of lordship.[18] *Herrschaft,* then, was an aggregation of rights and obligations that included executive and judicial powers, especially authority over subjects. It was not only the basis of noble authority, which became institutionalized with the formation of Estates, but also a foundation for state-building.

Important dynastic families (*Hochfreie*) had already appeared as advisers and guarantors of contracts made by rulers during the eleventh century, but their emergence into fully developed Estates began only in the middle of the thirteenth century, when the upper nobility, or lords (*Herrenstand*), first acted independently in the succession struggles after the extinction of the Babenberg dynasty. They were soon joined by the lesser nobility, or knights (*Ritterstand*), and, more than a century later, by the clergy and towns.[19] The preconditions for membership of the clergy and towns in the Estates were more complex than for the nobility, but, in essence, after 1500, next to *Unmittelbarkeit,* landed property, and residency, members of the First Estate (*Prälatenstand*) were required to possess autonomous powers over their financial administration, since this enabled them better to meet the monetary demands of the crown.[20] What distinguished royal (*landesfürstliche*) towns and markets that belonged to the Estates from the other urban centres was *Landesunmittelbarkeit* derived from direct *Herrschaft* over the community, in this case possession of lower jurisdiction. However, it appears that the financial strength of a town rather than legal authority was often more important in determining its ability to attend assemblies of the Estates. The claim of the Habsburgs that the towns and markets that constituted the Fourth Estate, and the First Estate, the clergy (or *Prälatenstand*), belonged to the royal domain (*Kammergut*) blurred the distinction between *Stände* and crown lands. But it had significant advantages for the ruler, since the claim that they did not have the same liberties as the noble Estates restrained the political activism of clergy and towns and opened them to extra demands for financial contributions beyond those granted at the *Landtage*.[21]

The frequency of dynastic power struggles, minority governments and subsequent internal wars and feuds during the late fourteenth and early fifteenth centuries contributed to the growing interdependence between rulers and elites, and to the development of Estates as a political force. Thus, in 1355, Albrecht II declared the Austrian possessions of the Habsburgs indivisible, and urged nobles and towns to oppose any successor who wanted to renew the divisions. Furthermore, in 1402, the crown called upon prelates, lords, knights and towns – who probably met for the first time in a common session – to declare and enforce internal peace (*Landfrieden*) by ending feuds and civil strife. Both events became the basis for direct intervention of the Estates during the following succession conflicts. The Hussite Wars of the early part of the century made yearly summons of the Estates an entitlement, and consequently the position of their representative, the *Landmarschall*, was consolidated.[22] Squabbles over succession and a series of minorities prompted the Austrian Estates to assume regency several times during the fifteenth century, and in 1451 the nobility even aided foreign military intervention and formed alliances with the Bohemians and Hungarians in their opposition to Frederick III. However, the growth of the Estates' political influence was facilitated considerably by the changes in the nature of warfare, especially the rise in the size and cost of armies, since this made it essential for the crown to call frequently upon its subjects to extend monetary contributions. This enabled the elites to demand greater control over internal affairs, in particular in the distribution of resources, resulting not only in constant bargaining with the ruler but also in the development of the Estates' own infrastructure, which became closely intertwined with central institutions headed by the Habsburgs.

Although the Habsburgs became more dependent on the *Stände* for financing and organizing military endeavours, the changing nature of warfare during the fifteenth century, especially the creation of an infantry, the strengthening of the artillery and the enlargement of armies, also enabled them better to co-ordinate the nobility and tie them more closely to their own interests. As elsewhere in Europe, the greater reliance on mercenary infantry troops broke the nobility's monopoly over warfare. Although the cavalry, and leadership over it, remained a focus of military activity for nobles, military service became more open to non-nobles, and increasingly subject to more uniform laws and regulations by the state. Thus the *Reiterrecht* of 1570 stipulated that all nobles who joined the cavalry had to be entered 'like others into the registry and bound to duties and obedience'.[23] By the late sixteenth century, the medieval military ban was entirely superseded by financial contributions from the Estates, allowing the Habsburgs to hire mercenary troops.[24] Together with other factors, enhancing the extraction of resources and the larger size of armies, which rulers could now muster during wartime, made it difficult, if not impossible, for great nobles to compete with them.[25] In the early fifteenth century, the emperors still had to worry that single knights, such as Franz von Sickingen, could muster their own armies of 10 000 soldiers.[26] But, a century later, the Estates of several territories had to unite all their resources in order to assemble about 25 000 men to confront Ferdinand II's army. Although the Habsburg ruler himself had to obtain over 1.5 million *florins* in subsidies from his allies to raise a slightly larger army, in other emergencies the dynasty was able to muster up to 80 000 men against the Ottomans. By the mid-seventeenth century, the dynasty was able to maintain a standing army of 65 000, and this had increased to about 100 000 at the end of the century.[27]

In addition to having larger and more expensive armies, the state elite gradually gained more centralized control over the military with the aid of a new administrative body, the Imperial War Council (*Hofkriegsrat*), established in 1556 by Ferdinand I in response to the perennial Turkish attacks on the Eastern frontier. Headed by a president and some five to seven members from the nobility, its function was to co-ordinate and centralize all the military affairs of the Habsburg territories, and during the seventeenth century it extended its influence to the Empire. Its primary duties centred on co-ordinating the provisioning and equipment of the wartime armies, and organizing the maintenance of defence works on the military frontier and in the city of Vienna. The raising and provisioning of troops for defensive purposes, and the upkeep of fortifications and soldiers along the military border with the Ottomans was largely in the hands of military commanders of the Estates and several regional War Councils.[28] Although historians have viewed this as a limitation of the power of the Imperial War Council, in fact it provided the Habsburgs with co-ordinating powers over the local Estates while maintaining their co-operation in financing and organizing military affairs. It testifies to the importance of the *Hofkriegsrat* in enhancing the dynasty's co-ordinating power that the Estates resented its influence and considered it as an interference with their long established monopoly over defence matters, to which they made large financial contributions. Even the regional War Councils were bitterly opposed by the Estates, and they tried unsuccessfully to dissolve the one in Inner Austria after it became clear that the Council was responsible only to the duke.[29]

Most resentment, however, was levelled against the Privy Council (*Geheimer Rat*) which, although medieval in origin, was given an independent existence and tangible form in 1527. Advising the emperor in all matters 'high, weighty and secret' pertaining to foreign and domestic policy in the Reich and other dominions, it was probably the most centralized of all the councils. Although it held a precarious dual position between the Empire and the disparate Habsburg lands, it became the chief instrument of the ruler in co-ordinating the activities of the other councils, the various provincial governments, and Estates. The chief officials of the household, the Imperial Vice Chancellor, and the heads of the Aulic Council, the *Hofkammer,* the Austrian Chancellor and the *Statthalter,* as well as at least one important royal representative of the Bohemian government, were all usually members of the Privy Council.[30]

Because of the perennial threat posed by the Ottoman empire, the *Stände* usually co-operated with the Habsburgs in military defence matters. Larger armies, coupled with monetary inflation, increased the Habsburgs' need for revenue and dependence on grants by the Estates, since ordinary taxes could not be imposed on their own subjects without their consent. The authority of the Austrian *Stände* to grant taxes was based on a thirteenth-century decree (1231) subjecting all new taxes to the permission of the *meliores et majores* (the better and greater men) of the duchies.[31] In the Austrian lands and Bohemia, direct taxation was collected regularly from only around the mid-sixteenth century. A form of property taxation, the *Gült,* became a permanent obligation in the Austrian duchy, even though the Estates insisted on granting it from year to year. While they rarely refused contributions, this allowed them to connect subsidies to the alleviation of grievances, and object frequently to increases. Collected from the peasantry, the *Gült* was a tax based on the self-assessed income of landowners from their peasantry. Income from manorial estate management, or *Eigenbetrieb,* was exempted, and all attempts by the crown to tax noble landholders personally, or substantially to improve the taxation system, which invited gross injustice and dishonesty, failed. None the less, a corrective step was taken in the late sixteenth century with a survey of peasant households on each landed estate, even though it was conducted in a slipshod fashion.[32]

Indirect levies were controlled by the rulers, but they generally farmed them out, and during the sixteenth century the Habsburgs frequently sold income from tolls and duties to noble landowners. By this time, the Austrian Estates had also obtained control over the most important excise taxes (*Ungeld* and *Zapfenmass*), which they usually granted only for specified time periods. In addition, the *Stände* not only collected these extraordinary taxes, but also all regular taxes, and determined the use of money grants, largely to cover military expenses. However, they did assume the repayment of considerable crown debts during this period, which they covered largely from the excise taxes. By the mid-sixteenth century it had become a regular feature of the bargaining process between Habsburgs (or their representative) and Estates at the provincial assemblies that the latter would present their grievances and demands before granting monetary contributions covered by taxation, while the former always made the point that aid was an obligation and insisted that redress might be forthcoming after financial contributions were promised during the session. As we shall see, this bargaining power at the *Landtage* secured the Estates their continued influence over internal affairs and, during the sixteenth century, enabled them to obtain considerable religious concessions.[33]

To respond more effectively and cohesively to the rulers' monetary and other demands, the Austrian Estates created their own permanent infrastructure, and at their new administrative centre, the *Landhaus*, they employed permanent officials to execute the decisions made yearly in the *Landtage* or Diets.[34] The designations varied, but in Lower Austria the most important among them, the *Landmarschall*, presided over the meetings of the lords as well as common assemblies and committees, and was paid and installed on the Estate's recommendation by the ruler. Because of his dual role as representative of the Estates and the ruler, the Habsburgs could sometimes exert their influence over this official, and this was particularly true in legal matters as the *Landmarschall* also presided over the *Landmarschallgericht*, a court which met two to four times yearly to decide, on the basis of *Landrecht*, cases involving members of the nobility and clergy (in secular matters).[35] The dual position of this official, who was recruited from the upper nobility, favoured finding a compromise in negotiations between Estates and Habsburg rulers. His representative, the *Landuntermarschall*, the highest official of the Estate of knights, was also chosen by the ruler upon recommendation of the Estates. Both of these officials were aided by about six to eight deputies (*Verordnete*), who were elected by the *Stände* and responsible for the general administration and execution of decisions made at the assemblies.

The Estates also employed a limited number of military officers who, besides maintaining defence works on their borders, levied horses (*Gültpferde*) for the military and mustered soldiers from the native populace.[36] In Lower Austria the highest of these officers were the *Generallandobrist*, elected by the *Stände* but confirmed by the ruler, and his deputy, the *Generalobristleutnant*. In order to provide the ruler with greater influence over military affairs, especially command over the troops raised by the Estates, it became common after the turn of the century to combine the office of the *Landobrist* with that of the *Landmarschall*. The Habsburgs had tried in vain to put the troops raised by the Estates under the command of their own officers, or at least to influence them by paying them directly through the Imperial treasury.[37]

The Estates' finances, especially the collection of taxes, were administered by a receiver general (*Einnehmer*, or *Einnehmerambtsverwalter*) and his staff.[38] Parallel to what they had done in military affairs, the Habsburgs established a central treasury (*Hofkammer*), during the early sixteenth century, headed by a president, aided by councillors (five in 1576) and some secretaries, in order better to control and co-ordinate the financial activities of the Estates. Most of the taxes collected by the *Stände* had to be delivered to the *Hofkammer* who would, on demand, hand it over to the office of the military paymaster (*Kriegszahlmeister*). Largely with income from royal domains, the treasury was also responsible for the payment of salaries, and the expenses of the court, including the central administration. The ability to become a genuine central treasury was certainly restricted, because the collection of all but a few extraordinary taxes remained in the hands of the Estates. However, as the tenacity with which the Estates tried to limit its sphere of influence indicates, the *Hofkammer* did become an important tool in regulating the Estates' activities and in co-ordinating the separate treasuries of the three regional governments in Tyrol, and Inner and Lower Austria (which also administered the income from Upper Austria, Hungary and Bohemia), all of which were accountable to the central treasury.[39]

Clearly, then, like other European monarchs, the Habsburgs had to rely on bargaining with the elites to enhance their revenues. But, because of their geopolitical position, they remained more dependent on them for much longer. Unfortunately, we know little about the Habsburg budget, partly because documents were destroyed, but also because the paymasters recorded mainly expenditure rather than receipts, perhaps in an effort to keep Estates and money lenders in the dark. We do know that income from ordinary or direct taxes granted by the Lower Austrian Estates doubled between 1562 and 1605,[40] and the figures for contributions by the other territories suggest a similar increase. But crown debts appear to have tripled during the sixteenth century.[41] This indicates that, while population growth and the pressures of war fostered the expansion of extractive capacity, inflation and larger military costs led to ever higher expenditure. As in the other hereditary lands, the population of Lower Austria rose moderately, by about a fifth between 1529 and 1618; but the prices of wheat, wine and cattle nearly tripled, and doubled for rye, barley and oats during the second half of the sixteenth century alone. This creeping inflation, which also extended to meat, affected the entire Danubian area as well as the Tyrol.[42]

The evidence is clear that war and inflation contributed to the chronic indebtedness of the Habsburgs throughout the sixteenth century, and to their continual efforts to supplement income by mortgaging, and eventually selling, much of their own domain lands (*Kammergut*) and by borrowing from various sources, including South German financiers. Moreover, at various times they were required to turn to the *Stände* to assume debt repayments, which, as we shall see, forced them to grant the Estates important concessions, among them religious liberties.[43] All of this inhibited the Habsburgs from using their expanded resources to further the growth of their co-ordinating power substantially, especially in terms of penetrating the country with their own officials, which would have provided them with more organizational autonomy. None the less, war and inflation did prompt the state elite to try to manage their capital resources more rationally, bringing the salt and iron mines of the crown under closer supervision, increasing output, and levying surtaxes on traditional tolls.

And in Lower Austria they initiated surveys of the size of the peasantry in order to enhance monetary contributions from the Estates.[44]

These and other efforts to intensify resource extraction with the help of the Estates, who also collaborated in military defence, were the building blocks enabling the Habsburgs to extend their infrastructural reach and co-ordinating power, albeit slowly. In the late seventeenth century the Lower Austrian *Stände* even agreed to approve financial contributions at ten-year recesses, which curtailed their influence over internal government substantially and prepared the way for the reforms of Maria Theresa in the mid-eighteenth century. During Maria Theresa's reign, much of the infrastructure of the Lower and Upper Austrian Estates was dissolved or integrated with the central administration, opening the way to ruling subjects directly.[45] The previous infrastructural dualism was therefore not as counter-productive as some historians have believed. Common interests in strengthening the military and financial capacity of the Habsburgs and the overlapping of officials assured the prevalence of co-operation between them. This does not mean that the Estates were wholly compliant, however, as they engaged the Habsburgs in difficult and continual bargaining over the competence of institutions and the extraction and distribution of resources.

Bargaining over judicial competence

The hybrid nature of early modern law made bargaining between Habsburgs and Estates over judicial issues especially contentious. Like most European monarchs, the dynasty listened to the advice of prominent political theorists, such as Jean Bodin and Justus Lipsius, who insisted that the essence of royal power was the ability to make and change laws by command, from which emanated all other attributes of princely authority, or *iura majestatis*, which some historians have defined, perhaps wrongly, as 'sovereignty'.[46] However, the increase in legislative activity of early modern monarchs was not so much an example of growing autocratic power as of an enhanced capacity to organize relations between dominant groups, and between elites and subjects. Attempts to bind subjects and lordship to positive law, the expansion of judicial and police functions, and the codification of laws, were all crucial steps by which the Habsburgs envisioned to strengthen the central co-ordinating power of the state.

Although the literature on the legislative power and jurisdiction of the Estates and the Habsburg rulers is confusing, it is doubtful whether the *Stände* ever had any independent rights to make laws, except in their function as regents during minority rule. Even though at times they assumed legislative powers, by the late sixteenth century the Austrian (and even Bohemian) Estates did not have independent authority to enact new laws.[47]

However, they did dispense lower (and often higher) justice at the local level, and participated in the codification of laws.[48] What was at issue in the various 'constitutional' disputes with the Habsburgs during the sixteenth and early seventeenth centuries was less the Estates' ability to issue legislation than the meaning and venue of their right to consent to princely legislation. It was not the ruler's authority to issue laws that caused concern, but rather the question of what exactly constituted the Estates' immutable customary rights and privileges, and whether they could be derogated and abrogated by the prince without the Estates' consent. Moreover, disputes evolved over whether the new courts of appeal instituted by the Habsburgs should have final jurisdiction in interpreting laws. Connected to these two issues were contests over the Estates' right to resist if rulers acted contrary to immutable customary rights and natural law, which were, as I shall show in the next chapter, also related to problems of religious reform and material survival.

During the Middle Ages, the Austrian duke was considered the protector of *lex regia*, the sphere of positive law, and *ius* – that is, justice or right (*Recht*), which was congruent with natural law, and connected to divine law. When *Recht* was in doubt, it was to be 'found' through judicial decisions in council of the *meliores et majores*, who together with the prince comprised the *Land* (the territory). Because consultation became consent in finding *Recht* (right), this opened the possibility for the claim that the ruler could be resisted if he proceeded against right.[49] However, late medieval norms of what constituted natural law were not stable and uniform, although since the thirteenth century jurists usually included contracts and pacts, property rights, and rights to a hearing and defence. Even more diverse and confusing were conceptions of customary rights and traditions, although all the Estates of the Habsburg domains, in response to challenges by the rulers, began to collect evidence for codifying them, and claimed that they were immutable because they were based on a contract to which the ruler was bound by natural, divine law.

Like other continental rulers, the late medieval dukes of the Austrian lands used the doctrine of *princeps legibus solutus* (the prince is not bound by the law) when asserting supreme jurisdiction over their own territory in relation to external powers, particularly *vis-á-vis* the Pope and the emperor, and when announcing their claim to make new or positive law in their lands.[50] The term *legibus solutus* was used interchangeably with *merum imperium, suprema potestas, plenitudo potestatis* and, at times, even with *potestas absoluta*. As Kenneth Pennington has shown, late medieval jurists interpreted these formulas to mean that the prince was above, or free from, positive law (for example, his predecessor's), which he could therefore alter. However, being bound by divine or natural law, he was not to change established or customary law without cause, and was bound by public and private contracts.[51]

Although Duke Rudolf IV claimed in the mid-fourteenth century that he could 'abolish every sort of liberty, right and custom', it seems doubtful whether he meant he could violate natural, or divine, law, especially since in practice he confined himself to making changes on his crown lands (*Kammergut*). Certainly, his sixteenth-and seventeenth-century successors meant to be bound by it, even if it was not always clear just what constituted natural law.[52] During the 1530s, when the unruly Bohemian Estates demanded the right of consent to changes Ferdinand I had made to what they considered their traditional rights (for example, free assembly and access to office), the Habsburg asserted his *plenitudo potestatis* (fullness of power), meaning that the Estates' rights had been posited through his will. In other words, what powers they exercised had been delegated to them by the ruler and belonged to the sphere of positive law.[53] While this was a controversial claim, most jurists considered authority over positive law not to be the same as *potestas absoluta* (absolute power), a notion that was connected to arbitrary or tyrannical rule, and rarely supported by German and other early modern theorists.[54] None the less, Ferdinand I's assertion is indicative of the Habsburgs' attempts to subsume customary under positive law. Since the ruler could change the latter for various reasons, but needed consent to derogate customary law, the Estates resisted such an equation and the issue remained a major source of conflict. Although the dynasty generally accepted the idea that changes to customary rights and privileges of the Estates that were anchored in contracts required their consent, by the early sixteenth century they began to require written proof for contractual claims and to assert the right to change customary law in the interest of the common weal and public utility.

In a draft of 1528 for the collection of legal norms (*Landrechtsbuch, or Landrechtsordnung*) of the Austrian duchies, Ferdinand I claimed that he had, like a king, sole legislative power in his domain, and that all decisions made by the Estates at the Diets required his sanction. His authority included not only the ability to make new laws, but also to change and replace customary law (*Gewohnheitsrecht*) and the *Landrecht*. He further asserted that custom became law if it was in use for at least ten years, and it remained in force as long as it was not overruled more than once (presumably by a court of appeal), and did not conflict with legislation. All positive laws and *Gewohnheitsrecht,* Ferdinand insisted, had to be subjected to reason (*'verstand und ... vernunft'*) and could be derogated and abrogated by the ruler if found to be against moral precepts (*'erberkhait und guet sitten'*).[55] None the less, the emperor added that he chose to exercise his legislative power with the consent of his Estates (*'mit rat und willen unserer landleut'*), although *de jure* he was merely bound by the divine law of nature and reason (*'götlichen gesezt der natur und vernunft'*).[56]

Ferdinand I's conceptions of his legislative power were thus in line with interpretations of Roman law by late medieval and sixteenth century jurists. Hardly innovators, they adhered to largely earlier notions of *princeps legibus solutus*, which gave the prince full authority over positive law, but not unlimited, arbitrary power. He was bound by divine, natural law, particularly the state of the realm (*status regni*), an amorphous concept that included legal norms, custom and traditions, such as the *Landesordnung;* these could not be abrogated without good cause, such as public utility, or the public good.[57] The emperor also supported another late-medieval notion, namely that consultation with the Estates guaranteed greater validity to changes in established law, although such counsel was not an independent right but, instead, an obligation that was derived from the prince's will.[58] However, Ferdinand did not stipulate whether he would consult a full assembly of *Landleut* (members of the Estates), and thus left it open to confine himself to the council and judgments *(Gutachten)* issued by assessors of the territorial court of appeal (*Landrechtsbeisitzer*), whom he appointed from members of the territorial Estates. None the less, being bound by natural law meant that the ruler could not overthrow arbitrarily established legal norms and rights anchored in contracts, although it remained unclear what was to be done if he did.

Ferdinand I's successors, who also stressed the divine sanction of their authority, were equally familiar with royalist theorists, such as Bodin and, particularly, Lipsius's art of Neostoic politics, which stressed the effective public projection of the ruler as upholder of religious and moral principles that bound together the Christian community. The Habsburgs cultivated their role of patriarchal house-fathers, whose authority could not be opposed, but who were not tyrants and, avoiding the wickedness of Machiavellian methods, observed customary and natural law.[59] Although they rarely used the concept of *potestas absoluta,* they claimed to have final authority in governing the Habsburg territories, particularly in enacting positive law. It was rare for Austrian Habsburgs to insist publicly, as did Archduke Ferdinand in 1598, that he had the *plenum imperium* (that is, fullness of power – *plenitudo potestatis*), which included religious sovereignty, and therefore did not require the consent of the Estates to implement the Peace of Augsburg in Styria. Interestingly, the Styrian Estates responded to the archduke's claim to have full Imperial power, by stating that he only had the '*absolutum et merum imperium*' over his royal lands (*Kammergut*) – that is, the ducal cities and markets. And, in a response to his reprimand, the Estates stated that they had always recognized him as their 'legal, natural, hereditary and mighty [*vollmechtigen*] territorial prince and thus *absolutum principem,*' but insisted that his *Imperium* did not extend to conscience. By invoking the term 'mighty' the *Stände* acknowledged the fullness of their duke's power (*plenitudo potestatis*), and equating this with *absolutum principem* was merely in line with contemporary theory that accepted the prince's authority over positive law. In their mind, supreme authority, or full power to command was not incompatible with being checked by natural, divine law, and neither contradicted the Estates' right of consent, nor their executive powers.[60] However, to conjure up the Estates' right to resist a tyrannical ruler in matters of faith was an issue over which contemporary theorists were more divided, and I shall return to this issue in the next chapter.

Ferdinand's own notion of his power was also not far removed from Bodin's belief that the power of legitimate rulers was constrained only by divine and natural laws, and that they therefore had to respect the liberty and property of free subjects, and honour previous contracts. Although Bodin eventually confined the ruler's need to seek the Estates' consent to new taxation, since it affected their property, he continued to recommended that a prudent king would consult with his Estates. Rulers were further bound by fundamental customary laws, and by 1576 Bodin had narrowed his definition of fundamental laws to observing the rule of succession and the preservation of the royal domain, but prohibited resistance to a sitting king in case of violation.[61] As we shall see later, in the early seventeenth century the *Stände* focused on these abrogations of natural law to justify their opposition to Ferdinand II, but also asserted their right to resist the ruler.

The Austrian and Bohemian *Stände* did not challenge Habsburg authority over positive law, and even asked the ruler to issue some *Polizeiordnungen* (literally, police ordinances), which the Habsburgs promulgated increasingly during the sixteenth and seventeenth centuries in order to regulate social and economic relations. Initially, the aim of police ordinances had been to correct disorder and preserve peace in the community where customary law did not provide a remedy, but this was extended by rulers to claim authority in correcting all disorder by enacting new laws. The crown even began to interfere with the local jurisdiction of noble landowners and issued a series of *Polizeiordnungen* to co-ordinate relations between peasant subjects and nobles, particularly economic dependencies (for example, labour services or *Robot*), often without the consent of the Estates.[62] Using complaints by the subject population in the form of appeals or revolts, the Habsburgs usually justified these police ordinances, which also attempted to regulate public behaviour and elite expenditure on luxuries, on the grounds of securing peace, law and order for the common weal, public benefit or utility, and even for coping better with military threats. Under the impact of the religious Reformation, *Polizeiordnungen* were also issued to establish norms for moral behaviour, and competed with ecclesiastical jurisdiction. In addition, the Habsburg rulers issued new *Ordnungen* for servants and urban guilds, although the Estates prompted these regulations frequently. Police ordinances thus provided an expedient to bind subjects and lordship more closely to positive law, although it is not entirely clear how they were implemented at the local level. It appears that at least some landowners added these state regulations to their own manorial ordinances (also called *Polizeiordnung*), which codified local customary law. This, and the fact that initiatives of the Estates lay behind some of the Habsburg ordinances, suggests that elites had an interest in the state's regulation of social relations through civil and criminal law, as long as law enforcement remained in their hands.[63]

Although jurisdiction over high and low justice remained exceedingly fragmented in the Habsburg lands until the eighteenth century, the crown had some success in bringing more unity to criminal justice (*Strafrecht*) in the territories that were united under a *Regiment,* a regional goverment. During the first half of the sixteenth century, procedures for the *Strafrecht* were codified in collaboration with the Estates in all of the Austrian hereditary lands, and the jurisdiction between higher and lower district courts (*Ämter*) was regulated and approved by the ruler in 1557 in a *Landesgerichtsordnungen* (not to be confused with *Landrecht*). In some areas, such as Styria and Carinthia, the Habsburgs even managed to appoint *Bannrichter,* their own judges who collected the evidence in criminal cases. Noble landholders, especially in Upper Austria, objected to this, because in Upper Austria the legally trained *Bannrichter* were appointed traditionally by the noble in charge of the district courts, the local Landgerichte. The office was soon abandoned in Lower Austria, together with Ferdinand I's attempts (in 1534) to bring criminal justice under the control of just four district courts.[64]

Autonomy over heritable seigneurial justice in the Austrian lands was also threatened by new courts of appeal, and the Estates put up considerable resistance to their establishment from the early sixteenth century. Criminal justice over noble subjects was dispensed by *Landgerichte,* or district courts, usually attached to larger landed estates of nobles. Even high justice over subjects' life (*Blutbann*) was largely in the province of these *Landgerichte.*[65] In order to have more influence over the heritable jurisdiction of nobles over subjects, Maximilian I had created an independent court of appeal (*Hofgericht* or *Kammergericht*) at the city of Wiener Neustadt, which accepted appeals from subjects and applied Roman Law. But the Estates managed to force its dissolution as an independent body by refusing funds for Maximilian's Italian wars. Its functions were taken over by the *Hofrat,* an Austrian Aulic Council attached to the Lower Austrian *Regiment,* over which the Estates had at least some influence, since the ruler was obliged to appoint local nobles as assessors, the *Landrechtsbeisitzer.*[66]

However, the *Stände* also resented the power of the *Regiment,* since its governor (*Statthalter*) and councillors were appointed by, and responsible to, the ruler. In 1519, the Estates of the five lands that had been united under one regional body, the *Niederösterreichische Regiment* (Lower and Upper Austria, Styria, Carinthia and Carnolia), resisted Maximilian I's will that the *Regiment* take over government after his death until his heir arrived. They refused to give homage until their privileges and rights were confirmed, and challenged the legitimacy of the *Regiment's* authority to act as regent. Claiming that it had been their long established right to rule the country during an interregnum or absence of the duke, they established their own government of sixty-four members in Vienna, appointed officials, printed money, and even administered the ducal domain. Charles v managed to divide the opposition members, but when Ferdinand took over the rule of the hereditary lands, he established a special court to deal with the leaders of the insurrection, among them two nobles, who were executed in 1522.[67] The *Regiment* retained its powers, but the government of Upper and Lower Austria was separated from the other three territories.

Another significant curtailment of the powers of the noble district courts (*Landgerichte*) was introduced in 1567, when all death and galley sentences (as well as proscription) were subjected to a review by the Aulic Council of the Lower Austrian *Regiment*.[68] When the Imperial Court moved permanently from Prague to Vienna in 1612, the Austrian Aulic Council was merged with the Imperial Aulic Council (*Reichshofrat*), the highest court of appeal for the Empire, and the Estates demanded in vain the re-establishment of a purely Austrian council where they had been assured at least that members of the Estates would interpret the law. Opposition to the Aulic Council, and bargaining with the Habsburgs over influence in the *Regimente* continued (particularly over the appointment of assessors and governors) and, as we shall see, reached a climax during the Counter Reformation.[69]

Clearly, the Austrian *Stände* were not willing to accept the Habsburgs' infringements on what they considered to be their customary rights, and their relations with Maximilian i and Ferdinand i alternated between collaboration with legal codification and police ordinances, and open rebellion. Prompted by the rulers, the noble Estates began feverishly to collect and codify their *Landesordnungen*, which, as drafts of *Landrechtsbücher*, provided an important tool in the continued bargaining with the Habsburgs over their rights and privileges. Such collection of rights, customs and rules concerning property and succession rights, court procedures and jurisdictions concerning the relations between members of the *Stände* and with the ruler were undertaken by all the Habsburg Estates throughout the sixteenth and seventeenth centuries.[70] By codifying their customary rights and privileges in the *Landesordnung*, the *Stände* hoped to fix them as *Gewohnheitsrecht*, while the Habsburgs intended to subsume them under positive law. It is not clear, however, why most of the *Landesordnungen* were not approved officially by them. Perhaps the Estates feared that this would transform customary into positive law, and so subject what they considered to be their immutable rights to changes by the ruler. Considering the nobles' notion of what constituted their rights, it also seems obvious that the Habsburgs must have had little interest in giving formal approval. As I shall show in the following chapter, by the early seventeenth century the Austrian and Bohemian noble Estates asserted their members' freedom from taxation, the right to high office, to call assemblies and approve not only taxation but also royal and ducal succession, to consent to declarations of war and peace, and to make independent defence treaties with confederates, especially when resisting unjust and tyrannical rulers.

However, the *Landrecht* did obtain a contractual character to which both the prince and the Estates were bound through the act of homage, or *Erbhuldigung,* when the ruler gave an oath to preserve the (unspecified) law of the land, and a ceremonial confirmation of the rights and liberties of the *Landleute,* who in turn swore loyalty to the prince upon succession.[71] This explains why, throughout the sixteenth and early seventeenth centuries, the *Stände* insisted on having their liberties confirmed before giving homage. This had become particularly important, because the Habsburgs had begun to request proof that specific rights had in fact been granted or confirmed by previous rulers, and to justify changes in customary law not only on the grounds of divine (moral) law, but also in the interest of the common good.[72]

Similar issues over customary rights were at the heart of conflicts between the Habsburgs and the Bohemian elites during the sixteenth century. When Ferdinand I summoned an emergency military levy during the Schmalkaldic War against German Protestants without seeking consent from the Diet (*Snem*), the Bohemian Estates (*Sjezdy*) rebelled in 1547, but ultimately were too divided and unwilling to use their smaller army offensively against the king. Next to a call for religious reform and unity, the largely Utraquist (Hussites of various persuasion) opposition of nobles and burghers demanded the initiative to assemble when the king was absent or refused to call a *Landtag,* and for discussing religious matters. Ferdinand I had denied them this right to free assembly.[73] How important changes in judicial competence were in this rebellion, and how this intersected with economic and religious interests, is evident from the Estates' request for confessional parity in all district and territorial courts, and royal councils, and the demand that all assessors (*Beisitzer*) of the territorial court (*Landgericht*) be chosen from a list established by and consisting of Estate members from each district circle. Previously, they had been selected by the king after consulting with some assessors and the Estates' officials. The Bohemian opposition also wanted to exclude the representatives of the royal law court (*Kammergericht*) from all urban and territorial law courts, and to prohibit the king from setting up special royal courts to judge disputes with the Estates. The territorial law court, controlled by Estates' officials and noble assessors, dispensed the *Landrecht* and remained the highest court of appeal, rather than the royal Aulic council, and even the place where charges were to be filed against the king. Furthermore, royal decisions against customary rights and privileges of the Estates were to have no validity, and the Estates could not be forced to obey such mandates of the king.

Apparently, in Bohemia too, the Habsburg king intended to eliminate customary law (the source of the Estates' rights) and restrict their privileges to those that could be supported by written documents. And the demands of the Estates cannot be viewed as an effort to preserve or gain legislative rights or 'sovereignty' over the king, as some have asserted; rather, they were designed to preserve their customary rights and privileges as fundamental laws which rulers could not abrogate or derogate without their consent, and to assert their right to resistance if the rulers did so.[74] It does not appear that the Bohemian Estates used natural law arguments explicitly to justify their rebellion, although there was much talk about protecting the common good (*Gemeinen Nutzen*), bringing to mind notions of late-medieval jurists who justified resistance if the prince violated natural law and broke previous agreements that protected the public good.[75] Ferdinand I obviously had a different view of their right to resist and, as he had done with the Lower Austrians, established a special court of law to punish the rebels, four of whose leaders were executed; over a dozen nobles lost property and were put under permanent house arrest. The king insisted that he had not violated any of the customary rights and privileges that the Estates could support clearly with evidence. This had for some time posed a problem, especially for the towns, since fire had destroyed many old documents.[76]

Although I shall pursue this further in the following chapter, it is already clear that during the sixteenth century the Habsburgs did not have extensive autocratic powers to control their elites or their common subjects. They faced locally segmented and heritable jurisdictions, and a plurality of authorities who made claims to share 'rights of majesty', which involved achieving their consent through continual bargaining over taxation, defence, and jurisdiction.[77] The Estates demanded that their proposition and opinions rendered at the Diets needed to be discussed and taken into consideration. Changes introduced by the ruler regarding their property and other customary rights without their consent justified their resistance. Nevertheless, as this chapter has demonstrated, elite opposition during the sixteenth century was an integral part of state-building, which was to a large extent the result of interactive claims and counter-claims of rulers and elites.[78]

While the Habsburgs avoided public claims to absolute power, they did follow the lead of Bodin and other jurists by asserting sole authority over making new laws. Although they accepted the idea that they were bound to contracts by divine and natural law, and could not alter customary rights without good reason or consent, they also began to require written proof of such rights. And, in contrast to the Estates, the Habsburgs viewed consent merely as consultation, and insisted that it and all the other rights they exercised were delegated by the ruler, thus denying the *Stände* the right of resistance, and challenging the status of customary rights as immutable.

In practice, it was impossible to deny the *Stände* the right to consent to taxation, to execute laws and participate in military defence, as well as to share in numerous other ways in the government of the territory. It was also difficult to abrogate their cherished privileges. Since Habsburg finances remained precarious and the size of their small *Hofstaat* was approximately 600–800 persons, they continued to rely heavily on the co-operation of local notables, nobles and Church authorities. As we have seen, the Austrian Estates co-operated to some extent in enhancing the legislative power of the Habsburgs, since, in the wake of increased urban and peasant unrest, they shared their interest in regulating the social order and moral life of their subjects. For similar reasons, they participated in codifying procedures for criminal law. However, they objected to attempts at bringing courts of appeal under state control, since this questioned their final judicial authority over their subjects, especially in decisions of life and death. Initially, they were more successful in resisting Habsburg attempts to subsume the *Landrecht* under positive law, and their efforts at beginning to systematize it made it a useful tool in bargaining with the prince. This, as well as attempts to bring some unity to criminal law, favoured territorialization. Indeed, the integration of the Austrian lands during the seventeenth century would have been impossible without these measures. By applying Roman law increasingly and extending legislative activity via the issue of *Polizeiordnungen,* and the establishment of central courts of appeal, the Habsburgs also managed to further their power to co-ordinate social relations and institute binding rules governing various activities of the elite, even though the execution of justice and enactment of the *Landesordnung* remained in the hands of the *Stände,* who also defended many of their other traditional privileges successfully.

The comparatively slow and piecemeal growth of the ruler's infrastructural power had much to do with the entrenched rights of the Estates in all the lands of the Austrian Habsburgs. Being late state-builders in an unfavourable geopolitical space delayed territorial consolidation, which had to begin with unifying each individual region. Integration was most successful in the Austrian territories, where the process had already begun prior to the Habsburgs. Yet even here the dependence of the dynasty on the regional Estates for taxation grants presented an important obstacle to consolidation, especially when changes in methods of warfare and inflation coincided with major conflicts with the Ottoman empire. But, necessarily, these developments provided incentives to enhance resource extraction and strengthen the financial and military infrastructure. Although this increased the interdependence and need to bargain with the regional Estates, shared interests in the security of the territory usually made the elites willing to co-operate in defence matters and thereby strengthen the military and financial capacity of the Habsburgs. This also developed the *Stände's* own infrastructural power, but the overlapping of their officials and administrative offices with central institutions ensured a certain degree of co-operation between them. Moreover, the Habsburgs began to reorganize and regulate the organs of government in a vertical manner. Thus, despite its limitations as a central treasury, the *Hofkammer* became a tool in regulating the Estates' activities in resource extraction and co-ordinating the different local treasuries, while the War Council started to regulate centrally the provisioning of armies and the maintenance of defensive works, which were frequently in the hands of the Estates. Larger armies further enabled the Habsburgs to better enforce punitive strikes against those who objected to increases in taxation and other measures, and eventually to establish a standing army. All of this prepared the way for more extensive state-building efforts during the eighteenth century.

In short, the seventeenth century symbiosis between Habsburgs and Estates was not a new phenomenon, and the political culture in the Austrian lands had been characterized by an ongoing bargaining between rulers and elites since at least the fifteenth century. Nevertheless, this interactive process was strengthened and transformed during the sixteenth century. The *Stände* certainly shared with their rulers an interest in extending the co-ordinating power of the state, but they also desired to enhance their own infrastructural capacity and preserve their customary rights as fundamental and immutable laws. As the following chapters will continue to demonstrate, the elite tended to view their participation in government as strengthening the co-operative power of ruler and Estates, and in this way they made an important contribution to territorial integration. However, there were limits to the communality of interests. The increased interdependence and need for consultation multiplied areas of conflict arising between them, which explains why co-operation continually alternated with Estate opposition. The Reformation proved to be a watershed. Successful bargaining became progressively more difficult as negotiations over religious reform were linked intrinsically to political culture and, together with problems in the distribution of resources, produced deep divisions among the elite.

2
Religious Reformations and Civil War

The Protestant Reformation posed an unprecedented challenge to secular authorities and had a profound effect on the interaction between ruler, elites and subjects. It accelerated social unrest among the peasantry and urban populations, and strengthened the opposition of the noble and urban Estates against the prince. Four crucial issues needed to be renegotiated between Estates and princes. First, who was to gain control of Church institutions and property. Second, who would have jurisdiction over the moral and social discipline of subjects? Third, finding a resolution to these issues opened new, or aggravated existing, 'constitutional' problems that governed relations between the prince, the Church and secular Estates. In areas of mixed confession, especially the Holy Roman Empire and the Habsburg lands, it was crucial to establish institutions or tribunals that could regulate relations and enforce agreements between the confessions. Fourth, contests arose over material issues not only with respect to Church property, but also with regard to the distribution of court patronage and the regulation of patron–client relations generally. Because religion was such an important bond cementing social ties, clientage system were necessarily affected by the changing balance between the various confessions.

In the German principalities, Protestant rulers eventually resolved these problems largely in their favour. Having become guardians or supreme heads of the Church, they not only extended their religious sovereignty but also their co-ordinating power over civil society through regulating the moral discipline and welfare of their lower subjects. Most of them settled the constitutional conflicts with their Estates in the interest of state centralization. The close alliance with the Counter-Reformation also provided Catholic rulers of South-German principalities with the opportunity to exert more central control over religious affairs, which helped them to widen the co-ordinating activities of the state. And imposing religious uniformity further prepared the foundation for social and territorial integration in Catholic territories.[1] However, confessional homogeneity was not achieved either easily or quickly, in part because new variants of

Protestantism spread during the late sixteenth century, and because some rulers and elites chose different religions to aid them in political contests. Even after internal sociopolitical struggles had settled down in most German principalities, serious constitutional problems remained unresolved at the level of Imperial government concerning the regulation of relations between the confessions and between princes and emperor until at least 1648.

Although closely connected to the situation in the Reich, the Habsburg dynasty faced the Reformation under circumstances that were far more complex and difficult than those of a small German principality, or those of larger, more unified, Western monarchies, such as France. The emergence of Protestantism coincided with the rise of the dynasty as a major European power, which meant that geopolitical considerations diverted much of its attention to major international conflicts. As the Habsburgs extended their power into Spain and overseas, and acquired the crowns of Hungary–Croatia and Bohemia, they became involved in wars with France and the Ottomans, a crisis of Imperial power, and numerous rebellions from their subjects. While Charles V was preoccupied with uprisings in Spain and wars with France (in Italy and the north west), his brother, Archduke Ferdinand I tried to centralize the Eastern patrimony, but soon became engaged in defending the newly acquired kingdoms against the Ottomans and the princes of Transylvania. In fact, from the beginning of Charles V's reign as emperor (1519–56) and Ferdinand's rule in the Austrian duchies (1521) and in the kingdoms of Bohemia and Hungary–Croatia (1526–7), war was a virtual constant until well into the second part of the sixteenth century. In the wake of the Reformation, the two Habsburgs also confronted major uprisings from the peasantry and urban subjects in the Reich and in their own lands, a war with German princes and rebellion from their Estates. Although they defeated popular uprisings, as well as opposition from the Schmalkaldic League of the largely Lutheran princes, and the revolt of the Protestant Bohemian *Stände* (1547), conflict with the German princes resumed during the early 1550s, culminating in the Peace of Augsburg of 1555, Charles V's abdication (1556), and the official separation of the Spanish dominions from the empire and the Eastern lands of the Austrian line.[2]

Difficulties in dealing effectively with Protestantism arose not only from the Habsburgs' geopolitical position and the onset of the Reformation at a late stage of state-building, but also from the entrenched position of their Estates over monetary matters, and the political and cultural heterogeneity that already characterized their composite state. This diversity explains to a large degree why Lutheranism could not obtain full dogmatic harmony in any one province, let alone across an entire duchy or kingdom. It certainly made inroads quickly in Hungary, and found fertile ground among Bohemian Brethren and Utraquists, who had preserved Hussite traditions.

Versions of Anabaptist beliefs spread across the Habsburg lands, with twenty-five different persuasions in Moravia alone, but, with the help of mainstream Protestants, these groups were soon brutally suppressed. By the late sixteenth century, Calvinism had found converts nearly everywhere. It was strong in Bohemia and became dominant in Hungary, where it was flanked by a variety of other religious movements, such as the Trinitarians and Unitarians of Transylvania.[3]

The situation in the Austrian lands provides an excellent case study for analysing in detail the difficulties the Habsburgs faced in dealing with religious reform, how this affected the relations with their elites, and the opportunities the Counter-Reformation offered to advance state power. Focusing on developments in the Austrian lands after the mid-sixteenth century, but being by no means confined to it, this chapter continues to provide a narrative of events as they pertain to changing relations between Habsburgs and noble Estates. It attempts to explain the attraction of Protestantism for nobles, and why the Habsburgs initially favoured compromise with them. After considering briefly the spreading Lutheran Reformation up to the 1570s, I then show the connections between developments in the Reich, Europe and the hereditary lands with respect to confessionalization and the struggle over Church property up to the resolution of the brotherly struggle between Emperor Rudolf and Archduke Matthias in 1612. Finally, I focus on the formation of active resistance by the Estates of the Habsburg lands, especially in Lower Austria and Bohemia, and the consequences of defeat up to the end of this phase of the Thirty Years' War in 1622. A profile of the Protestant groups that evolved in Lower Austria between 1618 and 1620 begins my exploration of why the conflict became a violent one.

Lutheran Reformation, Church patronage and compromise

Lutheran ideas spread very quickly into the hereditary lands, where the elite was well acquainted with humanist critiques. The urban and noble Estates of Upper, Lower and Inner Austria, who began to petition the Habsburgs to introduce the true 'Evangelium' as early as 1525, adopted some Lutheran practices after 1530, but declared their support for the Augsburg confession officially only in 1556, after the Peace of Augsburg. Although many Austrian nobles had appointed Lutheran-minded preachers to their parishes very early, changes in ritual and church services were introduced very gradually throughout the century.[4] One of the reasons for this was the continued hope for Church reform and union, at least between Catholic and Lutheran persuasions. Such expectations remained particularly strong in the Austrian lands, where the Protestants did not manage to establish a consistory or a superintendent, and Ferdinand I petitioned the

Papacy and Church council to introduce the chalice for the laity and marriage for priests, as well as other reforms.[5] In 1541, Luther still noted similarities in church services between the two confessions in the Reich, and the Imperial court councillor, Georg Eder, remarked in 1585 that in Vienna one could not distinguish among the various persuasions, and this made persecution difficult.[6]

Visitation reports indicate that the moral and financial condition of the Roman Church in the hereditary lands required prompt reform measures. Monasteries and convents had few members. Many of the clergy displayed a lax attitude towards chastity and asceticism, and clerical recruitment was dismal. Reform, which was largely dependent on the initiative of the Habsburgs, met with serious obstacles. As elsewhere in their domains, relations between the crown and the Catholic Church in the Austrian lands were complex, and the power of the prince over religious affairs rather limited.[7] With the exception of small areas under the control of the two small bishoprics of Wr. Neustadt and Vienna, which were dependent on the Habsburg rulers (who presented candidates to their sees), Upper and Lower Austrian Catholic churches were largely under the jurisdiction of the bishoprics of Passau and Salzburg. This presented a serious obstacle to Habsburg influence over the Church, because the prince bishops of Salzburg either tried to steer an independent course or were, like Passau, controlled by the Bavarian Wittelsbach, whose members supplied most of its bishops, at least until the end of the sixteenth century, and guarded their own jurisdiction carefully against Habsburg encroachments. Thus the Wittelsbach archbishop of Salzburg objected to a visitation of churches in the Austrian duchies (1543–4), which Ferdinand I had ordered. Even where the Habsburgs exerted influence, as in the bishopric of Vienna, overlapping jurisdictions and competition with the other dioceses, the university and city of Vienna, and the duke, limited effective Church reform.[8] According to reports of Councillor Eder to Duke Albrecht V of Bavaria, the conditions in the Passau see were still dismal in 1577, in part because of a lack of priests, but also because its officials seem to have had little interest in imposing religious reform in Upper and Lower Austria; even some of the top clergy still lived in '*publico concubinatu*'.[9]

The Habsburg rulers exerted greater influence over the dioceses of Inner Austria, such as Gurk, Lavant, Seckau and Laibach, which co-operated readily with them in instituting Catholic reforms. This probably explains why the ducal Counter-Reformation was more successful in the late sixteenth century in Inner Austria than in Lower and Upper Austria.[10] However, the Habsburg dukes had made a crucial step in the development of territoriality and increasing their co-ordinating power over the Church during the late Middle Ages, when they gained the right to nominate (*ius praesentandi*) bishops in the Austrian lands even though this did not include Passau or Salzburg. Moreover, they obtained the protective advocacy (*Schirmvogtei*) over monasteries, freeing these institutions from the advocacy of bishops and noble landlords. It provided rulers with monastic patronage rights and the ability to impose the appointment of noble clients on monasteries. As advocates (*Vogt*), the Habsburgs were regulators of churches' secular affairs, and monastic property could be administered as part of the crown lands. This justified the ruler's to claim aid and counsel, usually in the form of heavy extraordinary taxes.[11]

The nobility, however, retained patronage rights (*ius patronatus*) over the lower Churches they and their families had founded, and this presented the most important obstacle to internal Catholic reform and measures of the Counter-Reformation in the hereditary lands.[12] The *ius patronatus* included the right of nominating the person to hold ecclesiastical office and benefice, and to Church income during vacancies, but it also obliged patrons to maintain Church buildings. The general supervision of ecclesiastical property of these lower Churches belonged to the advocacy (*Vogtei*), a function which could be combined in the same person with the *ius patronatus*. The rights of a *Vogt* could vary greatly. He might only receive a payment for financial or other services rendered, but he could also hold judicial authority and feudal rights over Church subjects, usually bringing entitlements to services and dues, but also obligations for protection and safeguard.[13] Although many Austrian parishes were attached to monasteries, the nobility thus had substantial power over religious matters, and material and sociopolitical incentives to adopt Protestantism. Various reports from the church visitations the Habsburgs commissioned (1528, 1544 and 1556), as well as repeated legislation, support this contention. They complain that many nobles and urban patrons left Church offices vacant, diverted income of benefices to themselves, replaced priests with salaried Protestant preachers of their choice, revoked family donations and, in effect, confiscated ecclesiastical property.[14] The barons of Jörger present poignant examples of such activities in both Upper and Lower Austria, sugggesting that other nobles shared Adam von Puchheim's sentiments that he and his peers were 'at the same time lords and bishops on our property; we hire and fire clerics and they have to obey us; church property was donated by our ancestors, therefore, it is ours.'[15] In the Austrian lands the question of leadership over the Protestant Church remained open, and such practices appear to have been widespread. In most German Protestant principalities, in contrast, it was clear that the ruler had the *jus reformandi* and administrative authority over Church endowments. Even though the Protestant reformers were against it, there were, none the less, similar confiscations of ecclesiastical property on the part of noble patrons in numerous areas.[16]

As the confessional map of Lower Austrian parishes established by Loesche suggests, the majority of the population had become Protestant by the late sixteenth century, particularly in the districts above and below the

Manhartsberg, located north of the Danube. This confirms others' estimates that about four-fifths of Vienna's population were Lutheran in 1564, and is in line with my own findings that about 90 per cent of the Lower Austrian nobility was Protestant in 1580. Conversion of nobles was also extensive in Upper and Inner Austria, as well as in Bohemia and Hungary, although it was less common in Croatia–Slavonia, perhaps in order to defy the Hungarian elites.[17] Unfortunately, we lack in-depth studies that analyse the motives of nobles for turning Lutheran. The acts of defiance of the Jörger family against orders by the Habsburgs to close their churches to urban and rural subjects suggests that some used religious differences as a means of opposing the extensions of the ruler's influence over them, and that nobles competed with the crown to have more control over the clergy and dependents on their domain. Pressures from subjects, even fear of rebellion, also seem to have played a role in the nobility's leaning towards Lutheran reform.[18] And, as we have seen, particularly important was the desire of landholders to appropriate tithes, benefices, and other Church income and properties, although the influence of humanism and the conviction that reform was essential for spiritual reasons cannot be ruled out. Evidently, in a context of theological uncertainty and a fairly tolerant atmosphere, many hoped for religious reform and a union of Catholics and Lutherans, at least until the 1570s. The commitment to Protestantism was therefore a very gradual occurrence, and it had multicausal roots. Spiritual and material interests were closely connected, both in adopting Protestantism and in rejecting a return to Catholicism.

Equally complex were the motives of the Habsburgs to remain Catholic. German Protestant princes may have been serious when they proposed that election of a Protestant ruler as Roman king was the only solution to the confessional problems in the Reich.[19] However, while some Habsburgs were sympathetic to Humanism and displayed a diplomatic spirit of accommodation, the dynasty never contemplated embracing Lutheranism seriously. There were good reasons for this, most important among them being that the ties with the Spanish line remained vital and strong, in spite of various political disagreements. The Austrians received much needed financial support from their richer Spanish relatives. Most important, during the sixteenth century there was a strong possibility that a member of the Austrian line would succeed to the Spanish throne, since all but one of Philip II's (1527–98) sons from his four marriages had died by 1599 and the Austrian branch still had plenty of male children. In fact, to position his line, Maximilian II had married Maria, a daughter of his uncle, Charles V, and had his two oldest sons educated in Spain. By the early seventeenth century, however, the situation had reversed, since all Maximilian II's numerous sons were left without heirs or had died. If Ferdinand II of the Inner Austrian line had remained without issue, Philip III could have claimed the Austrian patrimony through his mother Anna Maria (Philip II's fourth wife), and his wife Margareth, both Austrian archduchesses. Strong prospects of adding the Polish crown to the Austrian line was probably another incentive for remaining in the Catholic fold during the late sixteenth century.[20]

Even without the Spanish connection, a Habsburg conversion to Lutheranism was not a viable choice as long as the dynasty continued to desire to secure the Imperial crown. The symbolism and traditions of the Holy Roman Empire remained closely connected with the Catholic Papacy, beginning with the coronation oath that obliged the emperor to protect the Catholic faith and to remain loyal to Papacy and Church. A change in direction had to wait for a more secular era. As explained earlier, in addition to enormous prestige, the title of emperor held great importance for the Habsburgs precisely because their territories were not held together by a single royal title, and neither the crowns of Bohemia nor Hungary–Croatia were terribly secure possessions, which may also explain the dynasty's flirtations with the Polish throne. As emperors, the Habsburgs also had access to important resources in the form of prestige, honours, titles, fiefs and positions, which they could distribute among clients; and they derived continued financial support from the Reich to support their struggle against the Ottomans. At the same time, the Reich needed the Habsburgs, still the strongest dynasty of the empire, in order to check the Ottomans and the Western powers. Most likely, then, the possibility of a Protestant emperor was debated periodically, only for the purpose of eliciting concessions from the Austrian dynasty.[21] The Habsburgs were not religious fanatics, and considering the enormous political implications, they contemplated their religious choices carefully.

Ferdinand I certainly remained a committed Catholic, even though he had an open ear for humanist critique. Despite continual internal and external conflicts, he reacted quickly to the dissemination of Protestant ideas in the hereditary lands, in Bohemia and Hungary. Commissions for visitations of religious communities were followed by a series of mandates designed to stem the flood of Lutheran books, to reform preaching, fill empty parishes, and enforce Catholic ritual. While he failed to achieve a union of the Bohemian Utraquists and Catholics against the Brethren and Lutherans, Ferdinand assumed the right to fill the Prague bishopric, which had been vacant for 150 years. In 1551, he called the Jesuits to Vienna, and a few years later the order also began to establish schools and printing presses in Bohemia and Hungary. Some of Ferdinand's measures drew strong criticism both at home and in the Reich, and since implementation depended on co-operation of noble and urban authorities, most failed to stem the tide. For this reason, he never relinquished his efforts to find a compromise and unite Lutherans and Catholics.[22]

By mediating the Peace of Augsburg (1555), Ferdinand I brought the religious wars in the Reich to a halt. Outlawing all other Protestant persuasions, the settlement recognized the Lutheran church of the Augsburg

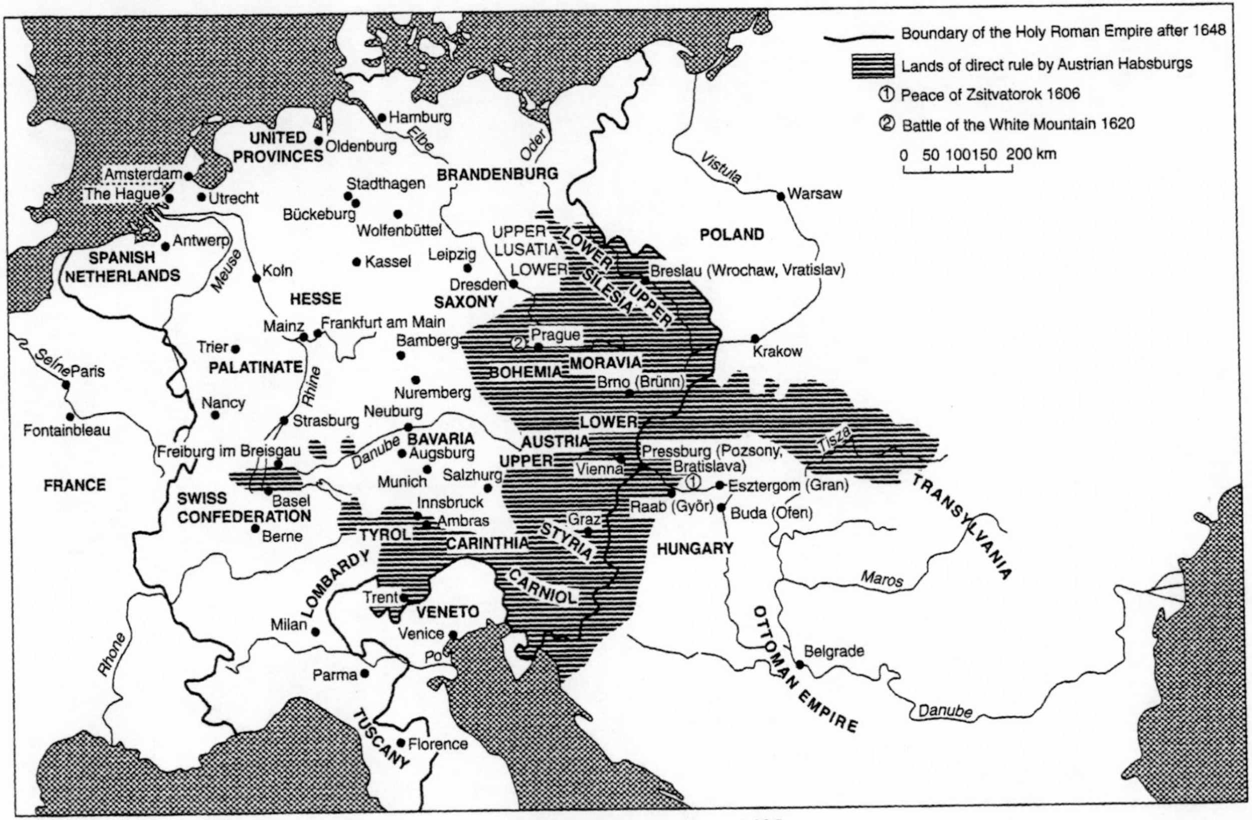

Central Europe about 1600

confession officially and subjected future conflicts between them and Catholics to arbitration by the law courts. While granting the secular Estates and Imperial knights the freedom to choose between the Augsburg confession and Catholicism, the most important resolution of the peace agreement stipulated that secular rulers were to determine the faith of their subjects, which was later summed up in the formula *cuius regio, eius religio*. Dissenting subjects were guaranteed the right to leave the territory, and Imperial cities of mixed confession were to establish parity between them. The Ecclesiastical Reservation prohibited further secularization of Church land, especially in the case of conversion by a Catholic prince-bishop.[23] Establishing a successful *modus vivendi* in the Reich for the next few decades, the Peace of Augsburg, however, also contained the seeds of future conflicts and could not withstand changes to the empire's confessional map. As this chapter shows, this was also true for the hereditary lands, where the Habsburgs initially were unable to enforce the formula of *cius regio, eius religio*.

Maximilian II (1564–76) continued his father's policy of building bridges between the two major confessions. Appealing for internal unity, he avoided persecution, built up Habsburg influence in the Empire, and generally pursued pragmatic strategies. Habsburg historians have viewed Maximilan's late Renaissance court and reign as the high point of Irenicism, because of his commitment to reconcile theological differences.[24] But the emperor never lost sight of the interests of his dynasty. Shortly before he began his reign he had pledged to remain Catholic, and afterwards he resisted the Estates' demands to allow the free exercise of Lutheranism, at least until 1568. Faced with the beginnings of an Estate-controlled Protestant Church in his territories, and concerned to protect the rights his ancestors had gained over Catholic institutions, Maximilian also established a *Klosterrat* (1568), a council under state control which was to secure Habsburg *Vogts-* and *Patronatsrechte* over monasteries and their attached parishes. The council managed the property of these foundations and parishes, appointed clergy, and generally became an important instrument of state control over the Church, as well as a bastion against the dissolution of Catholic institutions, so resembling the Spiritual Council (*Geistlicher Rat*) of other German Catholic princes.[25]

The financial weight of renewed war with the Ottomans (1566–8) forced the emperor to grant the Lower Austrian noble Estates the rights to exercise freely the Augsburg confession 'on and in all their castles, houses and estates for themselves, their servants and relatives', and 'in the countryside and attached churches also for their subjects'.[26] This freedom cost the *Stände* the considerable sum of 2 500 000 Gulden to cover Maximilian's debts. He insisted in a letter to his brother, Archduke Ferdinand, that he had made this concession out of necessity and against his will.[27] Indeed, since the total debts of the Habsburgs in 1564 amounted to 12 million Gulden, he conceded similar rights to the noble Estates in Upper Austria (1568), and verbally approved the *Confessio Bohemica* (1575), under which various Protestant groups in Bohemia united, although he prohibited its publication. Further, Archduke Karl granted the free exercise of the Augsburg confession to the noble Estate of Inner Austria (1572–8).[28] However, sovereign towns and markets, and subjects on crown lands, were excluded from these concessions. In the Austrian lands, the Protestant noble Estates received only verbal promises that permitted them to establish schools and appoint Lutheran preachers to their residences in sovereign towns and markets. Such omissions later allowed the Habsburgs to ban religious services in noble urban residences, to make urban centres – most of which were crown lands – the focal point of Counter-Reformation activities, and to divide the urban and noble Estates. The ambiguous wording of the written provisions also left an opening for other prohibitions in the future.

In Inner and Lower Austria Lutheran leaders soon drafted a so-called *Agenda* that regulated the form of worship, and this was sanctioned by the Habsburgs. Since the Upper Austrian Estates wanted their own *Agenda,* to which the crown could not agree, their religious privileges were never ratified formally. Apparently, Lutherans in the hereditary lands were unable to overcome theological differences and agree on a *norma doctrina* that might have led to the establishment of a consistory and a superintendent, two prerequisites for a unified Protestant Church. As in the Reich, the theological disputes were particularly disruptive between orthodox Gnesio-Lutherans, led by Matthias Flacius Illyricus (Matij Vlačić, 1520–72), and the followers of Melanchthon, whom the Flacian circle called 'Philippists' and accused of being crypto-Calvinists. Next to developing a resistance theory that claimed to avoid sedition, the Gnesio-Lutherans stressed original sin as the substance of human nature, denied that the human will co-operated in salvation, and resisted the rule of the prince in church matters.[29] Expelled from Saxony, many Flacians (Gnesio-Lutherans) came to the Austrian duchy, where the noble Estates desperately needed Lutheran preachers and wanted to establish a Protestant Church in the wake of the 1568 concessions. Flacianism thus gained support from leading members of the Estates, including the *Landmarschall* and the deputies. It also had a strong following among prominent noble families, such as the Puchheims and Geyers, residing in the area north of the Danube, especially the district above the Manhartsberg and, to a lesser extent, below the Manhartsberg. Melanchthon's followers, the 'Philippists', were close to the humanist position of Johannes Sturm of Strasburg, and were represented by the president of the court treasury, Reichart Streun (or Strein) von Schwarzenau (1536–1600), and a group of younger nobles with property along the Danube between Linz and St. Pölten. Between them stood those who were undecided, or lacked the theological knowledge to make a choice.

Unfortunately, we do not know the proportion of nobles who belonged to either the Flacians or the Philippinists.[30]

Many nobles and preachers of the Flacian persuasion resisted the introduction of the Lower Austrian Protestant *Agenda* of 1571 and established instead, like Veit Albrecht of Puchheim, their own rules of religious service on their Estates. Together with the resistance of many Flacian preachers to accept the compromise *Formula Concordiae* established in Württemberg and Saxony in 1577, the refusal to co-operate with the visitation of 1580 contributed to the failure to establish a territorial Protestant Church. However, by the beginning of the 1600s, a faction of the Lower Austrian noble Estates, aided by the death of a number of Flacian leaders and lack of recruits, finally succeeded in 1588 in banning preachers from using Flacian terminology, prohibiting further disputes and telling noble Church patrons to disengage themselves from theological debates. After 1590, Flacianism clearly lost momentum in the region, but Protestant unity remained difficult to achieve because Calvinism had spread into the Habsburg lands.[31] Prohibited by the Peace of Augsburg, nobles did not publicize conversions to the new faith, and it is therefore also impossible to determine the size of the Calvinist minority. The Lutheran Church in the Austrian territories remained a body without a head, which in fact served the interests of the largely Protestant noble Estates, who continued to control religious affairs and educational institutions in the countryside, and even in major towns. However, during the last decades of the 1500s, Protestantism was on the defensive as the relatively tolerant atmosphere of Maximilian's reign gave way to a more militant mood in the Catholic Church, and among princes and nobles under Rudolf II (1576–1612), who moved his court to Prague.

Confessionalization, counter-reform and the conflict over Church property

Several factors explain why attitudes hardened on all sides, and the empire became confessionalized. The Council of Trent in 1563 concluded with a reaffirmation of central Catholic doctrines, and the adoption of its decrees in most Catholic areas closed the doors to compromise between Lutherans and Catholics, even though the Habsburgs continued to harbour some hope for unity in their domain. As the Papacy launched a Catholic renewal by setting up nuncios in major cities, such as Prague, Graz and Vienna, and encouraged the Jesuits to take a harder line and increase their activities, Lutherans responded during the late 1580s by defining doctrine and ritual more clearly in order to end internal squabbles and delineate themselves clearly from Calvinists and Catholics.

Two further events contributed to the emergence of a mood of assertiveness and distrust on both sides. The Spanish Habsburgs' renewed war against the rebellious Netherlands led to a separation between

Catholic and Protestant provinces, with the latter adopting republican forms of government. In 1566, Protestant iconoclasts had stormed Catholic churches and monasteries, and the subsequent bloody Counter-Reformation and plundering by Spanish governors (the Duke of Alba and Don Juan) prompted Dutch Calvinists to retaliate during the 1570s. Their successful revolt against the Habsburgs certainly provided German Protestants and Estates in the hereditary lands, Bohemia and Hungary, with an example of successful defiance against the Habsburgs. It also spread fear among Catholics about Protestant plots. The other event, the St. Bartholomew's Day massacre of 1572 in France left, in turn, a long-lasting apprehension among Protestants across Europe regarding Catholic conspiracies aimed at exterminating them, but also heightened Catholic suspicions about counterplots.

Transgressions of the 1555 settlement added further to the increase of religious and political tensions. Besides the abandonment of confessional parity in many Imperial cities, the continued conversion of authorities, especially the turning to Calvinism of important counts, princes and electors with seats in the Imperial Diet, such as the electors of the Palatinate (1562) and the prince of Anhalt (1596), unsettled the power balance and problematized the fact that Calvinists had been left out of the religious settlement. But at the centre of the most explosive conflicts was the issue of Church land. Many Protestant rulers continued to annex Catholic property, in part because it helped them to eliminate the disruptive overlap of temporal and spiritual jurisdiction. The lands of many secular princes lay in up to ten different spiritual jurisdictions and this inhibited Church reform and the conversion process in their territories.[32] Gaining greater control over Church property and co-ordinating power over the clergy was also an integral part of continued state-building.

Frequently, Protestant nobles saw their socioeconomic survival threatened by their exclusion from profitable benefices and prebends of cathedral chapters, and had protested against this from the beginning. In the North-German Protestant lands the Ecclesiastical Reservation was therefore continually breached as cathedral chapters remained a material basis for sons of Protestant nobles and a means eventually of secularizing Church property. Unsettling as they were to the confessional power balance, these practices led continually to conflicts over seats and votes in the Imperial Diet.[33] When Lutheran-minded nobles were elected to bishoprics (as in Bremen or Magdeburg), they managed to obtain the emperor's enfeoffment (*Lehensindult*), providing interim access to secular authority and rights, such as a vote in the Imperial Diet, while awaiting papal confirmation. Whether or not this was forthcoming, the *Lehensindult* served many as a foundation for the seizure of ecclesiastical territory and property. But after the conclusion of the Council of Trent, appointments of Lutherans to Church benefices became more difficult, and the emperors became unwilling to bestow an interim *Lehensindult*. Naturally, this contributed to the hardening of confessional fronts.

Another means of secularizing ecclesiastical territory was when a bishop turned Protestant. A serious threat to Catholics was the conversion of the archbishop of Cologne, Gebhard Truchsess von Waldburg, in 1586. An Imperial elector, his refusal to abandon the territory, even after marriage, would have given Protestants a majority in the electoral college. War seemed likely, but Waldburg was bought off, and instead Cologne became a cornerstone of southern Catholicism under the leadership of the Bavarian Wittelsbach. Military conflict threatened to occur again after the Strasburg bishop tried to deprive Protestants of prebends (1583), leading to division and the election of two bishops, although the final compromise (1607) secured the bishopric for the Habsburgs and strengthened their political position in Alsace.[34] Protestant elites began to fear their ruin when the highest court, the *Reichskammergericht*, or Imperial Chamber Court, favoured a Catholic interpretation of the Peace of Augsburg in the cases of four monasteries (*Vierklösterstreit*) and declared the secularization of Church land and confiscation of ecclesiastical property by secular authorities in their territories to be illegal. Many Protestant rulers and princes anticipated that a flood of Catholic demands for the restitution of Church lands would inaugurate their economic and political ruin.

However, in most cases, actual economic decline was probably not the reason for the nobility's and princes' desire for Church land. As elsewhere, the demographic upswing and subsequent price inflation during the sixteenth century created incentives to increase agricultural production and to extend domain land.[35] But, as I shall show in Chapter 6, at the same time demographic change contributed to fears of material decline, since a greater number of noble children created problems where primogeniture was not practised and land was not easily divisible. Moreover, price inflation increased expenditure, especially for rulers who needed to pay for much larger and more expensive armies than before, and who could not raise taxes easily.

The struggles over Church resources had serious constitutional consequences, since they weakened the effectiveness of Imperial institutions in securing peace. As guarantor of the Peace of Augsburg, the *Reichskammergericht* had gained much authority after 1555 and enjoyed some success in this function. But when it had to rule on the critical issue of Church property, the Imperial Chamber Court, constituted on confessional parity, frequently could not arrive at a majority decision. Consequently, final judgment was passed on to the Imperial Diet (*Reichstag*), only to politicise issues further. At times, the emperor stopped the appeals against decisions of the highest court to the *Reichstag*, while the Protestant Estates, increasingly fearing the lack of impartiality of the courts, began to boycott the committee of deputies (*Deputationstag*) which, towards of the end of the 1500s, began to deal with appeals. Deferring arbitration to the Imperial Aulic Council

(*Reichshofrat*) which was controlled by Habsburgs and Catholic councillors and, in competition with the *Reichskammergericht,* acted as a high court, especially in cases concering Imperial fiefs, only aggravated further Protestant perceptions of the partiality of the courts and fear of the 'Catholic danger'. All this paralyzed the major institutions that were to enforce and guarantee the peace, and opened the possibility of renewed civil war.[36] In the years 1608–9 violent conflict became increasingly likely and, resembling a rehearsal for 1618–20, these developments illuminate the internationalization of confessional controveries.

Renewed war with the Ottomans between 1592 and 1606 quelled the explosive mood across the Reich only temporarily, and in 1608 strife over interpreting the Peace of Augsburg with regard to Church property deepened confessional polarization, leading to a breakdown of negotiations at the Imperial Diet. Particularly threatening to the Protestants was the Imperial Aulic Council's siding with the Catholics of Donauwörth and the subsequent occupation and re-Catholization of the Imperial city, where the duke of Bavaria had been ordered to execute the Emperor's ban. The weakness of Imperial power during the simultaneous conflict between Emperor Rudolf and his brother, Archduke Matthias, over the Habsburg patrimony, brought to fruition the dreams of the Calvinist elector of the Palatinate and Prince Christian of Anhalt for a Protestant international alliance under their own leadership. In May 1608 they formed a Protestant Union, a defensive pact in opposition to the Catholic interpretation of the Peace of Augsburg, which was joined eventually by nine princes and seventeen cities, with the Palatinate holding the Directorium and Prince Anhalt as leader. The Union had links with the Netherlands, England, and the Austrian, Hungarian and Bohemian nobilities. Competition between rulers of different confessions over the succession of the strategically important Jülich-Berg (1609–10) encouraged closer connections between the Protestant Union and the French king, Henry IV, and threatened to bring Europe to the brink of a major war that was only averted by the murder of King Henry. Catholics had responded in 1609 with the formation of a League of South German prelates, which was extended in 1610 to include the ecclesiastic electors (Mainz, Cologne and Trier), the Burgundian circle, and the Austrian Habsburgs, with the duke of Bavaria assuming leadership. This Catholic League counted on the support of Spain, the Papacy, and electoral Saxony, which had returned to Lutheranism and loyalty to the emperor.[37]

Events in the Reich paralleled and were closely interwoven with developments in the hereditary lands and Bohemia, where Protestants followed the Catholic offensive closely and hoped to form useful alliances. In turn, the combined efforts of the Wittelsbach and Habsburg dynasties in re-Catholicizing their territories and recovering Church lands were viewed with suspicion and fear by Protestants in the Reich. Shortly after Rudolf's accession to the Imperial throne, he displayed his allegience to the Catholic Church and the doctrine of transubstantiation by attending, in 1578, the important festival of Corpus Christi in Vienna, which ended in a skirmish (*Milchkrieg*) symptomatic of the new mood of fear in the wake of the St. Bartholomew's Day Massacre (1572) and iconoclasm in the Netherlands.[38] We know little of Rudolf's personal views on religion, but he certainly followed the strategies recommended by Jesuit advisers and set out by his family, even though officially he was not part of the secret meeting at Munich in 1579 attended by Archduke Ferdinand of Tyrol, Archduke Karl of Inner Austria, who had married a Wittelsbach princess, and Wilhelm, Duke of Bavaria.

At Munich the dukes outlined a counter-reform programme for the Inner Austrian lands with the explicit purpose of provoking Protestant opposition, which would serve as a pretext for withdrawing all former religious concessions. Following the model that the Wittelsbach had pursued in Bavaria, they spelt out in detail the strategies Karl of Inner Austria was to pursue. At first, the duke was to prohibit all practices that went beyond past concessions, such as the attendance at Protestant services by subjects of sovereign towns, and the building of new Protestant churches, presumably on crown lands. This, it was anticipated, would lead to disobedience and attacks on Catholics by the secular Protestant Estates, which would provide justification for expelling Protestant preachers from the ducal domains (*Kammergut*). Protestant resistance would also permit the duke, on the basis of the *cuius regio, eius religio* clause of the Peace of Augsburg, to abolish all previous concessions, although he was advised to do this indirectly ('fein tacite et per indirectum absorbirt, cassirt, und aufgehebt sein werden'). If the Estates resisted, they should be separated, and the duke seek help from the emperor, the other archdukes and Bavaria; he was also advised to ask the Papacy and Spain for financial contributions in order to hire soldiers and strenghen fortifications. Further measures recommended as supporting 'this work' were the prompt replacement of Protestant privy councillors with Catholics, and the general preferment of Catholics with offices and honours; foreign landholders in the territories should also be urged to appoint only Catholics to offices. And, in order to appease his conscience, the duke should seek absolution from the Papacy, presumably for breaking a contract and thus divine law.[39]

Archduke Karl (1564–90), assisted by a new Inner Austrian nunciature and the Jesuits, was fortunate in finding eager and reform-minded bishops to implement these measures, such as Martin Brenner of Seckau (1585–1618), Georg Stobäus of Lavant (1585–1618), Thomas Chrön (or Hren) (1597–1630) of Laibach, and Christoph Andreas von Spaur of Gurk (1573–1603). They soon began exerting pressure on Protestants in sovereign towns and markets, a campaign that was continued ruthlessly by Karl's son, the future Ferdinand II. Resistance by subjects, Estates, and polemical preachers were met with further repression. Protestant books were burnt, preachers and teachers banished from urban centres, and their churches and schools closed. Those who refused conversion could emigrate, but there were disincentives to this, since they had to provide the fiscus with 10 per cent of their property's sale value.

Clearly vital for the success of the Counter-Reformation in Inner Austria was the support of energetic bishops and the comparatively strong Habsburg control over the dioceses, as was the proximity to the Ottomans, with whom war had been resumed in 1596. This made it difficult for the Estates to use financial contributions as a bargaining tool against repression, although they appealed to Protestants in the Reich and to the other hereditary lands for assistance. Furthermore, open resistance was very difficult to justify, since the crown lands clearly had not been included in the agreements, and Archduke Karl had not even ratified the noble Estates' concessions in writing. Nor did Ferdinand confirm them at his succession, although the Lutheran nobility was assured personal religious freedom (until 1628), further inhibiting the capacity of the Inner Austrian Protestant Estates to resist the ruler in questions of faith.[40] All of this helps explain why, in 1619–20, they did not join the Lower and Upper Austrian and Bohemian Confederations.

The strategies spelled out for Inner Austria at the Munich Conference became the blueprint for other Habsburg lands as well. However, elsewhere the situation was more complicated, in part because of competing ecclesiastical jurisdictions, but mainly as a result of conflict between Emperor Rudolf and Archduke Matthias, which enabled the Protestant nobles to reassert themselves. Rudolf II's governors (*Statthalter*) of Lower Austria, his brothers, the Archduke Ernst (1576–94), (spurred on by his Jesuit confessor, Georg Scherer) and later Archduke Matthias (1595–1608), as well as the devout councillor Eder and the infamous Melchior Khlesl, launched a parallel assault on Protestantism in Lower Austrian urban centres. There, Protestant religious services had been held in urban noble residences, and were as open to burghers as their country churches were to peasants of neighbouring Catholic lords. After preachers and Protestant services were banned from the city of Vienna, its burghers made a last attempt in 1579 to obtain religious concessions in a 'stormy petition' to Archduke Ernst, but were instead punished by the removal of Protestant officials from city government. By 1581, the Lower Austrian Protestant Estates had been forced to discontinue religious services at their Viennese *Landhaus*, to close its school, and to abandon their book trade. Khlesl enforced the conversion of sovereign towns vigorously, although his success was limited by nobles who continued to hold religious services on landed estates on the outskirts of urban centres.[41] In 1590, the bishop, recently appointed General Reformer (*Generalreformator*), recommended a number of schemes to remove the three remaining bastions of Protestantism in the vicinity of

Vienna, including diverting water from the stream flowing to the Estate of Inzersdorf in order to force its Protestant owner, Hans Adam Geyer, to sell the property to a Catholic neighbour. Making certain that Catholics would buy Protestant property for sale was apparently a common strategy used to restore Church land; another was to withdraw ducal fiefs with churches from Protestants whenever possible.[42]

Khlesl further recommended terminating all ennoblements of Protestants and replacing Protestant officials with Catholics, a strategy that was instituted rigorously in urban administrations, but, as I shall show in Chapter 4, more cautiously applied at court.[43] Previously, Archduke Ernst had been concerned that he could not implement firm actions against Protestants because they and their relatives occupied most councils and military positions. Indeed, he felt he could not even rely on his own guards, who were under the command of two Protestants.[44] During the 1580s, councillor Eder asked the Bavarian dukes repeatedly to urge Emperor Rudolf to replace Protestant officials with Catholics at the Imperial court, and reported dutifully each success in Catholic appointments.[45] But Eder also suggested that the confession of some of these new servants and Catholics converts was suspect. In his mind, they were 'neither cold, nor warm', but Aulic Christians (*Hofchristen*) who insisted they were Catholic, but not Jesuit-Catholic, a distinction he did not appreciate, since anyone who was not 'Jesuitic' (*jesuitisch*) was not Catholic.[46] Still, in 1604, Cardinal Khlesl reported with satisfaction that the Catholics were more numerous in offices than the Protestants.[47] However, we do not know whether this was achieved through conversion, or what proportion of Catholics served the crown, but I offer a detailed analysis of the changing confessional composition of the Habsburg courts in Chapters 5 and 6.

During the last decade of the sixteenth century, attempts at re-Catholicization combined with economic problems to trigger a series of peasant uprisings (1595–7) in Upper Austria , which soon spread into the northern parts of Lower Austria (1596–7). The Protestant nobility, at first sympathetic to the rebellion, helped to crush it once they realized that the peasants also had social and economic grievances against their seigneurial lords.[48] The Catholic *Landeshauptmann* of Upper Austria, Hans Jakob Löbl, used the rebellion as a pretext to pursue even more forcefully the re-Catholicization of the province, borrowing the methods employed in Inner Austria.[49] In 1598, Emperor Rudolf demanded the complete restitution of Catholic churches that Protestants had taken over and converted illegally in the Austrian lands.[50] The fears which this and the other strategies generated enabled Calvinist nobles, particularly the Upper Austrian, Georg Erasmus von Tschernembl, to take over leadership of the Protestant Estates in the early seventeenth century.

Even though during the 1580s a similar programme of Counter-Reformation was designed for the lands of the Bohemian crown, it was slower to begin. Jesuits founded colleges and seminars, and Rudolf enhanced the prestige of the restored archbishopric of Prague and inititated reforms of monasteries. But only under the leadership of the bishops Johann Lohelius and Franz Dietrichstein did re-Catholization gain momentum after 1600. Particularly successful was the strategy to appoint Catholics to the most important positions, who then, like the Bohemian chancellor, Zdeněk Lobkovic, prompted Rudolf to dismiss Protestant officials and persecute radical Protestants. In addition, both the crown and the Catholic Church were successful in enlarging their landholdings so that the nobility's share of landed property diminished between 1529 and 1603. Catholic schools became well-endowed, and in the early 1600s the Catholic Church could afford to become a creditor to urban centres.[51]

Under the tutelage of a handful of Catholic nobles, the Jesuits introduced the Counter-Reformation to royal Hungary, although here it remained rather circumscribed. Since the Peace of Augsburg had no validity for the kingdom, the powerful Hungarian Protestant nobles resisted efforts to restore Catholicism. Rudolf's attempts to introduce more agressive measures, such as prohibiting the discussion of religious grievances at the Diet, and the confiscation of Protestant churches while waging war with the Ottomans, were rather foolish, since they endangered border security. When, in addition, the king tried an important Lutheran magnate, István Illésházy, for sedition, the Protestant Estates felt betrayed and supported the uprising by István Bocskai, who was elected prince of Transylvania in 1604 and proclaimed king of Hungary by a substantial proportion of the Diet.[52]

These events in Hungary helped Rudolf's ambitious brother Matthias to organize forces against the emperor and, since Rudolf was reluctant, was given authority by the other archdukes to make peace with the Ottomans. Concluded at Zsitvatorok in 1606, this peace was to last for half a century. Less stable was the Vienna Treaty of 1606, which acknowledged Bocskai as ruler of Transylvania and secured Hungarians far-reaching political and religious concessions, including religious freedom for Lutherans and the Reformed Church, the recall of Jesuits, an independent treasury, the instalment of local nobles to offices, and the election by the Estates of a royal representative (*Palatin*). Concerned about the mental stability of Rudolf, the Habsburg family designated Matthias as its acting head in a secret agreement of 1607, who then proceeded to form an alliance with the Protestant Estates of Hungary, Lower and Upper Austria, and Moravia, thus allowing him to march against Rudolf in 1608, force his ratification of the treaties and secure these territories for himself.[53]

It soon became evident that Matthias had no intention of rewarding his Austrian allies with religious concessions comparable to those of the Hungarians. In fact, he responded to demands for freedom of worship on the part of urban Protestants by rashly imprisoning a prominent Protestant nobleman, Hans Adam Geyer, who had reopened his church to Lutheran services on his property near Vienna. It was a provocative reminder that the Protestants had lost hundreds of churches in the recent past, and that the Habsburgs were determined to continue the restitution of Church lands to Catholics. And the ensuing conflict reveals clearly the important connection between the interpretation of religious concessions and competition over Church property. Matthias and the Catholic Estates wanted to confine the place where Lutheran nobles and their subjects could exercise their religion to the estate where the lord resided and to parish churches over which he or she had patronage rights, excluding those where they possessed only the advocacy (*Vogtei*). Pointing to the stipulation that the settlements of 1568–72 were not to harm the Catholic religion, the court further insisted that subjects of Catholic landlords were not allowed to attend services in Protestant churches.[54] This initiated a defensive alliance among the Protestant Estates of Upper and Lower Austria, who decided to give homage (*Erbhuldigung*) only after verification of their religious freedoms and a clearer, more favourable interpretation of them, claiming that it was customary for a new ruler to confirm their privileges before *Erbhuldigung,* and that they became his subjects only thereafter. Matthias' hopes to imitate the uncompromising Ferdinand of Inner Austria, who would rather forgo homage than make concessions, were dashed, since, as we saw earlier, the international situation was much more favourable for the Upper and Lower Austrian Protestants. They withdrew to the well-fortified town of Horn, where 166 nobles from both provinces signed a defensive alliance, or Confederation, in October 1608. Matthias and Khlesl feared that the Protestants planned to establish a 'free republic' and seek help from Rudolf and the Bohemians, or from Protestant rulers in the Reich, a number of whom had just concluded a formidable union. Both sides began to prepare for war, but Matthias eventually gave in, and in March 1609 signed the so-called *Kapitulations-Resolution,* after which the Estates paid him homage.[55]

The concessions of this *Resolution* improved on the rights given by Maximilian II and clarified some important issues. Nobles and their subjects received the right to the free exercise of the Augsburg confession in all rural castles and houses in their possession. Moreover, Protestant subjects living in Catholic parishes were not to be denied the exercise of their faith and Protestant nobles could open their churches to them. Matthias also had to agree to the establishment of an impartial court to decide all cases concerning ecclesiastical property. Apparently, judgement of such cases had been taken away from the court of the (Protestant) *Landmarschall,* the Estates' highest official, and given to the Court Chancery, which, not surprisingly, had decided cases in favour of Catholics. The Protestant nobility further demanded confessional parity in the distribution of all court appointments, but Matthias only promised to distribute important offices among the old native nobility without consideration of confession. Concerning the religious freedom of towns and markets, the urban Estate had to be satisfied with verbal assurances that the Emperor would renew the toleration of Lutherans, allow the return of preachers, and reopen the Protestant school at Linz.[56]

Meanwhile, the Estates of Bohemia and Silesia also formed a defensive Confederation and, presenting Rudolf with their own bill for loyalty, compelled him to sign the Letter of Majesty in 1609 which guaranteed the members of the three Estates freedom of faith and practice to all groups under the Bohemian Confession, the establishment of Protestant schools and churches, even in urban centres (*'Städten, Städtlein und Dörffern'*), control over the university, and the administration of a reorganized Protestant Consistory by an assembly of *'Defensors'* of the Estates. A new, impartial court of justice was to be established to decide disputes with the crown and between the confessions, although this was not included in the Letter itself. The Moravian Protestants were satisfied with Matthias's verification of their previous religious rights and verbal promises concerning the status of the towns.[57] Matters did not end here, however, and in 1611 Matthias had to seek support from the Protestant Estates once more against his brother, Rudolf, who had also opposed Matthias's election as German king and attempted forcefully to regain his lost authority with the help of his younger nephew, Archduke Leopold. Compelling Rudolf to abdicate, the Bohemian Estates offered Matthias the crown. After his brother's death in 1612, Matthias succeeded Rudolf as Holy Roman Emperor.

Towards civil war

Under pressure from Catholic advisers, Spain and the archdukes, Matthias continued working towards weakening Protestantism. In the Austrian lands he did not promulgate the Capitulation and pursued the re-Catholicization of urban centres, reviving the struggle over the status of sovereign towns as an Estate. Habsburg confessional strategy was aided by the refusal of the Catholic Estates to accept the 1609 agreements and, instead, form a Union in February 1610 (three months before Henry IV of France was murdered by the Catholic, François Ravaillac) comprised of twenty-nine lords, eighteen knights and sixteen prelates in order to secure the survival of their faith and churches. Renewed quarrels erupted among the *Stände* of Lower Austria as Catholics revived their attempts to control the Estate's administration, leading to the instalment of an equal number of deputies, elected from both confessions, although the issue continued to disrupt the sessions of the Estates. The crown also replaced the leadership of the Lower Austrian Estate of Lords with a Catholic *Landmarschall*, and mediated a settlement of the conflict over the Estates' treasury in favour of Catholics, forcing the Protestant Estates to collect taxes from their own subjects to cover expenses incurred during the conflict of 1608–9.[58]

Catholics remained unyielding when the Protestant *Stände* demanded the establishment of an impartial court, as stipulated in the Resolution of 1609, declaring that, not having participated in the agreement, they were not bound by any of its resolutions. Conveniently, the Habsburgs did nothing to satisfy the remaining conditions. Nevertheless, in 1614, danger of war with the Ottomans, Transylvania and Venice forced Matthias to honour at least his promise of 1611 to call an Estates General to Linz. Although the dream of the Protestant Estates for a defensive Confederation between the Austrian lands floundered on mutual distrust, the demands of the court for financial aid were rebuffed with the argument that war seemed unlikely.[59] Khlesl accused the Protestants in a letter to Archduke Ferdinand of Inner Austria of resolving 'to rather leave Transylvania to the Turks than grant his Majesty finances for war'.[60] But he continued to harass them and in 1615 closed a number of important churches outside Vienna, prompting the Protestant Estates to renew their demand for the establishment of an impartial court and a special council (*Hofrat*) for Lower Austrian affairs. By 1620, the Protestants had lost over 200 churches. Over a third of the parishes in the district above and below the Manhartsberg, the centre of the opposition, had been restored to Catholics; in the district above the Vienna Woods, the proportion was a little over a quarter, while the area below the Vienna Woods had few Protestant churches to begin with.[61] Catholics merely responded to the request for an impartial tribunal with complaints that Protestants had continued with great zeal to annex Catholic property, but refused to sell their own estates to them, especially when it included a parish.[62]

Relations between the confessions, and between Habsburgs and Estates, also deteriorated again in the Bohemian territories. In return for offering Matthias the crown in 1612, the Protestant Estates presented demands which might have turned Matthias, in the words of one of his privy councillors, into a king of gypsum (*'un rè di stucco'*).[63] Next to the right to collect taxes and muster troops, they asked him to approve a defensive union of all the Habsburg lands in order to protect their religious and other corporate rights. For the Protestants, this would have provided a guarantee of enforcement of the agreements with the ruler and the Catholics, but for the Habsburgs such an endorsement would have amounted to acknowledging the Estates's right of resistance, and put a stop to re-Catholicization. Matthias therefore avoided this by utilizing the conflicts between the Bohemians and the Estates of the other lands under the Bohemian crown, who resented their 'incorporated' status and wanted to secure more autonomy *vis-á-vis* the dominant Bohemians. Approving the previous Bohemian–Silesian Confederation, since it had not been directed against the Catholic faith, he postponed all further demands to a future meeting of the Diet.

While some Bohemian nobles thought the move of the Imperial court from Prague to Vienna would provide them with more independence, it distressed many others, who considered it as abandonment and probably foresaw the losses of patronage. Together with Matthias's refusal to call another Bohemian Diet for about three years in order to avoid dealing with Protestant demands, the move of the court was indeed inopportune. However, financial needs and the possibility of renewed troubles with Transylvania and war in the south-east also forced the Emperor to call a Bohemian Estate General for 1615. Khlesl had suggested that Matthias propose a confederation of Habsburg lands that served defensive purposes, externally and internally. Not suprisingly, the Estates avoided pressing their demands, and Matthias and his privy councillor succeeded in exploiting once again the power struggles among the Estates, who in the end approved taxes for five years.[64] None the less, this Diet had radicalized large sections of the Protestant nobility and turned many of them toward an anti-Habsburg course.

As in the Austrian lands, Catholics refused to accept the Letter of Majesty of 1609, and since they were obtaining important government and military appointments, tensions soon escalated between the confessions. Moreover, in Bohemia and Moravia, the Counter-Reformation continued to progress on royal and Church lands. In Silesia, disputes erupted with the bishop of Breslau over the building of Protestant churches and schools, culminating at times in the closing of churches, the expulsion of preachers, and in 1616 the execution of a burgher by the bishop. As elsewhere, competition became fierce over appointments in, and control of, the Estates' administration.

Despite these and other problems, Ferdinand of Styria, known for his actions against the Styrian Protestants, was elected in June 1617 to succeed Matthias as king of Bohemia. Evidently, many moderate, non-Catholic Bohemian nobles still hoped to secure their rights through constitutional means. They may have been appeased by Matthias's renewed patronage of Protestant nobles after appointment of Catholics to important Bohemian offices had reached a high point in the decade before 1609. However, with Ferdinand's election, a strong minority began to view open confrontation as their only hope of protecting their material and political rights. Stressing the religious aspects of their conflict in order to unite the various regional opposition groups against the Habsburgs, they were soon confirmed in their vision for a defensive alliance when two urban Protestants and the promient leader of the Protestant nobility, Heinrich Matthias Thurn, who had voted against Ferdinand, lost important and lucrative positions. This faction of the opposition decided, in a meeting prior to the defenestration, to attempt co-ordination with the Protestant Estates of other territories.[65]

It is hardly surprising that the Bohemian's revolt against the Habsburg Court in 1618 was triggered by renewed disputes between Protestants and Catholics over Church land. The events leading up to war further demonstrate the close connection, even fusion, between material, cultural and political factors in the conflict between ruler and Estates. They also suggest that the absence of impartial courts and failure to trust Habsburgs and central councils in arbitration played a crucial role in pursuading many Protestants that a violent confrontation was preferable to further negotiations. Even before their rebellious acts in May 1618, the Protestant opposition had become convinced of the need to protect their rights with a military alliance among the various Habsburg lands.

In order to clarify how distrust and issues of insecurity among the parties contributed to the failure of negotiations, it is essential to review the key events leading up to civil war and to the defeat of the Confederates. The Protestant citizens of Braunau (*Broumov*) and Klostergrab (*Hrob*) had erected two churches on the property of Catholic lords, insisting that this was in accordance with their right to build churches on the royal domain, since Church land was royal land (*Kammergut*). Although the Habsburgs had insisted previously that the First Estate, the Church, belonged to the *Kammergut*, the Emperor denied this claim and maintained that the king was merely protector rather than owner of the Church. Since the city of Braunau belonged to a Benedictine monastery, the Court decided the complaint by its abbot in his favour. In addition, Matthias transferred the right to oversee all pastors on royal domain to the archbishop of Prague, preparing the way to the conversion of parishes and subjects. In 1614, the archbishop closed the Protestant church that had been built on his domain in Klostergrab. Despite complaints by the Estates, the court continued to aggravate the situation by putting royal officials in charge of appointing urban councillors, and issuing instructions in 1617 that gave royal judges the power to determine whether ecclesiastical lands were administered in accordance with their founding charters. Since most Church property had been established by Catholic patrons before the Hussite and Protestant Reformation, it was clear to non-Catholic nobles and towns that Ferdinand intended to deprive them of all their churches with attached lands and benefices.[66] This was, of course, not a petty issue, nor was it a purely spiritual affair.

The citizens of Braunau refused to surrender their church, but the archbishop of Prague tore down the one at Klostergrab and demanded the conversion of its citizens. A meeting of the Estates called by the Protestant defensors for March 1618 was attended mainly by nobles, since the urban deputies had been dissuaded from appearing. The emperor responded to their grievance by threatening to arrest their leaders if they summoned another Diet on their own. When Catholics and government officials proceeded to divide the Protestant clergy by reviving Utraquist (Hussite) ritual (which was closer to Catholicism), the Bohemian defensors defied the crown and called another Diet, which met on 21 May 1618, attended by approximately a hundred noblemen, but only six urban representatives. Two days later, on 23 May, called to respond to emperor Matthias's command to close the Diet, the Protestants, led by the Count of Thurn, went to the royal castle, where events took a more radical turn, ending with the throwing from the windows of two Imperial representatives (*Statthalter*) and a secretary, perhaps in a deliberate attempt to murder them. The event was not without its ridiculous moments: the victims survived the defenestration, probably by landing on a dung-heap, although Catholics insisted it was the Virgin Mary or angels who softened the fall.[67]

Justified as a defensive measure, the Bohemian Estates soon prepared for military confrontation, entrusting the admininistration to a Directorium of thirty, headed by the eminent Wenceslas von Ruppa, while Count Heinrich Matthias von Thurn and Count Colonna von Fels were put in charge of military affairs, even though they had little practical or theoretical training. Protestants across Europe expressed their sympathies with the rebels, and the elector of the Palatinate promised military aid from the Union. Some Catholic advisers, including Cardinal Khlesl, counselled Matthias not to give in to the Estates' demands, and viewed the insurrection as an opportunity to end all opposition by force once and for all. The archdukes Ferdinand and Maximilian in particular urged a military solution, and in July 1619 managed to remove by force Matthias's trusted adviser, Melchior Khlesl, whom they blamed for delaying war against Bohemia. Although the exact reasons for the Cardinal's 'abduction' remain uncertain, considering his own agitations against the Bohemian Protestants, it is evident that he considered confessional and political stability in the Reich to be a precondition for success against Protestants in the Habsburg lands, and had hoped to come to an agreement with the German princes over the administration of Protestant bishoprics. However, the Catholic League, the ecclasiastical princes, the Papacy and Spain saw the protection of the Ecclesiastical Reservation as the cornerstone of re-Catholicization and, supported by the archdukes and the Catholic party at court, worked against compromise and Khlesl's so-called *Kompositionspolitik*.[68]

By early August 1619, an Imperial army of 12 000 under the commands of Count Buquoi, Count Dampierre, and Baron von Khuen passed into Bohemia but, with support from Silesia, the anti-Habsburg forces soon outnumbered them, and the Bohemian Directory refused, as had Matthias earlier, mediation attempts of the moderate Protestant, the Moravian Karel of Žerotín, and of the elector of Saxony. They particularly objected to the emperor's 'intolerable and dangerous' demand for unilateral disarmament, but expressed a willingness to negotiate during an armistice.[69] After some initial successes, the Bohemian forces soon encountered difficulties with finance and the hardships of winter, and the Protestants utilized a stalemate in early 1619 to search for allies. Although the Palatinate, the Netherlands, and Savoy promised aid, England merely offered Lord Doncaster's service as a mediator. Matthias, while awaiting the arrival of Spanish auxiliary forces, suggested the Bavarian duke as leader of the negotiations, but the emperor died on 20 March, 1619, in the midst of these preliminary talks. His successor, Ferdinand of Styria, continued to show himself willing to bargain with the Bohemians.[70]

While the Protestant opposition prepared for a projected meeting, they also negotiated a closer alliance with the Silesian and Lusatian Estates. But the Moravian Estates under Žerotín's leadership were more resistant, probably because about a third of its nobles who also held the most important positions, were Catholics. Since the Protestant Union and the Austrian Estates demanded their inclusion, an alliance with the Moravians was essential and, in April, Bohemian troops entered Moravia, where large parts of the Protestant nobility and the towns received them enthusiastically. Then, after removing most of the Catholic leadership, the Moravia Diet agreed to conclude an alliance with the Bohemian and Silesian Estates.[71]

Matthias's death also provided an opportunity for more radical action on the part of the Upper Austrian Protestants, who, under the leadership of the Calvinist Georg Erasmus von Tschernembl and Gottfried von Starhemberg, set up a Directory, deprived Ferdinand of income from his domain lands, and agreed to aid the Bohemians. Encouraged by this, the Lower Austrian Protestant *Stände* joined them in refusing to recognize Ferdinand as archduke of Austria, even though Archduke Albrecht, the legal heir to the throne, had transferred his rights to Ferdinand. According to the Protestants, the country was in an interregnum, giving the Estates the right to rule. When the refusal to recognize Ferdinand as legitimate successor became untenable, the Austrian Protestant Estates refused homage, on the grounds that he must first confirm their rights and privileges. In other words, they demanded some contractual guarantees before they would become Ferdinand's subjects, believing they had good reason to mistrust Ferdinand II, who had a reputation for proceeding against Protestants and being 'a slave of the Jesuits'.[72]

Still hoping for Ferdinand's capitulation, the Lower Austrian Estates tried to bargain with him again in early June 1619. But instead of concessions, the delegation led by Paul Jakob von Starhemberg and Andreas Thonrädl were urged to join the archduke against the approaching enemy. Apparently, Thurn was advancing toward's Vienna with Bohemian troops, probably to secure the safety of the protesters. But by the time he reached near the city, Ferdinand had also obtained reinforcements, and Thurn decamped after receiving word from the Hungarians suggesting alliance. Stressing carefully the need for protection against foreign and Imperial troops, a large section of the Lower Austrian Protestant Estates quickly withdrew, as they had in 1609, to the city of Horn, began levying troops, and set up their own *Direktorium*. At the same time they renewed their willingness to pay homage to Ferdinand as long as he first confirmed the eight religious privileges they had obtained since 1571. Again, he refused on the grounds that these were 'private matters' (*Privatbegehren*), and never before had special privileges been confirmed before paying homage. In 1608 Matthias had also insisted that religious demands by the Protestants represented private grievances or interests that had nothing to do with paying homage, an act in which all Estates must participate. But, drawing attention to precedents in 1577 and 1609, the Estates remained at Horn, and only Catholics, four Protestant nobles and seven Lutheran urban delegates appeared at the *Erbhuldigung* set by Ferdinand for 10 September.[73]

By July 1619, the articles of Confederation between the various lands united under the Bohemian crown had been drafted. This document, which I will discuss in more detail in the next chapter, was not a constitution in the sense of a *Landesordnung*, which spelt out the fundamental laws and legal order or the realm, but rather a defensive alliance between the regions to protect such fundamental laws (for example, the elective nature of kingship) and other legal rights and privileges held by the Estates. On 16 August, the Lower and Upper Austrian Protestant Estates joined the Confederation with two separate agreements, in order to keep their own *Landesordnungen,* independent leaderships, and different sovereigns. The Bohemian Confederates proceeded to depose Ferdinand as King of Bohemia on 19 August, and a week later elected Frederic of Palatinate as their new ruler.[74] While the opposition in all three regions claimed the right to resist a tyrannical prince, the Habsburgs rejected their justifications and declared their actions to be seditious rebellion against all fundamental and positive laws. I shall explore this important discourse in more detail in the following chapter.

Meanwhile, Ferdinand had left for Frankfurt to present himself for election as emperor. In July he had rejected renewed proposals for negotiation by the English envoy, Lord Doncaster, but in order to proceed with his election as emperor (on 28 August 1619) he had consented to the Electorial College, facilitating mediation with the Bohemians in November. As usual, Ferdinand favoured bargaining only when placed under considerable pressure. By this time the Imperial army had been greatly strengthened with troops Spain had enlisted in Italy and Flanders, war had spread into Moravia, and the Bohemian troops suffered a number of defeats. During the autumn, an advance towards Vienna and an effort by their new ally, the prince of Transylvania, Gábor Bethlen, to rescue Protestant forces failed, because the emperor received unexpected aid from a Hungarian opponent of the Transylvanian prince, which forced Bethlen to retreat.[75]

In November 1619, Frederic v of the Palatinate, the son-in law of the English king, accepted and received the Bohemian crown, making further negotiations with the Confederates unproductive because the Habsburgs would rather have given up what was left of Hungary than these rich territories. Moreover, Bohemia in the hands of a Calvinist had also tipped the confessional balance among the Imperial electors in favour of Protestants. By January 1620, when the Protestant Diet of Royal Hungary elected Gábor

Bethlen 'prince of Hungary', it became clear that Hungary, too, might be lost. However, while Ferdinand was negotiating alliances with German princes and waiting for further reinforcements, he concluded a truce with Bethlen, who suffered from a lack of both troops and finances. The Habsburgs left most of northern Hungary to the prince and agreed to end the war against the Bohemians and Austrians 'under reasonable conditions'.[76]

The situation was certainly not promising for Frederic V; with finances drying up, he faced mutiny and peasant uprisings. Neither the Protestant Union nor the other patrons of the new king provided much financial aid, although the Union promised to protect the Palatinate, Denmark offered a loan, and England sent some financial aid and an infantry regiment for the defence of the Palatinate. Only the Netherlands provided significant, albeit sporadic, monthly instalments of 50 000 florins, and in the end some regiments. The frenzied search for new allies did bring minor sums from Johann Ernst of Saxe-Weimar and promises of artillery from Sweden. And in March, Gábor Bethlen decided that it was time to reunite with Bohemia against the emperor, albeit in return for financial aid, and a few months after joining the Austro-Bohemia Confederation in April 1620, the Hungarian Protestant Estates proclaimed the Transylvanian prince as king of Hungary on 20 August. However, only a small Hungarian contingent reached the Battle of the White Mountain to aid the Austro-Bohemian forces.

Ferdinand was in a much better position than was Frederic V of Bohemia. He had managed to neutralize members of the Protestant Union with promises of compensation for restored church property, and gathered allies into a grand Catholic coalition. Bavaria and the Catholic League were to recruit 30 000 troops during the spring, and the Papacy promised 200 000 florins. The Duke of Bavaria was assured the electoral dignity, possessions in the Palatinate, and Upper Austria as security. From Spain, the emperor extracted 1.6 million Spanish crowns for the spring campaign against Frederic's Palatinate, and his brothers-in-law, the Polish king and the grand duke of Tuscany, also promised aid. In March 1620, a special deal provided Ferdinand II with military aid from Johann Georg, the elector of Saxony, who was to occupy Silesia and Lusatia. Somewhat surprisingly, two old foes, France and Savoy took neutral positions.[77]

It now became important for the Habsburg to negotiate with the Lower Austrian Protestant Estates, or at least to divide them, in order to secure his core lands on the south-eastern flank. In May, he finally agreed to confirm their privileges and religious rights as they enjoyed them at that moment, provided that they abandoned all their alliances. The leadership of the Estates had moved to the city of Retz (Horn having been captured by the Imperials), but it refused to give up the Confederation and demanded that Ferdinand make peace with all neighbours and confirm their privileges as they had held them under Matthias. Objecting to further bargaining with the 'Retzer', the emperor gave a verbal promise to this effect to the noble Estates alone, and after they had paid homage. Even though the *Stände* had only his word that he would provide a written declaration later, and still no security about how their concessions would be interpreted, Ferdinand succeeded in splitting the Protestant camp. Next to nineteen prelates, sixteen cities and sixty-two Catholic nobles, well over a quarter of the Protestant noble Estates paid homage on 13 July.[78]

In late July 1620, the army of the Catholic Liga under the Bavarian duke occupied Upper Austria and forced the Protestants to pay homage to him, and in August it marched into South Bohemia, joining the Imperial forces, while the Saxon elector began his campaign against Lusatia. As Spanish troops under Ambrogio Spinola began the offensive against the Palatinate in September, England made another futile effort to mediate a peace. Finally, on 8 November, 1620, the Catholic forces defeated the Confederate army in less than two hours at the Battle of the White Mountain, outside Prague. Frederic V, who fled the city, continued to fight the Liga with some of his allies but lost the Palatinate during the Fall of 1622.[79] Bethlen and the Hungarians signed a peace with Ferdinand II in January 1622, through which the Transylvanian renounced the royal crown in return for the title of prince of the Holy Roman Empire and a number of Hungarian counties. This ended the first phase of the military conflict in the Habsburg lands, which has been defined mistakenly as the 'Bohemian War', or Bohemian phase of the Thirty Year's War.

Ferdinand soon punished the Bohemian opposition and re-established his power wherever he could. Ten nobles and seventeen burghers, the leaders of the uprising, were executed in Prague in June 1621, and their mutilated corpses exposed for years on Charles Bridge. During the next few years, 680 others were sentenced, with confiscations of property (166 lost all) or monetary fines. About half of the Estates' landed property changed hands, being sold or given to loyal Catholic clients, and much of the ecclesiastical lands were restored. About 300 Moravians faced a similar fate, although the twenty death sentences handed down to their opposition leaders were commuted. By 1622, the non-Catholic clergy had been expelled, including the old Utraquists (Hussites), and in 1624 Catholicism was declared as the only official religon. In 1627 and 1628, the Bohemian and Moravian nobility was given the choice to convert or to emigrate, and only the Silesian Protestants continued to be protected by the Saxon prince. A revised 'constitution' (*Landesordnung*) of 1627 secured the hereditary succession of the Habsburgs and control over judicial appeals, which previously had been in the hands of regional institutions. The clergy was added as an Estate, and a salt tax instituted to restore the Catholic Church's finances. The Habsburgs further tightened control over admittance of new members to the Estates (*Inkolat*), and curtailed the influence of the towns and local officials. In Bohemia, Moravia and Silesia, the territorial treasuries were put under direct rule of the *Hofkammer* in Vienna, and the crown generally increased its administrative co-ordination over these lands, even though the local administrative structures remained largely untouched. Particularly crucial was the transfer in 1624 of the Bohemian Chancellery to Vienna, which soon attempted to harmonize judicial procedures, thereby aiding the integration of Bohemia and its restructured nobility. The Estates lost the ability to propose legislation, their voice in suggesting royal officials, and all other new freedoms they had assumed with the act of Confederation, but they retained the right to approve taxes and many of their older privileges. In time they regained some lost ground, such as the ability to make representations, which is one reason why historians no longer support the traditional interpretation, viewing the defeat of the opposition as destruction of the Bohemian Estates as a political force. Older historians also tended to compare the renewed *Landesordnung* with the rights claimed by the Estates during the rebellion, rather than with the authority they held prior to it, and thus exaggerated their loss of power.[80]

In the Austrian lands, the punishment of the opposition was milder. Sixty-seven Protestants, mainly nobles, were proclaimed as rebels and their property confiscated, but a number were pardoned and their landed estates returned for a fine. Only about a dozen Lower Austrian nobles were forced to leave the country, and the other members of the noble Estates were not compelled to convert or migrate. However, Ferdinand II soon ordered the expulsion of all Protestant clergy and schoolmasters, and church patrons had to appoint Catholics to their parishes. Moreover, only Catholics could become the servants of crown and Estates. Considering that the practising of Protestantism, including the reading of non-Catholic books and sermons, was prohibited after 1628, it is surprising that in 1647 almost two-fifths of the noble families still defined themselves as 'evangelisch'. Athough the Peace Treaty of Westphalia (1648) secured for the noble Estates the right to attend religious services outside Lower Austria, the next generation, if they had not already been raised as Catholics, converted. Protestant churches were gradually brought under the patronage of Catholics, continuing the process that had begun earlier. Without princely patronage, schools, preachers, churches, or a base in the towns, Protestantism was destined to decline.[81] In Upper Austria, re-Catholicization was continued more cautiously after a series of peasant uprisings shook the province during and after 1625, and secret Protestantism seems to have survived longer than it did in Lower Austria. But since the Upper Austrian Estates had refused continually to pay homage to Ferdinand, in April 1627 he ordered the noblility to convert or migrate, although a number of nobles had already left the region before the Bavarian occupation.[82]

It is evident, then, that an obstacle to prolonged religious peace was that all parties viewed the settlements in the Reich and in the Habsburg lands as being temporary, and wished to extend their interests in a context where success could only occur at the expense of others. As a consequence, the institutions that were to enforce the agreement either did not exist, or became dysfunctional, and the various parties developed rigid dispositions, opening the way for the complete breakdown of bargaining. However, knowing what could have prevented armed conflict does not necessarily provide full insight into the causes of rebellion. But before I can explore this matter further, including the motivations of the participants, it is necessary to establish the background of Protestant nobles who opposed the Habsburgs, and compare it to those who did not.

Noble opposition and loyalists in Lower Austria: a profile

A collective profile of the Protestant nobility is particularly important, since we lack sufficient personal testimonies to illuminate the social and economic factors that prompted some Austrian nobles to join the Bohemian rebels, while others decided to pay homage or remain on the sidelines. Despite a number of inaccuracies, the contemporary lists of men who were proscribed or paid homage do provide a means of ascertaining the background of Protestant nobles in early 1620, and suggest reasons for the different political choices they made. Statistical analysis can be an important aid to historians, pointing to factors that a study based on the stated intentions of historical actors may not reveal, since causes are not necessarily identical with conscious aims. At the same time, statistics alone are not enough, needing to be supplemented with an evaluation of motives and a consideration of matters that may degrade or add to the usefulness of the data.

Although some statistical information exists on the Bohemian nobility, there are serious flaws in the way it has been analysed and presented. In constructing and interpreting statistics one must be careful to resist the temptation to superficiality. For example, in order to show whether a relationship existed between political activisim and economic background it is insufficient to determine that 39 per cent of the total number of nobles who joined the opposition were small landholders. It is essential also to know what proportion this constituted of the entire Protestant nobility, including its loyal members, which reduces the proportion of small property owners who joined the rebels to 29 per cent. Even this does not tell us much about whether a significant correlation exists between the variables. To determine this it is necessary to use the statistical method of hypothesis testing. Doing so shows the number of small estate owners we could expect to join each group (loyalist or rebels) had they been distributed evenly and given the total size of the Protestant nobility and small landholders among it. For example, in the case of the Lower Austrian Protestants, the number would be eighty-two ('expected value'), with eighty-nine in fact joining ('observed value'). This suggests that small landholders were overrepresented among the opposition party. However, the method of hypothesis testing further indicates that the difference between eighty-two and eighty-nine is not large enough to deduce that the correlation between size of landholding and political activism is significant.

In the following analysis I define as 'loyalists' those seventy-seven nobles (a quater of the Protestant nobility) who paid homage to Ferdinand II in 1620 (and earlier) and refrained from further actions against the crown.[83] The government also compiled lists of nobles who should be proscribed, and those who failed to give homage but had remained passive during the conflict. These allow me to determine that a large number – over a third (102) – of the Protestant nobility remained in active opposition, but even more – about two-fifths (121) – stood on the sidelines.[84] Having adjusted these lists for greater accuracy, I apply the term 'active opposition' to those nobles whom Ferdinand II proscribed because of military involvement on the side of the Confederates, or because they had participated in at least two other rebellious acts and signed the Confederation, the Retzer *Jurament,* or joined the Directory set up at Horn.[85] At least a third (30) of the 'active opposition' fought in the Confederate army; if we include those whose engagement in battle was doubtful, but possible, the proportion would be nearly a half.[86]

While it was relatively easy to distinguish Loyalists from Active Oppositionists, it was more difficult to decide who were the remaining Protestant nobles and how to define them. Since they clearly refused to pay homage, but did not engage in any other activities of the Confederates, I classified them as the 'passive (or moderate) opposition'.[87] Some may have had religious scruples about active resistance yet remained convinced that they should not give in to Ferdinand's demands. Those who were willing to pay homage but had been unable to travel to Vienna were included among the Loyalists, while the few nobles who claimed that they had been prevented by the rebels from paying homage were eliminated from all the groups for the purpose of analysis.[88] If we combine the active and passive opposition, then nearly three-quarters (223) of the entire Protestant noble Estates, with a fairly even distribution among knights and lords, contested Ferdinand II's rule in early 1620 (see Table 2.1).

If we consider the social and economic profiles of Protestant nobles who joined the various groups, it is evident that the old nobility (those who had received their diploma more than a hundred years before) were disproportionally present among the Active Opposition, while new members were more inclined to take a passive position. None the less, hypothesis testing cannot confirm a significant correlation between political activity and social status, suggesting that antagonism between the new and the old nobility was not a crucial factor in determining political activism. However, since the Catholic noble Estate consisted largely of new members who had

Table 2.1 Division of the Protestant noble Estates, 1620

Estates	*Loyalists*	*Passive resistance*	*Active opposition*	*Total of known cases*
Lords	37 (25%)	58 (39%)	54 (36%)	149
Knights	40 (26%)	63 (42%)	48 (32%)	151
TOTAL	**77 (26%)**	**121 (40%)**	**102 (34%)**	**300 (100%)**

received recent status promotion, Chapter 4 will investigate the possibility of whether the older Protestant nobility had especially strong reasons for resenting the growth of Catholic newcomers and feared that Catholics would soon outnumbered them, so undermining their own influence.[89]

Wealth, or more accurately the size of landholding, also appears to have had little influence on the Protestant nobles' political choices. Although the small landholders were over-represented, especially if we combine active and passive opposition, a cross-section of rich and poor property owners joined with the landless.[90] This does not mean, however, that political dissent was unrelated to economic deprivation. As we saw earlier, many Protestant nobles had to relinquish control over Church land. Chapter 6 examines whether and how the growth in the average size of noble families, and the subsequent pressure on available land or positions at the Habsburg court affected their material position.

Similarly, young men were no more likely to join the resistance than to join the loyalists, although they were slightly over-represented among the former.Territorial origin also had little effect on political choices, although there was a tendency among recent arrivals from areas in the Reich to be loyal or among the passive opposition, while 'natives', who had been residing in Lower Austria for at least three generations, had a greater presence among the active opposition. However, statistical significance emerges when considering where in the four administrative districts of Lower Austria nobles resided. Those from the district above the Manhartsberg (north-west of the Danube) were clearly over-represented among both the active and passive opposition, but men from the district to the east of (or below) the Manhartsberg tended towards active protest, especially among the knights.[91] Proximity to Bohemia seems to be the most obvious explanation for this. However, as we observed earlier, in these two districts, Protestants had been forced to restore the highest proportion of churches. Chapter 6 explores whether the fact that the district above the Manhartsberg also had the largest number of small landed estates, or other material factors, played a role in political activism. The variable that is most strongly related to the political positioning of Protestants towards Ferdinand II was office-holding (see Table 2.2). In fact, probably only one or two men of the active resistance held active administrative positions at court.[92] The passive opposition can be distinguished clearly from the rebels in this respect, since fourteen of them were employed by the Habsburgs, especially in military positions. However, most of the Protestant princely servants (twenty-four) remained loyal.

We can conclude, then, that the active and passive resistance combined showed a slight preponderance of small landholders (especially among the knights) under the age of forty, and an over-representation of men who resided in the district north-west of the Danube, and were country gentlemen. The active resistance in particular counted few, if any, princely servants among them.

Loyalists, on the other hand, were distinguished from the other two groups by the disproportionate presence of men aged over forty with medium-sized estates, although this was statistically insignificant. Particularly decisive was the large incidence of nobles from the areas south of the Danube, and of princely servants among those who paid homage to Ferdinand. The remainder of this book will determine whether exclusion from offices was indeed the common experience that united the opposition, and whether this was the result of confessional policies, court versus country conflicts, or had other causes.

Although few sources exist to determine the motives of those among the three factions, it is possible to examine more closely the background and fortunes of a few typical representatives of each group, and it is important to do so in order to find reasons for their political choices. The Kollonitsches, an old family of the Croatian–Styrian lesser nobility, who had also been present in Lower Austria for a number of generations, serves as an excellent example to illuminate differences in motivation, since its individual family members took up various positions in the conflict. Typical of loyal Protestants from the Estate of Lords was Seyfried Kollonitsch II. His grandfather had studied law and rose to a position in the Habsburg administration, and his father, Georg Seyfried, had been rewarded in 1583 with a baronage for services to the Habsburgs. Seyfried's loyal positioning during the rebellion seems to have been prompted by the desire not to compromise his own and his family's gains. He was ambitious, protecting not only his inheritance – property in Hungary and a substantial estate in Lower Austria – but still had faith that he could further his own career in office-holding, which, indeed, showed promise. Ferdinand II confirmed Seyfried's honourary appointment as chamberlain and used his talents as a military commander. Loyalty to the crown, it appears, depended on loyalty to his family, a number of whom were also Catholic. It was certainly stronger than his allegiance towards the Protestant Estates, as Seyfried distinguished himself fighting against the forces of Gábor Bethlen. In 1621, at the age of forty-nine, he was promoted to field marshal.[93]

Table 2.2 Political affiliation and office-holding among Lower Austrian Protestants, 1620

Affiliation	*Household*			*Administr.*			*Military*			*Estates*			*Landadel*			*Total*
	o	*e*	*d*	*o*	*e*	*d*	*o*	*e*	*d*	*o*	*e*	*d*	*o*	*e*	*d*	*o*
Loyalists																
Lords	6	3	+3	4	2	+2	5	2	+3	4	2	+2	20	31	−11	39
Knights	1	0	+1	5	2	+3	3	2	+1	2	3	−1	30	33	−3	41
Total	**7**	**3**	**+4**	**9**	**4**	**+5**	**8**	**4**	**+4**	**6**	**5**	**+1**	**50**	**64**	**−14**	**80**
Passive opposition																
Lords	3	4	−1	4	3	+1	2	3	−1	0	3	−3	50	46	+4	59
Knights	0	0	0	1	3	−2	4	3	+1	3	5	−2	55	51	+4	63
Total	**3**	**4**	**−1**	**5**	**6**	**−1**	**6**	**6**	**0**	**3**	**8**	**−5**	**105**	**98**	**+7**	**122**
Active opposition																
Lords	1	4	−3	0	3	−3	0	2	−2	3	3	0	50	42	+8	54
Knights	0	0	0	1	2	−1	1	3	−2	8	4	+4	38	39	−1	48
Total	**1**	**4**	**−3**	**1**	**5**	**−4**	**1**	**5**	**−4**	**11**	**7**	**+4**	**88**	**81**	**+7**	**102**
All	**11**			**15**			**15**			**20**			**243**			**304**

Notes: *o* = observed value; *e* = estimated value; *d* = difference between o and e.
The realized value for the combined Estates is 34.08, and the null hypothesis is rejected at the 1% level. The nobles who fought in the Confederate army were included among the Landadel (Active Opposition). The base number is higher than the actual number of Protestants because some of them held double positions.

His younger brother, Ernst Kollonitsch, also a distinguished military commander, was even more ambitious than Seyfried, and went so far as to convert to Catholicism. It appears that the rebels took revenge for this conversion when they plundered and burnt down his castle, but in 1637 Ernst was finally rewarded for his loyalty and suffering with the rank of count. Seyfried's other brother, Hans Georg, however, remained a devoted Protestant. He refused to pay homage, and, having lost his small estate because of debts, went into the service of a Protestant prince, the Duke of Brunswick. Clearly, then, the Kollonitsch family members made some astute choices in order to protect and further their material interests.

However, as we have seen, only about half of the Protestants who paid homage to Ferdinand II in fact had positions at court to protect. Many, such as Niklas Gienger, a member of the Estate of Knights, were never in the service of the crown, but were social climbers who feared their ascendance might be jeopardized. Gienger's grandfather, a Swabian, had been ennobled in 1544, and his father, Jakob, founder of the Lower Austrian branch, pursued a career in the financial administration and acquired landed property. Niklas himself enlarged his inheritance substantially, married a baroness (Maria Windischgrätz), and in 1608 received the title of baron, probably for supporting Matthias in his struggle against Rudolf. None the less, further upward mobility of the family was delayed, and admission to the *Herrenstand,* which brought important social and economic entitlements, occurred only in 1635. Niklas was committed to the cause of Protestantism, had joined the opposition and signed the Horner *Bund* in 1608. It is therefore possible that status insecurity – his diploma had to be verified by Ferdinand before he could be admitted to the Estate of Lords – was a factor in Niklas's decision in 1620 not to rejoin the opposition but to pay homage to the emperor.[94]

Three members of the Althan family provide insights into why some Protestant nobles remained moderate in their opposition to the Habsburgs. Belonging to the old Swabian nobility who had come to Lower Austria during the late fifteenth century in the service of the Habsburgs, they established several branches and between them accumulated substantial landholdings in the province. Christoph Althan, privy councillor and president of the court treasury, was particularly successful in enlarging the family fortune; in 1574 he was raised to baron and admitted to the *Herrenstand.*[95] His eldest son, Michael Adolph, converted to Catholicism in 1598 and advanced quickly in the officer corps. Like many of the proselytes, he was raised to the rank of Imperial count in 1610, amassed a fortune, and became the most illustrious and successful member of his family at the time. However, his Protestant relatives remained unaffected by his elevation in rank and remained barons. Wolf Dietrich Althan, Michael's brother, a minor officer (*Rittmeister*) in his youth, was elevated in 1604 by Matthias to chamberlain. He acquired a small estate which eventually was his only source of income, since Ferdinand II did not confirm his appointment. Wolf Dietrich and his youngest brother, Quintin Leo, and cousin Wolfgang Georg did not join the active Protestant opposition, but refused to pay homage. Quintin merely held a temporary position with the Estates (1605), but he had more than 400 peasant households on his estate to support him.[96] Wolfgang Georg had risen to the position of Aulic councillor in 1617, but was not confirmed in this position when Ferdinand II took power.

The over representation of socially mobile barons and other nobles among the loyal party and passive opposition seems to confirm the conclusion that the eldest son of the Althan family chose to protect family property and opportunities, and that it was also most probably family strategy that prevented its Protestant members from joining the active opposition. While frustration and dissatisfaction with their meagre careers can explain why they declined to pay homage, and the refusal to convert may speak for their spiritual convictions, one should not rule out the possibility that the family covered its options and protected clientage networks should the Confederates win. That many noble families, particularly among the lords, pursued similar strategies is further supported by the fact that only a few (less than a third) *Herrenstand* families of mixed confessions had members who joined the active opposition. Although the rebels were somewhat more numerous among knightly families with mixed religious backgrounds, they also had a higher proportion of Protestant relatives who paid homage to Ferdinand II, thereby covering their options. It is also clear that, among clans who were entirely Protestant, the smaller families (those that included only one or two males over the age of twenty) tended to be more cautious in their political choices, and only about a third had members who joined the active opposition, whereas the proportion among the larger families was substantially higher, with over half of the knightly families and more than three-quarters of the *Herrenstand*'s lines having members who belonged to the active opposition. None the less, these larger, all-Protestant families tended to have at least one family member who paid homage, and among the lords this proportion was higher (nearly two-thirds of the families had a loyal member). All of this supports my contention that the majority of families tended to be risk averse, and diversified their 'portfolio', especially with respect to patron–client networks, and cover their options in case the Habsburgs were to win the conflict. If some family members might be proscribed, the other loyal or Catholic one might be able to obtain a pardon, retain their property, or at least hold a debt on it. In many cases, events proved them to have been correct.

This does not mean that religious conviction played no role, since many Protestant nobles emigrated by choice when confronted with conversion, while others clearly did not pursue strategies of diversification. Besides, the pursuit of family interests does not necessarily negate the existence of individual religious conviction, since neither refraining from participation in the rebellion nor paying homage to Ferdinand was incompatible with the Protestant faith. Conversion, of course, was another matter, but here personal disposition of family members, or their confessional indifference, could have been utilized to suit family strategies. It is noteworthy that, while some historians believe that in pre-modern times personal wishes and inclinations were subordinated to family or community concerns, they exempted religious preferences. However, throughout this book I shall continue to show how family interests intersected with personal faith.

Unfortunately, the only existing full biography of nobles who were active in the rebellion concerns itself with the leader of the Upper Austrian opposition, Georg Erasmus von Tschernembl. While he exerted considerable influence over the Lower Austrian Protestants, as a Calvinist he was not representative of the Lower Austrian opposition.[97] More typical was Georg Andreas Hofkirchen, of an ancient native family which had received a baronage in 1464.[98] His father William I, a Lutheran, rose to the position of president of the Imperial War Council (*Hofkriegsratspresident*) and first field marshal (1578), but Georg Andreas only held a command (*Oberst*) over an infantry regiment in 1608, a military sphere not very popular among the old upper nobility. Actively involved as a deputy of the Estates in the Horner opposition in 1609, the Lower Austrian Protestant Estates made him general over their *Armada* in 1619. He signed the Confederation, and from 1619 onwards fought with his forces on the side of the Bohemian rebels.[99] Several factors seem to have contributed to Georg Andreas's radical opposition to the Habsburgs. Like his ancestors and relatives, he was a fervent champion of the cause of Estates and Lutheranism, and one of his brothers, Wolfgang von Hofkirchen, had been prosecuted by the Habsburgs for these activities. Two years after Wolfgang was forced to vacate the important post of acting governor (*Statthalteramtsverwalter*) in 1601 to make room for a Catholic, the Lower Austrian Estates had sent him to Protestant courts abroad to gain support for the Protestant cause. The mission was unsuccessful, and on his return he was arrested for high treason. His trial dragged on until it was dismissed in 1609, two years before his death.[100] Not surprisingly, three of Wolfgang's surviving sons joined the rebels: Wilhelm III, for example, signed the Confederation and the Retzer *Jurament,* and became a member of the Directory; and Lorenz V, who signed the Confederation, emigrated to Brandenburg to avoid proscription.[101] None of them had ever been in the employ of the Habsburgs before 1620, providing another strong reason to consider active opposition as the proper choice to defend their faith and their family from social and material decline. Georg Andreas had also lost three large seigneuries he held in lien from the crown to Catholic lords, a typical Habsburg strategy to reward Catholic clients, and restore Church property.[102] Even though he was one of the larger landholders among the Protestant nobles – in 1620 the value of his confiscated property amounted to more than 260 000 gulden – his debts exceeded his assets by nearly 74 000 gulden. This may not be evidence of material problems, since he did not find it necessary to sell any of his numerous estates to cover this debt. Neither of Georg's sons, Hans Bernhard and Hans Rudolf, were able to pursue careers at the Habsburg court, and both joined the opposition. The former served in the Confederate army and later emigrated, while the latter confined his activity to signing the Confederation and Retzer *Jurament.*[103] Despite their active involvement – only one of the family's adult males remained cautious during the revolt – the Hofkirchens were Lutherans, not Calvinists, as some historians have assumed.[104]

Prominent among the opposition were the barons of Puchheim – ten of the fifteen members living in 1620 were proscribed rebels. The family was one of the few native clans who could trace their baronage back to the early thirteenth century. Like the Hofkirchens, the Puchheims had a long tradition of supporting the Estates' cause, and from the beginning they were leaders in establishing and retaining Protestantism in Lower Austria. Complaints from prelates against family members who opened their Protestant churches to peasants from Catholic parishes were numerous. However, their material interests were as strong as, and perhaps indistinguishable from, their religious commitment, since complaints against their seizing Catholic church property were just as common.[105] None of the fathers of the men who joined the active opposition among the Puchheim family had been able to pursue distinguished careers at court. Although a few held positions as chamberlains, or as councillors in the Lower Austrian *Regiment,* these appointments were hardly befitting such a prominent and ancient family. The only prestigious honorary office, the *Obersterbtruchsessamt,* which had been in the family for many generations, was bestowed on their only Catholic member, Johann Christoph Puchheim, after the death of Georg I. Nor had any of the rebels ever held a position at court, although Otto Herman had a short-lived military career as *Obristleutnant,* and, in 1608, held a commanding position with the Estates.

In contrast, Johann Christoph, from the Göllersdorfer line, was richly rewarded by the Habsburgs for his conversion to Catholicism in 1603. Only twenty-five yeas old, he was appointed to the War Council (*Hofkriegsrat*) in the same year. As first master of ordinance (*General-, Feld-, und Hauszeugmeister*), he also received the title of *Oberst*. A member of the Catholic Union since 1604, Matthias raised Johann Christoph in 1612 to the rank of count, which was pertinent only to himself and his heirs, thus excluding his Protestant relatives. By 1616, he was among the three largest landholders in Lower Austria and owned nearly half (at least 1600) of the peasant households belonging to the entire family.[106]

The city and seigneurie of Horn, which belonged to Reichard Puchheim, had been the centre of the Protestant opposition in 1608–9 and became its meeting place again after 1618. For this reason, Reichard was arrested as early as 1619, when the city of Horn was captured by the Imperials. His brother, Johann, who had established a printing press in the service of Protestantism on this estate, was proscribed in 1620. Reichard had debts, yet he had claims on the crown amounting to 50 000 gulden, covering at least half of his outstanding obligations. Evidently, a large number of other rebels had debts, although we do not know the exact nature of, or reasons for, these obligations, nor how many of the loyal or moderate nobles were also indebted. But given the diversity of material backgrounds, financial difficulties do not appear to have been important in determining whether or not a Protestant joined the active opposition.

Andreas (the Older) and Dietrich of Puchheim, proscribed because they had signed the Confederation, the Retzer *Jurament,* and were active in the Directory and in the Confederate army, had debts on their small estates, but only those of Andreas were substantial. Yet, their brother Johann Bernhard, who also had insignificant landholdings, paid homage in 1620. And one of Johann Bernhard's cousins, Otto Herman, who had no debts on his small estate, with twenty-five peasant households, compromised himself during the revolt.[107] Of the four Puchheims who did not join the active opposition, but refused to pay homage, Bernhard had considerable tax arrears, but also substantial claims on the crown. But his brother, Wolf Adam, who possessed a large seigneurie (*Heidenreichstein*) had lost some villages to pay tax arrears.[108] As was observed above, level of wealth was not strongly correlated with political activism.

The case of the Landaus further confirms this conclusion. One of the richest landowners among the Protestants, Hartman Landau, who had more than 1000 peasant households on a single estate, belonged to the old native nobility who had received a baronage only in 1564. He signed the Confederation and the Retzer *Jurament,* but appears to have died before he could be proscribed. His property was not confiscated, perhaps because one of his brothers, Ehrenreich, who was quiet during the uprising, had a title to half of the estate.[109] His other four brothers belonged to the passive opposition, but two of Hartman's cousins, Erasmus and Georg, were proscribed rebels, and their property in Lower and Upper Austria was confiscated. Their combined assets amounted to the enormous amount of 800 000 gulden, which exceeded their considerable debts.[110] However, the Landaus appear to have resented deeply their exclusion from office-holding, and the rebels from the Landau family shared this fate with the Puchheims: by 1620 none held a position at the Habsburg court. Erasmus and Georg Landau both had been chamberlains under Matthias, but the appointment was not confirmed by Ferdinand. Hartman and his five brothers, most of whom were in their thirties, never held posts.[111]

Among the knights who joined the opposition, many were also indebted, but again the pattern was not consistent enough to be considered a decisive factor for involvement in the revolt. Wolfgang Steger, from an old native noble family, had a small estate worth nearly 50 000 gulden, but his outstanding debts were nearly as large. He was never offered an appointment at court or in the military, and was proscribed for signing the Confederation and serving the Protestant Estates as a deputy.[112] On the other hand, Wolf Polani, also from the old native nobility, was not indebted when the crown confiscated his small estate for having fought in the Confederate army.[113] Another knight, Jonas Hillebrand, of new origin and admitted to the *Ritterstand* in 1601, had his two estates worth more than 120 000 gulden confiscated because he had signed the Confederation; they were free of debts.[114]

Equally instructive are the backgrounds of two other rebels from the *Ritterstand*. Wilhelm Kren, who was proscribed for unknown reasons, had a small property and no debts. His Catholic relative, Ulrich (probably his uncle), was ennobled in 1582, admitted to the Estate of Knights in 1599, and rose to high office (privy councillor in 1612) with a degree in law, but Wilhelm never held a position at court. As the case of Zacharias Starzer shows, this was not because he had not studied law.[115] Starzer, one of the leading personalities of the opposition, descended from wealthy Viennese merchants. After receiving his law degree in 1590, he was ennobled (1598) and admitted to the *Ritterstand* (1603). His talents were not recognized by the Habsburgs, but the Estates used him for various functions. After joining the Confederates, he became an active member of the Directory, was sent frequently on diplomatic missions to Protestant foreign allies, and therefore was one of the most compromised rebels. His houses in Vienna and his vineyards were confiscated, but Zacharias, who had no heirs, did not live long enough to suffer from his ruin.[116]

We can conclude, then, that over the long term the Protestant Reformation offered opportunities for Habsburg state-building that required altered relations with their elites. In particular, it allowed them better to assert their ecclesiastical patronage and advocacy rights, and thereby extend their co-ordinating power over the Catholic Church. As we saw earlier, through the tool of *Polizeiordnungen,* which attempted to regulate moral behaviour and social discipline, they slowly but steadily expanded their co-ordinating power over nobles, clergy and common subjects. None the less, all of this was accomplished with great difficulty and at huge cost. Initially, the dynasty suffered significant setbacks in political centralization as a consequence of the coincidence of major wars with the Protestant Reformation, and this helped to cement unity among the elites, putting them in competition with the Habsburgs in an effort to gain control of the Church and its property. Although the Augsburg settlement brought decades of peace to the empire, it was unable to cope with this problem and the unstable balance of power created by the continued advance of Lutheranism and Calvinism. One of the obstacles to extended peace was that Catholics, Protestants and emperors all viewed the treaty of 1555 as being temporary, and all wished to extend their advantage at the expense of the others. As a consequence, the institutions that were to guarantee and enforce the settlement became progressively impotent.

This resembled developments in the Habsburg lands, where the dynasty, ironically, could not enforce the formula of *cuius regio, eius religio*. After the mid-sixteenth century, war, financial problems, and the explosive situation in the Reich prompted compromise with the Protestant elites, but the agreements also suffered from ambiguities and continual transgressions. In fact, by instituting a rigorous counter-reform programme the Habsburgs hoped to find cause to rescind these religious concessions. The advance of Calvinism, the absence of an impartial court to settle conflicts, the threat of having to restore more Church land, and provocative measures, such as prosecuting important nobles, helped to radicalize the Protestant opposition in Bohemia and Austria. Moreover, the Council of Trent, as well as events in France and the Netherlands, further added to the hardening of fronts and the confessionalization of political and social relations, culminating in the formation of international and regional 'defensive' unions among both Catholics and Protestants. This further encouraged the leadership of both camps to pursue more radical action. Of course, war was not inevitable, and a willingness to set up impartial courts to arbitrate a new compromise might have arrested military conflict. However, the parties involved did develop rigid dispositions, and became increasingly willing to replace bargaining with violence.

Religion and political factors certainly played an important role in the contest, but they were inseparably fused with material issues, particularly competition over ecclesiastical property and court patronage. In Lower Austria, we observed that there was a strong correlation between political activism and office-holding, and very few Protestant nobles who joined the active opposition were princely servants. Furthermore, some nobles appear to have made rather astute political choices in 1620, suggesting that they pursued conscious strategies serving the interests of their families rather than unthinkingly acting out of corporate or religious loyalties. All this indicates that, in addition to the conflict over Church property, material causes played a crucial role in the political choices nobles made. To determine exactly how important the role was, it is necessary to explore first the subjective intentions of Protestant nobles and Habsburgs, and whether the nobility considered itself divided into court and a country factions. Analyzing the political claims the various actors made is particularly relevant in determining which factors contributed to the breakdown of bargaining in 1618–20. The next chapter therefore turns from the chronological account of political culture and actions in its specific historic setting to a closer analysis of the cultural and social symbols of political protest as communicated in the political discourse between the Protestant Estates and Catholic court during the first phase of war.

3
Discourse of Division, 1618–20

Public political discourse rarely reflects accurately the conscious intentions of actors, nor does it invariably provide a clear account of the real causes behind events since people may hide, for various reasons, their motives and goals, or may not be fully aware of all the factors that influence their actions. Especially in early modern times, the threat of reprisals by the authorities tended to distort political expression. Moreover, political discourse may in various ways merely duplicate the dominant discourse. This is certainly true of the exchange of propaganda between the Protestant and Catholic leadership after the defenestration in 1618, which reflected discursive norms of medieval and early modern natural-law arguments. These nearly always justified collective violence as a 'war for a just peace,' that is, as a means to protect the unity of justice and peace. War manifestos of early modern Europe therefore blamed the other side for breaking the peace, and war aims became identical with legitimation. The documents I have used in this chapter express this by covering the twelve most common justifications for war in early modern Europe, such as fighting heretics, protecting subjects against an enemy, enforcing contracts and rules of succession, putting down a rebellion, defending rights (religious or political), and obtaining restitution for injustices. Hegemonic goals were considered to be inappropriate grounds for fighting wars, and declaring material interests were thought especially unacceptable.[1]

Declarations of motives and goals by agents themselves, then, can be highly misleading, and they must be supplemented by other texts. But, at the same time, the public dialogue between Protestants and Catholics after 1618 suggests that the discourse of just war left room for stressing particular grievances (including material ones), with motives and meanings that were specific to the context and concerns of participants. Although the interpretation of these documents with respect to intentions and causality is necessarily tentative, it is possible to determine what claims the protagonists made, especially how they constructed the motives and actions of their opponents, which they contrasted with a desirable self-image, and how they viewed the gulf that separated them. This contributes to an understanding of the kinds of political identity each side wished to foster among themselves and communicate to their enemies and friends, and how they wanted their public to view the other side. It also sheds light on the accepted rules of legitimate political action, and how these shaped political choices and relations. However, this discourse was not fully representative, since the leadership of the active Protestant opposition and the Habsburg rulers and their closest advisers rather than the Protestant Estates or the Catholic Court at large dominated it.

Considering the high cost of early modern war, this chapter centres on exploring the question of why the Habsburg rulers and nobles resorted to violence. It was not only the large military expenses, which the parties considered carefully (judging by the attempts to find monetary subsidies from their allies), that should have made bargaining a preferable choice. More important was the danger each side confronted if the other won the war. The Habsburgs risked losing their economically and politically most important territories as well as the title of emperor, which would have transformed them into minor rulers. Likewise, as the Protestant nobles were repeatedly reminded, they risked their life and property if the Habsburgs were victorious.

Surprisingly few scholars address the question of why groups and their leaders cannot come to an agreement that would be preferable to war, although many rational choice theorists in political science and economics, believing that bargaining and co-operation always outperform conflict, explain violence as being a result of the absence of rational acquisitiveness. The logic here is straightforward. Because violence destroys productive assets, some form of contract or agreement has the potential to make all parties better off. Thus, rational and acquisitive people would never fight. To deduce this conclusion rigorously, however, it has to be assumed *inter alia* that everything of value is subject to continuous variation, and that people will always be willing to trade something of what they have for something they lack – provided the rate of exchange is appropriate. Some political scientists also believe that there is always a continuous range of peaceful settlements and that the issues in disputes are perfectly divisible, especially in periods before nationalism. Thus, James D. Fearon asserts that the problems over which the leadership in armed conflicts negotiate allow for 'many possible settlements' and that they can 'pay each other sums of money or goods ..., or make linkages with other issues, ... making any issues in dispute perfectly divisible.'[2]

Why, then, did the parties in the Habsburg lands resort to violence after 1618? An obvious answer would be miscalculations, but, as we have seen in the previous chapter, the two leaderships had no basis for overestimating its chance of victory and did not lack significant information about the capacity or willingness of the other side to fight. But if war was not the product of rational miscalculation, was it then the result of the parties irrationally believing that the outcome of war would be more profitable than the result of bargaining? Some economists and political scientists might indeed reply in the affirmative, pointing to religious emotions underpinning irrational choices, and noble material culture characterized by conspicuous consumption lacking rational acquisitiveness. However, as I demonstrate in Part II, such interpretations would fail to understand noble interests and the nature of symbolic and social capital in noble society. For now it suffices to recall that, considering the political space in which they operated, the Habsburgs' preference for the Catholic faith was a politically astute choice, and that few German princes and Austrian nobles lost sight of their material interests in their fervour to introduce spiritual reform. After all, a large part of why Protestants and Catholics of the Reich sought to come to a new arrangement after 1555 concerned disputes over territorial acquisitions and Church property. The question remains of why they were not able strike a new bargain over these goods?

I have no doubt, then, that early modern monarchs and their elites had self-interests, including material ones, and that they considered the benefits and risks of war, but I also think at these interest are best understood in terms of how the protagonists defined and acted upon them. To understand why they preferred war to negotiating a settlement, this chapter explores how they themselves made sense of the situation they confronted, and how they publicly defined their motives for engaging in war. In particular, it examines whether they considered everything of value as continuously divisible. After analysing how the Protestant leadership presented the intentions and actions of Catholics and Habsburgs, I focus on their political grievances and claims with respect to political authority and the theories of resistance they proposed, concluding with a reading of the political propaganda and response of the Catholic court. It is important to consider the public discourses of the Estates in both Bohemian and Austrian territories, because they show considerable similarities, suggesting that they were constructed through a co-ordinated effort. Moreover, the comparison helps to explain the separate Confederation agreements between them. However, I pay more attention to Protestant political rhetoric, because the evidence available to me was much richer than the sources reflecting the claims of the Habsburg rulers and their Catholic advisers.

Endowments and defining the Catholic other

It is tempting to construct a 'court and country' dichotomy in the Habsburg territories, even though historians of England have expressed doubts about the existence of a division between court culture and country life.[3] Court life did become a principal target of literary production by

Austrian Protestant nobles during the first half of the seventeenth century, which also reveals a fairly uniform self-perception that was dominated by the Lutheran ethic of *pater familias*. However, there was considerable continuity in the critique of court life in Germanic literature from the Middle Ages to the late eighteenth century, and not only humanist and Protestant literature criticized the court on moral grounds, but also Catholic writers, such as Antonio de Guevara and Adam Contzen, contrasted the supposed vices and depravities of the court with the virtues and benefits of rural life (*Landleben*).[4] As I showed in the previous chapter, the Lower Austrian Protestant and Catholic Estates were institutionally separated more clearly than the English elite, since few of the Austrian Protestant nobles who joined the Bohemian opposition were part of the Imperial court and thus strongly resembled a 'country party'. But we also observed that the Austrian Protestants were divided internally and clearly took different political positions during the last phase of the conflict, suggesting that it is necessary to re-evaluate in more subtle ways how seventeenth-century elites viewed the gulf that separated them, and how this contributed to the breakdown of bargaining.

In their public discourse during the two years following the defenestration neither Protestant Estates nor Catholic courtiers perceived much of a cultural gulf separating them in terms of court and country ethics. Although the Protestant opposition did not glorify pastoral country life, or vilify corruption at the Imperial court, they clearly identified the latter with Catholicism and the *Land*, or country, with Protestantism, but presented this dichotomy largely in terms of different conceptions of the political order.[5] And if the Protestant leadership frequently portrayed their conflict with Catholics in moral terms as a conflict between good and evil, this anti-court rhetoric was also related closely to their political propaganda. It defined Catholic courtiers clearly as a dangerous 'other', a *Partei*, or 'party', of interest,[6] whose discriminatory policies threatened Protestants with cultural erosion, the loss of political rights, material endowments and even life. This depiction of the other side was closely interwoven with self-presentations, and the 'evil' intentions of the Catholics were counterpoised with their own honest and righteous goals which aimed at protecting the territory, the Estates' rights, and the Protestant religion.

The identification of the Austrian Estates with the 'country' had its roots in medieval tradition which viewed the *Land* (country or territory) as consisting of both the territorial prince (*Landesfürst*) and the members of the Estates (*Landstände, Landleute*). But during the sixteenth century the Estates usually identified themselves alone as the 'Land',[7] and in the correspondence, memoranda, and manifestos the Protestant leadership produced between 1618 and 1620, the country and *Landstände* became synonymous with Protestantism because most of the nobility and towns had become Protestant. For example, the 'Historical and Diplomatic Declaration of the

Rights and Liberties of the Estates of the Duchy of Lower Austria' of 1619 was composed by the Protestant faction but written in the name of all the Estates, as if the clergy did not belong to them.[8] Such terminology ignored the fact that the First Estate consisted of Catholic clergy and thus underlined conveniently the divisions between the two confessions and the Protestant claim that the Church was part of the crown lands (*Kammergut*) but the towns and markets were not.

Before 1618, the Protestant Estates were careful in issuing public insults against Catholics, and avoided portraying them as a wholly separate community of interest, even after rumours began to circulate periodically about Catholic plots aimed at the destruction of Protestantism in the Empire.[9] One reason for this caution was connected to the hope of gaining support from some of the Catholic members of the Estates. This was particularly important to the Bohemians, who tried to persuade the Catholic majority in Moravia that the liberties of the political *Stände* at large had been threatened by the Habsburgs.[10] But after the defenestration it became standard terminology for the Austrian and Bohemian Estates to focus on accusing 'the evil councillors, our enemies' of the destruction of peace, justice and 'barbarian tyranny'.[11] After Khlesl's removal on 20 July 1618, it was particularly convenient to attack the former director of the privy council. In the opinion of the Austrian Estates, Matthias had been poorly advised by the Cardinal, 'a man composed of roguishness, deceit, impertinence, greed, and arrogance'.[12] The Bohemian Protestant leaders also blamed him and his assistants (*'mitgehülffen'*) for the policies at court which aimed not only at the destruction of the Protestants but also the political Estates at large. Khlesl, who was 'not educated in a bakery, as some think, but in the ancient Machiavellian school', had misled and deceived Protestants continually, and even acted without the authority of the emperor, Matthias.[13] They had therefore been forced into opposition by the threats of these 'harmful and poisonous councillors and archenemies of the Protestant religion, Khlesl and his gang', who took over and ran the government at will.[14]

Even though the identification of Catholicism with the court was at first not always stated overtly, the actions of the 'evil' officers and court officials were soon connected to Catholic interests.[15] The 1619 'Manifest' of the Protestant leaders of the Austrian Estates was particularly direct in making the 'advice of all Catholics' responsible for the attacks on their property, liberty and religion, and identified the court with 'Catholic courtiers and soldiers'.[16] And the portrait they painted of themselves in the process contrasted sharply with that of the Catholic courtiers, since their own goals were 'loyal, honest, necessary and unavoidable'.[17] The Bohemian Estates in particular liked to insist that they were 'honest people', 'loyal patriots and lovers of the fatherland', who were always 'obedient subjects' with a 'loyal Protestant heart'.[18]

Much of the public rhetoric of the Protestant leaders seemed to be aimed at reassuring supporters and opponents that their actions were not directed against Habsburg authority, and thereby guard themselves against charges of sedition. Thus the 'Second Vindication' of the Protestant Bohemian Estates (1619) claimed that they never intended to offend Ferdinand 'in the least, nor to recruit and establish a military defence against him', but had been forced into opposition to protect themselves by the actions of 'harmful and poisonous councillors'.[19] Like the declarations of the Austrian Estates, a large part of the Second Vindication was designed to stress publicly that the Protestants were not seditious. In fact, it was a response to the accusation of an anonymous pamphleteer who (pretending to write in the name of the Protestants) had called them 'rioters' (*Rebellen*) and their actions a 'true rebellion' (*purlautere Rebellion*).[20]

Resenting these allegations, the Bohemian non-Catholic Estates presented themselves as defenders of the kingdom and protested against the devastations, 'tyranny and cruelty' of the Imperial army against men, women and children, the shedding of innocent blood, and the unjust imprisonment of peasants and members of the Estates. They were forced, they insisted, to raise troops and organize their defence in order to prevent more bloodshed.[21] Like the Austrian Protestant leaders, they maintained that no one could blame them for their defensive actions considering that the 'destruction and decline of the Protestant Estates had been planned'.[22] They had set up a military defence to protect themselves against the enemies of their religion and opponents at court.[23] Furthermore, not only their religious but also their political liberties had been violated, so that the grievances of the Bohemian Estates, 'flooded this territory like the Deluge' (*Sündtfluth*). More specific complaints were also directed against their 'religious enemies' and advisers at court, who had acted illegally against them, taken their property and destroyed the kingdom and peace.[24] Committing a *crimen laesae majestatis* (*Majestätsbeleidigung*) alone could result in the ban (*Acht*) and confiscation of one's property, and the Protestants had good reason to worry. After all, nobles of the territory of Teschen in Silesia had been charged with this crime for merely forming a union,[25] and a number of powerful Moravian and Austrian nobles, such as Karl von Žerotín (the Older) and Wolfgang von Hofkirchen had been tried on the grounds of sedition since 1600.[26]

The public expressions of the Protestant leadership sought to vindicate their military actions and union, and invoke fears of losing life and property. The Jesuits in particular were frequently portrayed as threatening the security of all non-Catholics. After expelling them from their territories, the Bohemian Protestant Estates claimed that the whole world knew that the Jesuits were the 'most malicious' (*hochschedliche*) instruments of the Papacy. Thirsting not only after the property but also after the blood of the Protestants, the Jesuits schemed daily at court against them.[27] The polemic of anonymous German broadsheets (*Flugblätter*) printed between 1618 and 1620 was particularly condemnatory and frequently depicted the Jesuits as lusting after Protestant possessions.[28] Powerful metaphors of blood were evident here, and in the 'Discourse on the Present State of Bohemia', a broadsheet written in 1618, some time after Khlesl's removal in July 1618. Claiming that the Pope and Catholics at large were thirsting 'after Lutheran blood', a thirst that the Jesuits helped them to quench, it warned that Catholic plots, and especially Khlesl's 'knavish trick' (*Bubenstück*), could lead to a 'great blood bath'.[29] Tschernembl, the leader of the Upper and Lower Austrian Estates, who had in 1609 invoked the spectre of a 'great blood bath', warned again in a letter to Ferdinand on 25 April, 1619 that all his lands, indeed the entire Reich, might become embroiled in war.[30]

It appears, then, that after the defenestration of 1618, the Bohemian and Austrian Estates made a co-ordinated effort to accuse Jesuits and Catholic advisers at Court, rather than the monarch, of evil intentions, and particularly for threatening the peace of 1555, and for plotting to kill Protestants and lusting after their property. But, as we shall see shortly, by 1619 the Protestant leaders also began to accuse some of the Habsburg rulers, such as Rudolf II, and in particular Ferdinand II, of similar evil intentions, and to claim that Jesuits and Catholic advisers had turned Ferdinand II into a tyrant in order to destroy Protestants. While the desire of the opposition leaders to vindicate their actions as legitimate resistance seems designed at least partly to reassure Lutherans at home and in the Reich who were concerned that they act within the confines of Luther's opinions on resistance, the public rhetoric of the opposition leaders was most persistent in claiming that Protestant security was threatened.

The non-Catholic Estates further expressed grave concern about being excluded from court patronage. Equity of the religions in court patronage had already been a major issue in the conflict of 1608, but it soon surfaced again. In 1610 the first recommendation of a memorandum to King Matthias on how to gain Bohemian support was to avoid confessional considerations in appointments to the privy council and other councils.[31] Habsburg confessional recruitment policies were also an issue for the *Reichsstände*, and five of the thirteen 'Gravamina of the Corresponding Protestant Imperial Estates' of 1613 concerned the preference for Catholics, particularly as councillors in the high court, or *Reichskammergericht*.[32]

The Austrian Protestant *Stände* thought it was a long-established practice that the Habsburgs were obliged to rule the country according to the Estates' advice, and install only their members to important positions. In the 'Manifest' of 1619 they claimed that Rudolf II had refused to appoint Protestant nobles to court positions, viewing this as an arbitrary, absolutist policy contrary to their established rights and liberties, and demanding that the 'entire administration of the duchy be established according to the counsel of the Estates'.[33] Implementing this would have restored full powers of consent to the *Stände* and effectively prevented the Habsburgs from favouring foreign or Catholic nobles as councillors. Most important, it would have moved control over court patronage entirely to the nobility. The Lower Austrian Articles of Confederation (1619) determined that Catholics had to honour the agreements between the Confederates, and that officials had to be appointed without considering differences of religion. The Upper Austrians stipulated in their Articles that all officials were to be nominated by the Estates and merely confirmed by the prince, and that no one was to remove Protestants from office as long as they were qualified and led a Christian lifestyle.[34]

An anonymous position paper (*Gutachten*) of 1618 on how the emperor could resolve the Bohemian problem peacefully recommended, among other things, that a change in the preferred appointment of Catholics to offices was essential to preserve the peace, and that the king should seek nominations of officials from the Bohemian Estates.[35] The preference for Catholics in offices was a major issue of the first 'Justification' (1618) of the Bohemian Protestant leaders, and about half of their complaints centred on this concern, the other on ecclesiastical property; it also had a prominent place in their 'Second Justification' (1619). Moreover, the Bohemian Articles of Confederation envisioned a future order where court patronage was reversed, with the highest offices filled only by Protestants who were nominated by the Estates. Catholics would have no jurisdiction over Protestants, but could hold less important positions as long as they declared official allegiance to the Confederation and recognized all other religious concessions.[36]

Although framed by discursive norms that justified their actions, the Protestant grievances expressed economic interest centred on their fear of losing court patronage and Church property. However, these were closely intertwined with their religious faith and helped shape their representation of Catholics as a hostile, evil other. And by creating a 'them and us' dichotomy, the Protestant leadership futher defined religious identities in a specific context of conflict. In part at least, the public rhetoric of both the Austrian and Bohemian Protestant Estates seemed designed to arouse fear of Catholic plots and attacks on Protestant lives, property and other endowments in order to muster support for their actions, and foster the conviction among all Protestants of the need for radical action in establishing better constitutional protections for their security. This does not preclude that they themselves did not genuinely believe that their security was threatened. Their persistent refusal to disarm despite the danger of severe repercussions and their discourse on resistance both support this.

Tyranny, security and resistance

By 1619, 'constitutional' issues began to play a prominent role in the Protestant discourse, and opposition leaders sought to secure guarantees that the Habsburgs would in future observe the contracts they made. In the language of modern economics, one could say that they faced the problems of 'moral hazard'; that is, with opportunistic action by Habsburgs and Catholics in a context where there was no contractual enforcement mechanism. They therefore proclaimed that they had to protect themselves against security threats by fortifying the Estates' right of resistance through a military union. Using natural law arguments, their public statements explained why they refused to recognize Ferdinand II as their ruler, and why they could not disarm or give up the Confederation. In the process they had to define what constituted their privileges and traditional rights.

In their open 'Manifest' of 1619, the Austrian Protestant Estates addressed 'all the European Powers concerning Emperor Ferdinand II's illegal and violently obtained accession and crucial destruction of the hereditary [Austrian] lands', and explained why they would not pay homage to the Emperor. They insisted that first he had to confirm their rights, privileges and liberties, end the war with their neighbours, return the property his army had taken by force, approve the Confederation, and 'arrange the government of Austria according to the advice of the Estates'. Any rational being who visited the territories where Ferdinand II and his brothers had created 'servitude, misery and ruin' would understand that they could not pay homage to this prince without conditions and guarantees.[37] Viewing the Confederation as just such an assurance, the Austrian Protestants alluded here to the contractual nature of homage and invoked natural law implicitly, which (according to most theorists) prohibited a ruler's violation of his or her subjects' property.

In their Second Vindication, the Bohemian Protestant Estates made similar claims but accused Ferdinand more strongly of breaking the fundamental laws of the realm.[38] After they deposed Ferdinand in 1619 the Bohemian opposition claimed that he had not been freely and properly elected, had taken over government while Matthias was still alive (against his own promises), violated the Letter of Majesty, and had begun a war against the kingdom with foreign troops, thereby cruelly destroying the country and the life of the people, including unborn subjects. Moreover, before he was accepted as king, Ferdinand had made plans to pass on the kingdom to Spain in the event that he died without heirs, as if Bohemia were an hereditary possession, which it was not. Although they did not point out specifically that the alienation of crown lands without consent was considered by nearly all theorists (including Bodin) to be a breach of natural law, the Estates felt that not only Ferdinand's actions, but also his previous acceptance by the Estates as king were in violation of their rights and privileges, and they therefore had no further obligation to him.[39]

The Austrian Manifest also asserted that Ferdinand II had begun a war with Bohemia and Moravia against their will and failed to protect them from the 'lustful plundering and cruelty of the Imperials', who were robbing them of their property and violating 'not only human but also divine law', which was congruent with natural law. The greater the crime and cruelty someone committed against them, they claimed, 'the more he was valued at court'. Within two years, Ferdinand had destroyed the 'delightful' territory of Lower Austria, while Upper Austria was exhausted and intimidated by soldiers and 'Catholic courtiers'.[40] This provided the *Stände* with the opportunity to define themselves as protectors of the territory's inhabitants against such weakness in a ruler, and they asserted the right to ascertain whether he had a legitimate claim to rule and the appropriate qualities. Along similar lines, the Bohemian Protestants presented themselves as defenders of the kingdom and the public good, and protested against the devastations, the cruelty of the Imperial army against men, women and children, the shedding of much innocent blood, and the unjust imprisonment of peasants and other subjects. They were forced, they insisted, to raise troops and organize their defence in order to prevent more bloodshed.[41]

The Protestant Estates were here invoking received opinion among continental jurists about the limits of princely power. Medieval tradition had obliged the monarch to protect the law and provide '*Schutz und Schirm*', and some jurists allowed for resistance to a prince who proceeded in a harmful manner, and who did not fulfil his obligation to protect his subjects.[42] Renaissance jurists continued to assert that rulers' authority was bound by natural law and therefore could not take property away from subjects without just cause; princes also had to uphold hereditary obligations. Even Bodin stressed that monarchs were bound by natural law to respect the liberty and property of free subjects, but according to him they were answerable to God alone for any breaches.[43] Of course, contemporary Protestant (*monarchomach*) resistance theories disagreed with the premise that the ruler could not be held accountable in this world. Clearly influenced by them was the anonymous document entitled '*De resistentia subditorum adversus Principem legitima*', claiming that in cases of brutal tyranny the '*custodes patriae*' had the right to protect subjects and resist the ruler. It was handwritten in 1600 and was most probably composed by the leader of the Upper Austrian Estates, the Calvinist Georg Erasmus von Tschernembl.[44]

Justifying resistance with natural-law arguments was an integral part of the Protestant leadership's public discourse. In addition to accusing Ferdinand of violating the life and property of subjects, and denying him legitimate rights to succession, they represented him as a tyrant who had to be opposed for abrogating customary rights without seeking their consent. The Austrian Manifest explained how some of their *Recht* had been destroyed by the Habsburgs, even though by customary law their duchy could not be ruled in an 'absolute manner'.[45] Clearly, as the title of the Manifest indicates, Ferdinand was a tyrant and a usurper, who had obtained rule of the territory illegally and without regard for property or tradition. Other Habsburgs, such as Ferdinand I, had attempted to impose absolute rule over the people, 'left the path of ... ancestors and weakened the liberty of the Austrians through Spanish force and tyranny'.[46]

Interestingly, the Estates conceded that they had at times co-operated with this political trend 'because at least it was only a beginning', and they had hoped for religious freedom in compensation.[47] Viewing the government of Maximilian II as 'milder' (*gelinder*), they accused Rudolf II's 'absolute rule' of destroying the legal rights and traditions of the provinces and of 'wrongful and illegal interpretation' of their religious concessions.[48] In addition to a long list of the Emperor's arbitrary actions in religious matters, the Manifest complained that he had violated their traditional liberties and rights, and closed court offices to Protestants. It further objected to unreasonably heavy military and other financial burdens, unjust arrests and punishment of private persons, the alienation of crown lands against their interests, and the publication of patents and legislation (that is, positive law), all without consulting the Estates ('*ohne uns um unsere Meinung zu befragen*').

While Rudolf detested 'the name of liberty itself', Matthias had restored their political and religious freedoms and 'reconstructed the sad condition of the administration according to the advice of the Estates'.[49] The Austrian Protestant leadership thus expressed some nostalgic affection for Matthias, who 'by nature was a good man', but ill-advised by his councillors, in particular Cardinal Khlesl. In contrast, they pictured Ferdinand II as having always acted against them arbitrarily and without just cause and legality, and, on the advice of foreigners, of taking over the government by force. The leader of the Upper Austrian Estates, Georg Erasmus von Tschernembl, also expressed publicly his concern about Ferdinand's unjust and tyrannical actions, and other noblemen, especially in Inner Austria, had viewed him for many decades as a bloodthirsty tyrant and 'slave of the Jesuits'.[50]

Like the Austrian grievances, the Bohemian Protestants put the violations of the Estates' religious freedoms at the beginning of a long list of reasons for their opposition. Thus the Second Bohemian Vindication complained about the destruction of religious peace by Jesuits and the king's advisers, the attacks on their religious liberties, the closing of their schools and churches, the forced conversion of their subjects, and the imposed censorship and infringements on urban centres. However, the list of political grievances was more detailed than those of the Austrian Estates. Besides complaints about their exclusion from office, the Protestant leadership set out a lengthy exposition about how the court had illegally manipulated the '*Landts Ordnung*', and voting in the Diets. But they, too, stressed that decisions concerning the kingdom had been made without their knowledge and against their will, implying that their consent was necessary in all matters.[51] Although Bohemian accusations about Ferdinand's tyrannical actions are less prominent, perhaps because they focused on the claim that his succession was not legitimate, references to the 'barbarian tyranny of Catholic courtiers' and the tyrannical action of the Imperial army were abundant.[52]

In short, Protestant rhetoric about tyranny aimed at justifying resistance against both a legitimate ruler turned tyrant by exercise, and a tyrant by usurpation, with the Austrian opposition focusing on the former, the Bohemians on the latter. Each associated absolute rule with arbitrary, tyrannical actions, which they connected with violations of fundamental laws (for example, changing succession rules and the alienation of crown lands) and customary rights without their consent. The Austrians even claimed a right of approving positive law, and, as we shall see, the Bohemian Confederation asserted similar entitlements.

How to hold rulers (who, as supreme legislators, claimed to be released from positive law and answerable to God alone for breaches of natural, divine law) accountable, was a problem that vexed many contemporary jurists and theorists. The Monarchomachs' answer was to establish norms for justified resistance, and Tschernembl's *Resistentia*, which drew on their ideas, was probably the inspiration for the public rhetoric of the Austrian Protestant Estates. Putting infringements of religious freedom at the head of reasons for justified resistance to the ruler, the *Resistentia* also stressed violations of customary and positive law, and the legal order (*ordo judicorum*) in general. It did not allow for everyone to oppose a ruler, and differentiated between the *princeps legibus solutus* and the *princeps legitimus*. The former wielded absolute authority over individual subjects, who therefore could not resist the ruler openly because originally they had sworn obedience to him without condition (*vicissima condicio*) and possessed no privileges and liberties. It was up to the *custodes patriae* to defy the ruler and protect these subjects in cases of brutal tyranny.[53]

Resistance to legitimate authority that had become tyrannical was the main focus of the *Resistentia*. Asserting that, since the *princeps legitimus* was bound by law and tradition, the *custodes patriae,* identified with the territorial Estates, could resist if the former violated the contract between them by destroying their liberties and customs. Serving as a constant check on royal power, the *custodes patriae* made certain that the ruler did not misuse his position, and, for this reason, it was essential that all positions were filled by members of the Estates (*Landleute*) rather than by foreigners. However, removing a ruler from the throne was left to the *rectores provincialium* (perhaps identical with an executive assembly, or *Directorium*), although they were advised first to attempt to reform him, to dismiss his councillors and ministers, organize resistance, and seek a union with neighbours. The example of the Netherlands was called upon as proof that justified resistance, which the author distinguished from seditious rebellion, can defeat rich and mighty rulers. Although the killing of a tyrannical ruler was not permitted according to the Bible, he asserted that it was not to be punished as murder.[54]

The *Resistentia* drew on a variety of resistance theories based on natural law arguments which had developed in France and elsewhere after St. Bartholomew's Night, such as François Hotman's *Francogallia* (1572), and has some similarities to the anonymous *Vindiciae contra tyrannos* (1577), probably authored by Philippe Duplessis Mornay.[55] But it resembles particularly *Du droit des magistrats* (1574) of Theodore Beza, Calvin's successor, which differentiated between tyrants who were usurpers and legitimate rulers who had turned tyrant, and insisted that private individuals could only exercise passive resistance. The *Resistentia's* distinction between *custodes* and the *rectores provincialium*, who could depose the ruler, is also reminiscent of Beza's differentiation between inferior magistrates (for example, urban majors and Estates' deputies), who held power over local areas, protected the contract with the ruler and organized resistance to a tyrant, and simple magistrates (such as the Estates in assembly), who served as a constant check on royal power. However, this aspect was better developed in the Bohemian Confederation, which made a clearer distinction between the role of the Estates as a check and the function of the defensors, who were to take the initiative in organizing resistance to the prince. Like the Confederation, the *Resistentia*, which makes specific reference to the Netherlands, was also influenced by the work of Johannes Althusius, particularly when it insisted that since, by nature, all men were free, they transferred to another the power to rule them through a reciprocal contract to which all parties were bound. Although Althusius's *Politica methodice digesta* appeared three years later (1603), Tschernembl, like the Bohemian noble leaders of the opposition, such as Karl the Older von Žerotín, and Wenzel and Adam Budovetz, had close connections with European resistance theorists and with each other.[56]

Influenced by such theories, the Austrian 'Historical Declaration' referred to the existence of a contract by which the *Land*, or Estates, had conferred rights of majesty on the ruler. Searching for evidence on the origin of this contract, the Lower Austrians claimed that, following the rulers of ancient Rome, the emperor had installed both the 'Land', and the territorial ruler as regent, and provided them with the *jus majestatis*. Emperor Frederic I, who in 1116 had turned Austria into a duchy, first gave rights of majesty, liberties and regalia (*'Hoheiten, Freihaiten und Regalia'*) to the *Land*, and only afterward's did he give the duchy to the new duke. The Estates interpreted this to mean that the duke had received his rights and liberties 'from the *Land*, and not the *Land* from him'.[57] In short, rights of majesty was the property of the Estates, who had delegated it to the prince. Although this logic is confusing, since it made the emperor the original owner of the *jus majestatis,* the argument for co-sovereignty between prince and Estates was in line with the Protestant contract theorists of the Holy Roman Empire.

It was not merely a medieval notion of consent that the Lower Austrian Protestants had in mind when the Historical Declaration asserted that the *Land* possessed rights of majesty and various other '*regalia*', some of which it held by itself, and others it shared with the prince. In return, the ruler held some powers for himself and others in common with the *Land*. As the Historical Declaration stated:

> the truth is, that the praiseworthy duchy of Austria possesses this [*jus majestatis*] and other regalia in such a manner, that it holds them in part for itself and in part with the prince in *reciprocè;* in part the prince has his *regalia* for himself, in part *communia* with the territory: so that one has part of the other (but without damaging each other's distinguished estate): and use it at appropriate times and *data occasione*.[58]

At the time, few jurists and theorists in the Empire seem to have had a clear idea of how 'co-sovereignty' was to be shared or distributed, but the topic attracted much attention.[59] As we have seen, supporters of royal power rejected the idea of consent as a partnership in sovereign power. Instead, they followed Bodin in viewing rulers as the source of all authority, although most agreed they were bound by natural law and were wise to seek the consent of the Estates in some matters.[60] It was largely in the Reich that Bodin's idea of indivisible sovereign rights was challenged. Thus, the notion of the Historical Declaration that ruler and *Stände* each held separate rights of majesty, reflects the work of Arnisaeus, who concluded that *jus majestatis* could be separated and distributed to several agents so that a fragment of it existed in each of them, and only comes together in the body as a whole.[61] It also recalls Christoph Besold's conception of shared 'sovereignty' in a compound polygarchy, which argued that powers of majesty could be shared with an inferior, and that supreme sovereignty was in the corporation (*collegium*) even when its head was above the other members.[62]

In the Declaration, the Lower Austrian Protestant leadership further provided an account of what they thought constituted their *jura majestatis,* which they saw largely as the right to approve the ruler's actions and decrees. From the right to freedom from taxation they derived their ability to grant all taxes (ordinary and extraordinary) at the assemblies of the political Estates, which they could also summon themselves when necessary. Also essential was the 'council and will' of the Estates in declaring war and peace, and in the case of a minority or vacancy, they had the right to govern the territory.[63] It is unclear why they did not repeat the Manifesto's claim that their approval of legislation was necessary, but they did assert the power to forge their own alliances within and outside the territory, and to have the ancient freedom to turn to an elector of the Empire for protection and safeguard (*Schutz und Schirm*) in case their own prince burdened them unjustly.[64] In short, the Protestant *Stände* asserted here the right to resist their duke if he proceeded in an illegal manner and thus threatened their own and his subjects' security. For most of these justifications they found historical precedence and support in customary law.[65]

Bohemian Protestant leaders also claimed in their public discourse the right to protect themselves through active resistance. Thus the 'Second Vindication' asserted that rulers everywhere were bound by law and tradition, and could not act arbitrarily ('absolute') against their subjects who had the right to resist all dictates directed against their 'soul, body and life, possessions and property'.[66] Against those who accused the non-Catholic Estates of acting illegally and wrongfully against God and the king, they stated that they could (but did not) offer religious proof that both the Estates and the ruler 'had been installed by God' and limited by him ('*circumscribirt*') with certain conditions and statutes. Bound by divine, natural law, the king could therefore exercise his *plenum dominium* only on his crown lands (*Kammergut*).[67] The Confederation, they asserted, was an old instrument to assure their security, and similar to a previous union with nearby princes and territories; in the past such alliances had been approved by the Habsburgs.[68] Exculpating their actions further, the Bohemian Protestants insisted on having a customary right to set up a *Directorium* in the absence of the king to protect the law and authorities against the 'common rabble' (*Gemeinen Poffel*), collect taxes in case of unrest, and arm themselves against threats by their opponents and enemies at court.[69]

Clearly, like the Austrian Protestants, the Bohemians were keen to distinguish between rebellion and just resistance, which was not to be punished as treason. As I showed earlier, the Second Vindication responded to accusations that Protestants were rebels who planned seditious attacks ('*auffrhürische attentata*') against the king,[70] and denied that they had made changes to the legal order (*Landts Ordnung*), or violated the authority and majesty ('*Authoritet und Hoheit*') of the king. Moreover, it claimed, the alliances among the Estates had been concluded in the best interests of the ruler, and they had not accepted another 'defensor' except God and his majesty.[71] This was before they accepted Frederic of the Palatinate as their new ruler.

In the 'Deduction', composed after the Confederation to explain publicly why they had deposed Ferdinand, the Bohemian Protestant leaders provided, in addition to a list of specific offences the Habsburg had committed, a general justification for their resistance and removal of the king. Citing Althusius, they grounded the legal order in divine and natural law and claimed that the Estates, who represented the people ('*universum populum*'), could freely elect their ruler.[72] The formal acceptance of a ruler ('*Annahme*') constituted a contract which bound both parties to act within the traditions and laws of the land and dissolved automatically through non-observance and abnegation. The Deduction further asserted that the king could not change the contractual conditions and basis of his '*Herrschaft*' on his own, and that the Estates shared powers of majesty with him.[73]

Instruments of security: the Austrian and Bohemian Confederations

The Confederation agreements further demonstrate the concern of the Protestant Estates to safeguard their entitlements, liberties and contracts with the monarch, and their anxiety over how to hold the monarch to contracts made with them. Arguing that it was impossible to bargain over the security of their souls, lives and property, they presented the union as a purely defensive instrument designed to guarantee their rights and protection against arbitrary government, insisting that the Confederation did not constitute a new *Landesordnung,* or constitution. As we have seen, it was a union between Bohemia, Upper and Lower Lusatia, Moravia, and Upper and Lower Silesia on the one hand, and an alliance between these territories of the Bohemian crown and Lower Austria on the other. Upper Austria concluded another separate Confederation with the Estates of the Bohemian lands, and later an alliance was added between them, Transylvania and Hungary. None of these defensive unions made changes to the existing legal order (*Landesordnung*).

In their agreement with the Bohemian lands, the Lower Austrian Protestant Estates reiterated that the purpose of Confederation was to defend not only their religious and political liberties, but also to obtain a 'better and more bearable government and administration of all the territories', and 'remedy and eliminate' their grievances (which they did not repeat). In order to preserve their political independence, each union acknowledged the authority of their respective rulers and stressed that each territory kept its own religious and political freedoms, laws and customs. They would serve their prince at all times as loyal subjects so long as nothing was intended or done against their 'religion, political privileges, Letters of Majesty, concessions, law, justice, freedom and old custom'.[74] The Confederation, the Lower Austrians declared, was both defensive and offensive ('*Defensivè und Offensivè*'), and directed against anyone who questioned the Union, or the rights and privileges of its members, or tried to sow discord, recommending war and bloodshed.[75] These claims to active resistance against a ruler who acted against their established rights were followed by promises of mutual support to defend and preserve them.

Like the Declaration and Manifesto, none of the Confederation agreements made specific reference to the opinions of theologians and reformers on resistance, probably because of the ongoing controversies about the subject and the concern of many Lutherans about whether or not the Estates were acting within the confines of Martin Luther's opinions on resistance. In 1608 the Inner Austrian Protestant Estates had declined to join the Union after consulting theologians in Wittenberg, who advised them against active opposition.[76] Yet in his '*Zirkulardisputation*' of 1539, Luther had modified his previous position, which allowed for passive resistance only, and opened a way for active defence by asserting that it was legitimate if the Papacy, or someone influenced by the pope (for instance, the emperor), began a war against the Protestant religion.[77] As we saw earlier, the Austrian and Bohemian Protestants had therefore stressed in their public justifications that Ferdinand, under the influence of the Papacy and Catholic Spain, aimed to destroy Protestantism in the Habsburg lands by military force. Melanchthon and some German princes further developed resistance theories that were based largely upon natural law arguments. And a substantial part of the Lutheran nobility of Lower and Upper Austria based their opposition on these older Gnesio-Lutheran theories allowing for active defence. Certainly, many of the arguments the Protestant Estates developed prior to Confederation were similar to these earlier Lutheran ideas, giving the right to active resistance to the inferior magistrates, and justifying open defiance against rulers who declared war on Protestantism, but also if they behaved in a tyrannical manner in the secular sphere.

While a group of Lower Austrian nobles obviously felt that passive resistance was the more appropriate response and stood on the sidelines of the conflict, a large proportion became actively involved in the uprising. It is therefore difficult to support the assertion of some historians that the Lower Austrian Protestants preferred to follow the Lutheran call for passive resistance.[78] It is also not tenable that the Lower Austrian Confederation Articles were less radical than those of the Upper Austrians. Although the former did not reiterate specific justifications for active opposition, the resistance clauses of the two duchies were in fact very similar.[79] Both were also relatively brief documents, because many of the stipulations on defence matters were covered in the Bohemian Articles.

Like the Austrian agreements, the Bohemian Confederation freed all the members of the Union from their duties towards the ruler if he acted against their religious freedoms, or the Confederation and its provisions. Several articles dealing with the Bohemian territories established the right to resist any order of the monarch and Bohemian Chancellery directed against their liberties, customs and the *Landesordnung* of any of the incorporated and confederated territories.[80] Nine further articles specified the violations against the Confederation that would justify the use of a '*General Defension*', which next to attacking the confirmed rights and religious privileges of Protestants, included the refusal to fill the highest offices solely with Protestants. Moreover, a general defence could be called if Catholic officials did not accept the Protestants' religious freedom, treated them as heretics, or in the case of anyone preventing the free meeting of the Protestant Estates or the defensors, and if one of the united territories attacked or left the Confederation. In short, the Bohemian Protestants claimed the right of resistance not only if the Articles of Confederation were not observed, but also if the established rights of each individual territory were endangered. In other words, if the Estates of the Austrian territories thought their liberties were violated by their ruler, the king of Bohemia would become their protector and the Confederates would have to come to their aid.

As defined in the Articles of Confederation, the Bohemian king was a contractual partner only in the sense that he was designated by the Estates of all territories to be the protector of the union.[81] Since each region retained its own laws and institutional arrangements, it is easily overlooked that the Confederation could not, and did not, define the legal authority of the Bohemian king, and touched upon his other powers only in relation to the defensive alliance between the various territories. It is therefore untenable to maintain that the Confederation 'denied the ruler all sovereignty', and left the king with so few rights that it was difficult to speak of a monarchy.[82]

Certainly, the Articles relating to the territories of the Bohemian crown curtailed some of the existing powers of the king, particularly in terms of installing officials. Being able to select only one from the Protestant candidates whom the Bohemian Estates would nominate for all top positions in their territories, restricted severely the monarch's control over court patronage, and indicates that the non-Catholic elite considered this to be an important endowment. Furthermore, the king needed the consent of the Estates to borrow money or to raise taxes, and to all propositions he made at the political assemblies.[83] Further limitations were imposed on the monarch in military affairs of the Confederation: he could not build fortifications, begin a war, or hire or bring foreign troops into another region without the permission of the confederated territories. The Upper Austrian Articles also stipulated that their ruler could not negotiate peace with foreign powers concerning their *Land* without their consent. The raising of troops was left to each individual territory, but the election of a general commander of a common army was in the hands of all the Confederates, presumably an Estate General which would have included the Austrian lands.[84]

Although in Bohemia twenty-four general defensors were to call assemblies of all the regional Estates in case a new king had to be elected and for the common meetings of the regional defensors, the Confederation Articles did not limit the king's right to call any other Estate General of the Bohemian lands or the regular territorial Diets.[85] Certainly, the general defensors, who were elected by and accountable to the Estates alone, assumed considerable powers and resembled Althusius's inferior magistrates, the *ephors*. They shared administrative powers with the king, and in case of a vacancy could even borrow money and govern the country.[86] In addition, they alone made preparations for the Confederates' military resistance against the ruler.

The regional defensors of the Bohemian lands thus received wide authority to investigate violations of the Confederation, and to make suggestions to the king or his governor on how to correct them, eventually submitting the grievances (*gravamina*) to the Estates for a decision on whether to call for defensive action. In other words, for grievances that concerned violations of the Confederation and fundamental laws, the general defensors had final authority.[87] However, this did not mean that the Bohemian king had no other independent judicial powers, or that the defensors acted as a court of appeal in legal cases. Like Althusius's supreme magistrate, the Bohemian monarch retained many co-ordinating powers and could promulgate legislative and administrative decrees, although these did require the Estates' consent. He also held other rights of majesty, such as issuing patents of nobility, minting money, identifying causes of war, and calling the Estates. In 1619, the Bohemian Estates also transferred to him authority over the armed forces, so that the king could 'administer and govern' (*zu verwalten und zu regieren*) them and defend the confederated territories, albeit in consultation with the high officers installed by the Estates.[88] The king was generally bound by the Articles of the Confederation and divine, natural law, which included, above all, observing the customs and laws of the land and other contractual obligations, such as the duty to consult with the Estates on important matters. The Estates also reformed the major political office and limited the power of the Bohemian Chancellery so that the monarch (or the Bohemians) could no longer use it as a central organ to control the incorporated territories.[89] In short, the ruler shared rights of majesty and the government of the kingdom with the Estates.

We can conclude, then, that while the Bohemian and Austrian Acts of Confederation differed, the Protestant leadership made similar political claims and justified the union as an instrument for protecting their life, religion, material endowments and customary rights against both Habsburgs and Catholics. The Protestant leadership asserted that they had conferred upon the ruler his rights of majesty, which ultimately was the property of the *Land*. Thus securing the Estates' claim to co-sovereignty, the Confederation would have restored, supplemented and protected the powers they had held before the Habsburgs' began their centralization efforts, and deprived the ruler of the power to continue Catholicizing their territories.

Although looking backward for many of the changes it envisioned, the Union of 1619 could have provided, under the leadership of the Estates, the basis for establishing a confederated state characterized by multi-level governance of plural communities, who would have had considerable rights to self-governance, yet were committed to provide mutual aid. At least the elites would have taken part in the legislative process through consent, meaning that the decision-making process was a joint one involving the ruler and the regional Estates. Such an alternative to the development of a centralized monarchical state was a distinct possibility in the lands of the Bohemian crown (Bohemia, Lusatia, Moravia and Silesia). While the Upper and Lower Austrian Estates refused to make a joint agreement even among themselves, the Bohemian alliance gave no territory a superior status, leaving each with independent powers and equal religious and political liberties. Furthermore, their Estates proceeded to provide centripetal federal structures by equalizing some inheritance and property rights, and establishing some common interests in trade and taxation.[90] Joachim Bahlcke is correct in viewing this short-lived phase as signalling a trend towards regionalism rather than a return to medieval particularism, although one should not overstress the importance of the *Confoederatio Bohemica* as a model of integration from below. The confederated Estates made no fundamental changes to their respective *Landesordnungen*, although they added some new elements by securing their right to justified military resistance and in defining the powers of the Bohemian king in relation to the Union.[91] It befitted such elites, whose preservation of social, economic and cultural capital depended so much on the patronage system, that they aimed to achieve their goals predominantly through gaining access and control of key offices.

'One God, one prince, one law':[92] the response of the Catholic court

Public representations of the Protestant opposition by the Catholic court and the political discourse of the Habsburgs is not as extensive as the sources of the Protestant *Stände*, and it was therefore imperative to consult private documents. Moreover, it is impossible to decide what following the views of the Catholic leadership attracted, in part because the divisions within the Catholic elite are difficult to determine. Some historians believe that, on the eve of the rebellion, the Catholic 'party' at the Imperial court was divided into two basic factions. One, under the leadership of Cardinal Melchior Khlesl and Matthias, leaned towards compromise with the Protestants. The other faction, led by King Ferdinand, opposing this as contrary to Habsburg authority and political interests, gained dominance after Ferdinand succeeded in removing Khlesl in July 1618. While I agree that a militant Catholic faction controlled the Habsburg court after 1618, the available records of public expressions and private correspondence of the cardinal and the two emperors do not disclose fundamental differences in their representation of the Protestant opposition, or in motives in this conflict. As I showed in the previous chapter, soon after the defenestration of May 1618, both Habsburg rulers and Khlesl rejected bargaining with the Protestant Estates on the grounds that their survival was at stake. Vilifying the non-Catholics as disloyal and evil subjects who had no cause or right to oppose the divinely established authority of the Habsburgs, they portrayed Catholics as the reasonable party in the conflict, who merely wanted peace and reconciliation, and sought to protect their faith and possessions from destruction by Protestants. They argued that impiety and heresy were the cause of all disobedience and endangered gravely Habsburg security.

By the late sixteenth century the Habsburgs and some Catholic advisers associated Protestantism with disloyalty, and attempted to create fear of a Protestant uprising among those Catholic advisers and German princes who still desired compromise. The spectre of a Protestant rebellion was also useful to justify more aggressive re-Catholization strategies, and the equation of disloyalty with Protestantism therefore became a common royalist polemic in other countries as well. In 1597, Archduke Ferdinand of Inner Austria expressed concern that the Austrian Estates wanted to establish a republic similar to that of the Swiss or the Dutch. This received support from the Venetian ambassador to the Imperial court, Zorzi Giustiniani, who reported on 25 May 1619, several months before the Confederation was concluded, that the Austrian and Bohemian Protestants were aiming at a form of government modelled on the Dutch Union and the Swiss Confederation which would reduce the Habsburg rulers to figureheads.[93] A response of the Imperial court to the Bohemian Confederation, entitled 'Bohemian Miracle and Quarrelhead, filled with Netherland Brains', argued along similar lines. Taking delight in equating the term '*confederatio*' with '*conspiratio*,'[94] Habsburg public rhetoric was designed to worry even Protestant princes and prompt them to ally, as had the ruler of Saxony, with the Habsburgs. Most important, to associate disloyalty, resistance and conspiracy with Protestantism helped to damage the medieval heritage of the Estates' claims to resistance.

After St. Bartholomew's Night, many Catholics in the Habsburg lands thought it possible that they might become victims of Protestant attacks,[95] but the Catholic councillor, Georg Eder, in considering Emperor Rudolf's fear of a Protestant uprising, felt that such worries were unwarranted. Even though there were many 'who liked to see revolt', many more were unwilling to act or were insufficiently wealthy to do so.[96] In 1590, the bishop and general reformer for Austria, Khlesl, was more willing to utilize anxiety about insubordination and disorder to push through measures in order to gain Church property for the crown and Catholics, as well as to implement actions against Protestant preachers and Protestant religious practices. Complaining to Archduke Ernst of Lower Austria that Catholics everywhere were constantly 'molested', he warned that confusion over religious matters had led people to forget about the law, and respect and obedience for political authority. In 1618, Khlesl, who had become Matthias's closest adviser, was confirmed in his opinions by the May defenestration, and asserted a month afterwards in a memorandum that ever since the heresy had begun there had been nothing but disobedience, rebellion, deceit and disrespect for all authority by non-Catholics.[97] Similarly, he wrote to the ambassador in Spain, Count Khevenhiller, that impiety and heresy were the cause of all insubordination and Habsburg misfortune. Heresy, he claimed, was a rebellion against God and the Church, and since the Protestants did not honour either, this explained why they could not be obedient to the ruler. In other words, Khlesl argued for the necessity of religious uniformity in order to guarantee loyalty to the Habsburgs. Warning Khevenhiller that the House of Austria and the Catholic religion were in danger of being destroyed by Protestantism, the Cardinal attempted to convince the Spanish king to support his Austrian relatives financially, but he also repeated the opinion that the Habsburgs rulers ought to proceed with swift action against the Protestant Estates in a letter to his client and friend, Baron Johann Eusebius Khuen.[98]

As the previous chapter has shown, Khlesl's promotion of religious unity was nothing new, and other post-Reformation rulers and political theorists, such as Justus Lipsius, considered religious uniformity to be essential for the establishment and maintenance of social and political cohesion, equating religious heterodoxy with diminishing royal sovereignty. Since the legitimacy of the early modern monarchs was held to be based on their God-given authority, it seemed logical to argue that rulers and their subjects should follow the same religion.[99] Ferdinand II, familiar with the work of Lipsius and Giovanni Botero, who considered the fear of God and religious conformity to be indispensable in establishing unitary state structures, was particularly convinced of the necessity for religious homogeneity. In his last will and testament dated 1621 the emperor instructed his son, stating that religious division led to factionalism, disobedience and the breakdown of government.[100] Ferdinand was particularly influenced by Thomas Campanelle and Gaspar Scioppius's call for one religion and a war against heretics. In his *Classicum belli sacri* of 1619, Scioppius even remonstrated against the damage caused by the leniency the House of Austria had exercised in religious matters, a warning Cardinal Khelsl had issued long before.[101]

In his correspondence with his client, the baron of Khuen, Khlesl also strongly disapproved of accommodation with non-Catholics, at least in the Habsburg lands. The Protestant Estates, Khlesl feared, knew that in the past the Habsburgs and Catholics tended towards compromise with them, an approach that had always worked in their favour.[102] In letters to Khevenhiller, he claimed that accommodation only strengthened the heretics ('Ketzer'), who could expand like a cancer ('*wie der Krebs*'), and shortly after the Bohemian defenestration he asked whether people still considered his previous warnings about rebellion to be a figment of his imagination.[103] The cardinal further advised against compromise in his memorandum of June 1618, insisting that the uprising gave the house of Austria a unique opportunity to rid itself once and for all of the Protestants. Since the prince's authority was God-given, no other action remained but to punish the non-Catholics quickly before they established a republic or worse.[104] Khlesl's memorandum, correspondence, and events subsequent to his dismissal, make it difficult to accept the traditional interpretation that the cardinal was removed by Archdukes Ferdinand and Maximilian because he wanted to compromise with the Bohemian rebels. However, as we saw earlier, many envied his influence and disliked his recommendation to come to an agreement with the German princes over the administration of Protestant bishoprics.[105]

Khlesl generally had no problems interpreting the causes behind the Bohemian rebellion. To him, the Protestant Estates were merely lusting after property and political power, wanting to replace the Habsburg government and officials with their own. Repeatedly making the point that the Protestants obscured all their political claims with religious motives, the Cardinal accused them of agitating and misinforming the German princes and, under a pretence of their conscience, accumulating crown property and subjects, with the result that when they 'rise up, protest and rebel, his Majesty ... will not have a span of space left in order to defend himself'. In fact, he thought that besides their residences, castles and monasteries, the Habsburgs already had little left of their possessions, and that the opposition was now after the ruler's head and authority. Surely, he continued with the same demonizing rhetoric that the Protestants used, this could only be an act of the Devil. And just as the Protestant leadership had contrasted the evil intentions of Catholics with a counter-image of their own legitimate aims, Khlesl portrayed the non-Catholics as devious, disloyal and evil rebels, with designs to depose their legitimate ruler, and to disturb the peace with the 'loyal', 'reasonable', 'patient', and 'tender-hearted' Catholics. They had shown nothing but mercy and grace towards the Protestants and merely sought reconciliation in order to protect God-given authority and preserve the country, peace and order.[106] Khlesl's vilification of the other side was, of course, no empty rhetoric, but aimed at defining the opposition to the Habsburgs as illegal and against the natural order; that is, divine law. As he put it in a letter dated 30 May 1618 to his friend, the baron of Khuen, secular authority was God-given, and he 'who opposes secular power, opposes God'. Wanting to impress upon the Habsburgs that their security was compromised, he urged them to take action which they could now justify easily.[107]

The Cardinal's warnings seem to have had an impact on Matthias, who was, of course, also trying to solicit financial support when he wrote in

1618 to Archduchess Margareth in Spain that he had no money to punish his 'disloyal subjects', and therefore might be forced to make an agreement with the Protestants, who were demanding that he dismiss all Catholic ecclesiastical advisers. He too expressed a fear that the dynasty could be deprived of its entire inheritance, and cried that he would 'rather be dead than be a lord in name only'.[108] The emperor suggested here that Habsburg security and the preservation of his possessions ideally required military solutions rather than any bargaining with the opposition.

Like Khlesl, the Habsburgs equated in their public discourse divine with natural law, and emphasized continually that their authority was 'legitimate and natural.'[109] Of course, this stress on the divine character of kingship merely reflected medieval political theory. But the equation of Protestantism with disloyalty, and the declaration of all political opposition as traitorous and illegitimate was more recent. In fact, the main reason why absolutist writers gave a new lease of life to medieval theory of divine right was to counter Protestant claims to active disobedience towards the prince.[110] Since royal succession in Bohemia and Hungary depended on approval by the Estates, it was doubly important to insist that Habsburg authority derived ultimately from God directly than from a contract with the people. The emperors thus took great care to portray the Protestant opposition as an illegitimate bid for power, and contrast this with their own lawful, ordained rule which respected the laws of God and nature, and in particular the fundamental and customary laws of their dominions.[111]

Matthias's and Ferdinand's public vilification of the Protestants thus had the same purpose as their Catholic advisers' rhetoric – namely, to deny the Estates the right to active resistance against a legitimate ruler. In addition to pointing to their God-given, legitimate authority, they countered Protestant claims that they were tyrants who disregarded the divine and natural order as well as fundamental and customary laws. Perhaps under the influence of royalist theorists, such as Hadrian Saravia, Eli Merlat and Jean Barivac, the two Habsburg rulers also liked to depict themselves as reasonable, fatherly protectors of the common good against the particularist interests and destructive force of the non-Catholic Estates.[112] Both emperors provided lengthy narratives and public accounts of events which contrasted their own efforts to secure the public good against the selfish interests of the Protestants, who were dishonest, disloyal and evil men, destroying the peace and the country, and merely lusting after material gains and usurping power.

So between June and December 1618, Matthias authored a series of open letters and statements linking his God-given, legitimate authority with patriarchal power, which could not be opposed, and contrasting the 'evil intentions'of the Protestant Estates with his own fatherly efforts to protect the public good, the laws of God, nature and established legal norms. Claiming that he never intended to destroy the Estates' rights, freedoms and privileges, he rejected the accusation that he had done anything to justify their military action. On the contrary, he had only treated them in a gentle and fatherly manner, and merely protected his subjects from the burdens the Estates had imposed on them.[113] In other words, he was not a tyrant, but the *pater familias* who protected the *res publica* and must be obeyed. In a letter of October 1618 to the duke of Saxony the emperor further invoked his fatherly authority and repeated his honest intentions, which were aimed at defending himself from the 'insults and injuries' to his 'Imperial and Royal rank and sovereignty'.[114] In his public pronouncements, Matthias also depicted the Protestant Estates' actions as illegal and selfish, accusing them of wrongfully taking over the government and finances, and burdening his subjects with heavy military contributions and quartering. Criticizing them for disobeying his orders to disarm, which was against Imperial law, he claimed they were threatening urban citizens who refused to join the opposition with the destruction of towns and unborn children. Emperor Matthias further represented non-Catholics as land hungry and greedy, especially in their efforts at confiscating Jesuit property as well as his crown lands, and warned them that their actions amounted to *lèse-majesté*.[115]

Ferdinand II also protested that the Protestant Estates were encroaching on his legitimate authority and powers, but, in addition, threatened them by attaching Ferdinand I's decree of 1525, which had ordered the execution of the Lower Austrian leaders of a rebellion claiming the right to rule the territory after Maximilian I's death.[116] He was particularly adamant in blaming the Bohemian Estates for their 'evil intentions', the 'shedding of so much innocent blood', the spreading of 'fear through violence', and for bringing poverty and destruction to his innocent subjects. Moreover, like Khlesl, Ferdinand II liked to deny that the Protestants had deep religious convictions and motives, and depicted them as concealing the political aims of their 'horrible rebellion under the cover of religion.' Advancing lies and taking by force urban and ecclesiastical property, the emperor cried, only further revealed to the world their greed and disloyalty. Clearly, they had no interest in conciliation, but merely wanted to 'spread the fire' into Moravia, Austria and Hungary.[117]

Ferdinand II was particularly fond of utilizing the Neostoic art of politics, projecting himself in the image of a Christian patriarch or house-father. Referring to previous 'fatherly warnings' and the fatherly disposition of the Habsburgs, the emperor emphasized, as had Matthias, that he merely protected the peace and his poor subjects, but he also threatened to restore with counterforce ('*Gegengewalt*') what the Protestants had taken from him illegally.[118] Insisting that the rebels' 'excess', and 'injuries of his Imperial and royal supremacy and dignity' *(Hoheit und Würde)*, were 'against all divine and secular law,' Ferdinand vowed to defeat the rebellion, and with the help of God and other princes, defend the rights and liberties of his dynasty to the 'last drop of blood'.[119]

Patriarchy, as a buttress to universal empire, and the house-father as head of the spiritual community and universal Church, were metaphors the Habsburg emperor was particularly fond of, both in public print and in Jesuit plays.[120] He also liked depictions of himself that reflected his claim to authority by divine right and mission as defender of the Catholic faith. Thus a woodcut of 1622 (opposite) shows Ferdinand II as Christ on the Mount of Olives receiving divine assistance in his dynastic mission as king and emperor. Moving from the top right to the bottom left, the engraving's narrative depicts the Devil leading the forces of rebellion across the Habsburg lands, while six electors are sleeping at Ferdinand's feet, who, praying with his crowns gathered around him, receives from an angel his laurels of victory and sceptres of royal and imperial authority. Praised by Lipsius as ideal Christian rulers, the Habsburgs from then on paid special attention to glorifying themselves as Imperial patriarchs who, possessing all the *virtutes regia* (such as *justitia, pietas, aequitas* and *clementia*), exercised their office for the common good of subjects, rather than ruling for their own private or secular interest, and respected established freedoms, rights and laws so that they could justify themselves before God. In short, it was their intrinsic qualities that guaranteed they would not transgress natural law. Being pious, righteous, fair, merciful and kind – in fact, a reflection of the sacred – the Habsburgs were always able to justify their actions before God, making all resistance to their actions unjustified.[121]

At the same time, Ferdinand II was as eager as Matthias to portray himself as protector of the freedoms, privileges and customary laws of Bohemia, and contrasted this with breaches the Protestant Estates supposedly committed against 800 years of tradition and the fundamental laws of the kingdom. Like previous Bohemian rulers, Ferdinand insisted, the Habsburgs had received the crown through hereditary succession and marriage contracts. For the emperor, hereditable accession was, as it was for many absolutist theorists, quite compatible with the idea that the Estates had a right to confirm a new king (although the Bohemian Estates viewed this as an election). The final point of his rhetoric was that he denied the Estates the right to accept a new ruler regardless of hereditary rights or other contractual arrangements made by their previous king. And, after their defeat, the Habsburg ruler quickly grounded the hereditary right to succession for his dynasty in the revised Bohemian *Landesordnung* of 1627.[122]

In this *Landesordnung*, Ferdinand II claimed that changes in customary law were limited only by the obligation to 'honour God, natural fairness, and concern for the community'.[123] Issued without seeking the consent of the Estates, he clearly reasserted his power as sole legislator and denied the Protestant Estates all authority to make or change customary and positive law, and most of all to establish 'a completely new form of government after their own will'.[124] When his councillor, Count Wilhelm Slavata, remarked in 1622 that all officials employed by the Estates had to swear an oath to the

king alone since otherwise it would not be evident that the monarch had the '*potestatem absolutam*', he too asserted that all their powers were derived from him.[125] Clearly, then, like his close circle of Catholic noble advisers and his Inner Austrian bishops, Ferdinand II considered his *jura majestatis* to be indivisible, and denied the Estates of the Austrian and Bohemian lands any *jus resistendi*. The punishment of the opposition leaders was an unequivocal assertion and enduring reminder of this.

Conclusion to Part I

Whatever the truth of their public rhetoric, it is reasonable to conclude that by the early seventeenth century the Habsburg rulers and their main Catholic advisers were convinced that establishing religious homogeneity in favour of Catholicism was essential for the maintenance of social and political order. In their political discourse they equated religious heterodoxy with diminished royal sovereignty, and Protestantism with sedition and disloyalty. Contrasting the opposition's illegitimate bid for power with the prince's God-given authority, the Habsburgs and their Catholic courtiers construed, in a mirror image of the Protestants' leadership, the actions of the other confession as illegal, violating the law and breaking the peace, and their motives as devious, dishonest, self-interested and evil. They too produced a counter-image of themselves as honest and reasonable, and claimed to protect the public good and the territory from the selfish, material interests of the Protestants. Portraying the Habsburgs' military activities as a legitimate defence to protect their life, soul, inheritance and security, the main purpose of this rhetoric was to discredit the opposition and deny the noble Estates the right of resistance. Bounded by the cultural repertoire, the Catholic leadership, like the Protestants', created further symbolic boundaries between the confessions and greatly sharpened religious identifications, which contributed to hardening relations between them and convince each side that compromise was not an option. In rhetorical strategy and form, then, the leadership's discourse of both confessions displayed considerable similarities. However, they disagreed fundamentally on how power should be divided, and how to secure contracts made between them.

Since the early sixteenth century, the Habsburg rulers claimed to have the sole authority to make new laws and to change or eliminate old ones, subject only to the rule of reason and moral precepts. While agreeing that their *jus majestatis* was bound by divine, natural law, they thought they had to justify transgressions against natural law before God alone. If they chose at times to seek the advice of the Estates, in their mind this did not constitute a sharing in their rights of majesty. Although the *Stände* could give consent to ordinary taxation, execute laws, and even participate in codification, the prince remained the sole law-maker, and all the power and authority the *Stände* possessed to help him implement his will derived from the monarch, and not the other way round. Resistance against Imperial and royal authority was therefore a breach of natural and positive law. In short, the Habsburgs thought that their *jus majestatis* was not divisible and could not be split up through bargaining like an ordinary, everyday commodity. It could not, therefore, be traded; it was either accepted or resisted.

However, as I showed in the previous chapters, the realities of power differed considerably from the theoretical claims of the Habsburgs, making it difficult to support the notion that Ferdinand II was in practice an absolute monarch. A gap also existed between contemporary absolutist theory and the practice of princely authority, a common characteristic of seventeenth-century European states. But the autocratic power of the Habsburgs, who had a very small administration to govern very disparate territories, and, after 1648, a tiny standing army, was particularly weak, so government continued to depend to a large extent on the co-operation of the elites. Nevertheless, they had made a start on increasing their co-ordinating power with the collaboration of the Estates, by systematizing the law, quickening police ordinances, and enhancing their tax resources and military strength. However, some of their centralizing efforts also met with opposition from their elites, especially attempts to introduce Roman law practices, and to gain central control over regional administrations and courts of appeal. Continued negotiations and compromise with the *Stände* slowed down state-building and at times were interrupted by breakdown and violence. But none of the sixteenth-century confrontations reached the magnitude and danger of the war of 1618–20, because only then did the political contest combine with confessionalization and Habsburg attempts to exert control over the endowments and cultural preferences of the Protestant elites. Disputes over the division of power thus constituted an integral part and ongoing problem in the bargaining process between elites and Habsburgs, and it was not long-standing 'constitutional' problems *per se* that caused the conflict. Rather, it was the fusion of spiritual issues and security considerations, and their interprenetration with concerns over the selective distribution of patronage, that made bargaining over constitutional matters highly inflexible and war a likely outcome after 1618.

Negotiations broke down not because religious faith led actors to make emotional, or irrational choices. Clearly, the Habsburg rulers were not religious fanatics but rather asserted a clear vision of their power and a method of protecting their patrimony. Since the legitimacy of the early modern monarchs was based largely on their God-given authority, they pursued strategies that imposed on their elites an ideology that made it easier to implement their vision. Catholicism seemed an astute choice in view of the close relationship between Protestantism and republicanism, and in particular, since the Austrian Habsburgs wanted to retain the emperorship, close relations with its Spanish relatives and a claim to their inheritance. However, their strategies failed to bring about the conversion of most Protestants and, instead, provoked opposition to the rule of the House of Austria across its territories.

Even before the Bohemians had elected another king, the Habsburgs and their closest Catholic advisers were convinced that to proceed with force was the best means by which to defeat Protestantism quickly. As we saw in the previous chapter, both Matthias and Ferdinand declared that the Protestants threatened Habsburg security and survival, and refused bilateral disarmament as a basis for negotiations in the manner suggested by the opposition. In his public discourse, Ferdinand II was particularly expressive of his intention to protect his inheritance with force, and viewed military defeat of the Protestant opposition as being even more pressing after the Bohemians had deposed him and the Austrian nobility joined the Confederation in 1619. In short, the Habsburgs considered Catholicism and their authority to be intrinsically connected, and competition for power to be a zero-sum game. Believing that their *jus majestatis* was indivisible, they were unwilling to accept the elites' demands for co-sovereignty, and viewed force as a prerequisite for their political survival. Power and security were issues over which they were not willing 'to trade', and this reluctance of the Habsburgs to 'swap' them for other things rendered bargaining highly inflexible.

By 1619, the Protestant opposition had also rejected bargaining. As we have observed, an issue which continually obstructed negotiations was that the Protestant leadership felt the Habsburgs could not provide them with sufficient guarantees that they would honour a bargain. Their public discourse shows that they too believed that they understood the other sides' motives perfectly, and feared that the Catholic court again had incentives to renege on a peaceful settlement. In particular, the Protestants' justifications for their Confederation and its articles suggest that they were especially concerned that any delay in forceful action on their part would result in Catholics growing too strong to be defeated. Therefore, the Austrian and Bohemian Protestant Estates presented their military union as essential in defence of their life, soul and property, and to secure their dominant position in offices. Only this, they argued, could give them a guarantee that the dynasty would preserve natural law, and in particular contracts and customary liberties. It must be remembered that the Habsburg rulers refused to bargain over religious issues at the political assemblies, and, most important, that there was also no external power to enforce contractual terms, thus ensuring that they would be fulfilled, since the main institutions for conciliation in the Empire had become paralysed, or were under Catholic and Habsburg control.[1]

Exculpating their action with resistance theories also led the Protestant Estates to develop their own conspiracy theories, which resembled those of the Habsburgs, and this discourse of division contributed further to making their bargaining positions rigid. While employing a similar rhetoric in viewing the conflict between court and country as a struggle between good and evil, the Protestant leadership also used it to underline their contrary conception of the legitimate political order. Defining absolutism as rule without consent and equating it with arbitrary action and tyranny, the Protestant opposition stipulated that rightful authority was bound by divine or natural law, which included upholding contracts and customary law, and protecting the life and property of subjects. But, in contrast to Habsburg political theory, its leadership claimed to have the right to hold the ruler to observing natural and positive law.

Justifying their resistance as legitimate, the Bohemian and Protestant Estates portrayed Ferdinand II, as well as some of his predecessors, as tyrants who acted on the advice of foreigners, Jesuits and the Papacy in violating natural law. Not only had the Habsburgs acted without just cause and consent, destroyed the liberties, life and property of subjects, and failed to provide them with protection (*Schutz und Schirm*), they had also derogated the judicial order and broken the rules of succession and recent agreements with them. According to the Protestant leadership, the ruler had a *plenum dominium* only on his crown lands, but otherwise was bound by an ancient contract that obliged him to share rights of majesty with the original owners of 'sovereignty' and guardians of public welfare, the Estates, who had the right to resist a monarch who broke this contract.

In stark contrast to the Habsburgs, then, the Protestant elite believed that *jus majestatis* was divisible. Naturally, both the Austrian and Bohemian Protestant leaders' notion of co-sovereignty envisioned gains of political authority for the Estates at the expense of the ruler. To secure the right to share in the decision-making process through consent in all matters of government, including war, peace, financial matters and even legislation, they also thought it essential to have access to, if not control over, political office. Furthermore, they claimed independent rights of majesty, such as mobilizing an army, calling their own assemblies, and forging alliances to protect themselves; and they also wished to restore the right to administer the country during vacancies. Although the Bohemian Articles of Confederation were more specific and radical in curtailing the rights of the king and securing control over patronage for Protestants, the grievances of the Bohemian opposition did not differ fundamentality from that of the Austrian opposition. Both put the damages to their rights and liberties at the top of their list of reasons for resistance, including the abrogation of religious freedoms, the exclusion from court offices and attacks on their property. Clearly, the Protestant leaders did not distinguish their religious from their political, social or economic aims, suggesting that these motives were linked inseparably in their minds. The preservation of the Protestant faith depended on securing the political rights of the Estates, and Protestant ideology provided support for strengthening their political authority and material endowments. And securing court patronage and dominating political offices had become crucial in shaping political, cultural and socioeconomic policies and practices.

Even though violence was ignited over the restitution of ecclesiastical property, and Protestant complaints about inequities in court patronage are persistent in the documents, previously historians largely ignored expressions of fear about material losses and, instead, stressed only the confessional or political aims of the opposition. And the few scholars who did note demands for reform and control of offices by the Confederates have frequently treated the issue as confessional in character.[2] My re-evaluation of the subjective evidence shows that it is impossible to deny the concern of the Protestant leadership with religion and political power, but that fear of losing material endowments played a crucial role in why they felt their security threatened and turned to violence after 1618, and these issues were intrinsically connected to cultural factors such as honour as well as personal and collective preferences.

Few Austrian nobles considered their faith to be variable, and most refused to bargain over conversion. There were good reasons for this intransigence. Conversion under the threat of material sanctions threw doubt on the honour of the convert, which had important implications in the forming of patron–broker–client relations with either the Protestant majority or with the Catholic minority. Since they were not secured legally, religion and honour, together with kinship and corporate loyalties, served as a significant moral bond to cement clientage relations. If a patron or client did not meet his or her obligations at least it was possible to impose moral sanctions and threaten the loss of reputation, or honour.[3] The Habsburgs understood the importance of such ties, and precisely because dangerous alliances against them could be cemented through Protestantism and corporate solidarity among members of the Estates they were determined to weaken these bonds.

Being second- or third-generation Protestants, many nobles had also internalized their religion. It had become a part of their '*habitus*', making it very difficult for them to convert, because religion defined their identity and preferences. As I shall show in Part II, these predispositions and preferences extended beyond personal interests to collective selves, leading nobles to defend the traditions and culture of their families, their social group and religion. Because they derived satisfaction from them, they considered the preservation of these conventions to be essential to their continued well-being. And this merging of collective allegiances with emotive properties of honour and faith added to the rigidity of their bargaining position.

Clearly, Protestant and Catholic interests were imbued with meaning derived from practices, traditions, norms of fairness and honour, and especially from religious beliefs. Fusing, like a ball of wax, the secular with the spiritual, particularly confessional identities with material interests and collective allegiances, made it difficult to reach a negotiated settlement. The main reason, then, why the parties preferred war to reaching a bargain was that the issues could not be divided perfectly, like land and money, or linked with other issues which enhanced divisibility.

It remains to be examined whether or not Protestants' fears about the loss of court patronage and material decline were sensibly based on concrete experiences, or were exaggerated phobias lacking a real foundation.

Part II

Court Patronage and Noble Strategies

4

Social Capital, Symbolic Power and Religious Conflict

Distributing noble titles and other honours was an essential element of exercising the prince's power as the most important patron. In most areas of Western and Central Europe it involved rulers in continual negotiations with their elites over the classifications that underpinned the social order, and this was an integral part of early modern state-building. In an effort to strengthen monarchs' co-ordinating power over their elites, many succeeded in obtaining sole control over defining social distinctions, thereby making access to social capital depend on their will. As this chapter will show, in the core Habsburg lands, this ability was contested and, in peculiar ways, eventually shared with the noble Estates. The religious conflict complicated this process considerably, because by confessionalizing access to upward mobility, the Habsburgs necessarily had an impact on strategies of reproduction among the Protestant nobility. And this development helps to illuminate further the close interconnection between material and spiritual issues in early modern Europe. Examining the bargaining over social classification and the real changes of the social structure of the provincial nobility highlights the role social factors played in the relations between the Habsburgs and their elites in the half century before the uprising of 1620.

Drawing on Pierre Bourdieu's definition of 'capital', this chapter first examines the significance of social status in aristocratic society, how it connected to elite strategies of social and dynastic reproduction,[1] and the conditions under which social mobility could lead to serious divisions within the elite, and between nobles and rulers. On the basis of data for the noble Estates of Lower Austria I argue that the possibility for open conflict was present when status mobility brought marked changes in the composition of noble society, which led to the rapid displacement of a significant proportion of its members. During the half century before 1620, the Habsburg rulers used court patronage to promote the rise of a new Catholic upper nobility. This resulted in the displacement of Protestant nobles, which undermined their strategies of social and dynastic reproduction, leading them to fear that their existence as a social elite was at stake. It was this fear that underpinned their revolt in 1620.

Social capital, symbolic power and social conflict

Upward social mobility and status were central parts of social capital, understood as a durable network of relationships maintained by material and symbolic exchanges. Noble title is the purest form of social capital, because it legally guaranteed the endurance of a particular system of social relations. Noble status not only authorized dominance over the peasantry but usually also assured access to the court, so facilitating political influence and social connections which could be used to acquire and enhance economic capital. Nobility was also the prerequisite for attending the assemblies of the noble Estates, which secured some influence in the affairs of the territory, especially over taxation, and was also crucial for determining the Estates' distribution of pensions and gifts. Thus, while social capital was not reducible to economic resources, it was never entirely independent of them. Consequently, some economic capital was usually essential to obtain a noble title in the first place, which could then serve to produce or reproduce other forms of profit, monetary or otherwise. For example, having once become a member of the group, a noble gained access to collectively-owned capital, such as prestige, tax exemption and other privileges, and to networks of social connections, which could underpin the further accumulation of material endowments.

Symbolic capital was an important form in which the various types of capital were legitimized, which explains why social capital was often not recognized as productive capital, but instead thought of as legitimate competence, indicated by prestige. Thus, a noble of high rank, richly endowed with patronage networks, was known to more people than he knew and was sought after precisely because of his prestige, which was, of course, the implicit acknowledgement of his ability to make his work of sociability highly productive. It must be stressed, however, that the strategies in the acquisition of social and symbolic capital varied greatly from individual to individual, depending on his or her socialization, and did not necessarily reflect a conscious 'maximizing strategy'. From the narrow standpoint of economic theory, they may seem to involve great waste, but in the long run, in 'real' societies (as opposed to the constructions of economists) sociability could be a solid investment. I therefore regard conflicts over distinctions as informal bargaining for access to a resource which could, in turn, secure other resources, and generate differential benefits, monetary or otherwise.

The social world of the nobility thus tended to function as a symbolic system organized by a logic of differences. Forming the basis of social identity, the hierarchy of noble titles served to define a sense of distance from others, while at the same time providing a common framework within which the members of nobility could understand their own and others' actions. In other words, distinctions formed the basis of the sense nobles had of their place in the world. Even though they generally tended to internalize their perceptions of their position, and social relations could become relatively stable or even rigid, the principles that legitimized the partitions of the social world were not fully secure and could always be called into question. For example, as this chapter shows, rapid social mobility opened the nobility to adulteration and thereby required a redefinition of status divisions. As a result, social classifications became the stakes in political conflicts. Bargaining between Habsburgs and their elites over the power to conserve or change the social world, by preserving or transforming the categories through which it was perceived, was part of an ongoing process which, once combined with confessionalization, contributed to the deterioration of relations between them, and between Protestant and Catholic elites.

One factor ensuring that bargaining over social advancement and classification was an ongoing process was that the nobility had to replace extinct members with newcomers, which exposed it to adulteration that could threaten its social identity and self-definition. However, social mobility did not lead automatically to overt conflict within the elite, or between nobles and rulers. Relative harmony was most likely when the demand for entry into, or ascent within, the nobility matched vacancies, commonly created by biological extinction or emigration, and when upward social mobility did not overtly threaten opportunities to the benefits accruing from social status. In contrast to this 'structure preserving change', social mobility could lead to conflict when it transformed the structure of the nobility, even if the basic aristocratic nature of society was not threatened. The possibility that such a 'type-preserving change of the social structure' would lead to problems in resolving conflicts arose because the turnover of members altered the distribution of resources between well-defined groups within the nobility, and restricted access to the various forms of capital for at least one segment of nobles.[2] In short, it would lead to what Jack Goldstone defines as 'turnover and displacement' of the various fractions of the noble class.[3] And those who suffered displacement, but could still draw on some resources, might turn to offensive strategies to preserve their threatened way of life. Consequently, the nobility, essentially a backward-looking class, could find itself in a situation where it had to become politically 'radical' in order to remain socially traditional, and willing to envision fundamental political changes as being necessary for the preservation of its traditional position and way of life. The Austro-Bohemian Confederation of 1619 should be viewed in this light rather than as a purely progressive development.[4]

During the half century before the uprising in 1620, rapid social mobility did lead to 'type-preserving changes' in the social structure of the Lower Austrian nobility. Intervening with their own agenda, the Habsburgs exerted a decisive influence over this process, even though their actions were constrained by demographic change and economic difficulties, as well as by the power of the noble Estates. Since they did so overtly, and to the detriment of very specific sections of the nobility, their policy was a contributing factor in prompting opposition and rebellion.

Holding a formal monopoly power over the granting of noble status, the Habsburgs, like most other state-building monarchs, created opportunities for status mobility. While social advancement was always the most common means for rulers to reward loyalty and service, the possibilities for upward mobility widened in the early modern period, primarily because of fiscal problems, warfare, and, in particular, the growth of central administrations.[5] Although the size of the Habsburg Court and its administration grew only moderately, it is evident that the increased need for officials trained in Roman law did facilitate the advance of new men into the nobility. Otto Brunner has shown that a change in career mobility occurred in the Austrian lands around 1500. During the later Middle Ages, when the core of the patriciate was composed of wealthy merchants and financiers, burghers moved into the nobility by connecting their wealth with royal offices (*Ämter)*, usually in independent financial functions, such as the collection of tolls and excise taxes, which were frequently farmed out to them. After 1500, by contrast, burghers moved increasingly into the nobility by means of careers in central administration.[6] This change is clearly evident from the composition of newcomers to the Lower Austrian *Ritterstand* (Estate of Knights) between 1570 and 1620. Over two-thirds of the new knights were princely servitors, and only about a quarter (eighteen) of them had made careers as *Amtsleute*. Moreover, the majority of these *Amtsleute* were, or had been, overseers of royal domains, and only a few held independent financial positions.[7] About another quarter of the new knights in royal service held positions in the central administration,[8] and about a third were incumbents of offices in the Imperial or archducal household.[9]

Most of the positions held by the newcomers to the *Ritterstand*, whether in the central administration, the household, or as *Amtsleute*, required judicial training. From the mid-1590s there was a marked increase in the number of newly admitted knights who completed their judicial training with a doctoral degree, and who were able to rise at a faster pace than before into high governmental offices. Rapid career advancement such as that experienced by Baptist Linsmayr, for example, was unusual during the previous period. Linsmayr studied at Padua and in 1567 received a doctorate in jurisprudence. Holding the title of Imperial councillor, he became procurator of the Lower Austrian Court Treasury (*Hofkammerprokurator*) in

1579. During the same year he was ennobled, and a year later admitted to the new *Ritterstand*. Linsmayr's appointment as councillor of the court treasury in 1608 brought him the title of baron, with the predicate 'von Greiffenberg'.[10] Equally dramatic was the career of Johann Paul Krauss von Krausenegg, who held a doctoral degree in jurisprudence, and moved from the position of councillor of the Lower Austrian *Regiment* (1595) to councillor of the court treasury (1603). He was installed as Aulic councillor in 1607 before he becoming president of the court treasury in 1611. Johann Paul was probably ennobled around the begining of the seventeenth century, admitted to the new *Ritterstand* in 1607, and, after receiving the baronage in 1613, was raised to the Estate of Lords (*Herrenstand*) in 1616.[11]

Although early modern rulers created opportunities for entry into the elite, certain independent factors, such as favourable economic conditions, were essential to provide them with a pool of men able and eager to enter the nobility. Most important was the existence of an urban patriciate who could afford to buy noble titles, or could obtain the educational qualifications necessary to rise in administrative office and finance a lifestyle and property appropriate for nobility. This was particularly important in the Austrian territories, as land was a necessary prerequisite for entrance into the Estates and for ascent to higher ranks. In comparison to England,[12] however, the economic conditions in Lower Austria were unfavourable for the advancement of men from the merchant class, and only a few of the knights admitted between 1580 and 1620 had in fact risen from this group. The main reason for the limited mobility of merchants was the decline of the political autonomy of urban centres in the hereditary lands, and, with some exceptions, the deterioration of their financial strength during the sixteenth century.[13]

Nevertheless, general conditions favourable to upward social mobility did exist in sixteenth-century Lower Austria. Two-fifths of the families belonging to the Estate of Knights in 1620 had been admitted during the previous four decades, and a large proportion – about a third – of these newcomers had been ennobled for only one or two generations (see Figures 4.1 and 4.2; and Tables 4.1 and 4.2).[14] The great majority of these new knights were descendants of burghers who had pursued careers as municipal office-holders. Some were sons of prominent town councillors, such as Michael Pittersdorfer, whose father had served for more than thirty years on the town council of Stein and Krems. Leopold and Jakob Hutstocker's father, Christoph, had been a municipal judge and mayor of Vienna, and the service of his ancestors in municipal office can be traced to at least the fifteenth century. In a few cases, engagement in a lucrative trade enabled families to buy property and to send their sons to university to study law, so as to facilitate their entry into municipal and governmental offices. The Händls, for example, having possessed a foundry for almost a century, then bought property, moved into municipal and governmental offices, and acquired a noble title in 1571.[15]

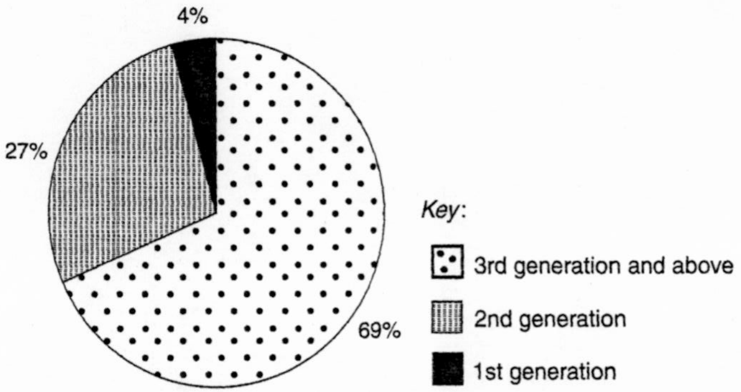

Figure 4.1 Age of nobility of knightly families, 1620

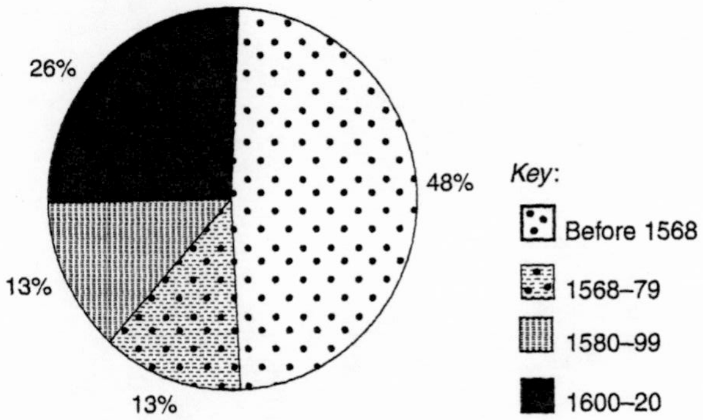

Figure 4.2 Social mobility of families into the Estate of Knights, 1620

Table 4.1 Age of nobility of knightly families, 1620

Noble status in	*Families*
3rd generation and above	62
2nd generation	25
1st generation	4
Total	91
Age of nobility unknown for	37

Table 4.2 Social mobility of families into the Estate of Knights, 1620

Admitted	*Families*
Before 1568	62
1568–79	16
1580–99	17
1600–20	33
Total	128

In the absence of an adequate pool of men with the wherewithal necessary for upward mobility, rulers could provide favourites with grants of land and other capital. During the sixteenth and seventeenth centuries, however, the Habsburgs were restricted considerably in the distribution of such resources, since inflation and war had plunged them into substantial indebtedness. Nevertheless, they did offer positions to 'foreigners'[16] at the Imperial and archducal courts, and this encouraged many nobles and burghers from other territories to move to Lower Austria. Thus, between 1580 and 1620 only about a third of the newcomers to the *Ritterstand* had been long-term residents of Lower Austria.[17] As I shall show below, this immigration was also stimulated by religious conflict, and the desire of the Habsburgs to distribute positions at court among the elite from some of their other territories.

While most of the newcomers to the Estate of Knights held financial and judicial positions, the background most common for ascent into the Estate of Lords was serving in important positions in the military or in the royal household. The largest portion (a quarter) of the newcomers to the *Herrenstand* were high officials in the military administration, or commanders of regiments. Alban Grässwein, for example, whose ancestors had served the Habsburgs for almost a century in judicial, court and military functions, distinguished himself in several military campaigns in Hungary and the Netherlands. A colonel and war councillor of Rudolf II and Matthias, he was raised to baron in 1607. In 1612, he was admitted to the Estate of Lords, and during that time he also obtained an important royal fief, Orth an der Donau.[18] The preference of the old nobility for active military service, or for positions in the military administration, is evident throughout the period. Such positions were a reminder of the nobility's feudal military functions, and consequently of special importance in distinguishing nobles from burghers, as well as signifying distinctions within the nobility itself. Rapid social mobility made it increasingly imperative to stress such distinctions. For example, about two-fifths of the families belonging to the Estate of Lords in 1620 had been elevated to baronial status since 1580 (see Figures 4.3 and 4.4; and Tables 4.3 and 4.4).[19] The second largest portion (a fifth) of the princely servitors admitted to the *Herrenstand* were officials and dignitaries in the royal household. While many of these positions were conferred on an honorary basis, they placed their incumbents in close contact with the ruler, and made them highly visible at court.[20] Salaries were clearly less important to many new upper nobles than the social and symbolic capital they could derive from court positions.

Whether rulers wanted to expand their administration, to restructure their nobility, or simply to raise cash through ennoblements, they were, in principle, not compelled to concern themselves with the question of whether there were sufficient vacancies within the nobility to absorb new

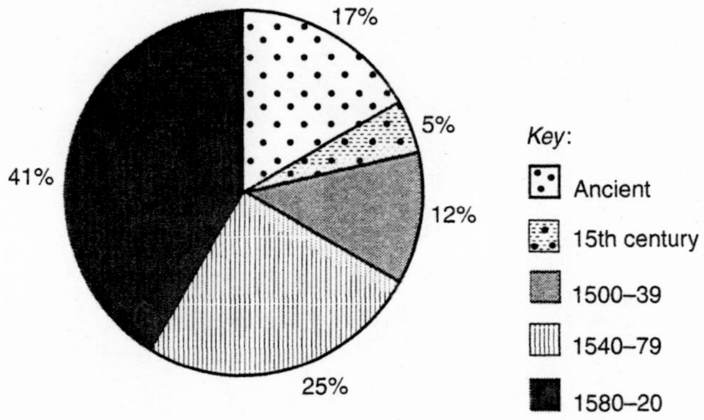

Figure 4.3 Social composition of the Estate of Lords by age of baronage, 1620

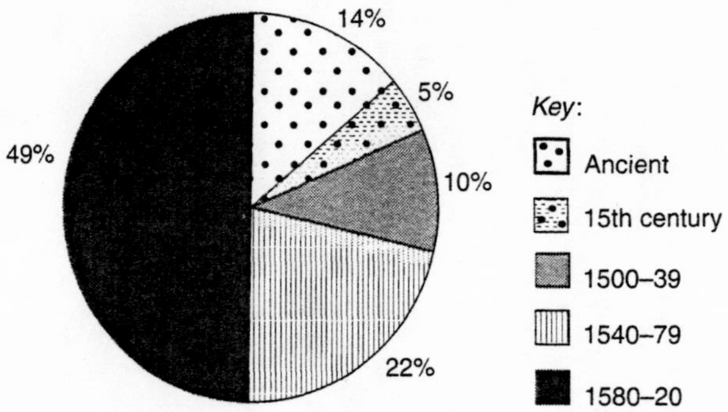

Figure 4.4 Social composition of the Estate of Lords by date of admission, 1620

Table 4.3 Social composition of the Estate of Lords by age of baronage, 1620

Age of baronage	*Families*
Ancient	14
15th century	4
1500–39	10
1540–79	21
1580–1620	35
Total	84
Status unknown	3

Table 4.4 Social composition of the Estate of Lords by date of admission, 1620

Admitted	*Families*
Ancient	12
15th century	4
1500–39	9
1540–79	19
1580–20	43
Total	87
Status unknown	0

members. However, a consequent growth in the size of nobility could lead easily to serious divisions within the elite, if not to opposition to the monarch's social policies. Therefore, other things being equal, rulers who could not also guarantee sufficient resources to avoid the crowding-out of members were wise to keep upward social mobility more or less in line with genuine vacancies.

Vacancies within the nobility were most commonly created by extinction of families in the male line. Emigration and downward social mobility also opened places, although the influence of both of these factors on social mobility is usually difficult to determine from the records. It is clear, nevertheless, that during most periods of its history, the nobility had to replenish itself with newcomers in order to continue its existence. Biological extinction depended to a considerable extent on the socio-economic fortunes of each family. And, as fortunes changed over time, so did the identity of the noble families. Thus, only ten of the noble lines belonging to the upper nobility of Lower Austria during the middle of the fifteenth century survived until the late eighteenth century, and the losses among the lower nobility were certainly higher.[21] A list drawn up in 1574 by the noble Estates records 118 knightly families that had died out during the preceding fifty years, and my own calculations reveal that during the following half century about another half (92) disappeared. A number of these families probably emigrated or experienced downward mobility, but the proportion of these is unclear, since such cases were treated in most records as if they had become extinct.[22]

The failure to reproduce because of high infant mortality, violent death or land shortages was also common to other European noble families. In Brandenburg, only a third (83 of 259) of the families that existed in 1540 were still around in 1800, and in Saxony about half of them disappeared during the century prior to 1550.[23] Tracing six generations of Bohemian lords, Jaroslav Honc calculated that, from the early sixteenth century, about a third of the lines became extinct in each generation.[24] In the county of Forez in south-central France, only five of the noble lines of the twelfth century survived as far as the French Revolution, and in England only sixteen of 136 peerage families living in 1300 survived to 1500.[25] Yet it is also apparent that the nobility could counteract extinction to some extent by increasing the size of the surviving families.[26] The other response was to admit new members. However, the relationship between the disappearance of noble families and the level of social mobility was not always a direct one. The nobility of early modern Bayeux, for example, experienced the lowest upward mobility during the period of high population losses, while it endured the largest influx of newcomers during the time of population expansion in the late sixteenth century. Clearly, then, social mobility was not only determined by demographic processes, but, as I shall elaborate below, also by the political and fiscal needs of rulers.

Type-preserving changes of the social structure

Over the long run, the Lower Austrian nobility proved itself able to regulate and maintain the size of its membership. Thus, between 1415 and 1720–27 the number of noble families increased by only about a quarter (from 210 to 265). Extinct families were clearly replenished by newcomers, while a growth in the number of individual male members was usually followed by a decline in the number of lines (and vice versa). This was particulary true during the period from 1580 to 1620, when the general population expanded in the Austrian territories by at least a fifth. This led to the growth in the average size of noble families, prompting a 17 per cent increase in male members. However, a 15 per cent decline in the number of lines prevented an expansion of the noble order (see Table 4.5).[27]

Once we differentiate between the lower and upper nobility, the possibility of two distinct responses to demographic pressure crystallizes. On the one hand, the lower nobility lost families and individuals mainly because of biological extinction, a loss that was made up by newcomers only as far as the availability of landed property permitted this. Altogether, the number of knightly families declined by a third (from 197 to 128) between 1580 and 1620. Despite the high rate of extinction – almost a half of the families disappeared during these forty years – the *Ritterstand* could not restore its membership to the previous level because the population increase during the sixteenth century put too much pressure on the available land.[28] While landed property, a prerequisite for admission to the Estates since 1572, was available for sale to newcomers because of the extinction of old families, it was not available on a scale sufficient to replace all those who died out, since the number of male children of the remaining families had risen. On the other hand, the extinction rate of the upper nobility was insignificant. Because the rate of social mobility was greater than the vacancies created by the disappearance of families, the Estate of Lords expanded by more than a half, from fifty-six to eighty-seven, families. Its individual male members more than doubled, from 119 males over the age of twenty in 1580 to 243 in 1620 (see Table 4.5).[29] Evidently, the growth in the average size of the

Table 4.5 Size of the noble Estates, 1415–1720/27

	Lords' Estate		*Knights' Estate*		*Combined*	
Year	*Families*	*Individual members*	*Families*	*Individual members*	*Families*	*Individual members*
1415	43	67	167	222	210	289
1580	56	119	197	281	253	400
1620	87	243	128	224	215	467
1720	160	280				
1727			105	111	265	391

noble family, which had caused the decline in the total number of knightly families because of added pressure on the available land, did not prevent the increase of families in the Estate of Lords. Since about half of the new families admitted to the lords had risen from the ranks of landed knights, the availability of property was of less significance for the renewal of its membership. However, the growth of the *Herrenstand* created further difficulties for newcomers to the *Ritterstand* to purchase land from this source. It appears, then, that the lower nobility declined precisely because social advancement into the upper nobility exceeded vacancies. In other words, while the knights show a strong relationship between extinction and social mobility, the ascent of families to the Estate of Lords was unrelated to demographic change.

Although the changes in the sizes of Bohemian and Moravian lords and knights, and in their proportions, are uncertain,[30] judging by the change in property owners between 1557 and 1615 it seem obvious that the knights experienced losses – perhaps as many as a third – from which the lords benefited in Moravia, while in Bohemia it was the towns and the crown that made the property gains.[31] Certainly, the social structure and rate of social mobility in the Bohemian lands need further investigation in order to determine their influence on the relations between the Habsburgs and the Estates.

In Lower Austria it is evident that significant type-preserving changes of the nobility's internal social structure occurred during the late sixteenth and early seventeenth centuries. The most apparent of these changes was the numerical decline of the lesser nobility and the growth of the upper nobility (see Figure 4.5). In 1580, three and a half times as many families,

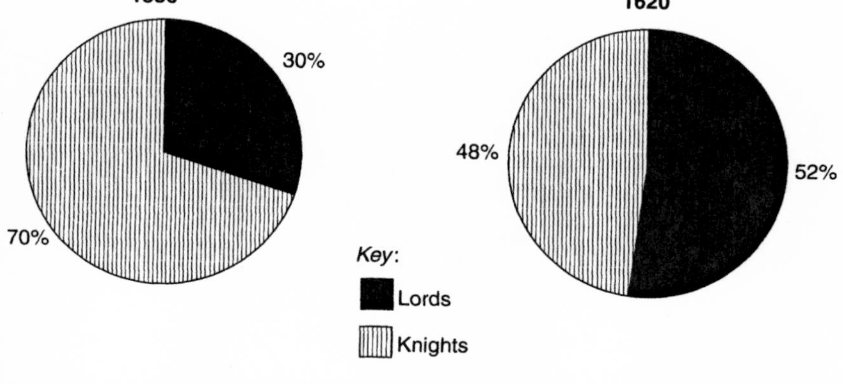

Figure 4.5 Distribution of individual members in the Lords' and Knights' Estate (combined)

and more than twice as many individuals, belonged to the Estate of Knights than to the Estate of Lords. By 1620, the knights only comprised a third (fourty-one) more lines than the lords, while the latter already counted nineteen more individuals. Nevertheless, the *Ritterstand* experienced a significant turnover in membership. About two-thirds of the ninety-two families who had disappeared were replaced by newcomers, so that approximately two-fifths of the families living in 1620 had been admitted during the previous four decades. Social ascent into the Estate of Lords was even higher: about half of the families living in 1620 had been admitted after 1580. However, since only a few (seven) of the old lords had become extinct, three quarters (forty-two) of the families living in 1580 still belonged to the Estate in 1620. It remains to be seen how these changes affected the religious and regional composition of the nobility.

Developments in Lower Austria parallel a similar growth of the high nobility and numerical decline of lesser nobles in European monarchies generally, where other rulers saw political and economic advantages in utilizing their power of social patronage to advance clients to high ranks. However, the growth–decline ratio was by no means uniform, nor have historians always appreciated the causal complexities behind changes in the size and structure of nobilities, or distinguished between the number of families and individual male members.[32] In particular, as we have seen, a simple comparison of the size of the nobility over time cannot reveal whether social mobility was characterized by absorption, or whether it led to displacement of members. In the case of Lower Austria, it appeared at first sight as though absorption was the prevalent pattern. Only a differentiation between upper and lower nobles made it evident that ascent into the Estate of Lords caused an expansion in the size of its families by a half between 1580 and 1620. This, together with the growth in the average size of the noble family, put pressure on the available land, prompting a numerical decline of a third in the lines belonging to the Estate of Knights. It must be stressed, however, that these type-preserving changes of the nobility's internal social structure did not in themselves provoke opposition to the Habsburgs, precisely because they could occur without social or economic displacement. However, once we further distinguish the effect social mobility had on Protestants and on Catholic nobles, it becomes clear that the Habsburgs' policy of withdrawing its patronage, in terms of status promotion, from the Protestant nobility opened them to the risk of social displacement, and this added a very dangerous ingredient to the process.

Confessionalizing the struggle over social classification

As the previous chapters have shown, during the 1570s the Habsburgs, under financial strain caused by a new war with the Ottomans (1566–8), granted the noble Estates and their subjects the right to exercise freely the Lutheran religion on their landed property and in their castles, in exchange for loan repayment.[33] At the same time, the noble Estates succeeded in limiting Habsburg control over social capital. This meant that after 1572 a precarious balance of power over social classification emerged between rulers and nobles. The emperors realized that making the elite dependent on them for the distribution of social capital was a crucial prerequisite to enhancing their co-ordinating power over social relations. Maximilian II's successors therefore attempted to strengthen their influence over social classification and impose their own vision of the social hierarchy. They did so by changing the rules and channels of elite recruitment and thereby transformed the composition of the noble Estates. To a large extent, their aim was to rid themselves of the unruly Protestant nobles by promoting the rise of a new, loyal and court-centred Catholic nobility.

Favouring Catholics in status promotion became a priority after the Protestant nobility had gained religious concessions. A clear line of action towards confessionalizing social mobility was especially imperative after the Lower Austrian nobility had succeeded, in 1572, in restricting the power of the Habsburgs over social classification.[34] From then on, two broad categories of nobility existed, as a distinction was created between the nobility and noble Estates (see Figure 4.6). Previously, any noble who possessed *Dominikalland* (demesne land) was considered automatically as a member of the political Estates. But after 1572 only those nobles who were formally admitted by representatives of the noble Estates had the right to attend political assemblies, to purchase tax-exempt land, and to claim trial and judgement by their peers. Although the ruler still granted all noble titles, the noble Estates – where Protestants held a majority – now decided who was entitled to the important benefits derived from noble status. As I shall demonstrate, this development created difficulties for the Habsburgs in pursuing their strategies, and complicated bargaining between them and the Protestant nobility, as well as between Catholic and Protestant Estates.

The nature of warfare, the centralization efforts of rulers, and their financial difficulties, helped to facilitate increased social mobility in other European countries, and this allowed many nobilities to gain greater influence over the regulation of the flow of newcomers.[35] Thus the noble Estates in various German territories, and in Bohemia, began to establish more stringent rules for ascent to their order, and for mobility within it. The Bohemian nobility in fact secured the right to regulate the admission of new members in 1554, long before the Lower Austrians.[36] Just how far the elites of the other lands were able to limit Habsburg power over social classification and mobility is uncertain. What is clear, though, is that the redefining of the rules for social mobility was aimed largely at clarifying the demarcation boundary of the noble Estates and fixing the distinctions within it, rather than simply closing the Estates to newcomers.[37] Moreover,

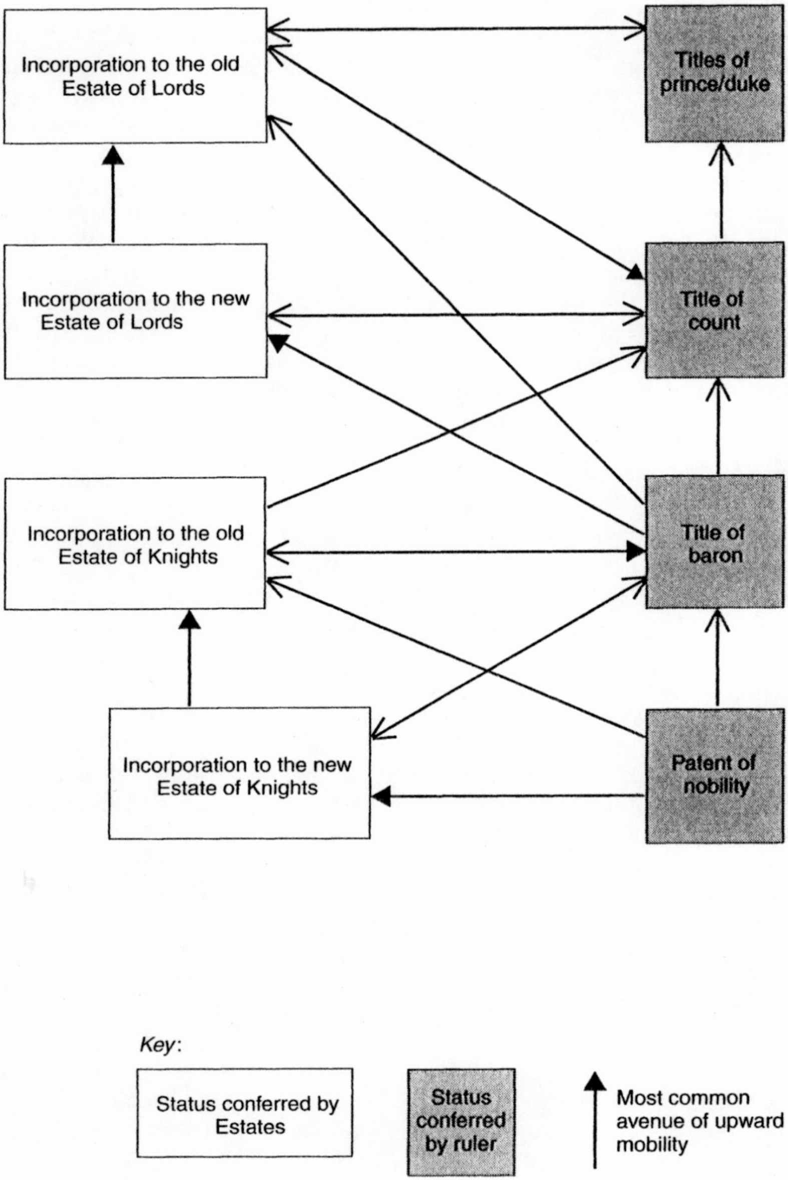

Figure 4.6 Possibilities of upward status mobility (after 1572)

the new rules did make it more difficult for commoners simply to assume noble status and gain access to collective benefits.

In Lower Austria, the new admission requirements stipulated that new members had to sign a written declaration (*Revers*), promising that they would comply with the customs and rules of the noble Estates, and accept the leadership of their older peers. Naturally, these customs stressed the distinctiveness of the noble lifestyle, such as abstention from usury and engaging in a bourgeois trade.[38] But the status requirements were clearly not designed to exclude newcomers, and provided for a relatively open social structure. While a simple diploma of nobility sufficed for admission to the Estate of Knights, applicants for incorporation to the Estate of Lords were required to hold the title of baron (*Freiherr*) or above (count or duke); in the latter case the regulations did not specify a particular age prerequisite for the title. New nobles could also rise to the Estate of Lords within three generations.

Social distinctions within each Estate also became more clearly defined, and both the *Herren-* and *Ritterstand* divided into a new and an old order in 1575. The Estate of Lords required that a family belonged to the new Estate for three generations before it was eligible to advance into the old order.[39] Although no specific lineage requirements could be found for admission to the old *Ritterstand*, it appears that a third degree of membership in the new Estate was also necessary before advancing to the old order. Matriculation into the old Estate conferred not only prestige to its occupants, but also important political powers. Thus old members could assemble in separate sessions, where they debated certain issues concerning their own order and, after 1612, decided the admission of newcomers. Moreover, they had precedence in voting at the common assemblies. Since decisions at all of the Estates' meetings were based on majority vote and the oldest members of each order would speak and vote first, the oldest members thereby had the most opportunity to influence and persuade the remaining voters.[40]

Although the status requirements did not provide the noble Estates with effective measures to close their ranks, they were at least designed to ensure that new candidates had the wherewithal to imitate a distinctive noble lifestyle. Thus new members had to pay taxes on a minimum *Gült* of 10 Pfund – a tax unit based on self-assessed seigneurial income from the peasantry – and within a year they were to purchase landed property worth at least that amount.[41] A new member also had to pay certain admission fees to the Estates' treasury. A newcomer to the *Ritterstand*, if native to Upper and Lower Austria, was obliged to pay 50 Thaler, and, if a 'foreigner', 100 Thaler. The fees required from the successful candidate to the *Herrenstand* were much steeper, as he was required to pay a total of 3026 Gulden if he had not previously belonged to the Estate of Knights. But if the candidate was advancing from the new *Ritterstand* to the Estate of Lords, his fee was reduced to 1840

Gulden, and a member of the old knights could rise at the low rate of 540 Gulden.[42] The high fees for admission to the lords were undoubtedly designed to control the flow of newcomers, since they represented three times the yearly income from a small estate, or an important court office, and about half the sum required to buy a small manor.[43] Although the Lower Austrian Estates frequently reduced fees, the requirement could be used to eliminate undesirable candidates. Moreover, the fees could be circumvented by using the *Ritterstand* as a stepping stone to advance into the *Herrenstand*. In this case, the Estate of Knights retained even greater control over social advancement. Clearly, the admission fees appear to have been designed to encourage the upward mobility of old, native knights, and to make the direct admission of new foreign nobility into the Estate of Lords more difficult. Lacking a pool of native Catholic nobles, the Habsburgs, as we shall see, frequently promoted Catholic nobility to the baronage from outside the province. Once they had obtained the required property in Lower Austria, they could not be denied direct admission to the Estate of Lords. The steep admission fees for direct entry into the *Herrenstand* were thus designed to limit the massive incursion of Catholic royal favourites. However, in one respect, the new matriculation rules also encouraged the admission of royal protégés, as they stipulated participation in a military campaign (either in the past or the future) against the Ottomans, or the provision of other services for monarch and country. This demand was contrary to the desire of the noble Estates to prevent the entry and ascent of royal officials and officers. Since the new rules were drawn up after negotiations between Estates and the court, it is evident that the service requirement demonstrates the success of the Habsburgs in retaining some means of influence over new incorporation.

Clearly, then, the powers of the Protestant nobility to control upward social mobility were limited not only because the Habsburgs remained the sole granters of noble titles, but also because they had managed to make service to monarch and country a prerequisite for admittance. It was thus difficult for the noble Estates to deny the admission of Catholic court nobles who held the required noble diploma and possessed landed property. In 1612, when fifty applicants waited for admission to the *Ritterstand*, the Estates had to acknowledge that the new rules had not limited effectively the incursion of 'undesirables'. They complained that the regulations were not applied consistently, and that the newcomers had found means of 'persuasion' for admittance without fulfilling the preconditions for membership. Indeed, numerous new knights had been ennobled for fewer than ten years at the time of admission. The knights therefore decided to raise the status requirements for new members, who now had to produce proof of nobility in the third degree (agnates and cognates).[44] Moreover, in future, the documents proving the qualifications of a new candidate had to be investigated by the *Landuntermarschall* (the highest official of the *Ritterstand*), the deputies and three other knights before a decision could be made by at least twenty members of the old Estate, and a common assembly of knights had to approve their decision. A similar admission procedure was observed by the *Herrenstand*, except that its highest official, the *Landmarschall*, passed the application and documentation of the candidates' qualifications directly to an assembly of twenty old lords. The possession of a baronial status obviously eliminated the need for a lengthy investigation of social origin. This also provided the Habsburgs with greater influence over admissions to the *Herrenstand*. In addition to the existing property requirements, the Estates decided in 1612 that landless knights had to deposit a sum of money in the treasury – the magnitude of which was based on the candidate's wealth – until property was acquired. The Estate of Lords fixed the deposit at 10 000 Gulden, at 5 per cent interest, equivalent to the amount required to buy a small estate. This change makes it apparent that the regulations requiring the purchase of property within a year had previously not been observed; the money deposit was to provide the Estates with a guarantee that taxes would be paid by landless nobles, and, more importantly, that the newcomers could afford to obtain the minimum of land required in the first place.[45]

However, admission requirements were not applied consistently, either before 1612 or thereafter. Indeed, the proportion of landless newcomers increased after 1612, and two of the three families admitted to the new Estate of Knights during the following eight years had been ennobled for just two generations. In total, almost a third of the knights admitted between 1580 and 1620 had been ennobled for fewer than twenty years.[46] As I shall show, the confessional conflict was the primary reason for these inconsistencies.

The discussions leading to the new regulations concerning social distinctions and social mobility during the late sixteenth and early seventeenth centuries reveal little about confessional hostilities. But they do show that the Protestant nobility felt threatened by adulteration. Already by the mid-sixteenth century they had begun to complain about land sales to 'foreigners', coming to Vienna to serve in the central administration, and who frequently moved into the nobility. The established, native nobility objected to the new origin and wealth of newcomers because these nobles 'desire to be equal to the old lords and nobles ... [and] are slowly buying up natives with their exorbitant wealth', a practice they believed could only lead to 'innovation and the change of old traditions'.[47] The old nobles in particular resented the new court nobles, who were royal creations and whose behaviour at the political assemblies frequently revealed loyalties to the crown rather than to noble interests. In 1572, the noble Estates asked Rudolph II to reject new nobles as office-holders unless they had reached the third degree of noble rank, but the emperor, pretending not to understand the reasons behind the demand, objected.[48]

Most of the Protestant opposition against the preference shown to Catholics in status mobility was couched carefully in secular terms, probably to conceal the symbolic and economic significance that social capital had for the survival of Protestantism. It is also possible that they did not want to disturb the atmosphere of religious toleration that officially prevailed – at least until 1608. They clearly desired to prevent a massive incursion of social 'inferiors', but the real and unstated objection to newcomers and foreigners was that the large majority of them were Catholics and royal officials. This is evident from the actual admission pattern. For example, the Protestant knights did not hesitate to admit newcomers even without a noble diploma when it suited their purpose. Thus, in 1579, a number of Protestant burghers who had been involved in a demonstrative confessional petition to the emperor, the so-called *Sturmpetition*, were admitted by the Estate of Knights without possessing a noble diploma, in order to protect them from royal punishment.[49] The admission practices reveal further irregularities, indicating that the religious conflict was of vital importance in explaining their erratic pattern. In 1608, mobility into the new *Ritterstand* came to a near standstill after more than a decade of substantial influx.[50] Moreover, the social, economic, occupational and geographic background of the knights was fundamentally different after 1609, and became more homogeneous compared to the preceding decades. Thus the new knights were of older nobility and had either served in the army or held no position at all; they possessed smaller landholdings, and frequently they were of foreign origin. Most important, nearly all of them were Protestant. Evidently, the xenophobia was directed only against Catholic foreigners. This contention is also supported by the alliance between the Bohemians and the Austrians in 1620.

A comparison of the admission frequency per confession and per decade clearly reveals the tug-of-war between Protestants and Catholics over membership (see Figure 4.7). With the strengthening of the Counter Reformation after 1580, the number of Protestant admissions to the Estate of Knights declined drastically. While the advancement of non-Catholic nobles doubled during the 1590s, the number of new Catholic newcomers more than tripled between 1600 and 1609. This advancement of Catholic knights was facilitated largely by the installing of a Catholic *Landuntermarschall* in 1595. Presiding over all the meetings of the *Ritterstand*, he could influence admissions by encouraging and manipulating the attendance of knights favourable to certain candidates. After the events of 1608–9 a Protestant was installed again as *Landuntermarschall*, which explains the drastic reduction in Catholic admissions. In fact, nearly all the knights incorporated to the new and the old Estates after 1609 were Protestants.[51]

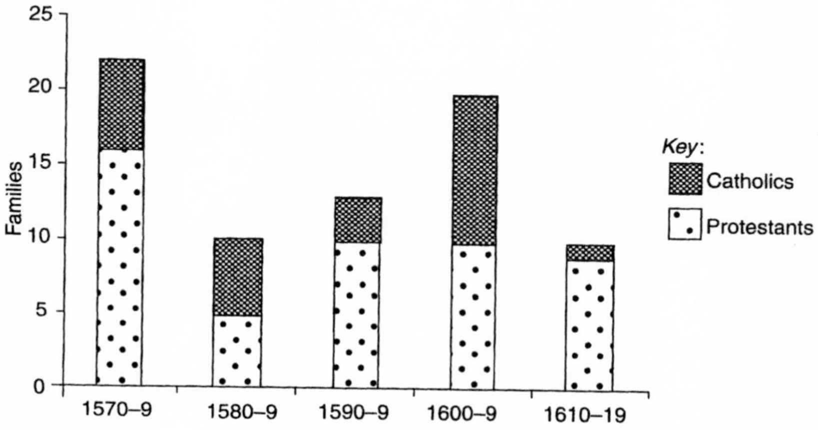

Figure 4.7 Admissions to the Estate of Knights by confession and decade, 1570–1619

Since the Habsburgs increasingly favoured Catholics with ennoblements, it is not surprising that the Protestants advanced older or foreign Protestant nobility to the *Ritterstand* in order to forestall the domination of the Estates by Catholics. Seen in this context, the complaints of the knights against new nobles, and the establishment of stricter admission rules regarding noble status in 1612, appears to have had a strong confessional ingredient rather than purely social roots. This contention can further be supported by the fact that after 1612 the admission of Protestants to the old Estate accelerated, even though the candidates frequently could not fulfil the new property requirements. Most were landless because they had recently emigrated from the hereditary lands (especially from Inner Austria) and from the Reich, and a large proportion were military officers.[52] While the incorporation of foreign landless nobles did not violate the admission rules, as long as they obtained property within one year, recently created Catholic nobles could be turned away on the grounds of the new status requirements. This explains why admissions to the new *Ritterstand* almost ceased after 1608. In short, since the Habsburgs began to exclude native Protestant burghers from status promotion, the Protestant *Ritterstand* had no choice but to admit old foreign nobility if it wanted to retain a numerical predominance over the Catholics. Even though the Protestant knights were thus able to curtail Habsburg influence over membership in the *Ritterstand*, Catholic families multiplied (from nineteen to thirty-three), increasing their proportional strength from about a tenth to a quarter, while Protestants lost almost half of their families (down from 179 to 99).[53] The diminution of the Estate of Knights was thus largely a consequence of losses among Protestants (see Figure 4.8).

The Habsburg rulers retained more influence over admissions into the Estate of Lords. Here, two-fifths of the families admitted between 1580 and 1620 belonged to the Catholic faith.[54] A comparison of mobility by decade and by confession into both noble Estates reveals similar but also contrary trends. Thus, after 1580, admissions of Protestants lords also suddenly declined (see Figure 4.9). Evidently, the accession of Archduke Ernst to governor (*Statthalter*) of Lower Austria, and subsequent efforts to strengthen the Counter Reformation, had a similar effect in both Estates. After 1590, however, the two noble Estates appear to have been involved in a confessional tug-of-war. While the number of Catholics admitted to the Estate of Knights declined during the decade after 1590, it increased in the Estate of Lords. The reason for this development in the *Herrenstand* must be sought in the succession of a Catholic (Sigmund von Lamberg) to the office of *Landmarschall* in 1592. Of some importance, too, was that Catholics already had a stronger numerical position within the Estate of Lords. This made a reaction against the promotion of Catholics more difficult. Yet, even though the office of the *Landmarschall* remained in Catholic hands throughout the period, Protestant mobility into the *Herrenstand* more than tripled between 1600 and 1609. Since about half of the new Protestant lords had advanced by means of military careers, it is clear that the Ottoman war exerted some influence on their increased admission during this period. The other, more important, factor appears to have been Matthias's attempts to muster and reward Protestant support for his

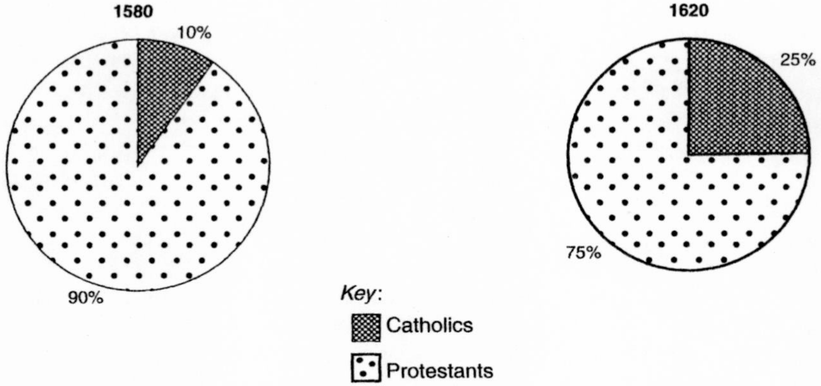

Figure 4.8 Distribution of confessions in the Estate of Knights, by family

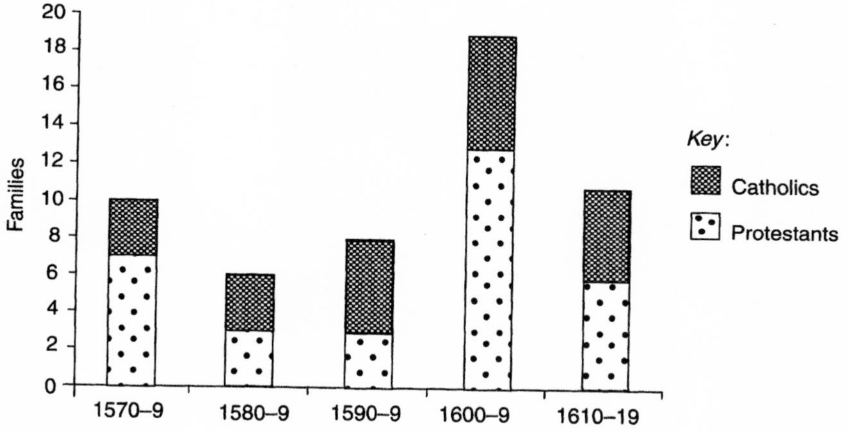

Figure 4.9 Admissions to the Estate of Lords by confession and decade, 1570–1619

schemes against his brother, Emperor Rudolf II. After this period of rapid ascent within the noble ranks, the Protestants were suddenly confronted by a complete reversal of royal policy, when Matthias, once in power, excluded them from promotion to the rank of baronage and above. As a consequence, Protestant admission to the *Herrenstand* declined by almost a half between 1609 and 1619, and after 1613 only one Protestant family (the Tattenbachs) was incorporated.[55]

Obviously, the *Landmarschall* and the Estate of Lords responded more readily to the status promotions and pressures of the Habsburgs than did the knights. In the admission of the Catholic Georg Leonhard von Stozzing, for example, it is known that Matthias pressured the *Herrenstand* to advance him.[56] Moreover, the Estate of Lords often had no choice but to admit royal protégés, since the barons, frequently of older landed nobility, were much more likely than newly-ennobled knights to fulfil all the admission requirements, which also did not specify the age of baronial status. However, since the *Ritterstand* – comprising the pool of older Lower Austrian nobility eligible for status advancement – was still largely Protestant, the Habsburgs had to promote lesser Catholic nobles from outside territories to the baronage. Consequently, three-quarters of the Catholics entered the Estate of Lords directly after being made barons. Moreover, the large majority (nine-tenths) of them were first-generation immigrants, typically from Styria. In contrast, only half of the Protestant families incorporated between 1580 and 1620 originated from territories outside Lower Austria, and about three quarters of them rose from the Estate of Knights.[57] Although the number of Protestant families slightly multiplied by about a third (from forty-four to sixty), the expansion of the Catholic camp caused the proportional strength of Protestant families in the Estate of Lords to decline, from about three-quarters to three-fifths. Overall, Catholic baronial families almost tripled (from fourteen to thirty-eight), and rose proportionally from a quarter to nearly two-fifths (see Figure 4.10).

The Catholic gains in both Estates were thus substantial, and explain the increased activism of the Catholic party during the early seventeenth century. It must be stressed, however, that this advance was mainly the result of social mobility rather than of conversions, which were surprisingly low; only about 6 to 9 per cent of the Protestant lines converted after 1580.[58] This loyalty of the Protestants to their faith remains to be assessed in a subsequent chapter. Despite the low rate of conversion, by 1620 the combined Catholic nobility had more than doubled, and by then comprised almost a third of the families and about a quarter of the individual members of the noble Estates. Because of the moderate gains in the Estate of Lords, the combined losses of Protestants are less striking. Nevertheless, the number of non-Catholic lines had declined by a third (from 223 to 159), and the proportional strength of Protestant families in the combined Estates had fallen from about nine-tenths to seven-tenths by 1620; the individual members were reduced to three quarters (see Table 4.6 and Figure 4.11). While they were still in the majority, the Protestant nobility had a legitimate fear that they would soon be outnumbered by Catholic nobles. Considering that the latter had a strong ally in the

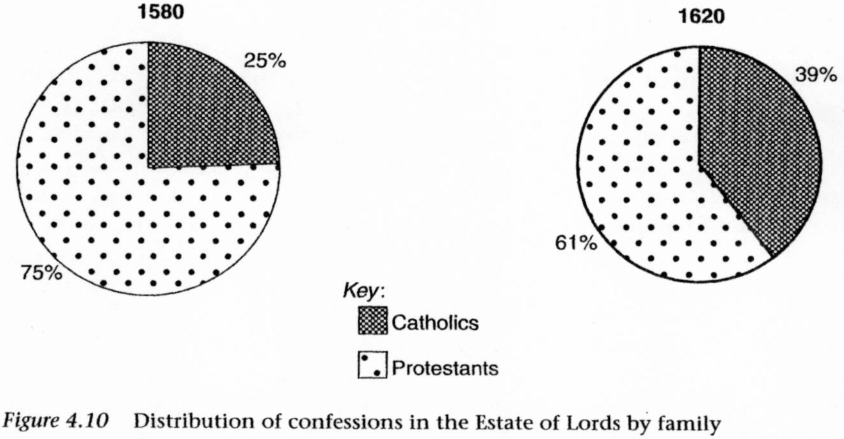

Figure 4.10 Distribution of confessions in the Estate of Lords by family

Table 4.6 Distribution of confessions among individual members of the Estate of Knights and Lords (combined)

Year	*Catholic members*					*Protestant members*				
	Knights	*Lords*		*Total*		*Knights*	*Lords*		*Total*	
			U	*No.*	*%*			*U*	*No.*	*%*
1580	28	20	1	48	12	253	99	93	352	88
1620	45	78	7	123	26	179	165	22	344	74

Note: U = confession uncertain for combined Estates.

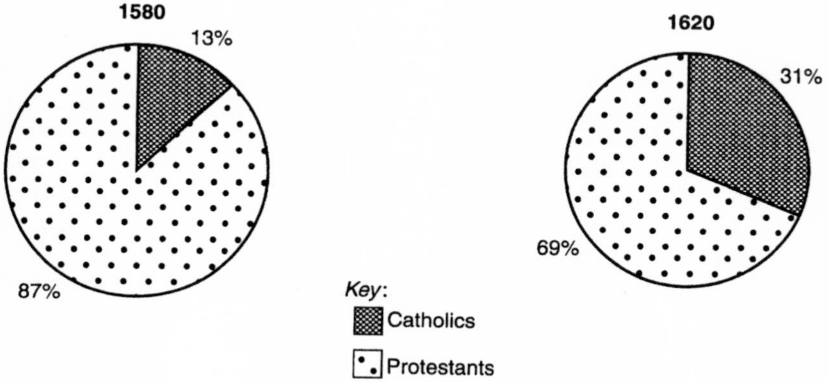

Figure 4.11 Distribution of confessions in the noble Estates (combined) by family

First Estate, the clergy, Protestant power at the political assemblies was already threatened.[59]

It should now be more understandable why noble status did not have a decisive influence on the political position that Protestant nobles took in 1620, and why old and new nobles were fairly evenly distributed among the three Protestant parties. Antagonism between the new and old nobility did not *per se* determine who joined the political opposition, because the confessionalization of social patronage by the Habsburg rulers overrode such intra-class conflicts. This does not mean, however, as some revisionists have concluded, that political opposition of early modern European elites was without social foundation. Clearly, the changes in the nobility's social structure and strategies of social reproduction were intertwined closely with economic, cultural and political problems. Because the various forms of 'capital' were mutually reinforcing, each being more or less dependent upon the other for the reproduction of noble power, a restriction on the access to one form of capital also meant a constraint on the access to profits (monetary or otherwise) derived from the other forms. Consequently, exclusion from the benefits of status mobility represented an attack not only on the religion, culture and social predominance of the Protestant nobility, but also on its continued existence as an elite. In short, social mobility was of great importance to the early modern elite, because status was a crucial resource for generating a whole range of benefits, and because social distinctions were an essential part of noble power and legitimacy.

The Habsburg rulers therefore had a strong interest in maintaining and increasing their ability to manipulate the social structure of the Estates, since this would enhance their power to co-ordinate elites and gain their co-operation in the state-building process. It is understandable, then, why redefining the rules and channels of elite recruitment could become an important factor in shaping relations between Habsburgs and Estates. The party who was able to transform or conserve existing social categories in ways that conformed to its own advantage would necessarily also alter social and power relations in its favour. Although bargaining between rulers and nobles over social classification was an ongoing process in early modern society, largely because of continual, and often rapid, social mobility, serious conflicts were most likely to occur when type-preserving changes in the social structure led to the displacement of a definite portion of the elite, and, moreover, did so very suddenly. During the half century before the rebellion of 1620, the transformation of the internal structure of the Lower Austrian nobility did lead to the rapid social displacement of the Protestant majority, and this played a crucial role in galvanizing the opposition against their monarch.

Along with European rulers generally, the Habsburgs obviously exerted considerable influence on social change and classification. It was primarily the increased need for men trained in Roman law to work in the central administration that led the Habsburgs to accelerate status mobility. The new nobles who entered the Estate of Knights had risen mainly by virtue of their judicial training and administrative functions in municipal offices to positions in the central administration, or in traditional *Ämter*. Different personalities, and conflicts within the dynastic family, also left their mark on the social structure, but the rulers' actions were limited by structural factors, notably demographic and economic changes. The population growth of the sixteenth century put pressure on the available land, thereby limiting social mobility into the lesser nobility. Because the noble population increased, and landholdings – a prerequisite for membership in the Estates – were frequently small and indivisible, the lesser nobles could not replace all the losses they suffered from biological extinction. Nevertheless, the high mortality rate facilitated the admission of a large number of new families to the Estate of Knights. Demographic change exerted less influence on mobility into the *Herrenstand*, because the lords could advance knights who already possessed landed property, and because the lords' landholdings still allowed for some divisibility. As a consequence, the upper nobility could expand in size at the expense of the lesser nobility.

None the less, the Habsburg rulers were able to turn these developments to their advantage and manipulate the transformation of the nobility's internal structure to benefit a new, and what they regarded as a more loyal, Catholic nobility. They were in fact less interested in creating a new nobility than in re-establishing confessional conformity among the elite, which they considered to be an essential prerequisite to strengthen their authority.[60] Since the Protestant nobles in the main refused to convert, and the Habsburgs were forced by financial considerations to make religious concessions, they had to use their power of patronage over social capital to reduce the size of the Protestant nobility, and thereby also provide enhanced incentives for conversion to Catholicism. Although Matthias had temporarily to bestow his patronage once again on the Protestants who sided with him against Rudolf in 1608–9, the expectations of the Protestant nobility were greatly disappointed when they suddenly realized that, in the future, the Habsburgs were determined to distribute social capital only to Catholics. Instead of bringing about the change gradually, Matthias and Ferdinand implemented their strategies for attaining dominance at a speed that minimized the chances of appropriate cultural adjustment.

The transformation of the noble Estates' social structure occurred despite the fact that in 1572 the Protestant Estates had been successful in limiting the power of the Habsburgs over social mobility. Their aim in establishing a dual system of nobility and Estates was to strengthen and clearly define social distinctions, rather than close the noble *Stände* to advancing commoners. Certainly, the established Protestant nobility resented the new nobility. However, the conflict of interest between new and old nobles was dwarfed by the religious divide, and its significance for the preservation of social capital.

However, for various reasons, competition over this form of Habsburg patronage differed in each noble Estate. In their choice of new members, the Estates depended on the pool of nobles and barons created by the emperor. If the emperor ennobled only Catholics, the Estate of Knights would eventually be unable to admit Protestant nobility; if he raised mainly Catholics to the baronage, the Estate of Lords had to choose new candidates among this favoured group. The noble *Stände* could avoid complete dependency on royal promotions by advancing foreign nobility, but this could operate only so long as the Habsburgs provided opportunities for such nobles. This limited the possibility of advancing many Protestants into the *Ritterstand* after 1609. But the Habsburgs had the most influence over admissions to the Estate of Lords and therefore began to concentrate on the advancement of a new and loyal Catholic nobility within the upper nobility, which prompted a numerical expansion of the *Herrenstand*. Because the pool of the native Catholic nobility was necessarily small, and the conversion rate low, the Habsburg rulers advanced foreign Catholic nobles increasingly. After 1609, the Protestant noble Estates were thus threatened from below by the advance of a new Catholic lesser nobility, and from above by the creation of a Catholic high nobility. Understandably, their attitude hardened, and they tried to prevent Catholic newcomers from entering the Estates. This reinforced the fears and intolerance within the Catholic party, and ossified relations with the Protestants.

It remains to be examined as to what extent the promotion of Catholics affected the Protestant elites and the composition of the Habsburg court. And, in order to understand more fully why Protestant nobles continued to hold on to their faith despite considerable material incentives to convert, it is essential to determine how far the nobility generally adjusted to the competition over court patronage from educated commoners and foreign newcomers, and what strategies of social reproduction it employed, especially with respect to the acquisition of cultural capital.

5
Advancing at the Imperial Court

Habsburg historians long ago noticed changes in the social and confessional background of servants at the Imperial court during the early part of the seventeenth century, but we still do not know the exact nature of the transformation, when it occured, and how it affected the composition of the administration and household. It remains uncertain if, and to what extent, Habsburg rulers favoured particular groups and factions with their patronage, and what impact this had on their relations with the elite, and on the state-building process. This chapter therefore examines the flow of Habsburg patronage in the form of court appointments as well as the social composition of the Imperial court. It further asks what kinds of resources the elite could acquire at court, and how the distribution of Habsburg patronage intersected with the dynastic reproduction and social identity of nobles. This will provide the requisite background to proceed, in the final chapter, with analysing the confessional distribution of patronage at the Imperial court, and how this affected the state-building process and relations between the Habsburgs and the provincial nobles.

As this chapter will show, careers in the service of the ruler had became important to nobles for securing both political influence and dynastic reproduction. However, since the demand for appointments at the Imperial court outstripped availability, competition for office was fierce, especially at a time when noble families had to provide for more children. This allowed the Habsburg rulers to strengthen their role as central patrons, and, by distributing patronage selectively, attempt to secure greater loyalty and cooperation from their elite. In particular, they weakened the stronghold of the old upper nobility at court, and in the process decreased the patronage flowing through the hands of local established noble families.

The transformation in the social composition of the court required a change in the meaning of merit and political loyalty. In addition to virtue, the Habsburg rulers required educational competence from their servants, including the nobility. Most important, in return for career advancement and other forms of patronage, the dynasty expected loyalty to the prince to take priority over all other personal and political bonds. Both changes served the state-building effort, and encouraged professionalism in the central administration and political cohesion. Eager to serve their own dynastic interests, the Austrian nobility adapted their strategies of reproduction to include new educational qualifications and cultural skills. But the demand for a Habsburg-centred loyalty proved more difficult to induce, because it came into conflict with religious identities.

In the following, I apply the word 'court' both to the government and to the ruler's household. This reflects contemporary usage, and the complex nature of the Imperial and archducal courts, where the household and the central administrative organs were still inseparably linked into a single system; this explains why a number of servants could hold appointments in both. When contemporaries used the term *Hofstaat* they therefore referred to the totality of people serving the ruler in the physical space occupied by him or her. *Hof* (or court) denoted the space where ruler and servants assembled, while the term *Staat* (state, abode, seat of government) reflected the patrimonial nature of a government that did not yet separate public and private spheres.

Centres of patronage and career opportunities

The Imperial court had to contend with multitudinous centres of political loyalty in the Reich, the most important being the Imperial Diet (*Reichstag*) and the Chamber Court (*Reichskammergericht*), which were open to the patronage networks and influence of the Imperial princes. In addition, the courts of the electors and other major princes in the empire were centres of patronage competing with the Imperial court in importance and splendour. Very few princes in fact attended court, believing that by doing so they would weaken their own symbolic power. And the more independent a territory was of the Habsburgs, the less likely would its elite be to seek patronage at their court. Instead, rich and powerful magnates would have their own court and attempt to build their own clientage networks autonomously. For example, Petr Vok of Rožmberk's court in southern Bohemia could compete with Rudolf's in Prague both in design and splendor. The Moravian magnate Karel Žerotín had an extensive network of brokers and clients, and connections all over Europe, including at the court of the French king.[1] This sheds light on why Rudolf II thought it important to reside at Prague, close to some of his most powerful subjects and their clientage networks. The existence of great noble clienteles may also explain why the Hungarian nobility had a small presence at the Imperial court before 1620, and why the less independent hereditary nobilities were overrepresented.[2]

Other competing centres of power and patronage were the archducal courts. Finding it difficult during the sixteenth century to rule their enlarged and diverse dominions through patronage from a single centre, the emperors governed with the help of relatives and their clienteles in various provinces, rather than giving extended powers to great nobles, as did the French monarchs.[3] After Ferdinand I's death in 1564, his three sons maintained separate and fairly independent archducal courts in Vienna, Graz and Innsbruck. Until 1621 there was also a Habsburg court at Brussels. When Rudolf moved the Imperial court to Prague (1576–1612), Archduke Ernst became governor (*Statthalter*) of Upper and Lower Austria and maintained another archducal court in Vienna. Although historians have focused on the divisive aspects of this development, putting the brokerage of Imperial patronage into the hands of loyal relatives had considerable advantages for building a broad provincial base of support independent of local magnates and, in the long run, helped to integrate the provincial governments. Nevertheless, the succession conflict between Rudolf and Matthias made it evident that the system of ruling indirectly through relatives could create its own difficulties, and these reflected the contradictions of clientelism. Like the great nobles in France, archdukes often built up their own power networks to rival Imperial influence, generating a high level of distrust and a poisoned atmosphere. Mutual interests among family members of the dynasty would then be transformed into bitter conflicts of interest, creating, as it did in 1608–9 a potential for civil war.

When the Imperial court returned permanently to Vienna in 1612 and merged again with the archducal residence and administration, this caused discontent not only among the nobilities of the Bohemian lands, who then had restricted opportunities to receive and broker Imperial patronage, but also among the lesser nobles of Lower Austria, who were deprived of patronage at an archducal court. After moving with his immediate entourage to Vienna, Ferdinand II dissolved the archducal court at Graz in 1619, so that a separate court remained only at Innsbruck until the Tyrolean male line became extinct in 1665. The subsequent dominance of the Imperial court and the fact that by the early seventeenth century it had become sedentary, testifies to the increased effectiveness of centralizing patronage at the Habsburg court.

Even though the expanding institutions of the provincial Estates represented another arena where patronage was dispensed, this became less independent of the crown. Certainly, the *Stände* distributed favours and resources, such as pensions and positions, directly to their own clients in the province and at the Habsburg court, and the yearly assemblies were occasions where connections could be made or brokered. However, in the hereditary lands, the Habsburgs had gained control over appointing the Estates' key officials, such as the *Landmarschall*, who could divert resources to loyal clients of the crown. Furthermore, beyond controlling the top positions, the local nobility had little interest in becoming officials in the less prestigious administration of the Estates. Serving the Habsburgs at court evidently offered greater benefits and was therefore more attractive to them, although restraints on expanding substantially the number of officials meant that the demand for service at the Imperial and archducal courts usually outran supply.

During the sixteenth and early seventeenth centuries the size of the *Hofstaat* fluctuated between 600 and 800 persons, excluding honorific positions but including all governing councils and the royal guards. The archdukes employed, at most, half of this number of servants, but the size of their courts depended on the number of family members present at any given time. The Imperial court grew significantly only during the late seventeenth century, and Leopold I employed 1966 servants, a number that did not rise significantly under Charles IV.[4] But throughout the sixteenth and seventeenth centuries the Imperial court (including the central administration) was still very small. The French kings engaged 12 000 officials as early as 1505, and about 80 000 in the first part of the seventeenth century. In 1657, Louis XIV's household alone comprised around 4000 people, and in 1639 Cardinal Richelieu maintained a household almost as large as the emperor, with 480 persons. And even the frugal Elizabeth I of England maintained twice as many officials as Emperor Rudolf II.[5]

The stronghold of the nobility over local justice (*Ämter*), and of the Estates over the administration of provincial affairs, was one of the reasons why the Imperial court remained comparatively small. Financial difficulties and the perennial threat from the Ottoman empire presented other obstacles to enlarging the Viennese court during the seventeenth century. An expansion of the city into the suburbs was facilitated only during the late seventeenth century, after the danger of a further Ottoman expansion became more remote. In the meantime, the Habsburgs had to house most of their servants by quartering them within the city gates, the crowded conditions of the city making this very difficult. Sometimes the quartermaster was unable to find adequate housing for over a hundred servants, and this was perhaps another reason why Rudolf II preferred Prague as his residence.[6] Probably because few nobles could live in the Imperial palace, the Habsburg court lacked the divertissments of the French court, and public festivities were largely confined to religious devotions and procession, at least until the late seventeenth century.

As we saw earlier, with such a small *Hofstaat*, the Habsburgs continued to depend on the local nobilities to govern the countryside and administer important legal, fiscal and military functions. Nevertheless, they had made significant progress in expanding their co-ordinating power in the hereditary lands before 1620 by establishing new, and centralizing existing, governing councils. While local nobles resented the elimination of local administrative institutions over which they had some control, they found it highly desirable to obtain positions in the new councils in order to extend their political influence at the centre. Naturally, the dynasty encouraged nobles to compete for appointments at court and did not hesitate to provide even powerful aristocrats with access to brokerage, in return for fostering elite support in the provinces by brokering benefits downwards to pro-Habsburg clients. To promote this, the Habsburgs resisted the sale of inheritable offices. Furthermore, the access of nobles to court positions was not an automatic privilege, as nobles liked to claim; instead, the ruler had the option, in principle, of dismissing them if they infringed the rules.

Noble families were certainly eager to have their sons serve the Habsburg rulers. Thus, towards of the end of the sixteenth century, more than half of the second-born sons of the upper nobility of the Austrian hereditary lands were courtiers, and another fifth were officers. The proportion of third-born and fourth-born sons employed at court was even higher, with more than two-thirds of them serving the crown. More surprising is the high proportion – about a third – of first-born sons of the upper nobility in the employ of the Habsburgs.[7] Naturally, the old upper nobility believed that certain appointments at court were its prerogative, and that the most prestigious and influential functions could only be performed by them, while the less important ones were to be assigned to nobles of new or lower ranks. As this claim came to be contested increasingly by educated commoners, nobles intensified their insistence on possessing an established right to serve the ruler, and that the hierarchy of offices at court should reflect and reproduce the existing social hierarchy. During the sixteenth and seventeenth centuries, the Habsburgs were largely unpersuaded, and frequently upset the homology between social status and the hierarchy of the Imperial court in order to enhance their role as central patrons, distributing their patronage selectively as a means of securing the loyalty of their elites.

Because the four highest honorary functions in the household, the *Erz- und Erbämter,* were hereditary and by tradition the preserve of the old lords of the hereditary lands, the dynasty had even before the sixteenth century deprived them of any substantial powers by installing people of their own choice to perform their functions on a daily basis. Since these people could be dismissed, especially by a new monarch, the Habsburgs could thus alter relatively quickly the power structure at their court. The hereditary incumbents performed their duties only during special ceremonies and festivities, which, however, gave them much prestige and a very profitable sinecure.[8]

In many ways the Imperial Habsburg household resembled a military regiment, a reminder of its medieval origins. This did not change with the introduction of the Spanish court ceremonial by Maximilian II (1564–76). However, the Spanish model strengthened the role of the monarch's close entourage in order to keep him more remote from his subjects, including his courtiers, a fact much resented, especially at the court of Rudolf II. Such distancing of the sovereign only furthered the influence of those who did have personal access to the ruler.[9] The incumbents of the four highest of these offices, the *Obersthofmeister* (master of the household), the *Obersthofmarschall* (marshal of the court), the *Oberstkämmerer* (master of the chambers), and the *Oberststallmeister* (master of the horse), wielded enormous political influence, since they were personally close to the ruler. The master of the household, who supervised court routine and personnel, could often combine unlimited access to the ruler with the directorship of the Privy Council, while the master of the chamber, organizing all matters concerning the ruler's bodily and spiritual needs, including his audiences, frequently ranked second after the *Obersthofmeister*. When the ruler travelled, the *Oberstkämmerer* was replaced by the master of the horse, a kind of transport minister in charge of stables and laager (*Wagenburg*), making this office also very desirable to nobles. The marshal of the court, the executive officer, had immense disciplinary powers not only over the household staff, but also over officials in the administration.[10]

Serving under the jurisdiction of these four men provided numerous other nobles with political influence and access to Habsburg patronage as well as other clientage networks. In a system where the exercise of royal power remained highly personal, having direct access to the ruler was vitally important. Personal contact with the monarch opened the way to obtaining favours, honours and other benefits, and to broker them downwards to clients, friends and relatives. A nobleman holding a leading position in the household, which was often combined with a seat in the Privy Council, could become very powerful indeed. Usually, therefore, the Habsburg rulers made special efforts to appoint people of their own choice to the top positions in the household, and to distribute a proportion of them to nobles from less-established families. Indeed, of a large sample of thirty-two nobles serving in key positions at the Imperial and archducal households between 1580 and 1620, a high proportion, almost a third, were new barons who had been in possession of their rank for fewer than fifty years.[11]

The Habsburg rulers also undermined the homology between the social order and the hierarchy of administrative offices. Old nobles had to compete with newcomers for appointments to the Privy Council, the Imperial Aulic council, the war council, the court treasury and the Austrian chancellory, all of which were crucial to protecting nobles' political and material interests. Although serving as a privy councillor was most attractive to the upper nobility, an analysis of the background of some forty Imperial privy councillors who served during the reigns of Rudolf II and Matthias, and who were installed by Ferdinand II in 1619–20, shows that the *Geheime Rat* was no stronghold of old aristocrats. Only about half of the privy councillors belonged to the baronage, and two-thirds of these were of new baronage. Merely a fifth held titles above a baron, while another fifth were lesser nobles, and a little over a tenth were commoners, usually trained lawyers.[12] Clearly, then, the Habsburgs chose its closest advisers carefully from various social groups, and they preferred the new baronage in their Privy Council.

During the early seventeenth century, the other central councils also became the preserve of specific noble groups. In 1576, positions in the prestigious Imperial Aulic council were shared almost equally between the high and low nobility and educated commoners, but by 1629 over a half of the councillors were lords. As in the Privy Council, the new baronage was preponderant among them.[13] The Imperial court treasury, which was dominated by the new baronage during the late sixteenth century, became in 1629 the preserve of the lesser nobility. This reflects the low esteem of positions in the financial administration, because financial matters carried the taint of a bourgeois occupation.[14] Only the presidency, which could lead to a seat in the Privy Council, attracted members from the upper nobility. Offices which required a formal legal education were even less desirable to the high nobility. Thus most of the Imperial vice chancellors belonged to the new, lesser nobility, because the office required some legal training, if not a doctorate in jurisprudence. By way of comparison, the presidents appointed between 1580 and 1620 to the Aulic council belonged to the high aristocracy of the Reich.[15] Service in the Imperial war council (*Hofkriegsrat*) became more desirable to the upper nobility during the early seventeenth century, probably because the status and salaries of the war councillors had improved by 1615. After that date, two of the five councillors were counts, and the other three barons, with the lower nobility excluded altogether. In contrast, in 1576, only one of the seven war councillors had held titles above that of a baron, and two even belonged to the lesser nobility.[16]

It also became imperative for the provincial nobility to secure positions in the new lower courts of appeal for the provincial, municipal and patrimonial courts, since this is where territorial laws (*Landrecht*) were revised. In particular, the lesser nobles of Lower and Upper Austria competed for positions in the *Nieder-Österreichische Regiment,* even though its officials did not belong to the inner circle of the Imperial court. But as councillors and assessors they would have close contact with the archducal court, and such positions in the *Regiment* served frequently as springboards to higher office in the central administration.[17]

Considering the importance of being close to the prince and his main advisers, it is understandable that the Austrian nobility had little enthusiasm for active military service. In addition, employment depended on warfare, at least until the establishment of a standing army, while the cost of equipment, and ransom in case of capture by the enemy, were considerable. A more profitable enterprise, which during the seventeenth century led to the rapid rise of a number of noble families, was regimental proprietorship. Such regiments and squadrons could be disposed of at the will of the proprietor, and commanding positions within them were even available for sale.[18] Surprisingly, regimental proprietorship was not very common among the Lower Austrian nobility, perhaps because it necessitated having a strong financial basis. It also removed nobles from the new centres of power. Pursuing a clerical profession was obviously difficult for the Protestant majority, which explains why even high Church positions became dominated by commoners, who frequently came from the Reich.[19]

Obviously, the Habsburgs entertained some of the wishes of the old nobility to distribute vacancies according to rank and, with some notable exceptions, commoners and lesser nobles were delegated to positions of inferior status.[20] They were barred from high office in the Imperial household and, at best, were appointed chamberlain, or master of the table. Even these positions were open more frequently to knights and commoners at the archducal rather than the Imperial court. Moreover, only a few lower nobles received military commands as high as an *Obrist.* In the central administration, knights could move up to the position of councillor in the *Reichshofrat,* the *Hofkammer* or the *Hofkriegsrat,* which might lead to status promotion. They could obtain a presidency only in the court treasury, but even then they were usually raised to the baronage upon appointment. The highest position most commonly available to knights was a councillorship in the court treasury or the Lower Austrian *Regiment.*[21]

Clearly, then, the most prestigious functions in the rulers' household, and most of the important positions in the bureaucracy, were distributed primarily to lords. Although the upper nobility continued to be the major recipient of Habsburg patronage, and in fact strengthened its presence at court during the early part of the seventeenth century, its claim to monopoly over high offices had been undermined by a new baronage. The latter had gained the largest share of positions in the Privy Council and the *Reichshofrat,* and secured an important place for itself in the Imperial household. In addition, a new, lesser nobility began to control the leading positions in the inferior branches of the bureaucracy, such as the financial administration and the vice chancellery; some of those with judicial training had also been able to advance to high offices. The old nobility would have preferred a recruitment policy that they themselves pursued in the administration of the Estates, in which the most important and prestigious positions were the preserve of the old nobility and distributed according to age of rank, while the inferior offices, especially in the financial administration, could be divided among new nobles and commoners.[22]

The court had become a point of contact not only for the Habsburgs and nobles from various social backgrounds, but also between the heterogeneous nobilities of different territories. This allowed the dynasty to use the court as a tool better to centralize its disparate dominions. However, judging by the regional background of privy councillors appointed in the forty years before 1620, the Habsburgs focused largely on integrating the German-speaking nobilities at the Imperial court. Thus, about a fifth of the privy councillors were indigenous to Lower Austria, another fifth came from the other hereditary lands, and the largest proportion – over a third – originated in the Reich. Only about a tenth of the privy councillors came from the Bohemian lands, and the nobles of Hungary and other territories were conspicuously absent.[23]

Giving preference to senior men when making appointments was not always observed by the Habsburgs. But, certainly, the highest positions were frequently reserved for older, and presumably more experienced, people. On average, lords and knights were forty years old when installed as councillors to the court treasury, the Aulic council and to the war council, although some could be as young as twenty-five at the time of their first appointment.[24] Privy councillors and council presidents were, on average, already in their early forties, and, as far as I can determine, the youngest candidate was thirty-one years old.

Advancement to important positions was generally a very slow process. Regardless of rank and seniority, the average waiting time from entering the service of the Habsburgs to obtaining a high post in the administration or household was fourteen years, varying in individual cases from two to twenty-nine years.[25] Although social connections and the favour of rulers could make a tremendous difference in speeding-up career mobility, social rank mattered little. Few differences existed among knights and lords, and between new and old nobles, in the speed of their advance. However, after 1580, religious affiliation became much more important for advancement at court. Protestants, once promoted, advanced on average five years more slowly than Catholics, and they were excluded increasingly from court appointments. I shall pursue this topic more closely in the next chapter.

Producing economic, social and symbolic capital at court

The nobility competed for Habsburg patronage as a means of advancement in the administration and household, not merely to enhance their ability to shape Imperial policies and territorial politics, but to ensure their own social and dynastic reproduction via access to various forms of capital available at court. A political office in itself had little value, unless it could provide its incumbent, his family, clients and friends with material resources. In turn, economic capital became most effective in pre-modern aristocratic society, when it was associated with social and symbolic power distributed largely by the prince. As we have seen, for many positions at court it was essential to have noble status, if not a specific rank, and without social connections it was more difficult, if not impossible, to gain an appointment. And networks of social relationships had to be sustained by both symbolic and material exchanges. Equally essential was the acquisition of cultural capital (including education) in the form of skills required for the production and reproduction of other kinds of capital. In other words, some degree of social and symbolic capital, cultural training and economic assets, were required to gain access to court offices and to yield political influence.

The financial gains available to nobles from office-building could be substantial, and it is not surprising that the new upper nobility originated in families who rose to prominence through service in the highest governmental offices. As I showed earlier, careers at court were important to provide income for the nobility's younger sons, and even a high proportion of first- and second-born sons of the upper nobility of the Austrian lands were employed by the Habsburgs. This suggests that noble families had become dependent on vacancies at court to provide for their numerous male children during this period of population growth.[26]

The substantial salaries of higher officials was obviously one reason for the desire to serve the Habsburgs, since they were equivalent to, and in some cases even better than, the yearly income from landed properties. Thus, during the late sixteenth century, the master of the Imperial household (*Obersthofmeister*) received a yearly salary of 4000 florins (or Gulden), and the yearly income of a privy councillor ranged between 1500 and 2000 florins. One could purchase a small estate with about twenty-six peasant households for approximately 5000 florins, and income from such a property might be as low as 1000 florins.[27] By holding double functions, an official could increase his income substantially, and some individuals were able to negotiate special salaries. For example, Privy Councillor Georg Ludwig von Leuchtenberg, who was also president of the Aulic council (1600–04), demanded a salary of 6000 florins before accepting the presidency for a second term, even though the usual remuneration for the position was set at 2000 florins.[28] None the less, salaries were generally commensurate with the prestige and importance of an office. Thus the president of the less prestigious court treasury received only 1200 florins per year, the councillors of the Imperial war council a mere 600 florins, and a similar position in the Lower Austrian *Regiment* paid between 400 and 500 florins.[29]

However, the attraction of salaries obtained from court appointments should not be overrated, since they were often paid irregularly and sometimes not at all. For example, Adam, Baron of Dietrichstein, the master of Rudolf II's court, frequently did not receive his full salary. Ferdinand II, who had inherited debts of about 20 million florins, was forced to melt down tableware and other plate to pay salaries to court servants. The Habsburgs often rewarded courtiers by mortgaging their crown lands (*Kammergut*) to them, which involved a considerable shrinkage of the court's landholding during the late sixteenth and early seventeenth centuries. Some nobles obtained permanent ownership of such landed property as a reward for loyal service, which often served as an old-age pension. For example, in 1611, the Privy Councillor Ernst Mollart received from Rudolf II an Imperial fief in Piedmont worth 100 000 florins, to which he retired seven years later. Sometimes loyal servants received extraordinary gifts, frequently in the form of gold, jewels, silver objects and precious stones. Adam Dietrichstein's accounts reveal that during his lifetime he received from the Austrian Habsburg dynasty a total of 129 600 Gulden just in the form of gifts, and another 53 000 Gulden from the Spanish Habsburgs. Despite the considerable expenses he had to pay in the service of the dynasty, in 1580 Dietrichstein had tripled his inheritance, and his wealth amounted to some 300 000 Gulden.[30]

As this suggests, many of the courtiers were able to amass fortunes from the appurtenances of their office, as well as their salaries. Besides gifts, land grants and sinecures from the crown, most officials at the Habsburg courts received gifts from their clients, which in many cases functioned as a substitute for the salaries the Habsburgs were so frequently unable to pay. Collecting such gratuities or honorariums for services performed was widely practised in the Habsburg household and administration. It is an anachronistic representation of historical situations in terms of categories of the present to judge these practices simply as corruption, since early modern officials were not modern-style bureaucrats with a civil service ethic and career structure, and contemporaries did not look upon gifts as bribery. Rather, they defined bribery as buying a favour in order to circumvent the law. This type of behaviour was clearly distinguished from giving presents to people who acted legally in providing service as a client or broker, such as helping to gain a position, to forge marriage alliances, or to speed up a case before the courts.[31]

Since custom and the status of the recipient regulated the level of gratuities, it is difficult to generalize about the actual income officials could derive from them. It was rumoured at court that in just five years of tenure as Imperial vice chancellor (1607–12), the Baron Leopold von Stralendorf had accumulated 200 000 Gulden in the form of presents. Privy Councillor Paul Sixtus von Trautson, who more than doubled the property he had inherited, was also reported to have enriched himself through such gratuities. More detailed is the evidence of how Johann Caspar von Ampringen, Grand Master of the Teutonic Knights, rewarded obliging courtiers for helping him to gain the release of the knights' property from the Imperial treasury. He provided gifts of gold worth about 600 Gulden to the chancellor, between 100 and 200 Gulden to the Imperial secretaries, and about 50 Gulden to a junior clerk.[32]

While the Habsburgs had an interest in encouraging this informal exchange, they made a concerted effort to avoid the sale of positions, especially on an hereditary basis. There is evidence, nevertheless, that the incumbents of very popular positions in the household, such as the chamberlains, had to pay a '*Taxe*' to the crown upon their instalment. However, these fees seem to have been relatively low; Hans Jacob von Kufstein, for example, paid only 30 florins when he was named Imperial councillor in

1607. Occasionally, positions in the household and the bureaucracy were passed on to an heir in return for money grants to the crown. But these were practices quite distinct from the proprietary rights many offices provided in seventeenth-century France.[33] The dynasty was thus sufficiently prudent to retain the sole right to make all important appointments in the army, administration and household, and to harness the distribution of court patronage for its own benefit, rather than allow it to be channelled into the hands of a few magnates.

Historians have often been puzzled why nobles were willing to serve the Habsburgs even though they knew they would be paid irregularly, if at all, and that the cost of display and living near the court would often outweigh income. No doubt, some may have served the Habsburgs idealistically, although there is little evidence to support the contention that material considerations were generally neglected. The key to the solution is recognizing the importance of prestige and status in gaining access to material resources. As I shall show below, the early modern Austrian nobility was well aware of the growing importance of the Imperial court as the central place from which they could enhance family resources. They knew that social connections forged at court were essential to facilitate status advance, pensions, profitable marriage alliances and positions for themselves, clients, friends and family members.

Although at present the available evidence makes it impossible to show exactly how patronage was brokered at the Imperial court, we can determine how nobles utilized connections to facilitate beneficial marriage alliances, and how kinship ties opened access to court offices and status mobility for themselves and family members. Certainly, by the early seventeenth century, the Imperial court had become one of the most important marriage markets. And an opportune marriage provided not only material resources, but also more intangible benefits. It could give a family access to another family's privileges, increase its prestige generally, and multiply clients and political supporters. Most importantly, the exchange of children provided an essential bond between patrons, brokers and clients, which also helped to guarantee trust among them.

Paul Sixtus Trautson's career serves as a good example to show the benefits of family connections and marriage alliances. His family belonged to very old nobility, who had been raised to the Estate of Lords only in 1541. In his youth he served as a page and chamberlain at the court of Maximilian II, where his father was master of the court. Advancing quickly through the combination of fortunate family connections and real ability, at the young age of twenty-eight he was appointed Aulic councillor, and only five years later, in 1581, to Privy Councillor and president of the Aulic council. After his instalment as master of the court (*Obersthofmeister*), Rudolf II raised him and his family to Imperial counts in 1598. Not surprisingly, following Paul Sixtus of Trautson's instalment, his less capable son, his older brother, Balthasar, and his nephew, Anton, were all appointed at various times as active Privy Councillors. In fact, until the eighteenth century, one member of the family was always advanced to this important office. Nevertheless, after 1600, Rudolf II, suspicious of Trautson's connection with Matthias, the emperor's brother, appears to have sent Paul Sixtus into retirement. His decision to side with Matthias was a wise one, even though he had to begin a new career at the archducal court. When Matthias became king of Hungary in 1609, he rewarded Paul Sixtus with the governorship of Lower Austria (*Statthalter*).

Five years earlier, Paul Sixtus Trautson had married Susanna Veronika, the sister of Leonhard Helfried Meggau, whose family had been raised to the baronage only three decades earlier (1572). The connection between these two Catholic families proved particularly beneficial to the bride's family. Paul Sixtus's brother-in-law, Leonhard Helfried Meggau, who had served as councillor in the Lower Austrian government since 1600, suddenly also received a number of high offices as Matthias's master of the chambers and master of the court. In 1612, both Trautson and Meggau received a seat in the Imperial Privy Council, and when Paul Sixtus Trautson died in 1621, Leonhard Helfried Meggau succeeded him as *Statthalter*. In the 1640s, the office passed to Johann Franz Trautson, Paul Sixtus's and Susanna Veronika Meggau's son and heir. Johann Franz married the daughter of the Privy Councillor, Georg Franz Prince of Hohenzollern-Heckingen, and also entered the Privy Council. This obviously helped his son to receive the rank of Imperial prince in 1711. By this time, the family also held extensive possessions of land.[34]

The example of the Trautson family suggests that important offices at the Imperial court were controlled by a few families who were connected by marriage and blood ties. Indeed, all the presidents appointed to the Imperial Aulic council between 1580 and 1620 belonged to the high aristocracy of the Reich, and were closely related by marriage. So were nearly all of the Imperial vice chancellors. Although the new baronage had made substantial inroads, intermarriage was clearly also very common among the families appointed to the Privy Council. However, marriage alliances frequently followed rather than preceded appointments, and this testifies also to the importance of the court as an arena for brokering marriage alliances serving to guarantee trust and loyalty between patrons, brokers and clients.[35]

The process of exchange at court between rulers as patrons and nobles as brokers and clients necessitated other interactions that legitimized and symbolized conditions of trust and obligation. Intermarriage and gifts were only two aspects of the strengthening of ties of allegiance. Court ceremony and public festivities were important ritual occasions that further supported and legitimated the patron–client exchanges between ruler and elite. They served to uphold the basic symbols of social identity and the sociopolitical hierarchy; for example, in the form of socially differentiated dress. The space and function that individuals were allotted according to rank at festive occasions also revealed publicly the close relationship between the relative standing of each group in the social hierarchy, and its access to the centre of power and patronage. It was especially important to publicize and emphasize symbolically the ruler's authority, and constantly to reinscribe the asymmetry of power, while at the same time affirm solidarity and mutual dependency between ruler and nobility, and between patrons, brokers and clients generally. It is hardly surprising, then, that conspicuous consumption and public ceremony increased as Habsburg patronage became more important and centralized at the Imperial court.

Although during the late sixteenth and early seventeenth centuries public ceremony was not yet as elaborate as it was to become subsequently, the Habsburg court had already become the primary space where nobles could display and seek recognition for distinctions in rank, wealth, influence and lifestyle.[36] Most early modern European rulers manipulated the desire of elites to attend court for this purpose. What distinguished the Habsburg from other courts was a greater emphasis on religious ceremony. The Austrian Habsburgs of the Counter-Reformation particularly cultivated an ideal of princely piety, which by the mid-seventeenth century became known as *Pietas Austriaca*. In public ceremonies, this piety manifested itself in an emphasis on the veneration of the Virgin Mary, the Cross and the Eucharist.[37] However, this focus of Habsburg public festivities on religious devotion changed little about the nature of display and its function in reinscribing distinctions of rank and authority. It only made it more public.

As I argued earlier, prestige or reputation were important means by which the various other forms of capital were acknowledged. To be known and highly visible because of rank and distinction was necessary to be sought after as patron or broker, and this was, essentially, symbolic capital. This acknowledgment of a noble's ability to convert social and symbolic capital into other forms of resources was the rationale behind the nobility's willingness to serve at the court without direct economic reward. It was also the reason behind the incessant striving of court society over seemingly empty honours, and the seemingly 'irrational' pursuit of all other forms of distinction, such as titles, conspicuous consumption or superior rank (*Präzedenz)* in processions and court ceremonies. However, as I shall show shortly, the strategies nobles employed to acquire social and symbolic capital did not necessarily reflect conscious maximizing strategies as modern economists understand them, but depended to a large extent on individual disposition and socialization.

Cultural capital and noble identity

The acquisition of cultural capital, including social skills, was essential for nobles to take full advantage of the patronage system, and to produce and convert social and symbolic power profitably. Even though status, kinship and patronage networks continued to be important factors for career advancement, the evidence also shows that education became an important prerequisite for patronage. In order better to compete with educated commoners for positions at the Habsburg court, noble families had to improve their cultural capital. As a German nobleman put it in the late sixteenth century, 'neglecting ... [studies] or quitting them prematurely means the decline of the nobility'.[38] Not only did nobles have to emulate the new educational practices, they also had to devise new ways of upholding social distinctions. As I will show, the acquisition of cultural capital at the prince's court became the primary strategy in achieving this goal.

Across Europe, the strategies of noble families in educating their sons had principally become more orientated towards serving the ruler at the court and in the army. The technical revolution in warfare necessitated, for success, the acquisition by warriors of competence in mathematics, fortification technology and tactics, just as courtiers and administrators needed formal training in the law, languages and rhetoric. Noblemen were now expected not only to be polished in manners and proficient in the military arts, but also to have a knowledge of the law, to speak foreign languages, and to display book-learning and organizational talents. Early modern monarchs encouraged the formation of an educated elite not only because they needed specially trained officials to deal with the new requirements of state centralization, but also to ensure a uniform culture among the state elite and standardize the means of cultural representation.[39]

However, this change caused discontentment, especially among some old nobles. Thus a seventeenth-century French nobleman complained that in his time, 'one made gentlemen study only to join the church; even they were mostly satisfied with just the Latin needed for their breviary. Those destined for the court or the army went to the academy. They learned to ride, to dance, arms, to play the lute, to leap, and that was all.'[40] And a Tudor gentleman asserted, 'I swear by God's body, I'd rather that my son should hang than study letters. For it becomes the sons of gentlemen to blow the horn nicely, to hunt skilfully and elegantly, carry and train a hawk. But the study of letters should be left to the sons of rustics.'[41] Evidently, the new educational requirements raised questions about social distinctions between commoners and the nobility, causing nobles to fear that educational achievement and merit rather than birth would become the main criteria for social advancement. Educational reformers and others campaigned increasingly against the ignorance of the nobility, and supported the idea that noble privilege had to be justified through public service. Good birth had to be coupled with virtue, which came to be defined not only as moral rectitude and devotion to God, but also as mastery of intellectual and technical skills.

Most noble families soon understood that the successful propagation of the social order and family enhancement depended not only on associating economic resources with social and symbolic capital but also to a large extent on the assimilation of cultural capital into the '*habitus*' of young nobles. *Habitus*, as the sociologist, Pierre Bourdieu, has defined it, is formed in the course of socialization by the family and other educational institutions, and, while it is durable, it can be modified by subsequent experiences. It is the product of internalized practices, structures, norms and ideas of a particular social environment, helping individuals to decipher their particular world and mobilizing them to pursue certain strategies and goals. These may be 'reasonable' without being the product of deliberate and systematic decision making. Thus, in the ideal case, when properly inculcated with noble culture, new generations of nobles will view their society as self-evident, and perceive opportunities for, and collaborate in, the requirements of social and dynastic reproduction.[42]

Reproducing culture, then, was essential to propagating social relations. In a society where action was much more co-ordinated through tradition than it is in modern times, and where legal prescription and normative structures (for example, prohibitions on nobles engaging in trade and commerce, and patrilineal transmission) made the conversion of non-material resources into economic capital much more complicated, it was especially important for the elite to endow its sons with a durable *habitus* that internalized noble culture, and in particular the skills to enhance the social and symbolic resources of the family, which could be used for material purposes. And with the advances that commoners had made in the acquisition of scholastic learning and in gaining access to the Habsburg court during the sixteenth century, it became doubly imperative that noble sons be better prepared academically for the changing roles of courtier, warrior and landowner. But to uphold the social divisions between nobility and commoners, it was equally essential that the nobility redefine the new educational standards to suit its own social identity by reinscribing traditional social distinctions in educational practices. To achieve these aims, noble families combined explicit, institutionalized education at schools and universities with implicit, diffuse socialization in an aristocratic, court-like setting at home and abroad.

These strategies were already apparent in the elementary education of young noblemen in the Austrian lands during the sixteenth century. Here, as elsewhere in Europe, the education of male children was generally reinvigorated by humanist and religious reformers, who promoted schooling that combined *pietas* with *eruditio,* and this, together with the new vocational needs, led to the establishment of many new schools in the Habsburg territories. Noble families sponsored their creation and began increasingly to send their young sons, usually around the age of seven, to the new urban *Gymnasia* or Latin schools. During the late sixteenth century the Protestant nobles, who were numerically predominant in Lower

Austria, preferred their sons to attend, for four to eight years, the newly-established Protestant schools of the provincial Estates (*Landschaftsschulen*), while Catholics, under the leadership of the Jesuits, sponsored Latin schools of their own to ensure the infusion of the appropriate religious identity. Although the ideal community of the Christian *ecumene* had split and new educational centres were no longer controlled by any single institutional power, both confessions focused on moral training and the teaching of reading and writing in Latin.[43]

Noble parents recognized that cultural capital was essential for family continuance when they stressed that their sons' education was to serve the 'honour of the family'.[44] They also realized that the best conditions for converting cultural capital into more concrete resources was via service to the crown. Since it was a prerequisite for most important positions at court, the instruction of Latin became a focal point of secular primary education. As a late-sixteenth-century elementary school regulation put it, 'nearly all offices deal in legal matters, and cannot be run without Latin'.[45] Considering the linguistic diversity in the Habsburg lands, it was particularly important that the elite was able to speak and read Latin, since this enhanced the state's capacity for co-ordination from the centre. Pupils also received basic schooling in some other languages and subjects such as history, rhetoric, geometry, music and philosophy (that is, logic, metaphysics and mathematics). Most of these primary schools served as a preparation for university attendance, and some of them even offered instruction in legal studies during a student's final year.[46]

Moral training was the other focal point of elementary education in the Austrian lands. Parents and humanist educators thought it essential to 'drum' moral virtue into the habit of young children. They viewed religious instruction as being particularly helpful for internalizing respect for authority and obedience towards parents. This was thought to be crucial for dynastic reproduction because it disposed children to put the interests of their family, or *Haus,* before their personal desires. Appropriately, the word *Zucht,* which in German means both discipline and breeding, was employed widely in the instructions for noble education, and the term *Hofzucht* was applied to the rules of courtly behaviour. Obviously, fostering discipline in education was equally important to condition the elite to obedience towards rulers. The fact that parents and authorities considered self-control of body and mind to be essential parts of the *habitus* of a successful warrior and courtier indicates that they did not lose sight of the vocational objectives of discipline. So, for all these reasons, late-sixteenth-century educational guidelines concentrated on punishment, drill and repetition. They regulated strictly every hour of the day, from six in the morning until bedtime, and recommended constant surveillance of pupils' behaviour.[47]

Together with the reading of ancient texts (in particular, Cicero), the inculcation of discipline and religious instruction were also designed to activate the supposedly natural predisposition of nobles to virtue, especially prudence, temperance and constancy. As Prince Karl Eusebius von Liechtenstein put it, 'fear of God' was the 'basis of all virtues', and noble virtue found its expression not only in piety but also in dignified and self-controlled behaviour, including bodily posture and gestures. The 'honour of nobility', his cousin Hartmann insisted, depended on 'good manners and gestures' (*gute sitten und geberden*). Late-sixteenth-century pedagogical guidelines for elementary education defined the posture for reciting texts, urged pupils to eat their food with 'good gestures', dress in a noble manner, and clean their bodies and change their clothes regularly. People had to be able to recognize by their appearance and behaviour that pupils were raised as nobles rather than peasants, a contrast that was also emphasized in Count Baldassare Castiglione's book, *Il Cortegiano* (The Courtier). In other words, the symbolic reflections of noble superiority had to be incarnated in the body itself. Moreover, as the proportion of pupils from urban classes increased around the begining of the seventeenth century, the nobility began to include in their sons' curriculum the teaching of fencing, music and dance. The purpose was to develop competence in traditional noble forms of behaviour, thus facilitating the distinguishing of nobility from commoners.[48]

Many parents of the upper nobility, and those who could afford to support aspirations for status mobility, continued to send their sons to serve in the households of relatives, friends, or patrons – usually between the age of seven and fourteen – where a private tutor instructed them in the company of other children in various academic subjects, moral virtues and bodily disciplines. That this practice became even more popular during the early seventeenth century was a result not only of the closing of the Protestant *Landschaftsschulen* during the course of the Counter Reformation,[49] but also because this type of education allowed for intereraction with social peers and immersion in a court culture. The Inner Austrian noble, Sigmund von Herbertstein, who had served in his youth as a page at a relative's court, remarked in his diary that the purpose of his foreign residence was to acquire both 'learning and court discipline'. As elsewhere in Europe, educational authorities in the Austrian lands also considered the early separation of young nobles from their families as being beneficial in itself for disciplining and moulding children's wills to family aims while at the same time furthering a certain amount of autonomy necessary for leadership.[50]

The new emphasis on courtly manners and the greater centralization of patronage at Court made it highly desirable to send young sons to serve as pages at the Habsburg court for a few years, where they received a thorough training in court etiquette and in the usual academic subjects. Only around twenty youngsters between the age of eight and ten, mainly from the upper nobility, found such honorary employment at the Imperial court in the late sixteenth century.[51] But similar opportunities were available to a few new and lesser nobles, especially at the archducal courts, and this was especially desirable when an archduke was next in line to the Imperial throne, since it could help to advance a family's position. Hieronymous Beck, for example, who belonged to the new lower nobility, learned social manners as a page at the Innsbruck court and was educated together with the sons of Ferdinand I. Beck's father was chief administrator of the royal domain (*Vizedom*) and money-lender to the crown, but Hieronymous, who later also obtained a degree in law, rose to be chancellor of the Imperial treasury (*Hofkammer*) and chief purveyor of the armies in Hungary. His sons, who made careers as military officers, were elevated to the barony in 1597.[52]

Already at the elementary level, then, the education of male nobles in the Austrian territories was orientated towards preparing them for a public life that focused on service at the Habsburg court. It combined formal scholastic instruction geared towards vocational qualification with informal training in a court setting that was crucial to internalizing cultural competency. Noble parents of the old and upper nobility thought it particularly important that the *habitus* of young nobles should incorporate skills in the maintenance, accumulation and conversion of social and symbolic capital. Training at a court acquainted them with practices in cultivating social connections, and in particular patronage networks. They could internalize an appreciation of the importance of patron–client relations in forging marriage alliances, enhancing noble status, and gaining access to various other assets which rulers distributed at court, including monetary, juridical, military and symbolic resources.[53]

Residence at court further provided young nobles with a practical appreciation of social distinctions, and with the skills for perpetuating social divisions through the cultivation of a lifestyle (for example, manners, tastes, dress, prestige and honours) that differentiated them from commoners. Habsburg historians often overlook the emphasis that early modern nobles placed on the pursuit of seemingly empty honours and social distinction (what Norbert Elias called 'prestige-fetish'), neglecting to recognize them as strategies that legitimized the dominance of the nobility and secured its dynastic and social reproduction.[54] Many of the educated urban classes could afford to buy landed estates, dress like nobles, eventually obtain noble titles, and compete for patronage at court, thereby threatening the symbolic and cultural capital of the traditional nobility. Nobles therefore needed to re-emphasize social distinctions, and did so by, among other things, advancing an educational model that stressed formal training as merely serving to develop the supposedly naturally inherited, superior capacity of nobles to moral virtue, valour, self-discipline and grace. The ruler's court provided the perfect arena for noble sons to acquire cultural competency, and the best field in which they later could display the distinctiveness of noble culture.[55]

The need to prepare young nobles for service at court, and the desire to infuse cultural capital with symbolic power that fortified the position of the nobility, explains why the cavalier's tour became an expensive addition to the education of nobles during the sixteenth century. Since judicial training had become necessary for many posts in both central and local administrations, as well as for managing landed estates, attendance at foreign universities became imperative. However, noble families, especially those from the old and upper nobility, made efforts to invest formal university education, which was tainted as an activity of the urban classes, with traditional symbolic meaning suited to its own social identity. As they had in primary education, noble families combined academic schooling with a diffuse training that focused on inculcating noble culture. In particular, parents emphasized visits or service at foreign courts in order to further shape their sons' *habitus* toward courtly practices and values.

In Europe generally, the increased enrolment of nobles at universities exceeded the rate of expansion of the nobility. In England, for example, university attendance by the titled nobility increased fourfold from 1580 to 1639; similarly, the proportion of noble students at the South German university of Ingolstadt rose from 4.4 per cent to 17.6 per cent between the late fifteenth and the late sixteenth centuries.[56] But we know relatively little about how the Habsburg nobilities adapted to the changes required of them in higher education, and how the acculturation process related to religious differences and competition over court patronage.[57] It appears that, while members of the Austrian nobility in the early sixteenth century still had to tolerate much mockery for obtaining a university education,[58] this dissipated as nobles patronized them more readily towards the end of the century. My own calculations on rather dispersed data indicates that university attendance among the Lower Austrian nobility (knights and lords) more than doubled after 1580, so that about a third (155) of those alive in 1620 had some higher education. Since the total population of the noble Estates had grown by nearly a fifth (from 400 to 467), the proportional advance (from over a tenth to a third) is particularly remarkable. Recall that the growth of the nobility was the result of a larger number of children for each family rather than the expansion of noble houses (which, in fact, declined by 15 per cent), so that families were faced with the cost of educating a larger number of children.[59]

A university education, as it was refashioned by the nobility, required considerable economic capital, in part because of the necessity of paying for the tutor who accompanied the young nobleman, usually around the age of sixteen, on his tour of foreign courts and countries.[60] The cost of this 'cavalier's tour' could amount to around 10 000 florins per year for one son of the upper nobility, which represented five times the income from some top positions, or the cost of a small estate.[61] Consequently, the sons of less wealthy noble families and commoners, who normally also had fewer connections to aristocratic courts, travelled for only short periods, while the richer and older families with elaborate kinship and social networks could afford to send their sons abroad for many years.

On average, young nobles travelled for one or two years and attended universities only briefly. Padua and Bologna were especially favoured by Austrian noble families for their legal training, but many Protestants also sent their sons to universities in the German territories, Bohemia, Geneva and the Netherlands. Johann Wilhelm von Stubenberg, for example, travelled through France, Italy, the Netherlands and Germany, and Georg Erasmus von Tschernembl even went to England. The considerable variety of universities and countries that noble sons visited can be explained partly by the various subjects that had to be studied in different places. Law was best taught at the legal faculties of Padua and Bologna, equestrian techniques had to be learned in Paris and Florence, architecture in Rome and Genoa, and fortifications in Holland, while military tactics could be studied wherever there was a theatre of war.[62]

Since the combining of university training with a cultural tour of foreign courts required both extensive social networks and substantial economic capital, higher education in fact served to deepen social distinctions, not only between commoners and nobles, but also within the nobility. University attendance was thus higher among the Lower Austrian upper nobility, the lords, than among the lesser nobility, the knights.[63] In 1620, over two-fifths (106 out of 243) of the lords, but only one-fifth (49 out of 224) of the knights, had some higher education; moreover, the new families among the lesser nobility were able to send a higher proportion of their sons to universities than were old ones. Thus, in 1620, less than a fifth (25 out of 130) of the old knights had attended universities, in contrast to over two-fifths (24 out of 59) of the new knights, most of whom had risen from wealthy urban families.

The established nobility reinforced the inscription of social distinctions via education by discrediting a university degree as a form of cultural capital acquired only by commoners and new nobles, while valorizing the non-academic aspects of the cavalier's tour as being inherently aristocratic. Thus, most nobles, especially those from the old, upper nobility, attended university only briefly to obtain a rudimentary knowledge of Roman law. While about a fifth of the university-educated knights obtained a doctorate, nearly all of them belonged to the new nobility, and had obtained their degree before they rose to the Estate of Knights. Once they were members of the *Stände*, their sons might also visit universities, but they would not acquire degrees. The refusal of the old nobility to earn terminal degrees was not uniform in all European regions, however. Nearly as many old nobles as new completed their university studies in Aix-en-Provence with a doctorate, for example. But, while not uniform, the disdain for the legal profession was shared by many families of the old and upper nobility in other countries.[64] The upper nobility of the Austrian territories certainly made it a sign of social distinction not to enter the legal profession. None of the upper nobles held a university degree unless it had been obtained before entering the Estate of Lords. In this manner, certification, which now had an overtly utilitarian purpose attached to it, came to symbolize the education of commoners or new nobles. Since a doctorate held limited prestige and identified the holder clearly as a commoner by background, it is not surprising that it caused embarrassment among the upwardly mobile. The composer of a list of Aulic councillors in 1629 annotated the name of Caspar Terz with the remark that he disliked the title of '*doctores*' since he had become a member of the noble Estates.[65]

Clearly, cultural capital, especially in the form of a university education, offered the urban classes opportunities for social advancement. However, because of the need in early modern society to assimilate into the nobility by obtaining noble titles and emulating the lifestyle that went with it, this mobility contributed to the constant rejuvenation and reproduction of the nobility as the supreme social group, rather than undermining its legitimacy. In this way, cultural and symbolic capital secured the continuance of noble dominance. It was further buttressed by the educational model that noble families constructed for the cavalier's tour, which stressed that formal training merely enhanced the inherited, superior abilities of nobles. The study of law was supposed to be coincidental and, to distinguish their sons from commoners and newcomers, the old upper nobility emphasized that the main purpose of the cavalier's tour was to develop the young nobleman's natural capacity for prudence, valour, grace and refined taste, all of which entitled them to serve the ruler.

It was imperative, therefore, for young noblemen to continue their informal education in aristocractic modes of behaviour in a court setting.[66] The Inner Austrian noble, Sigmund von Herbertstein, reported in his diary on how, as a young man, he had followed the court of Maximilian I for some time in order to observe courtly practices and manners ('*des Hoffswesen erlernnen*'), and to meet courtiers, reflecting how much the familiarization with court culture had become part of the educational model.[67] Many Austrian nobles also visited foreign courts, and even served foreign rulers, during their cavalier's tour; thus Johann Wilhelm von Stubenberg spent some time at the court of the ruling count of Oldenburg, and Georg Raimund von Gera and Adam von Herbertstorff were sent to the court of the duke of Palatinate-Neuburg. Not only Austrian nobles considered such contacts with foreign rulers and nobles to be important, but noble parents throughout Europe also found it desirable that their sons should cultivate, in the process, an international network of friends and patrons. Like other rulers, the Habsburg emperors therefore tried to prohibit – without much success – service at foreign courts and the attendance of foreign Protestant schools. Besides a desire to ensure confessional homogeneity, the Habsburgs seem to have worried that young nobles were being exposed to new ideas, and in particular, to contractual political theories.[68]

As an alternative, after visiting a few universities, some Austrian nobles went to the Imperial or archducal court to carry out ceremonial functions, usually when they were between eighteen and twenty-two years old. Most frequently, they served meals as a *Truchsess*, and thereafter might be installed as *Fuerschneider* (meat-cutter) or as *Mundschenk* (cup-bearer). Such service in the household provided young noblemen with the opportunity both to complete their socialization and to advance to higher offices, especially if they already had forged (or were then able to forge) important social connections, or belonged to the upper nobility. They might become chamberlains, heads of departments in the household, or seek careers in the administration. For example, the baron Paul Sixtus von Trautson, who in his youth served in Maximilian's household, later became his chamberlain. The baron Seyfried Christoph von Breuner made a career by rising from the household of the archducal court in Graz to become privy councillor and president of the court treasury.[69]

The emphasis on transmitting the symbols and meanings by which nobility was recognized and legitimated should not detract from the specific vocational purpose of the cavalier's tour. On the contrary. The instructions some fathers of the upper nobility proffered for the education of their sons during their travels stressed explicitly the conversion of cultural capital into positions at the court or in the army. For example, Hartmann von Liechtenstein advised his sons to gain qualifications on their cavalier's tour in such a manner 'that today or tomorrow you can become *ministros*'.[70] This included the study of law and other academic subjects, such as languages, geography and history. In addition, they had to learn geometry, mathematics and architecture, which were useful skills for military careers.

None the less, the amount of time noble sons were to spend on the study of these scholarly subjects amounted to no more than three to four hours a day, whereas the remainder of their day was devoted to developing competence in traditional knightly skills, defined as noble *Exercitien,* such as fencing, riding, dancing, music and various games. Many of these practices had changed since the late Middle Ages, or were in the process of being transformed. For example, nobles had to learn how to ride a horse like a '*cavalliero*', rather than like a knight in uniform, and equestrian skills included complicated exercises for courtly festivities and ballets. Together with the study of military tactics and fortification technology, learning these skills was supposed to provide an understanding of form, order and hierarchy, which parents considered to be prerequisites to internalizing discipline, obedience and an appreciation of the social order.[71]

The *Exercitien* were also valued for enhancing self-control through bodily discipline. Self-control was itself a sign of noble virtue, but fathers also expected the exercises to encourage in their sons that physical grace which was needed for moving in 'high social circles'.[72] Particular attention was to be paid to their posture, which had to be upright, and gestures, which were to be measured and deliberate, and on graceful bodily movements in general, all of which supposedly distinguished natural, inherited nobility. In order to acquire competence in courtly behaviour, fathers urged their sons to visit the courts of princes or high dignitaries at lunch or dinner, and during holidays, so that they could observe noble conduct and display during festivities, ceremonies and meals. It was particularly important that they internalize the symbols of social distinctions in the order of precedence, in fashions of dress, and in other forms of conspicuous consumption, which were regulated at court according to rank. The upper nobility also put a new stress on collecting antiquarian curiosities during the cavalier's tour, and on developing an aesthetic appreciation of the arts, architecture and music, as well as refining other tastes that enhanced social distinctions symbolically.[73]

Clearly, noble fathers in the Austrian territories wanted their sons to internalize modes of behaviour and schemes of appreciation that distinguished them from commoners and prepared them for court life. Not surprisingly, courtesy-books that provided practical guidelines to a courtier's conduct, especially Castiglione's *Book of the Courtier*, became very popular during the sixteenth and seventeenth centuries. Several Latin and nine German editions were printed before 1700, with a possible readership of 27 000 in the German-speaking lands. Italian editions also existed in the libraries of Austrian, Bohemian and Hungarian noblemen, and the work was much debated among German speaking humanists. The Spanish bishop, Antonio de Guevara, copied much from Castiglione's *Courtier*, especially in his 'Advice for Favourites and Doctrine for Courtiers', even though his other work provided a humanist critique and satire of court life. Since the 'Advice', translated into German in the late sixteenth century, was popular and available in Austrian noble libraries, Castiglione's book obviously had an impact on Habsburg nobilities, and much of its prescription on style of behaviour was emphasized in the education of Austrian nobles.[74]

Like Castiglione's courtier, noble sons were to acquire distinctive tastes and cultivate perfection, harmony and grace in their appearance and behaviour during their cavalier's tour. They also tried to aquire a manner of behaviour defined by Castiglione as *sprezzatura*, which concealed what had been learned as a skill behind an appearance of being naturally accomplished, spontaneously and without effort.[75] This may represent, as Peter Burke believes, 'the construction of the self as a work of art', but it also shows how important the unconscious embodiment of cultural competency into *habitus* had become for nobles in the work of social reproduction.[76] Instructive here is the pride which sons of the old Austrian nobles felt as people recognized their high rank simply by their skilful behaviour and superior taste when they were travelling *incognito*, which they did in order to save on costs of display when on tour.[77] Passed down through generations and acquired early in life, cultural competence, complemented by scholastic learning, was to confer self-certainty in the legitimacy of aristocratic culture. Old nobility only had to be what they were, whereas social upstarts had to prove themselves because they were what they were as a result of what they did. As Bourdieu puts it, 'unselfconsciousness is the mark of socalled "natural" distinction.'[78] Although well-to-do commoners or new nobles could easily emulate the outward appearance of nobility, cultural capital in the form of an effortless superiority in lifestyle and manners took generations to cultivate.[79] Therefore, the older the family, the greater the possibility of perfecting the inherited inclination of young nobles toward virtue, graceful manners and distinctive tastes.

The strategies of the old and upper nobility to reinscribe social distinctions in educational practices makes it possible to understand why the trend in Habsburg Austria towards a scholastic education was accompanied by an equally strong tendency to teach courtly behaviour. Some historians have claimed that this signified a shift, around 1600, from travels concentrating on university study to a cavalier's tour serving primarily the acquisition of court etiquette and social skills.[80] However, it seems doubtful that such a change occurred at this time, or subsequently, considering that university attendance continued to increase in the decades after 1600, and that the educational strategy of the Liechtenstein family in the mid-seventeenth century did not differ substantially from the aims of the Herbertstein family during the sixteenth. In fact, lesson plans for the cavalier's tour show that the time noblemen devoted to the study of academic subjects in fact increased.[81] Evidently, by the early seventeenth century, scholastic training through university attendance had become more widely accepted as being essential for career advancement and family continuance, and noble families had finally resolved the tensions and problems posed by the new type of education. They strengthened the formal education of their sons by paying greater attention to the new vocational requirements, while simultaneously reinvesting all cultural capital with symbolic meaning which better suited their social status and position. As noble identity became defined increasingly by courtly ideals, specific cultural practices became even more essential in distinguishing old nobles from newcomers and commoners. And this synthesis and reconstruction of the educational model became the ideal of noble schooling throughout the seventeenth century. Even though not all of the lesser nobles could afford to emulate it completely, the cavalier's tour had become essential in completing the socializing process of young noblemen.

Redefining virtue and the conversion of cultural capital

The evidence suggests that the social mobility of educated commoners and the transformation of the educational model created an incongruity between social practices and the principles of noble legitimation. As I showed in the previous chapter, this had already led to struggles between nobles, Habsburgs and newcomers over social classification. Simultaneously, debates developed over conceptions of nobility, especially categories of virtue and merit. As with redefining the rules of admission to the noble Estates, and the reconstruction of the educational model, the central issues were whether and how to change the categories through which people perceived social advance and legitimized nobility. The Habsburgs, newcomers, and even nobles of the Austrian territories, aimed at modifying the position of the old nobility within the scheme of social classification, albeit in different ways.

Because the Habsburgs were in the process of changing the flow of court patronage, they had a stake in altering the rules that legitimized noble dominance. Recall that upward mobility of urban families into the nobility was high, and the ascent of new men within noble ranks rapid, changing the composition of the Lower Austrian nobility and the Imperial court. Two-fifths of the families belonging to the upper and lower noble Estates in 1620 were newcomers, and a substantial proportion of the top positions at the Imperial court were given to new barons. Recall also that two-thirds of the Imperial privy councillors from the upper nobility, and a third of the men appointed to the highest positions in the household, belonged to the new baronage. Habsburg rulers, it appears, considered merit to be equal to noble virtue, but believed that virtue could be acquired within one generation through education and service.

This social advancement of commoners prompted critics of nobility, mainly from the urban classes, to challenge publicly traditional noble conceptions of virtue and merit, and to develop new ideas that lent theoretical support to upward mobility. Some of the judicial tracts of the time were particularly offensive to the nobility, since they argued that title of doctor itself conferred noble status. This idea, based on a reinterpretation of the Roman law definition of *militia inermis* (unarmed military), considered the status of doctor, especially the *doctor legum*, as a form of public service that was equal to the noble status of the warrior. In short, these critics believed that education itself conveyed noble virtue. Other theorists focused on legitimizing the act of ennoblement by the prince, on the grounds that a noble title could be granted by the ruler without any reason, and certainly did not have to be justified by birth and natural ability (*sanguis sive virtus*). The opposition to these views was vehement, and argued strongly against the notion of a *nobilitas scientiae sive literaria* because an academic title could not be inherited and nobles did not even try to obtain certification.[82]

Obviously, the nobility felt threatened by adulteration, and feared that merit would become synonymous with educational qualifications. The older nobles particularly preferred the traditional notion that they inherited superior moral, mental and physical virtues, and believed that virtue alone was of sufficient merit to legitimize the socio-political dominance and privileges of the nobility. As I showed earlier, Austrian nobles considered important and prestigious offices at court and in the military to be their preserve, insisting that noble virtue equalled merit. The old and upper nobility in particular felt that the hierarchy of offices should reflect and reproduce the existing social structure. But this came into conflict with the Habsburgs, who, in order to enhance their authority and control over patronage, aimed to upset the homology between social stratification and court hierarchy by advancing a new upper nobility.

The older nobility resisted the Habsburg conception of virtue and merit. The Upper Austrian nobility complained in 1586 that persons of low birth could 'rise to high positions, status and honour merely through the means of studies'.[83] The nobility of Lower Austria demanded repeatedly during the late sixteenth and early seventeenth centuries that the Habsburg rulers not show preference for educated commoners in offices, and regulate more strictly social distinctions, especially in conspicuous consumption. They even asked Rudolf II to reject new nobles as office-holders unless they had reached the third degree of noble rank.[84] Although the emperor ignored this demand, we saw in Chapter 4 that during the late sixteenth century the Lower Austrian nobility was successful in restricting the power of the Habsburgs over noble classifications, and established the rule that only members admitted by the nobility into the Estate of Knights or Estate of Lords were entitled to the important economic benefits and privileges derived from noble status. In addition to creating a new distinction between nobility and noble Estates, the nobles initiated a series of rules for regulating social mobility that aimed to clarify the demarcation of nobility and fix the distinctions within it, rather than simply close the Estate to newcomers. They clearly defined the lifestyle, economic capital and social status required for entry into the noble Estates, and for mobility within them. Even though, after 1612, these rules required new nobles to produce proof of nobility in the third degree (agnates and cognates) for admission to the Estate of Knights, the recruitment practices of the noble Estates indicate that they remained a relatively open elite who accepted the idea that noble virtue could be acquired through service and training, albeit only after three generations. In other words, virtue had to be passed on through generations, and new nobles had continually to prove their worth and perfect their virtue. The Austrian nobility had thus reconstructed a conception of virtue and merit that was compatible with the new educational model it advanced, reinforcing the idea that education merely enhanced its inherited capacity to virtue.

The attitude of the established nobility naturally caused resentment among learned men from the urban classes, including poets and scholars, such as Sebastian Franck and Nicodemus Frischlin. The latter often used abusive language in condemning the nobility for its arrogant refusal to consider men with high academic titles as equals, and reprimanded nobles collectively for their lack of moral virtue and cruelty towards the peasantry. Frequently, German nobles silenced such critics with imprisonment and exile, and engaged theorists of nobility in their defence. The Austrian nobles did not sponsor their own theoretical response to critics. However, Protestant nobles of Southern Germany appear to have commissioned Cyriacius Spangenberg's *Adels Spiegel* (Mirror of Nobility), which was written between 1591 and 1594.

The work was certainly known among the Austrian Protestant nobility, and its ideas were congruent with the conceptions of virtue and merit they expressed in their opposition to Habsburg recruitment policies and in their revision of admission rules to the noble Estates.[85] It also reflects the ideas of other defenders of nobility in the Reich who grounded noble ethic in Christian versions of ancient moral philosophy, and emphasized the virtues of *pietas* (moral strength), *prudentia* (wisdom, good judgement), *temperantia* (moderation, self-control), *liberalitas* (kindness, generosity), *constantia* (endurance, dependability) and *fortitudo* (physical strength, courage).[86]

Spangenberg's Christian humanism maintained the link between virtue and nobility by insisting that it was virtue that ennobled. And he insisted that nobility 'is not derived from right of birth, but it is virtue that leads to distinction. He who is always devoted to virtue, proves to be of true nobility. He who sins in a beastly way, cannot be truly noble'.[87] Nobility, he believed, was not a natural state, because everyone descended in some way from Adam. Nevertheless, Spangenberg reasserted the legitimacy of nobility by stressing that it was instituted by God, because rulers needed aid and counsel, and he affirmed that a natural superiority of body and mind could be inherited. Like other German moral philosophical tracts of the late sixteenth and early seventeenth centuries, Spangenberg differentiated between a Christian nobility of virtue (*nobilitas virtutis*) and a political nobility (*nobilitas politica*). The latter had to possess the internal virtues of the former, but in addition required external confirmation of its distinction (*Vorzug*), such as possession of political authority (*in Obrigkeit sitzen*), a good reputation with others, and honours and titles bestowed by the prince. *Nobilitas politica* could be inherited (*Erbadel*), but it was also bestowed by the prince for service and other merit. It could be bought or assumed, which Spangenberg associated negatively with acquisition by force (*Gewaltsamkeit*). While acknowledging the existence of a nobility of learned men, he did not equate this 'weisen Adel' with political nobility, since the former still had to obtain noble status through the proper channels. Stressing service to country and community ('Vatterlandsheil') for all political nobility, Spangenberg considered it particularly important for newly-created nobles. He displayed a positive attitude towards new nobility, especially when a title was obtained by a devout man for service or courageous deeds, but stressed repeatedly that old and inherited nobility were a superior Estate if supported by a virtuous lifestyle.[88] In addition, he emphasized the virtues of learning in literature, rhetoric, philosophy and ethics (but typically not in law), as a useful adornment and sign of noble distinction. Clearly, then, Spangenberg wanted to give legitimacy to legal or new nobility, and lent support to the idea that it was an old custom and right of rulers to ennoble commoners. At the same time, he was willing to buttress the idea of the superiority of inherited nobility as long it was sustained by a virtuous lifestyle reinforced by education and service.[89]

Spangenberg's theories were therefore compatible with the notion that old nobles in the Austrian territories had come to accept: namely that their predisposition to virtue had to be activated through proper upbringing and formal education.[90] As Sigmund von Herbertstein put it: 'it was not enough to be born of noble and virtuous ancestors'. He opposed the idea that nobles could simply base their virtue on the deeds of their ancestors; rather, they should be required to prove their nobility through their own virtuous actions.[91] The Austrian nobility could more easily accept the right of rulers to create new nobles on the basis of education and service (*virtus civilis*) once it had reconstructed the new educational model, made it congruent with its own conception of nobility, and refined the external boundaries and internal divisions of the social structure. From that time, new nobility had to prove the virtue it acquired through education and service for at least three generations. Only then would they be able to act like true nobility, and gain admission into the noble Estates in order to benefit from the privileges and freedoms the nobility deserved by right of birth. For upstarts, virtue and merit were earned through intergenerational accumulation and habituation. In contrast, old nobles, who had inherited a capacity for virtue, merely needed to activate their natural superiority of mind and body through individual upbringing.[92] Nevertheless, by the early seventeenth century they were accepting academic training readily as a shining reflection of this superior ability.

The contest over categories of noble virtue thus led to a redefinition of merit that included academic qualifications orientated towards service of the ruler. The Austrian nobility accepted this idea, but only after reinscribing traditional social distinctions in the new educational model. In the process, the established nobility also agreed to transform traditional meanings of noble virtue. From then onwards, prudence had to include scholastic training and valour, complemented by knowledge in mathematics, fortification science, and skills in dancing and games fashioned by the court. Furthermore, liberality and temperance became orientated towards courtly manners, gracefulness and *sprezzatura*. Even notions of *constantia* and *pietas* were imbued with new meaning as the religious struggle prompted the Habsburgs further to transform conceptions of merit by equating loyalty with Catholicism. However, as I shall show presently, on this issue the Protestant nobility proved unwilling to accommodate them.

Similar struggles over cultural and symbolic capital are evident throughout Western Europe. But in the Austrian territories they differed because there they coincided with the Counter Reformation. For the Protestant majority, the differences between rulers and Estates over religion complicated the conversion of cultural and symbolic capital into other resources, and this threatened the dynastic reproduction of the Protestant nobility, as an examination of confessional differences in the acquisition of cultural capital and the effect education and religion had on the competition over court patronage between Protestant and Catholic nobles demonstrates.

It testifies to the importance of social and dynastic reproduction that few differences existed in the educational strategies of Protestant and Catholic nobles, both combining the learning of vocational skills with the transmission of the symbols and meanings of noble culture. Although the Jesuits offered more uniformity, both confessions centred the elementary curriculum on the *humanitas christiana*. The aims and structure of higher education were also surprisingly similar, although Protestant nobles attended Catholic universities in Italy as well as centres of learning in non-Catholic territories. The main difference in the education of Protestant and Catholic nobility lay in the study of religious dogma and the inculcation of distinct religious identities with different practices and values.[93]

Between 1580 and 1620 another difference emerged in the frequency of university attendance, at least among Catholic and Protestant nobles from Lower Austria. Since it has become commonplace to assume that Protestants put greater emphasis on learning, it is noteworthy that, with about two-fifths (48 out of 116) of its sons attending universities, the Catholic nobility still had a higher proportion of males with higher education in 1620 than did the Protestant nobility, a third (105 out of 322) of whom had enrolled at universities. This had less to do with different emphases placed by Catholic and Protestant families on learning but, instead, can be explained by the Habsburgs' rapid advancement of educated commoners and lesser nobles into the Catholic noble Estates of Lower Austria, leading to a tripling of university-educated people among the Catholic noble Estates (knights and lords). Nevertheless, by 1620 the Protestant nobility had almost caught up with the educational level of Catholics, which had been proportionally much higher in 1580.[94] Thus the percentage of Protestant nobles (knights and lords) who attended universities more than doubled (from 41 to 105) between 1580 and 1620. This was achieved mainly by Protestant families of the upper nobility, whose university-educated members more than tripled (from 22 to 74) by 1620, so that the proportion of Protestant lords with higher learning increased from about a quarter to nearly a half.[95] Although the number of Protestant knights with higher education came close to doubling (from 19 to 31), the proportion of Catholic knights, two-fifths of whom had registered in universities, was still large compared with a fifth of the Protestant knights.[96]

When considering how many of the Lower Austrian nobles with university education found employment with the Habsburgs in 1620, it becomes clear that most of the Protestants among them were unable to convert the cultural capital they had acquired during their cavalier's tour into other resources. Only about a fifth (14 out of 74) of the university-educated Protestant lords were in Habsburg service. This compares very unfavourably to the three-quarters (23 out of 32) of the educated Catholic lords who belonged to the service nobility. The cultural capital of the Protestant knights had suffered even greater devaluation, with only two of the thirty-one university educated among them employed by the crown.[97] Since the talents of such a high proportion of university-educated Protestants remained unused, the higher educational level of Catholic nobles cannot explain why the Habsburgs preferred them over Protestant servants.

This chapter has shown, then, that despite the existence of a number of competing centres of patronage, the Habsburg court had become a central 'marketplace' where members of a diverse elite strove to enhance the resources of their families. However, exchange was focused not merely on economic but also on symbolic, social and cultural capital. In fact, these various forms of power were intrinsically intertwined and essential to noble reproduction. Status, prestige, honour and cultural capital underpinned patronage relations at court and were all necessary to take full advantage of the patronage. In fact, the display of symbolic, social and cultural capital at court had become imperative for their conversion into material resources.

The increasing desire for patronage and presence at the Imperial court helped the Habsburg rulers to better regulate social relations among the elite and to co-opt nobles into supporting state-building efforts. In particular, court patronage fostered the integration of a new state elite and tied it more closely to the dynasty's interests. But not all of these efforts were successful. Certainly, the Habsburgs were able to eliminate an over-dependence on old, established aristocratic families in key positions of the household and administration. At the same time, they observed some of the established rules of recruitment according to rank and seniority, and distributed their favours among men from various regions, even though they preferred the Catholic elites of German-speaking lands as their servants. The nature of clientelism required that rulers balance factions and stabilize the competitive atmosphere they created with the selective distribution of their patronage. But, as I shall show in the following chapter, the Habsburgs ultimately failed to harness the disintegrative forces of clientelism, largely because they confessionalized their strategies of recruitment far too rapidly, without allowing for appropriate cultural adjustment.

This chapter has argued that the Habsburg court was a force for social change which promoted the transformation of the cultural habits of nobles as they realigned their strategies of reproduction and social identities to meet the new requirements in serving rulers. The pursuit of distinctions in the form of rank, behaviour and taste, had a civilizing effect on nobles. They shed some of their habits of violence, and slowly began to apply a new professionalism in their careers. The new rules of conduct and sociability also imbued the court with enhanced splendour and prestige, allowing it to set the standards of behaviour and taste for elite society at large.

This transformation did not involve overt Habsburg coercion, because the new requirements at court intersected with the interests of noble families. Dynastic reproduction and enhancement in early modern society depended to a large extent on the collective embodiment of noble culture, especially its symbolic order, into the *habitus* of young sons. Reproducing noble culture in this way also helped to secure continued noble dominance of the social structure. But innovation was involved. As I showed in this chapter, the changes that occurred in social relations during the sixteenth century in connection with new educational standards at court required an adjustment of the symbolic framework. In order to uphold existing divisions between nobles and commoners, while accommodating changed educational necessities, families of the established nobility reinscribed traditional social distinctions in a new educational model and imbued vocational values with social purpose. In particular, they refused certification and combined academic schooling with training in court culture.

Adapting cultural practices to the principles of noble legitimation also required that the nobility counter its critics and the Habsburgs, who equated virtue and merit with education. In order to enforce their own conception of merit, which they believed was derived only from noble virtue, Austrian nobles insisted that education simply enhanced their inherited capacity for virtue, and that scholastic training orientated towards service was merely a manifestation of that mental and physical superiority that entitled them to leadership. Refashioning conceptions of noble virtue and merit, and reconstructing the external boundaries and internal divisions of nobility, opened the possibility for noble families to accept a reorientation of education to include scholastic training and university attendance. While families of the upper nobility greatly improved the educational qualifications of their sons, the lower nobles, and especially the older families among them, were less able to do so because of the high cost of the cavalier's tour. This deepened the social and economic divisions within the nobility.

Differentiating educational qualifications by confession revealed that Protestantism did not lead automatically to a higher level of education, and that the Counter Reformation complicated the conversion of cultural and symbolic capital into other forms of resources for the Protestant nobles. Even though Protestant families, especially among the upper nobility, had by 1620 almost succeeded in catching up to the level of Catholics in higher education, their cultural capital had become practically worthless. As the following chapter shows in more detail, the Habsburgs began to equate merit and loyalty with Catholicism, and favoured Catholics with their patronage, suddenly confronting Protestant nobles with an incongruity between their *habitus* and the real conditions surrounding them. Their unwillingness to convert in the face of such incentives and pressures shows that, before 1620, the Habsburg Court was unsuccessful in fully transforming and homogenizing noble culture.

6
Confessionalizing Court Patronage

Although historians have noted that by 1650 few Protestants were serving at the Imperial court, they have not explored the religious composition of the court very much, either before or after the Battle of the White Mountain.[1] Instead, they have concentrated on the impact of defeat on the Protestant opposition in Bohemia, and in particular on the distribution of noble landholdings. This is unsatisfactory, because the changes induced by Habsburg patronage, demography and social mobility on the structure of the Imperial court prior to 1620 were, in fact, crucial. And they were, in turn, fused with counter-reformatory strategies, material interests, and the state-building process, so it is difficult to understate their overall historical importance. Here, in the final chapter of this book, I argue that increased rivalry between the Catholic and Protestant elites over vacancies at court was a major cause underpinning the formation of a grand alliance against Habsburg policies by a section of the Protestant nobility. Because the rulers' patronage flowed almost entirely in the direction of new Catholic men, very few Lower Austrian Protestants were in Habsburg service in 1620, and the Imperial court was dominated by a Catholic faction. This explains why, as I showed in Chapter 2, hardly any of the Protestant nobles who joined the Confederates held appointments at Court. Forced to withdraw to the countryside, a substantial proportion of the Austrian Protestant elite began to organize their opposition under the banner of religion and corporate rights.

I begin with a statistical analysis of the confessional composition of the Imperial court, which provides the requisite background for highlighting the extent and impact of Habsburg recruitment strategies on provincial nobles. A detailed examination of the allotment of offices to Lower Austrian nobles follows, and further illuminates how confessionalizing court patronage affected the distribution of landholding and fuelled competition between Protestants and Catholics. Finally, determining the actual confessional, social and economic divisions between court and country nobility makes it possible to evaluate the impact of court patronage on the political position Protestant nobles took in 1620.

Rechannelling patronage at the Imperial court

Habsburg strategy to force the religious conversion of the Protestant elite by denying them access to the centres of power was planned carefully long before 1620. As was noted in Chapter 2, in October 1579 the Habsburg archdukes resolved in a meeting with the Catholic Duke of Bavaria to provoke Protestant opposition in order to have a pretext for withdrawing all their religious concessions. Part of this counter-reform programme stipulated the replacement of Protestant officials with Catholics, and to begin the process in the Privy Council.[2] A few months earlier, the Catholic privy councillor, Dr Eder, had swept away concerns that there were not enough Catholics around to replace Protestant servants in the event that they all resigned simultaneously from their posts in protest. Pointing out that many nobles would be unable to 'eat their soup' (*nicht die Suppen vermöchten*) without service to the crown, he was convinced that the Catholic faith could be saved only by stopping the 'harmful' preference of Lutheran officials at the Imperial court, and replacing them with Catholics.[3] But the really important question is: how successful were the Habsburgs in implementing the policy of 1579 during the following half century?

The evidence appears contradictory. We do know that, in Inner Austria, Archduke Charles II soon gave preference to Catholic officials, especially in his Privy Council, and his confessor reported in 1580 that the 'situation was finally at a stage where those who did not wish to become Catholic would be dismissed'. A list of officials installed by his successor, Archduke Ferdinand, shows that the policy was also implemented in all other Inner Austrian councils.[4] In contrast, the sources, such as Eder's reports to the Bavarian archdukes, suggest that the replacement of Protestant servants at the Lower Austrian Court progressed at a snail's pace. Contradicting this is Cardinal Khlesl's satisfied report of 1604 that Catholics were more numerous at the archducal court than Protestants. However, we do not know whether this was an acute observation or an effort to appease the militant Catholic faction.[5]

Eder also wrote in 1582 about the Imperial court, regretting that even though a beginning had been made at promoting Catholics, this was soon abandoned in favour of Protestants who seemed to have better kinship networks.[6] Rudolf II, wanting to remain neutral, is supposed to have selected his advisers from both confessions, or preferred individuals with weak confessional commitments, at least during his early reign. Such observations are based on Councillor Eder's scathing reports to the Bavarian duke that one could not tell with certainty what faith prevailed among many 'court Christians' (*Hoffchristen*), particularly among those who had converted to Catholicism.[7] It appears, however, that towards the end of the sixteenth century Rudolf did give in to the more radical plans of his family, in both Austria and Spain, to re-Catholicize his territories, and on 24 August, 1599, the anniversary of St. Bartholomew's Massacre, he dismissed a few of his Protestant advisers, replacing them with Catholics.

Evidently, then, progress in eliminating Protestants was intermittent. As we observed in Chapter 2, Matthias's need for allies from both Catholic and Protestant camps in deposing his brother gave non-Catholics new hope, which was further nurtured by their contacts with Protestants in the German territories and Europe at large. During 1607–9, the Austrian Protestant Estates had also demonstrated their ability to form an alliance to bargain with the Habsburgs, and in 1609 they had obtained Matthias's promise to make appointments according to qualifications rather than religious affiliation.[8] In the case of the Bohemian administration, Matthias certainly continued to give preference to Catholic servants, although we know little about the composition of the court at Prague.[9] Furthermore, we saw that between 1618 and 1620 renewed grievances of both the Bohemian and the Austrian Protestant opposition regarding their continued exclusion from court patronage suggests long-term success in filling court vacancies with Catholics.[10]

Indeed, the analysis of the religious background of top servants in the Imperial household and administration shows that a new Catholic nobility was already dominant in the most important offices before 1620. A number of honorary sinecures traditionally held by nobles of the hereditary lands was firmly in the hands of new Catholic families. Thus the post of *Erbland-Obersthofmarschallamt* (master of the household) had been given to a Catholic family, the Trautsons, from the Tyrol, in 1531, and they were raised to the barony just ten years later. The Harrach family, also Catholic, had been *Erblandstallmeister* (master of the horse) from 1552, the year when the family advanced to the barony. When old, high-ranking, Protestant families became extinct, or were disgraced or converted, the Habsburgs would reward the remaining few Catholic families of old nobility with honorary sinecures.[11] In August 1620, the Austrian branch of the Breuners, a Catholic family from Styria, who had been residing in Lower Austria for three generations and had been barons since 1550, were invested with *Erbland-Oberstkämmereramt* (master of the chambers) after the barons von Eitzing, an old Lower Austrian Protestant family, had become extinct in the male line. The barons von Rogendorf, another old indigenous Protestant family who held the post of *Erbland-Hofmeisteramt* (master of the court), were replaced by the Catholic barons von Trautson in 1620 as a result of Georg Ehrenreich von Rogendorf's conviction for treason.[12] In addition, the Habsburg emperors clearly favoured Catholics in the most important non-hereditary positions in the household. In fact, only five of the twenty-five top household officials appointed by Rudolf II, Matthias, and Ferdinand II, and whose confession could be identified, belonged to the Protestant faith.[13]

The confessionalization of Habsburg patronage was also effective at the level of the administrative councils. Nearly all of the presidents of the Aulic council, and Imperial vice chancellors installed between 1580 and 1620, belonged to Catholic families.[14] Moreover, the background of some forty privy councillors who served during the reigns of Rudolf II and Matthias, and who were installed at the beginning of Ferdinand's reign, reveals that the Imperial Privy Council was a stronghold of Catholics long before 1620.[15] Only two of these privy councillors belonged to the Protestant confession, and they were exceptional. Heinrich Julius, Duke of Braunschweig-Wolffenbuettel (1607–13), a German prince and Lutheran, was probably the most active and able of Rudolf II's privy councillors. Although opposed by the Catholic faction, he managed to retain the trust of Rudolf, who appointed him master of the court (*Obersthofmeister*) and director of the Privy Council. It speaks for Heinrich Julius's diplomatic abilities and moderate attitudes that he continued in service under Matthias until his sudden death.[16] Equally exceptional was the position of the other Protestant privy councillor, Wolf Sigmund Losenstein, whom Matthias appointed *Obersthofmarschall* in 1612. A moderate among the Protestant faction, he was also one of the few councillors who belonged to the ancient nobility of the hereditary lands. Although it is remarkable that Ferdinand II confirmed his appointment, he actually removed him from active service.[17]

Clearly, then, Habsburg strategies of replacing Protestants with Catholics had a profound effect on changing both the social and the confessional composition of the Imperial court and, with it, power relations. As we observed in the previous chapter, the emperors favoured new barons and nobles as servants, but it also appears that their social status was subsidiary to their religious background. Since the pool of old Catholic nobles was relatively small in the territories where the emperor resided – Bohemia and Lower Austria – it is not surprising that many of the new barons and nobles employed by them originated in other territories, and particularly in the Reich. Despite his complaints about the slow re-Catholization of the Court, Privy Councillor Eder was, in fact, well aware of the difficulties in finding Catholic servants. When Rudolf II urged Matthias in 1605 to dismiss his Austrian privy councillors, the Archduke declared that it was difficult to replace them with Catholic candidates.[18] Matthias had, of course, not only a confessional agenda, but also sought to placate his friends among the Austrian Protestant nobles, whose support he still needed to wrest the throne from his brother. This may also explain why Rudolf favoured German over Austrian nobles with his patronage. However, Matthias, once he achieved his goals, soon pursued a similar strategy of distributing his patronage to Catholic men, and for this he too had to rely frequently on nobles and commoners from other German principalities.

The Protestants' criticism of the Privy Council, which I outlined in Chapter 3, takes on a new significance when we consider that the council had become a stronghold of a new, Catholic nobility which also came largely from 'foreign' territories. It also puts into perspective a policy established in 1617, which stipulated that Aulic councillors had to be chosen equally from the Reich, from Lower Austria and from Upper Austria.[19] Apparently the proportion of Lower Austrian nobles among the Imperial Aulic councillors had declined significantly after 1576 as a consequence of replacing Protestants with a new Catholic baronage.[20] Both the demand of the Estates for a representation of local nobles in the Imperial Aulic council, and the request of 1618 for the re-establishment of a purely Austrian Aulic council, would have increased the presence of Lower Austrian Protestants in the central administration, and testify to the dissatisfaction of the nobility of the hereditary lands with the distribution of court patronage. However, the Austrian *Hofrat* was not re-established, and the demands for regulating appointments by territorial origin were ignored consistently.

Unfulfilled ambitions: career advancement of provincial nobles

It remains to be investigated what effect the confessionalization of Habsburg patronage at the Imperial court had on provincial nobilities, and how this influenced internal divisions and political choices between 1618 and 1620. Focusing again on the case of Lower Austrian nobles, two major trends stand out. First, after 1579, employment opportunities at court were declining at all levels for the old, indigenous members of the noble Estates. Second, those principally affected by this change were Protestant nobles, who tended to belong to old local families.

The lesser nobility was affected most visibly by the decline in Habsburg patronage. Thus, between 1580 and 1620 the number of Lower Austrian knights in the service of the crown declined by nearly a half (from ninety-one to forty-nine),[21] with the proportion of princely servants among the entire *Ritterstand* decreasing from about a third to just over a fifth (see Table 6.1).[22] As we observed regarding the composition of the Imperial court in the previous chapter, lesser nobles frequently were installed as councillors in the court treasury, or held other subordinate positions in the financial administration. They also found employment as councillors or secretaries of the lower courts, or as managers (*Pfleger*) and foresters (*Forstmeister*) on crown lands.[23] However, opportunities for knights in the last two categories declined by 1620, because the Habsburgs had also made it a policy to employ foreign Catholics and non-noble officials to administer crown lands. This practice was much criticized by the *Stände* at their assemblies.[24]

On the surface, the opportunities for the Lower Austrian high nobility remained similar to what they had been in 1580, with the total number of lords serving the Habsburgs slightly increased. However, there were significant changes in the distribution of lords within various offices, and a substantial growth of the country nobility (*Landadel*), who served neither the Habsburgs nor the Estates. The proportion of lords with appointments in the administration and the household diminished by about a fifth (from

Table 6.1 Distribution of offices among Lower Austrian knights, 1580 and 1620

Position	*1580*		*1620*	
	Knights	*%**	*Knights*	*%**
Household	20	7	7	3
Political/judicial administration	23	8	16	7
Financial administration	14	5	8	4
Other positions	16	6	–	–
Military administration	4	1	4	2
Military service	14	5	14	6
Total of crown's servants	**91**	**32**	**49**	**22**
Estates' servants	23	8	17	7
Total service nobility	**114**	**40**	**66**	**29**
Confederate army	–	–	19	8
Landadel	**168**	**60**	**142**	**63**
Knights holding double functions*	–1		–3	
Total	**281**	**100**	**224**	**100**

Note: *Percentages have been rounded off. Since some nobles held double positions (usually in both the household and administration), they had to be counted in both categories and then deducted from the total in order to arrive at the correct base number.

seventy-three to fifty-seven), and it is only because the officer class had multiplied (because the country was in a state of war in 1620), that in absolute numbers the lords in Habsburg service remained virtually at the previous level.[25] Recall, however, that membership in the Estate of Lords had more than doubled since 1580. With the number of offices remaining fairly stable, it is clear that many of the newcomers found themselves excluded from Habsburg patronage. This had the effect of increasing the ranks of the country nobility fourfold (from 43 to 163). Consequently, the ratio between country nobles and those serving the crown and Estates reversed, so that in 1620 only about a third of the Lower Austrian lords belonged to the 'service nobility';[26] in 1580 it had been around two-thirds (Table 6.2). The proportion of courtiers among the lords in the Habsburg administration and household alone had declined from about three-fifths to one-fifth, which in part reflects Ferdinand II's preference for Inner-Austrians. Only two members of the Lower Austrian Estates (Adam and Hans Bernhard von Herbertstein) were holding important positions in the household in 1620, and even they belonged to the Catholic branch of a Styrian family. If we combine the figures for lords and knights, then the proportion of princely servants among the Lower Austrian nobility

Table 6.2 Distribution of offices among Lower Austrian lords, 1580 and 1620

Position	*1580*		*1620*	
	Lords	*%**	*Lords*	*%**
Household	36	28	24	10
Political/judicial administration	25	19	17	7
Financial administration	5	4	8	3
Other positions	1	1	3	1
Military administration	6	5	5	2
Military service	5	4	23	9
Total of crown's servants	**78**	**61**	**80**	**32**
Estates' servants	8	6	11	4
Total service nobility	**86**	**67**	**91**	**36**
Confederate army	–	–	11	4
Landadel	**43**	**33**	**152**	**60**
Lords holding double functions*	–10		–11	
Total	**119**	**100**	**243**	**100**

Note: *Percentages have been rounded off. Since some nobles held double positions (usually in both the household and administration), they had to be counted in both categories and then deducted from the total in order to arrive at the correct base number.

declined from about two-fifths (169 out of 411) to a little over a quarter (129 out of 481).

Obviously, the Habsburgs no longer favoured Lower Austrian nobles with their patronage in the form of court appointments. This was not only a consequence of Ferdinand II bringing his Inner Austrian entourage to the Imperial court, but also the result of confessionalizing patronage. The rapid succession of rulers during the early seventeenth century and the extinction of old knightly families, the majority of whom belonged to old indigenous families, helped to facilitate the replacement of Protestants by Catholic newcomers from other territories. Most important, the merging of the archducal with the Imperial court at Vienna in 1612 enabled Emperor Matthias to rid himself of about two-thirds of the Protestant officials from Lower Austria. By 1620, Lower Austrian Protestant nobles serving in administrative offices alone had declined from 122 to 43.[27]

The confessionalization of merit and patronage restructured the social composition of the territorial service nobility profoundly and led to the emergence of a large group of 'unemployed' nobles. Once we differentiate between the lesser and upper nobility, and between new and old nobles, it is apparent that the old Lower Austrian knights in particular were affected by reduced opportunities at court. Thus the number of old Lower Austrian knights serving the Habsburgs declined dramatically, by nearly four-fifths (from fifty-four to eleven) after 1580, so that about a tenth (or eleven) of the old knights were princely servants, and more than four-fifths (eighty-nine plus fourteen employed by the Confederate army) of the old *Ritterstand* were neither employed by the Habsburgs nor by the Estates in 1620.[28] In contrast, crown servants among the newly-admitted knights greatly outnumbered the old members (Table 6.3).[29]

Career opportunities also diminished for the old Lower Austrian lords, and in 1620 the proportion of the princely servants among them had declined, from about two-thirds to one-third (Table 6.4).[30] Consequently, those without office or charge among the old Estate of Lords more than tripled (from twenty-five to eighty-one).[31] However, among the newly-admitted members, the country nobility also increased fourfold (from eighteen to seventy-one). And because in the new *Herrenstand* members had multiplied more rapidly (it had more than doubled) than the old Estate, the proportion (over one half) of 'unemployed' people was in fact substantially smaller among the new lords than among the old, nearly two-thirds of whom were without a position. In fact, by 1620, the newly-admitted members had benefited from Habsburg patronage to such an extent that the

Table 6.3 Distribution of offices among old and new knights, 1580 and 1620

Position	*1580*				*1620*			
	Old	*%*	*New*	*%*	*Old*	*%*	*New*	*%*
Crown's servants	54	24	37	66	11	9	38	37
Estates' servants	22	10	1	2	11	9	6	6
Service nobility	**76**	**34**	**38**	**68**	**22**	**18**	**44**	**43**
Confederate army	–	–	–	–	14	11	5	5
Country nobility	**150**	**66**	**18**	**32**	**89**	**71**	**53**	**52**
Total	226	100	56	100	125	100	102	100

Table 6.4 Distribution of offices among old and new lords, 1580 and 1620

Position	*1580*				*1620*			
	Old	*%*	*New*	*%*	*Old*	*%*	*New*	*%*
Crown's servants	41	57	37	65	37	29	43	34
Estates' servants	6	8	2	3	3	2	8	6
Service nobility	**47**	**65**	**39**	**68**	**40**	**31**	**51**	**40**
Confederate army	–	–	–	–	6	5	5	4
Country nobility	**25**	**35**	**18**	**32**	**81**	**64**	**71**	**56**
Total	72	100	57	100	127	100	127	100

service nobility among them outnumbered those among the old *Herrenstand.*[32] This was a reversal of the situation in 1580, when courtiers had been more numerous among old members.

As the previous analysis of status mobility and of the background of top officials at the Imperial court revealed, the Habsburg rulers were advancing new men because they were Catholic. In other words, they were, in principle, not opposed to advancing old and established nobles had they not tended to hold on to the Protestant faith. The confessionalization of court patronage explains, then, why the losses of positions among the old members of the noble Estates coincided with the decline of office-holders among Protestants, and why the gains by newcomers were almost entirely absorbed by Catholics. Since the majority of the old, established nobility were Protestants, the Habsburgs were forced to appoint Catholic newcomers from territories other than Lower Austria. The effect this had on the Lower Austrian Protestant nobility was devastating. In 1580, the Protestant knights had outnumbered Catholic members of the Lower Austrian *Ritterstand* in all offices at court, and they had dominated the Estates' administration (see Figure 6.1).[33] Despite the fact that in 1620 the Protestants still constituted a majority, the Catholic knights held both a

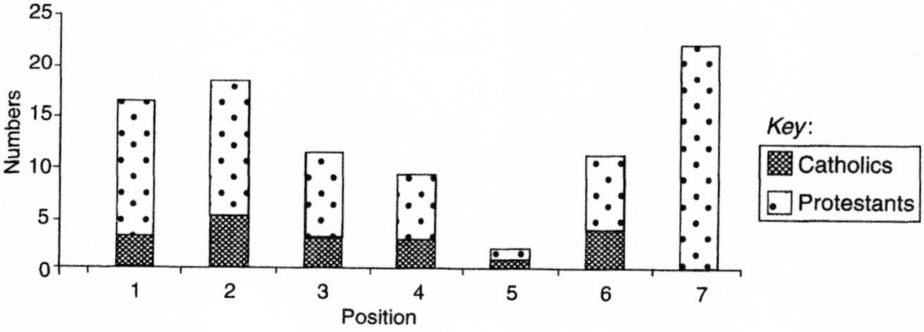

Key to positions:
1. Household
2. Political/judicial administration
3. Financial administration
4. Other offices
5. Military administration
6. Military service (excluding Confederate army)
7. Estates' organization

Figure 6.1 Numerical distribution of positions among Protestant and Catholic knights, 1580

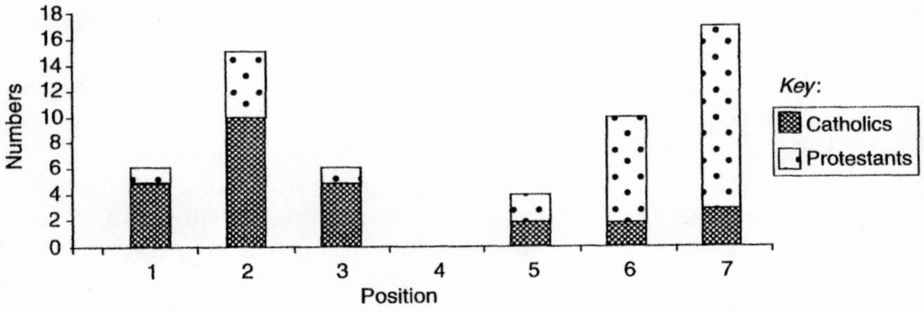

Key to positions:
1. Household
2. Political/judicial administration
3. Financial administration
4. Other offices
5. Military administration
6. Military service (excluding Confederate army)
7. Estates' organization

Figure 6.2 Numerical distribution of positions among Protestant and Catholic Knights, 1620

greater number of positions and the most important functions at court (see Figure 6.2).[34] As a consequence, the number of Lower Austrian Protestant knights who served in the household and in the administration diminished by almost four-fifths, with the result that in 1620 only about one-tenth of the Protestant knights were serving the Habsburgs. Even if we counted those employed by the Estates among the service nobility, less than a fifth of the Protestants belonged to it in 1620; four decades earlier it had been around two-fifths (see Table 6.5).[35] In contrast, the Lower Austrian Catholic knights increased their numerical presence at court by more than two-fifths, so that three-fifths of the entire Catholic *Ritterstand* were still employed at court and in the army in 1620, even though the Catholic Estate had multiplied its members. Although the number of those among the Catholic knights who were merely country nobility had become more numerous as well, proportionally this *Landadel* remained stable at about a third (see Table 6.6). This compares very favourably to the four-fifths of the Protestants knights who were country nobility.

Clearly, then, because the majority of Protestants belonged to old indigenous families, it was largely the old Lower Austrian knights who had lost positions to Catholic newcomers, who came predominantly from the other hereditary lands. Only where the Protestant knights preserved their dominance, in service with the Estates, did the old native nobility prevail.

However, since the Habsburgs had advanced Catholic newcomers from Lower Austria, and the Estates had tried to counterbalance this with admissions of Protestant knights from the Reich, the total loss of positions among the native knights was not as dramatic as it was in the Estate of Lords.[36]

Not surprisingly, the gains made by the new members of the Estate of Lords, who originated largely from other territories, were also a consequence of the confessional recruitment strategies of the Habsburgs. As in the *Ritterstand*, it was mainly the old, Lower Austrian Protestant lords who lost positions, while the new Catholic members of the *Herrenstand*, who frequently were not native to the province, retained or improved their presence among the servitors.[37] Only Protestant lords suffered from the loss of position by the Lower Austrian *Herrenstand* in the Imperial household and in the bureaucracy, while Catholics increased their numerical presence in these centres of power. Even in the military, where the Protestants made some gains, they were outnumbered by Catholic lords and held fewer commanding charges. Because, by 1620, the pool of old and native Catholic lords had grown, they were even more numerous than Protestants serving in the household. In short, in 1620, Lower Austrian Catholic lords outnumbered Protestants in all offices except those administered by the Estates. But even here, new Catholic barons from the other hereditary lands had made some gains (see Figures 6.3 and 6.4).

In total, in 1620, the princely servants among the Catholic Estate of Lords nearly tripled (from seventeen to forty-five). Even though the members belonging to the Catholic *Herrenstand* had grown substantially, a higher proportion – nearly three-fifths – of them were employed by the Habsburgs in 1620, and only about a third were strictly country nobility.[38] While this does represent a multiplication of the Catholic *Landadel* compared to 1580, it was still substantially lower than among the Protestant lords, the great majority of whom were merely country nobility. In fact, the proportion of Lower Austrian Protestant lords employed by the crown in the household and the administration had declined two-thirds by 1620. If one includes those who served in the Habsburg military (but not in the Confederate army), then the Habsburgs had withdrawn more than half of the positions and charges that the Lower Austrian Protestant lords had held in 1580. And proportionally, the princely servants, who previously had constituted about half of the Protestant *Herrenstand*, declined to just over a tenth. Since a small proportion (five per cent) served the Estates, well over three-quarters of the Protestant lords held no position at all in 1620, although some served in the Confederate army. In 1580, fewer than half of the Protestant lords had belonged to the *Landadel*. How far the Lower Austrian noble Estates had divided along confessional lines into a court and country nobility is especially evident when we combine the figures for lords with those of knights. About three-fifths of the Lower Austrian Catholic nobility served the Habsburgs in 1620, compared with only a little over a tenth of the combined Protestant nobility (see Figure 6.5).

Table 6.5 Distribution of offices among Protestant knights and lords, 1580 and 1620

	1580						1620					
	Knights	%	*Lords*	%	*Sum*	%	*Knights*	%	*Lords*	%	*Sum*	%
Crown's servants	71	28	51	52	122	35	19	11	24	14	43	13
Estates' servants	23	9	8	8	31	9	14	8	8	5	22	6
Country nobility (*Landadel*)	159	63	40	40	199	56	146	81	133	81	279	81
Total	**253**	**100**	**99**	**100**	**352**	**100**	**179**	**100**	**165**	**100**	**344**	**100**

Table 6.6 Distribution of offices among Catholic knights and lords, 1580 and 1620

	1580						1620					
	Knights	%	*Lords*	%	*Sum*	%	*Knights*	%	*Lords*	%	*Sum*	%
Crown's servants	19	68	17	85	36	75	27	60	45	58	72	59
Estates' servants	–	–	–	–	–	–	3	7	3	4	6	5
Country nobility (*Landadel*)	9	32	3	15	12	25	15	33	30	38	45	36
Total	**28**	**100**	**20**	**100**	**48**	**100**	**45**	**100**	**78**	**100**	**123**	**100**

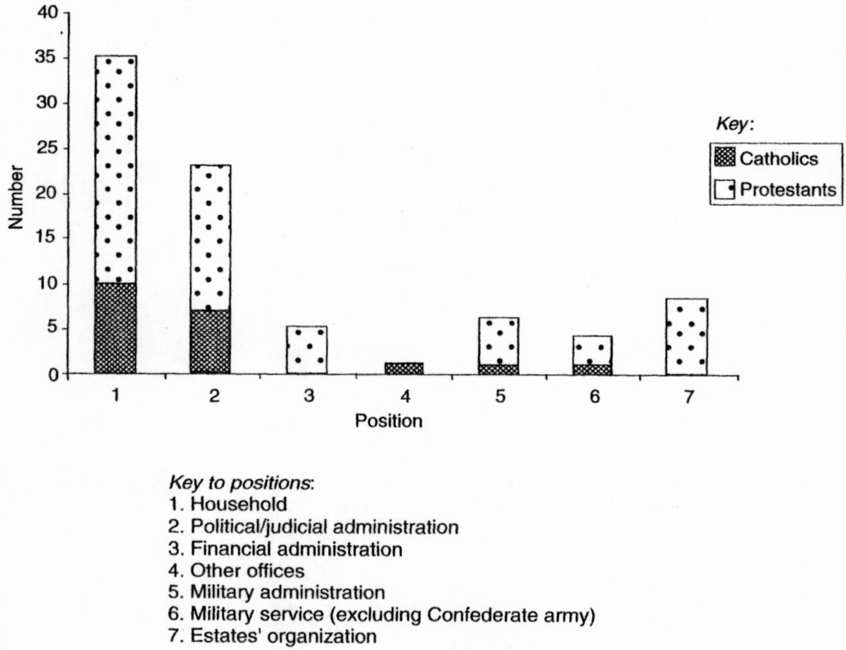

Figure 6.3 Numerical distribution of positions among Protestant and Catholic lords, 1580

The frequency of appointments of Lower Austrian nobles to the major councils further illuminates the impact that the confessional distribution of court patronage had on the provincial nobility. Surprisingly, the appointment of Lower Austrian knights to the Aulic council and court treasury,[39] and of Lower Austrian lords to the Privy Council and to the four top household positions, nearly doubled between 1600 and 1620. However, rather than reflecting a preference for Lower Austrians, or a multiplication of offices, this high frequency of appointments was a consequence of the rapid rise and fall of favourites during the last decade of Rudolf's reign, and of the changing of the guard at the time of Matthias' and Ferdinand's succession. It shows that the Habsburgs utilized the rapid change of rulers and the move of the Imperial court to Vienna during the first decades of the seventeenth century to replace Protestant members of the Lower Austrian Estates with Catholic newcomers.

Differentiating the rate of appointment to the most important councils at court by confession supports the contention that the Habsburgs

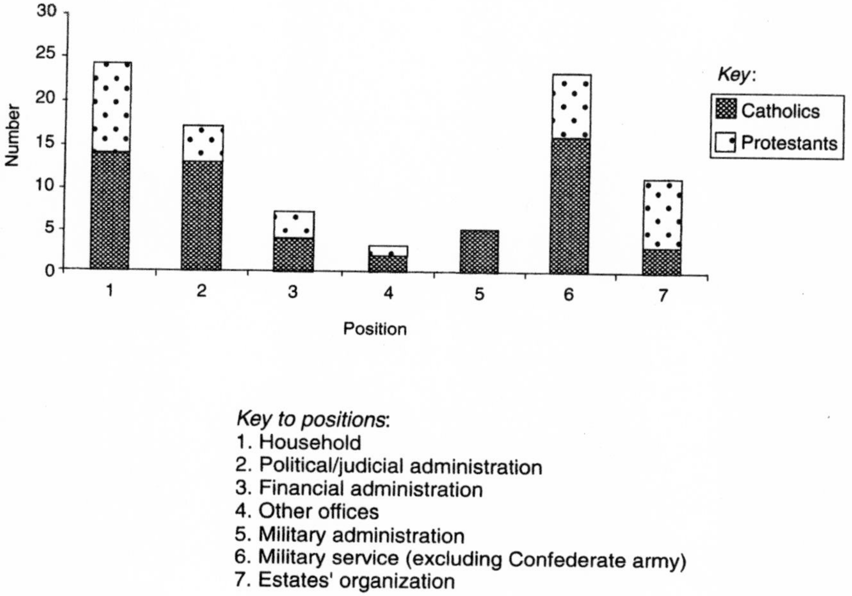

Figure 6.4 Numerical distribution of positions among Protestant and Catholic lords, 1620

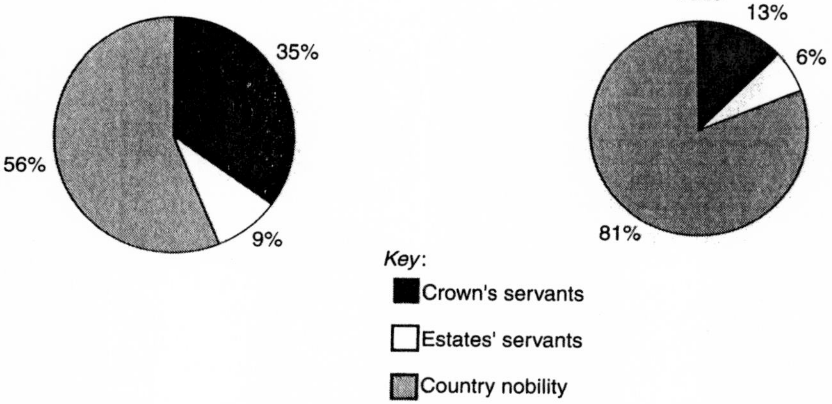

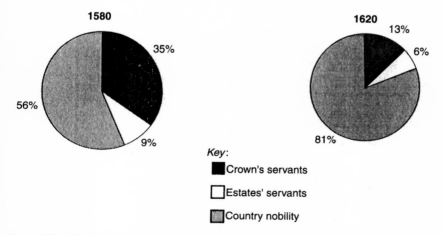

Figure 6.5 Distribution of offices among Protestants (lords and knights combined)

were most successful in confessionalizing patronage during the two decades after 1600. As I showed in the first section of this chapter, before 1600, Catholic lords already dominated the Imperial Privy Council, the office of president of the Imperial Aulic council, and the four top household offices, but they took over the presidency of the Aulic council only after 1604, and of the *Hofkammer* shortly before 1620. Similarly, the ratio of Protestant and Catholic lords who belonged to the Lower Austrian Estates and were appointed to the three major councils (Imperial Aulic and war councils, and court treasury) reversed only after 1600, with two-thirds of them becoming Catholic.[40] The elimination of Lower Austrian Protestant knights from these councils was particularly prominent in the decade after 1609. Less than a third of the Lower Austrian *Ritterstand* appointed to the Aulic council and court treasury were Protestants; but between 1580 and 1609 non-Catholics constituted about half of the new appointees from the provincial nobility. Furthermore, confessional parity in the appointment of knights as councillors to the Lower Austrian *Regiment* gave way to a preference for Catholics after 1600.[41] All of this confirms again the decline of Matthias's taste for Austrian men who did not share his Catholic faith, at least after he had utilized their support in obtaining some of his brother's crowns; it also evidences the impact of Ferdinand II's better-known preferences for Catholic servants.

Clearly, then, in the decades before 1620, Protestant nobles had much cause to worry about their social, economic and cultural continuance. The practice of the Habsburgs to equate merit and loyalty with Catholicism, and to deny all but a tenth of the Lower Austrian Protestant nobility access to essential resources at court, was all the more disappointing at a time when noble families were larger and court-patronage had increased in importance. Moreover, Protestant families had put much time, effort and money into improving the educational qualifications of young nobles with the very objective of facilitating better access to court patronage. As we saw in the previous chapter, the proportion of Lower Austrian Protestant nobles (knights and lords) who attended universities more than doubled (increasing from 41 to 107) between 1580 and 1620, and virtually caught up with the educational level of Catholic newcomers, which had been proportionally much higher in 1580. However, within a few decades, their cultural capital had become devalued and most of the Lower Austrian Protestant nobles were unable to convert it into other types of resources. Only about a fifth of the university-educated Lower Austrian Protestant lords were servitors, which compares very unfavourably to the nearly three-quarters of the educated Catholic *Herren* who belonged to the service nobility.[42] The cultural capital of the Lower Austrian Protestant knights had become even more devalued, and only two of the thirty-three university-educated nobles among them were employed by the Habsburgs in 1620.[43]

The careers of particular individual nobles further illustrates the impact the confessionalization of merit and court patronage. The Lower Austrian Protestant knight, Karl Pacheleb, could, like his ancestors, still count on Habsburg patronage during the late sixteenth centry, but this was denied to his son. Karl's father, Johann Baptist, the grandson of a Viennese magistrate, held a degree in jurisprudence, and rose from the position of procurator at the court treasury to Aulic councillor. It is uncertain when he was ennobled, but he acquired substantial property in 1559 and was considered a member of the Lower Austrian Estates before 1568. Karl himself studied at Tübingen (1558) and Padua (1562), but since the family was already ennobled, typically he refrained from obtaining a doctorate. He was soon appointed to the judicial post of *Hofdiener* in the Imperial household and rose to the position of *Regimentsrat* in 1579. Another nine years passed before he became councillor at the court treasury, a position he seems to have held for only one year. He became involved in Estates' politics but died some time after 1594. However, Karl Pacheleb's son never held any position. He joined the Protestant Confederation of 1608 and in 1614 was prosecuted by the crown for holding religious services on his manor near Vienna. He died shortly afterwards as the last male of his line.[44]

The contrasting careers of Catholic knights indicate that recent noble origin was not the primary reason for Pacheleb's slow career, or for the fate of his son. Thus the Catholic Johann Baptist Weber the Elder, who had received a doctorate from Bologna, was admitted to the Estate of Knights only in 1568. He had emigrated from Swabia, bought a sizeable seigniory and quickly advanced to high office. In 1565, at the age of thirty-seven, he was appointed Imperial vice chancellor, a function that also gave him a seat in the Privy Council. His son, Johann Baptist II, managed to become an Aulic councillor without much trouble. Although he spent some time at the universities of Bologna (1597) and Siena (1600), he did not obtain a doctorate. In 1609, five years after he had joined the Catholic Union, Johann Baptist II was appointed *Regimentsrat,* and in 1614, councillor of the court treasury (*Hofkammerrat*). Although his career path was similar to that of the Protestant, Karl Pacheleb, it took the Catholic knight only half the time to advance to the court treasury. Moreover, Johann Baptist Weber II continued to be favoured with Habsburg patronage. In 1615, in his mid-thirties, he was appointed to the prestigious Aulic council, and seven years later raised to the barony.[45]

Equally illuminating as to the difference religious affiliation made in advancing at the Habsburg court after 1600 are the careers of Lower Austrian lords. Wolfgang Eitzing (1538–1613), a fervent defender of the Protestant faith, belonged to a family of the old native baronage, whose members rose to prominence during the sixteenth century. Incumbents of the honorific office of hereditary chamberlain, Wolfgang's father, Christoph, and his uncle, Oswald Philipp, had been provincial governors

(*Statthalter*) and privy councillors. An older cousin, Michael II, had served as privy councillor and chamberlain to Maximilian II and Rudolf II. In stark contrast to these relations, only one of Wolfgang's four surviving brothers, Paul (1546–92), held a relatively unimportant position, that of Imperial ambassador at Constantinople. Wolfgang Eitzing himself received positions of some importance, but he advanced at a comparatively slow pace and never attained the prominence of his father and uncle. Beginning his career as assessor at the territorial court, he became councillor of the Austrian treasury in 1582. It took another ten years to rise to councillor of the Imperial court treasury, and finally in 1598, at the age of sixty, he was appointed as its president.[46] It is unclear whether he resigned or was dismissed by Rudolf, but he certainly was not reappointed by Matthias upon his succession, possibly because of his active involvement with the Protestant Confederates in 1608–09.

Nevertheless, his successor as *Hofkammerpresident*, Wilhelm Seemann, was also a Protestant. From a Bavarian family who had settled in Upper and Lower Austria during the late fifteenth and early sixteenth centuries, his ancestors had been employed as estate managers, and his father, Georg, who was admitted to the Lower Austrian Estate of Knights, had been appointed to the Aulic council. Wilhelm, who had attended the universities at Padua, Siena, and Bologna (1572–4), began his career in 1585 at the age of thirty-three in the administration of the Upper Austrian Estates. It took eight years to become councillor of the provincial government (*Regiment*), and another nine years to follow his father to the position of Aulic councillor. Upon his promotion as president of the treasury in 1609, at the age of fifty-seven, he was, like many supporters of Matthias, raised to the rank of baron and admitted to the Estate of Lords. Yet, like his predecessor, Seemann also left his job within a year, for reasons that are not entirely clear.[47]

The employment opportunities of Catholic lords, such as Leonhard Helfried von Meggau, provides an instructive contrast to Seemann's and Eitzing's career. Leonhard Helfried was admitted to the old Estate of Lords of Lower Austria in 1576, and after studying jurisprudence at the universities of Padua, Bologna and Siena, he became chamberlain of archduke Maximilian in 1595 at the age of eighteen. Even though Rudolf II dismissed him from his posts because of his close relations with Matthias, Meggau was well rewarded, and advanced to high office in Matthias's Privy Council and the household immediately after 1608. Ferdinand II even raised the family to become Imperial counts, and provided them with the hereditary sinecure of *Oberst-Erbland-Hofmeister* of Austria.[48]

Few, if any, Protestant nobles could have been ignorant of the benefits a conversion to Catholicism could bring them after Karl von Liechtenstein and his brothers Maximilian and Gundacker gave up Protestantism between 1599 and 1602. Their family belonged to the ancient nobility of the Austrian lands, and they also held property in Moravia. Like his father and grandfather, Karl had been an ardent Protestant and leader of the Moravian Estates. It is unclear whether this presented obstacles to him in entering the service of the emperor, although even his uncles and brothers were only in the employ of the archdukes. The exact reasons for Karl's conversion remain ambiguous, but it is clear that, just one year later, Rudolf II appointed him as director of the Privy Council and master of the court, when he was only thirty-one years old. Considering that the Habsburgs owed his family 410 000 Gulden, he had to manoeuvre carefully, but, when the time was opportune, he sided with Matthias against his brother. Liechtenstein was well rewarded, and in 1608 received the title of prince, followed in 1614 by the duchy of Troppau in Upper Silesia. Not surprisingly, his brothers' careers also improved markedly, and by the middle of the seventeenth century about a fifth of all the land in the kingdom of Bohemia belonged to the family, in reward for loans as well as for conversion and service to the dynasty.[49]

The redistribution of landed property

The accumulation of property by the Liechtenstein family suggests that the confessionalization of court patronage had affected the distribution of landholdings among Catholic and Protestant nobles already before 1620. In the past, Habsburg historians have emphasized instead how the Habsburgs rewarded loyal Catholics with land expropriated from Protestant rebels in the decades immediately after their defeat, and how this affected landholding patterns, especially in Bohemia.[50] They also claimed that, having sold many of their crown lands, the dynasty lacked resources to strengthen significantly the position of the Catholic nobility as landed proprietors before 1620.[51] All this neglects to recognize the transformation that occurred prior to 1620 as a consequence of confessional recruitment. An analysis of the distribution of landed property among Lower Austrian nobles between 1580 and 1620 shows that the Habsburgs managed indirectly to alter the allocation of land among the confessions.

The present stage of research on the Austrian nobility's landed wealth does not allow us to draw many definitive conclusions about its overal economic position before 1620. Historians of other European nobilities, however, have put to rest older debates about the possibility of economic decline among nobles during the late sixteenth and early seventeenth centuries and instead asserted that they adjusted successfully to economic change throughout the early modern period.[52] We still need to know more on the relative economic fortunes of various groups within the nobility in order to answer some of the questions left open about this process of accommodation. In particular, it remains unclear how the response to inflation and an emerging market economy varied with social and economic background.

None the less, the evidence we do have suggests that the Austrian nobility as a whole did not experience economic decline, even though most noble landholders were unable to profit significantly from higher prices for agricultural products, largely because manorial farming was relatively small. The income of a sample of fifty-eight landholdings for the period 1560 to 1620 shows that, on average, only about a third of it was derived from noble self-management (*Eigenwirtschaft*) of fisheries, forests and rural industries, and the cultivation of manorial land.[53] Because noble landowners derived most of their income from fixed peasant rents, they usually combated inflation by increasing other feudal obligations, or inventing new ones, and by utilizing seigneurial monopolies more effectively.[54] Even though rural industries did not grow substantially, the amount of arable land did expand, even doubling in some areas during the half century before 1620.[55] Moreover, in the case of about a third of the sampled fifty-eight landed estates, the proportion of noble revenues from manorial self-management increased from less than a third to two-fifths during the two decades before 1620.[56] This suggests that at least a part of the Lower Austrian nobility was able to adjust relatively quickly to changing economic conditions. The fact that the Habsburgs were indebted to numerous nobles, the restoration of many noble castles and the greater frequency of the cavalier's tour during the late sixteenth century support the idea that many noble landowners adapted successfully. However, as I shall show below, it is also the case that changes in the distribution of peasant households among Lower Austrian nobles indicate that the economic gulf between rich and poor nobles was widening, and that the nobility confronted problems of providing for more children as families grew in size. The indebtedness of nearly two-thirds of the estates confiscated from the Protestant rebels after 1620, most of which was the result of accumulated interests on loans, further suggests that adjustment to economic change was very uneven in the Austrian territories.[57]

Even though at the present time we cannot determine conclusively whether income from noble landholding declined or not, it is possible to make a fairly reliable comparison of the number of peasant households attached to each landed property in 1580 with those in 1620, and thus estimate the broad structural transformations in the relative size of landholdings among different noble groups. Three major changes stand out in the distribution of landed wealth between 1580 and 1620.[58] First, economic inequality between nobles was on the rise, caused largely by a remarkable increase in landless nobles. Second, the lesser nobility suffered a significant decline in size of landholdings and a high turnover of property. And, third, the Catholic nobility made important gains at the expense of Protestants.

As I observed earlier, in 1620 Lower Austrian noble families had, on average, at least a fifth more male adult children than in 1580. Although this appears to be a rather moderate growth rate, it only pertains to sons over the age of twenty. We can safely assume that in 1620 noble families also had to pay more dowries to a larger number of daughters than in 1580. Most important, when evaluating the effect of population growth, it is imperative to note the disproportionate effect it had on marginal groups, such as younger, unlanded sons of elites, especially when landed resources were scarce.[59] For example, if twenty nobles produce twenty-four sons but can pass on only twenty landed estates, four of the sons will remain without property. At the same rate of growth, these twenty-four sons will have to provide for twenty-nine sons, and so nine will become landless in the next generation. The general population would have increased by only 20 per cent, but the marginal population of the landless would have expanded by 125 per cent. In Lower Austria, where landed property frequently was small and thus effectively indivisible, the number of landless nobles rose by about 150 per cent between 1580 and 1620, clearly at a much faster rate than the general population, which increased by only about 20 per cent.[60] This puts into proper perspective how rivalry among the elite over vacancies at court, and other patronage, was fuelled by long-term demographic change and by the limitations of the agrarian structure. Furthermore, this occurred precisely at a time when warfare and inflation also put limits on the Habsburgs' distribution of resources to the elite.

The increase in the number of landless nobles in Lower Austria, and upward social mobility, changed the distribution of landed property considerably, making it more unequal, especially among the lords. Thus, in 1580, about half of the Estate of Lords' peasant households belonged to the upper quartile of the *Herren*, but in 1620 this proportion already owned over three-quarters of the peasantry (see Tables 6.7 and 6.8). And this growing inequality can be explained largely by the quadrupling of lords without property. The Estate of Knights multiplied its landless members by only about a half. None the less, in 1620, the upper quartile of knights already possessed three-quarters of the peasant households belonging to the *Ritterstand*; in 1580, they had held only around two-thirds of the peasantry (see Tables 6.9 & 6.10). Clearly, then, the survival of a larger number of sons put pressure on the available land in Lower Austria, increasing inequalities of landed wealth within the elite and nourishing competition over landed resources.

As we saw in Chapter 4, demographic change made it difficult for the lesser nobility to replace extinct families with new admissions to the *Ritterstand*. Recall that, between 1580 and 1620, the number of knightly families declined by a third, while the upper nobility increased its lines by about a half. The consequence of this high social mobility of knights into the Estate of Lords signalled not only a numerical decline of the *Ritterstand*, but also a decline of landed wealth belonging to the knights as an order, since the Estate lost more than half of the peasant households held in 1580. Two thirds of these households were transferred to the Estate of Lords by knights who were newly

Table 6.7 Concentration of peasant households among lords, 1580

Size	*No. of lords*	*No. of houses*	*Sum of lords*	*Sum of houses*	*Percentage sum of lords*	*Percentage sum of houses*
0	21	0	21	0	17.6	0
1–49	11	335	32	335	26.9	1.0
50–99	11	851	43	1 186	36.1	3.7
100–199	17	2 536	60	3 722	50.4	11.7
200–299	10	2 493	70	6 215	58.8	19.5
300–399	13	4 603	83	10 818	69.7	33.9
400–499	15	6 687	98	17 505	82.4	54.8
500–599	8	4 326	106	21 831	89.1	68.4
600–799	9	5 732	115	27 563	96.6	86.3
800+	4	4 360	119	31 923	100.0	100.0

Table 6.8 Concentration of peasant households among lords, 1620

Size	*No. of lords*	*No. of houses*	*Sum of lords*	*Sum of houses*	*Percentage sum of lords*	*Percentage sum of houses*
0	104	0	104	0	42.8	0.0
1–49	22	732	126	732	51.8	1.8
50–99	20	1 516	146	2 248	60.1	5.6
100–199	29	4 214	175	6 462	72.0	16.2
200–299	16	3 987	191	10 449	78.6	26.2
300–399	16	5 607	207	16 056	85.2	40.3
400–499	12	5 437	219	21 493	90.1	54.0
500–599	9	5 024	228	26 517	93.8	66.6
600–799	11	7 883	239	34 400	98.3	86.4
800+	4	5 404	243	39 804	100.0	100.0

Table 6.9 Concentration of peasant households among knights, 1580

Size	*No. of knights*	*No. of houses*	*Sum of knights*	*Sum of houses*	*Percentage sum of knights*	*Percentage sum of houses*
0	51	0	51	0	18.1	0
1–49	104	2 747	155	2 747	55.2	12.1
50–99	49	3 526	204	6 273	72.6	27.7
100–199	51	7 389.5	255	13 626.5	90.7	60.1
200–299	13	3 339	268	17 001.5	95.4	75.0
300–399	6	2 051	274	19 052.5	97.5	84.0
400–499	3	1 334	277	20 386.5	98.6	89.9
500–599	4	2 297	281	22 683.5	100.0	100.0

Table 6.10 Concentration of peasant households among knights, 1620

Size	*No. of knights*	*No. of houses*	*Sum of knights*	*Sum of houses*	*Percentage sum of knights*	*Percentage sum of houses*
0	79	0	79	0	35.3	0
1–49	82	2 204.5	161	2 204.5	71.9	20.7
50–99	30	2 103	191	4 307.5	85.3	40.5
100–199	21	2 974	212	7 281.5	94.6	68.5
200–299	8	1 807	220	9 088.5	98.2	85.5
300–399	2	698	222	9 786.5	99.1	92.0
400–499	2	847	224	10 633.5	100.0	100.0
500–599	0	0	224	10 633.5	100.0	100.0

admitted to the Estate. Moreover, established lords purchased a tenth of the property of knights, so that the Estate of Lords augmented its overall holdings of peasant households by about a quarter.[61]

In addition to the transfer of land between the *Stände* caused by social mobility, property turnover because of sales was very high during the forty years prior to 1620. Although this may have been beneficial for increasing property values, the growing inequality in size of land holdings suggests that it had an unsettling effect socially on the less well-to-do nobles. Thus, the frequency of property turnover was highest among small estates; that is, those with fewer than fifty peasant households attached to them. The district above the Manhartsberg was particularly affected by this because it had the largest number of small estates. In total, nearly half of the property belonging to the Lower Austrian knights in 1580 had changed hands by 1620, not counting estates that were part of a dowry or transferred to an heir. Again, this high mobility of landed estates was a consequence of the high extinction rate among old knights and admissions of new members, who often purchased the property they left behind. Among the lords, buying and selling was half as frequent as in the *Ritterstand*, because their rate of extinction was substantially lower and because the newly admitted lords, who rose mainly from the Estate of Knights, already possessed landed property.

Evidently, then, the high turnover of landed estates was facilitated not only by demographic change, but also by the social and confessional recruitment strategies of the Habsburg rulers. Their impact was most evident in the Protestant *Ritterstand*, and most effective in the redistribution of large and medium-sized property.[62] Thus the high losses of peasant households among medium- and large-size property owners belonging to the Estate of Knights were incurred largely by the Protestant knights, while it was predominantly Catholic lords who acquired property in these categories. Altogether, the Protestant *Ritterstand* lost nearly two-fifths of its estates and peasants between 1580 and 1620, which constituted the entire losses of the Estate of Knights. Although the Protestant lords increased their small and medium-size landowners by about a quarter, because before 1608 Matthias had also promoted many Protestant supporters from the lesser nobility to the *Herrenstand,* the combined Protestant Estates lost about a third (65 of 194) of its landowners with medium- to large-size holdings and more than a quarter of its total peasant holdings (see Table 6.11).[63] In contrast, the small landholders among the combined Catholic Estates remained relatively stable, while its members with medium- and large-size landed property more than doubled. It is especially significant to note that, while only two Catholics held property with over 400 peasant households in 1580, by 1620 there were nine, and three of the four largest landholders in Lower Austria belonged to the Catholic Estate of Lords (see Table 6.12).[64] Combined, the Catholic Estate of Knights and Lords more than doubled their peasant households, and on average had almost twice as many peasants per landed estate than Protestant nobles.[65]

Nevertheless, the Catholic nobility also expanded it landless members, which multiplied by a factor of six (from eleven to sixty-five). In 1620, they constituted more than half of the combined Catholic noble Estate, and had become especially numerous among the lords. This pattern was similar to the Protestant nobles, whose landless members increased most rapidly in the *Herrenstand* (from fifteen to sixty), and nearly doubled (from 61 to 117) among both Protestant knights and lords. While those without property constituted only just over a third (117 of 344) among the combined Protestant nobility, in absolute numbers they comprised nearly twice as many nobles without landed property than did the smaller Catholic Estate.

The Protestant nobility was particularly disadvantaged because less than a tenth (10 out of 117) of their landless members were employed by the Habsburgs in 1620; in 1580 it had been almost a third (eighteen out of sixty-one). In sharp contrast, more than half (thirty-seven out of sixty-five) of the landless Catholic nobles were in the service of the crown in 1620. Although their proportion had been higher (nine out of eleven) in 1580, one must keep in mind that, at the time, the Catholic Estate was extremely small, and a statistical analysis becomes less relevant when dealing with low base numbers. It is clear, however, that the Catholic newcomers to the Lower Austrian Estates experienced considerable difficulty in obtaining land holdings from the established Protestants, which increased competition over landed resources between the confessions. Nevertheless, the Catholic faction could multiply its land holdings significantly at the expense of non-Catholics, who themselves suffered from land shortage because the larger number of male children put pressure on the available land.

We can conclude, then, that the redistribution of peasant households and landed estates within the nobility was caused by demographic change and shifting patterns of social mobility that favoured the emergence of a new and expanded upper nobility, recruited largely from among non-native Catholics. It was largely the Protestant nobility, and especially the

Estate of Knights, who were affected by losses of peasantry and landed property, which were absorbed primarily by the newcomers among the Catholic nobility. This does not mean that individual Protestant nobles necessarily experienced financial difficulties, only that there was a significant redistribution of property within the noble *Stände* that was unfavourable to Protestants. This process strengthened the Catholic Estates in relative and absolute terms, so adding to the fears among Protestants as to their capacity to sustain their bargaining power *vis-à-vis* the ruler and the Catholic faction. Moreover, both Protestant and Catholic nobles experienced difficulties in obtaining land for their numerous sons, and this added to the competition between the confessions over the distribution of resources, increasing each side's desire to gain an advantage over the other, and decreasing their willingness to resolve conflicts through negotiation.

None the less, it appears that, as a group, the nobility in the Austrian lands was able to adjust to economic change during the late sixteenth and early seventeenth centuries, and that declining incomes from landed property was most probably not a factor in nobles' decisions to join the Bohemian Confederation. This confirms the observation made in Chapter 2, that there was no significant correlation between size of landholding and the political position Lower Austrian Protestant nobles took in 1620. Small landholders were slightly over-represented among the active opposition, but this can now be explained by a significant presence of Protestant nobles from the area below the Manhartsberg, a district that also had the largest number of small landed estates in Lower Austria, and where the highest proportion of Church property was restored to Catholics. Although the evidence does not allow us to conclude that small landholders suffered from declining incomes, they did experience particular difficulties in passing on property to a larger number of male heirs, who were also unable to obtain positions at the Habsburg court, especially if they were Protestants.

Table 6.11 Numerical distribution of peasant households (PH) among Protestant knights and lords, 1580 and 1620

	Unlanded: 0 PH			*Small: 1–49 PH*			*Medium: 50–399 PH*			*Large: 400+ PH*			
	Knights	*Lords*	*Combined*	*Knights*	*Lords*	*Combined*	*Knights*	*Lords*	*Combined*	*Knights*	*Lords*	*Combined*	*Total*
1580	46	15	61	89	8	97	111	42	153	7	34	41	352
1620	57	60	117	71	18	89	49	59	108	2	28	30	344
Total	+11	+ 45	+56	–18	+10	–8	–62	+17	–45	–5	–6	–11	–

Table 6.12 Numerical distribution of peasant households among Catholic knights and lords, 1580 and 1620

	Unlanded: 0 PH			*Small: 1–49 PH*			*Medium: 50–399 PH*			*Large: 400+ PH*			
	Knights	*Lords*	*Combined*	*Knights*	*Lords*	*Combined*	*Knights*	*Lords*	*Combined*	*Knights*	*Lords*	*Combined*	*Total*
1580	5	6	11	15	3	18	8	9	17	0	2	2	48
1620	22	43	65	11	4	15	12	22	34	0	9	9	123
Total	+17	+37	+54	–4	+1	–3	+4	+13	+17	–	+7	+7	–

Conclusion to Part II

Part II of this study has demonstrated that the complaints of the Protestant opposition about the debilitating impact on them of the selective distribution of Habsburg patronage to Catholics were based on concrete experiences. The confessional allocation of various forms of resource dispensed at court was central to the deterioration of relations between Protestant and Catholic elites, and between Habsburg rulers and Protestant nobles, during the half century prior to 1620. However, although this part of the book emphasized material motivations, it also shed light on the complexities of converting immaterial forms of resources into material ones, and the interpenetration of ideal and material interests.

Unwilling to forgo the Imperial title, and their Spanish inheritance, the Habsburg dynasty considered religion to be the primary bond tying the nobility to their regime. After 1579, they began to create a new Catholic court nobility, who would become the bearers of a homogenous Catholic court culture that legitimated and supported their political claims. In order to encourage conversion to Catholicism, the Habsburg rulers denied the Protestant elite access to their patronage, but most Protestant nobles in fact refused to abandon their faith. Since the pool of old Catholic nobles was relatively small in the territories where the court was located, the crown recruited newcomers from other territories, especially from the Holy Roman Empire.

As the analysis of the religious composition of the Imperial and archducal courts showed, a new Catholic nobility already dominated the top positions and military commands on the eve of the rebellion, and not just after 1620. This preferential recruitment of Catholics had a profound effect on the provincial nobility, since only about a tenth of the numerically much larger Protestant nobility of Lower Austria was still employed by the crown in 1620, compared to nearly two thirds of the Catholic nobles. The Habsburgs were also successful in redefining the rules and the channels of social recruitment, thereby transforming the social structure of the provincial nobility. Aided by long-term demographic and economic forces, this fostered the social displacement of the Protestant majority, a redistribution of landed property, and the numerical growth of the Catholic nobility, which more than doubled in Lower Austria. This was essential for the formation of a new Catholic court nobility.

The confessionalization of court patronage was devastating for Protestant nobles, because it occurred at a time of population increase, requiring them to provide for a growing number of male children. By the early seventeenth century, noble families had become dependent on vacancies at court, not only in order to provide for their younger sons, but also for their eldest sons. Moreover, Protestant nobles had invested heavily in education so they could enhance their families' social capital and cultivate patronage networks at the Habsburg court, which were essential for forging marriage alliances, enhancing noble status, and gaining access to various other resources. And the court had also become the major arena in which nobles acquired cultural capital and displayed symbolic power. Clearly, Protestant nobles no longer had access to the major instrument of social and family reproduction, the Habsburg court, and their clientage networks were impaired as a result. Not surprisingly, then, the confessionalization of court patronage fermented opposition among Protestant nobles to the regime and played a significant role in their rebellion of 1618–20.

Although Part II has emphasized the importance of material factors, this book overall has applied a conjunctural model exploring the short-run factors that promoted political volatility and the ways in which these connected with long-term socioeconomic, cultural and political problems. As we have seen, the insistence of the Habsburg rulers on imposing religious uniformity, and the subsequent contests concerning cultural policy, sharpened the ongoing negotiations with local elites regarding judicial competence and autonomy. As spiritual issues fused with concerns about security and discontent as to the selective allocation of resources, bargaining over judicial power and political authority became highly inflexible, so contributing to the outbreak of violence.

However, the impact of deep-seated differences of conviction, and of preferences for political centralization, on the conflict of 1618–20 has been exaggerated. Certainly, religious identities framed the different visions of the Protestant leadership and the Catholic state elite about the political order, especially over the nature of consent and how to ensure that rulers observed natural law and custom. But alone these issues were not sufficient to bring about a grand alliance of Protestants against Ferdinand II. Religious and political divisions crystallized as conflict because they were fuelled through the selective allocation of Habsburg patronage. This is particularly evident from the fragmentation of the Protestant camp in Lower Austria, since those who had favourable chances of gaining access to court offices, and the various resources connected to them, took a loyalist position in 1619 and in 1620. In short, it was the merging of religious issues and bargaining over political authority with the confessional distribution of patronage that facilitated the formation of the Confederation among the Protestant Estates of several Habsburg territories.

This study also sought to shed light on the question of why the Protestant nobles clung with such tenacity to their faith rather than to convert under the threat of their demise, especially considering that material factors and access to the Habsburg court were so central to family enhancement. Their commitment was certainly very strong, as most continued to hold fast to their religious beliefs even after military defeat, although their sons did convert gradually to Catholicism after 1620. Protestant nobles, in general, were clearly capable of adjusting their *habitus*, and they accommodated rather well to the acculturation process in education. However, this took place gradually over nearly a century and the adjustment was, for the most part, not incompatible with their *habitus*. In contrast, the confessionalization of Habsburg patronage was implemented very rapidly, and was in tension with the religious identity of Protestant nobles.[1] In 1620 they were for the most part second- and third-generation Lutherans who had fully internalized their faith, and the values and rituals associated with it, through both socialization and everyday practice. Their confessionalized identity had become an intrinsic part of their *habitus*, so that their interests and perceptions of their position in society were fused deeply with their faith, and, understandably, they became fixated about preserving it. Protestantism provided them with an essential conceptual framework for underpinning and sustaining the very traditions of noble society, including the proclamation of themselves as champions of the Estates' traditional political rights in their conflict with the Habsburgs.

However, by the early seventeenth century, it was increasingly clear that there was an incongruity between their *habitus* and the objective conditions surrounding them. This disjunction occurred rather quickly. Before the seventeenth century circumstances still allowed the Protestant nobles to remain optimistic about the survival of their faith in the Habsburg territories, even with regard to retaining a dominant position within the existing order. They remained numerically predominant, and the Habsburg rulers continued to need their support in dynastic quarrels and financing wars. Emperor Matthias had rewarded many non-Catholics with status promotion (and, at times, with offices), and had, like his predecessors, often shown a willingness to bargain and compromise with them in disputes. By the early seventeenth century, the Counter-Reformation had made limited progress in Lower Austria, while the Protestant Estates built up impressive international contacts. Hopeful about the victory of their faith in the empire, Protestant families even invested heavily in the cultural capital of their sons.

However, in the decade prior to 1620, Protestant nobles faced an entirely new situation, being confronted suddenly with a mismatch between their *habitus* and real opportunities. Even though they had adapted to the new requirements in education, and had reconstructed aristocratic virtue to suit the social identity of nobility, the Habsburg equation of merit and loyalty with Catholicism rendered impossible the conversion of this cultural capital into other resources. Only a political victory over the Habsburgs could have preserved the *habitus* of the Protestant nobles, including their religious identity, and secured the material reproduction of their families. Thus, one discontinuity lent support to another.

After the defeat of the Protestant opposition, the Habsburgs were relatively successful in sustaining the incentive structures that secured the co-operation of the elite, at least in their Austrian and Bohemian territories, by channelling selectively to loyal servants various resources vital to noble dynastic reproduction. As the new state elite helped to extend the co-ordinating activity of the monarch into new areas, the Habsburg court increasingly became the most important arena of patronage, eventually destroying, or at least neutralizing, competing centres of loyalty. Court patronage, now fully confessionalized, continued to be a main technique of Habsburg government. In fact, we cannot understand how the early modern Habsburg state functioned without recognizing the central role of patronage in co-opting and co-ordinating elites.

None the less, even with the usual qualifications, it is fanciful to apply the notion of absolutism to the Habsburg monarchy even after 1620, since centralization continued to progress slowly. The nobilities of most territories retained their influence, and the dynasty depended on their collaboration in resource extraction and their participation in extending the state's co-ordinating power. But it was this co-operation that eventually facilitated a larger, and more effective, centralized administration and army, enabling the state to regulate rather than merely to co-ordinate society. In this process, it is difficult to view the Habsburgs as being instruments of the dominant class; rather, they were agents with interests of their own. While they shared certain goals, particularly with respect to dynastic reproduction, the interests of the nobility were as diverse as the groups that comprised it, so that willingness to co-operate with the ruler always depended on a variety of factors. Still, the history of the relations between Habsburgs and elites in Austria and Bohemia during the following two centuries is testimony to the fact that tightening the interpenetration between early modern rulers and nobles strengthened both state power and the dominant social group.

Notes and References

Introduction

1. Hans Sturmberger, *Aufstand in Böhmen. Der Beginn des dreißigjährigen Krieges* (Munich/Vienna: R. Oldenbourg Verlag, 1959).
2. J. V. Polišenský and Frederic Snider, *War and Society in Europe, 1618–1648* (Cambridge University Press, 1978), p. 55; see also Polišenský's *The Thirty Years' War*, trans. Robert Evans (London: Batsford, 1971).
3. Prominent among these is Jaroslav Pánek, 'The Religious Question and the Political System of Bohemia before and after the Battle of the White Mountain', in R. J. W. Evans and T. V. Thomas (eds), *Crown, Church and Estates. Central European Politics in the Sixteenth and Seventeenth Centuries* (New York: St. Martin's Press, 1991), pp. 129–48. We still lack a recent monograph of the Bohemian side of the conflict. However, Christine van Eickels has made the Silesian participation in the Bohemian Confederation the topic of her book *Schlesien im böhmischen Ständestaat. Voraussetzung und Verlauf der böhmischen Revolution von 1618 in Schlesien* (Colonge: Böhlau Verlag, 1994); see also Josef Válka, 'Moravia and the Crisis of the Estates' System in the Lands of the Bohemian Crown', in Evans and Thomas, *Crown, Church and Estates*, pp. 149–57; Karolina Adamová, 'K otázce česko-rakouského a česko-uherského konfederačního hnutí v letech 1619–1620' [The Question of the Bohemian–Austrian and Bohemian–Hungarian Confederation Movement of 1619–1620] , *Právnéhistorické studie*, 29 (1989), pp. 79–90; and Václav Bůžek, 'Nižší šlechta v předbělohorských čechách (Prameny, metody, stav a perspektivy bádání)', [The Lower Nobility of Bohemia at the time before the Battle of the White Mountain (Sources, Methods, State and Perspectives of Research)], *Český časopis historický*, 1 (1993), pp. 37–53.
4. Myron P. Gutmann, 'The Origins of the Thirty Years' War', *Journal of Interdisciplinary History*, XVIII (Spring 1988), pp. 751–2. However, Gutmann also complains that the origin of the *Thirty Years' War* has not been discussed sufficiently in recent treatments of the war. The English literature on the Thirty Years' War is extensive; recent works include Stephen J. Lee, *The Thirty Years' War* (London: Routledge, 1991); Geoffrey Parker, *The Thirty Years' War* (Boston, Mass.: Routledge, 1984); and N. M. Sutherland, 'The Origins of the *Thirty Years' War* and the Structure of European Politics', *English Historical Review*, 107 (July 1992), pp. 587–625.
5. In this book, the term 'Austria' refers to the archduchy of Austria; that is, the hereditary lands of Lower and Upper Austria. Although at times I include the Inner Austrian territories of the Habsburgs, this will be made clear. The focus of the statistical data, however, is on Lower Austria. The sociopolitical structures of these lands were similar and their nobilities closely related.
6. I define 'elite' as the most powerful and wealthy groups in society. In the Austrian lands of the sixteenth and seventeenth centuries, this included the groups (landed nobles, highest Church officials, urban representatives) who were incorporated into the Estates or *Stände*. There were, in addition, nobles, clergy and burghers who were not members of the *Stände*, but who were sufficiently

wealthy to be considered on an equal footing with those incorporated in the Estates, but usually they were politically less influential.

7. Charles Tilly's important work provides a convincing chain of cumulative causation in which geopolitics and technological change brought about the expansion of armies, prompting greater efforts on the part of rulers to extract resources from their subjects and to create central administrative institutions. In short, war made the state, causing resistance from subjects and leading to further increases in the 'extractive bulk of the state'. See his *The Formation of National States in Western Europe* (Princeton, NJ: Princeton University Press, 1975), pp. 73–5; and, more recently, *Coercion, Capital and European States, AD 990–1992* (Cambridge, Mass.: Blackwell, 1992). Michael Mann, who supports Tilly's basic conclusions in his *The Sources of Social Power,* vol. I: *A History of Power from the Beginning to A.D. 1760* (2 vols) (Cambridge University Press, 1986), has stressed particularly that the revenue-extractive strategies rulers were able to employ to meet geopolitical challenges determined the size and character of the infrastructure and type of regime a state developed. For example, 'absolutist states' developed where states depended on the difficult extraction of land taxes to finance armies, forcing rulers to construct larger bureaucracies to coerce subjects. Critics of this approach have insisted, however, that the size of administrations was connected rather with the practice of venal offices, and that the extraction of commercial revenues in fact required larger and better-trained personnel; see Thomas Ertman, *Birth of the Leviathan. Building States and Regimes in Medieval and Early Modern Europe* (Cambridge University Press, 1997), ch. 1.
8. The recent literature on state-building by historians is extensive. For some national overviews, see Michael Braddick, *State Formation in Early Modern England, c. 1550–1700* (Cambridge University Press, 2000); James B. Collins, *The State in Early Modern France* (Cambridge University Press, 1995); Julian Goodare, *State and Society in Early Modern Scotland* (Oxford University Press, 1999); Hagen Schulze, *States, Nations and Nationalism. From the Middle Ages to the Present,* trans. W. E. Yuill (Cambridge, Mass.: Blackwell, 1996); and Peter H. Wilson, *Absolutism in Central Europe* (London/NewYork: Routledge, 2000).
9. Paula Sutter-Fichtner, 'Habsburg State-Building in the Early Modern Era: The Incomplete Sixteenth Century', *Austrian History Yearbook,* XXV (1994), pp. 139–57.
10. Berthold Bretholz still emphasized this aspect in the early twentieth century in *Neuere Geschichte Böhmens* (Gotha: F. A. Perthes, 1920).
11. Otto von Gierke was the major representative of this view; *Das deutsche Genossenschaftsrecht,* Vol. I: *Rechtsgeschichte der deutschen Genossenschaft* (Berlin: Weidmann, 1868); see also Anton Gindely, *History of the Thirty Years' War,* trans. Andrew Ten Brook (2 vols.) (Freeport, N.Y.: Books for Libraries Press, 1972), and Petr Chlumecký, *Carl von Zierotin und seine Zeit, 1564–1615* (Brünn: A. Ritsch, 1862), who offer similar interpretations for the Habsburgs and their Estates.
12. A principal prepresentative of this historiography was Otto Hintze, 'Weltgeschichtliche Bedingungen der Repräsentivverfassung', *Historische Zeitschrift,* 143 (1931), pp. 1–47; and 'Typology der ständischen Verfassung des Abendlandes', in *Abhandlugen zur allgemeinen Verfassungsgeschichte,* 2nd ed. (Göttingen: Vandernhoeck and Ruprecht, 1962), pp. 120–39. Marlene LeGates, 'Princes, Parliaments and Privilege: German Research in European Context', *European Studies Review,* 10 (1980), pp. 151–76, summarizes some of these debates among German scholars.
13. Victor S. Mamatey, 'The Battle of the White Mountain as Myth in Czech History', *East European Quarterly,* XV(3) (Sept. 1981), pp. 335–45, provides an overview of Czech historiography.

14. Brunner's *Land und Herrschaft: Grundfragen der territorialen Verfassungsgeschichte Südostdeutschlands im Mittelalter*, 1st edn. (Baden bei Wien, 1939); 3rd ed. (Brünn: R. M. Rohrer Verlag, 1943) has remained influential despite its Nationalist Socialist overtones and purpose, and has been translated recently; Otto Brunner, *Land and Lordship. Structures of Governance in Medieval Austria*, trans. from 4th, revd. ed. by Howard Kaminsky and James Van Horn Melton (Philadelphia, Pa.: University of Pennsylvania Press, 1992), p. 363. Hans Spangenberg had already considered the emergence of the estatist state in, *Vom Lehnstaat zum Ständestaat. Ein Beitrag zur Entstehung der landständischen Verfassung* (Munich/Berlin: R. Oldenbourg, 1912).
15. F. L. Carsten, *Princes and Parliaments in Germany from the Fifteenth to the Eighteenth Century* (Oxford: Clarendon Press, 1959); Fritz Hartung, *Deutsche Verfassungsgeschichte vom 15. Jahrhundert bis zur Gegenwart*, 5th edn. (Stuttgart: Koehler, 1950).
16. See, for example, Dietrich Gerhard, 'Ständische Vertretungen und Land', *Festschrift für Hermann Heimpl zum 70. Geburtstag am 19. September 1971* (Göttingen: Max Planck Institut für Geschichte, 1971), pp. 447–72, who suggested that this dualism was not overcome until the nineteenth century.
17. Sturmberger, *Aufstand in Böhmen*, p. 99.
18. See, for example, Grete Mecenseffy, *Geschichte des Protestantismus in Österreich* (Graz: Böhlaus, 1956) and Victor Bibl, 'Die katholischen und protestantischen Stände Niederösterreichs im XVII. Jahrhundert. Ein Beitrag zur Geschichte der ständischen Verfassung', *Jahrbuch für Landeskunde von Niederösterreich* (JbLkNÖ) 2, NF (1903); pp. 167–323. Gustav Reingrabner's, *Adel und Reformation. Beiträge zur Geschichte des Protestantischen Adels im Lande unter der Enns während des 16. und 17. Jahrhunderts* (Vienna: Verein für Landeskunde von Niederösterreich, 1976), offers no new interpretation of the conflict.
19. Like contemporaries, I apply 'court' to both the government and the ruler's household.
20. Robert Bireley, 'Ferdinand II: Founder of the Habsburg Monarchy', in R. J. W. Evans and T. V. Thomas (eds), *Crown, Church and Estates. Central European Politics in the Sixteenth and Sevententh Centuries* (New York: St. Martin's Press, 1991), pp. 230–1, 240.
21. Jeremy Black, 'Recent Work on European Absolutism', *Teaching History* (Jan. 1988), pp. 39–40, has asked these questions.
22. See Thomas Ertman, *Birth of the Leviathan. Building States and Regimes in Medieval and Early Modern Europe* (Cambridge University Press, 1997), ch. 1, for succinct review of these debates. However, Ertman's own differentiation between patrimonial and bureaucratic constitutionalism and absolutism suffers from a similar problem, and his argument will not hold up if applied to the entire complex of the Austrian Habsburg lands.
23. Nicholas Henshall claims this in *The Myth of Absolutism: Change and Continuity in Early Modern European Monarchy* (London: Longman, 1992), pp. 1–3. For more balanced overviews of the debate and treatment of the subject , see Richard Bonney, 'Absolutism: What's in a Name?' *French History*, 1(1) (1987), pp. 93–117; Heinz Duchhardt, 'Absolutismus – Abschied von einem Epochenbegriff?', *Historische Zeitschrift*, 258 (1994), pp. 113–22; Phyllis K. Leffler, 'French Historians and the Challenge to Louis XIV's Absolutism', *French Historical Studies* (1985), pp. 1–21; Black, 'Recent Work on European Absolutism', and especially John Miller's 'Introduction' in John Miller (ed.), *Absolutism in Seventeenth-Century Europe*, (London: Macmillan, 1990).

24. Rudolf Vierhaus, *Germany in the Age of Absolutism,* trans. Jonathan B. Knudsen (Cambridge University Press, 1988), pp. 88–9.
25. Henshall, *The Myth of Absolutism,* p. 141.
26. Nicholas Henshall claims that there was little difference between the medieval and early modern state. He fervently charges historians with having 'assiduously asked the wrong questions. They have investigated the socio-economic basis of "absolutism" when they should have explored the vagaries of high politics and personalities'. Henshall welcomes newer political studies that swing the spotlight away from the preferences of French scholars, who study 'history "from the bottom up"', especially 'cat massacres by Parisian apprentices or contraceptive practices among the peasants of Provence'. He feels that 'Rebels and poachers remain bigger business than the protagonists of authority'. *The Myth of Absolutism*, pp. 5, 173. It is unfortunate that new trends in history writing frequently tend to go from one extreme to another. Thus, while social history was inclined to neglect political history, revisionists such as Henshall prefer to undervalue economic and social factors. And this reaction is typical of much of the other criticism levelled against the traditional social conceptions (Marxist and non-Marxist) of the relations between rulers and elite in Western European historiography.
27. In fact, few historians have offered alternative concepts. A notable exception is James B. Collins, who applies 'judicial monarchy' to French government from the thirteenth to the late fifteenth centuries, 'legislative monarchy' until the early seventeenth century, and 'administrative monarchy' to describe its specific nature during the seventeenth and eighteenth centuries; see *The State in Early Modern France* (Cambridge University Press, 1995), p. 3. However, I find these divisions confusing, particularly the distinction between judicial and legislative monarchy since these governmental functions overlapped at all times. Moreover, administrative monarchy conjures up inappropriate images of the modern bureaucratic state.
28. See, especially, Marc Raeff's work, *The Well-Ordered Police State. Social and Institutional Change through Law in the Germanies and Russia, 1600–1800* (New Haven, Conn.: Yale University Press, 1983); Peter-Michael Hahn, '"Absolutistische" Polizeigesetzgebung und ländliche Sozialverfassung', *Jahrbuch für die Geschichte Mittel- und Ostdeutschlands*, 29 (1980), pp. 13–29. R. W. Scribner's examination of policing at the grass-roots calls into question the existence of a well-ordered police state in his 'Police and the Territorial State in Sixteenth-century Württemberg', in E. I. Kouri and Tom Scott (eds), *Politics and Society in Reformation Europe* (London: Macmillan, 1987), pp. 103–20; Karl Vocelka, 'Public Opinion and the Phenomenon of *Sozialdisziplinierung* in the Habsburg Monarchy', in Charles W. Ingrao (ed.), *State and Society in Early Modern Austria,* (West Lafayette, Ind.: Purdue University Press, 1994), pp. 119–40, gives the problematic a different, and interesting twist.
29. Polišenský and Snider, *War and Society in Europe, 1618–1648* (Cambridge University Press, 1978), p. 55; see also Polišenský's, *The Thirty Years War.*
30. Polišenský and Snider, *War and Society,* pp. 55–6.
31. Miroslav Hroch and Josef Petráň also focused on the inherent contradictions within the Bohemian form of *Grundherrschaft,* which involved a 'combination of some capitalist elements with methods of purely feudal exploitation', but argued that the leadership, which was in the hands of the wealthiest feudal lords, was motivated by their exclusion from positions of power; *Das 17. Jahrhundert. Krise der Feudalgesellschaft?,* trans. Eliška and Ralph Melville (Hamburg: Hoffmann

and Campe, 1981), p. 147. For a review of Czech literature of the period between 1526–1620, see Jaroslav Pánek, 'Das Ständewesen und die Gesellschaft in den Böhmischen Ländern in der Zeit vor der Schlacht auf dem Weissen Berg (1526–1620)', *Historica*, XXV (1985); and Bůžek, 'Nižší šlechta v predbělohorských čecháh', pp. 37–53. Eila Hassenpflug-Elzholz, *Böhmen und die böhmischen Stände in der Zeit des beginnenden Zentralismus. Eine Strukturanalyse der böhmischen Adelsnation um die Mitte des 18. Jahrhunderts* (Munich: R. Oldenbourg, 1982) summarizes the historiography for the subsequent period.

32. See Jonathan Dewald, *The European Nobility, 1400–1800* (Cambridge University Press, 1996), esp. ch. 1, for a review of debates.
33. R. F. Schmiedt, 'Vorgeschichte, Verlauf und Wirkungen des Dreissigjährigen Krieges', in Max Steinmetz, (ed.), *Deutshland von 1476 bis 1648: von der frühbürgerlichen Revolution bis zum Westfählischen Frieden* (Berlin: Deutscher Verlag der Wissenschaften, 1967), pp. 271–383. For a review and bibliography of Marxist historiography, see Klaus Deppermann, 'Der preussische Absolutismus und der Adel. Eine Auseinandersetzung mit der marxistischen Absolutismustheorie', *Geschichte und Gesellschaft*, 8 (1982), pp. 538–53; on Engels' contribution, see M. C. Howard and J. E. King, *A History of Marxian Economics*, Vol I: *1883–1929* (Princeton, NJ: Princeton University Press, 1989), chs 1 and 2.
34. Perry Anderson, *Lineages of the Absolutist State* (London: Verso, 1979), pp. 18, 54–5.
35. L. Makkai, 'Die Entstehung der gesellschaftlichen Basis des Absolutismus in den Ländern der österreichischen Habsburger', *Études Historiques*, 1 (1960), pp. 630–67.
36. However, some Marxists emphasized that absolutist rulers needed a degree of autonomy from the nobility in order to protect it. For a critique of the Marxian equilibrium and dominant class theories by sociologists, see Theda Skocpol, *States and Social Revolutions* (Cambridge, Mass: Cambridge University Press, 1979), pp. 3–46; and Edgar Kiser, 'The Formation of State Policy in Western European Absolutism: A Comparison of England and France', *Politics and Society*, 15 (1986–7), pp. 259–96.
37. On pre-1945 historiography, see the overviews of James Van Horn Melton, 'Continuities in German Historical Scholarship, 1933–1960', and Winfried Schulze, 'German Historiography from the 1930s to the 1950s' in Hartmut Lehmann and James van Horn Melton (eds), *Path of Continuity. Central European Historiography from the 1930s to the 1950s*, (Cambridge University Press, 1994), pp. 1–47. For an overview on general historiographical trends see Karin J. MacHardy, 'Crisis in History: Or Hermes Unbounded', *Storia della Storiografia*, 17 (1990), pp. 5–27; MacHardy, 'The Boundaries of History and Literature', in Gisela Brude-Firnau and Karin J. MacHardy (eds), *Fact and Fiction: German History and Literature, 1848–1924,* (Tübingen: Francke Verlag, 1990), pp. 11–35; MacHardy, 'Geschichtsschreibung im Brennpunkt postmoderner Kritik,' *Österreichische Zeitschrift für Geschichtswissenschaften*, 4(3) (1993), pp. 337–69.
38. Peter Feldbauer, *Herren und Ritter*, Vol. 1: *Herrschaftsstruktur und Ständebildung* (Vienna: Verlag für Geschichte und Politik, 1973), and *Der Herrenstand in Oberösterreich. Ursprünge, Anfänge, Frühformen* (Vienna: Verlag für Geschichte und Politik, 1971); Herbert Knittler, *Städte und Märkte*, Vol. 2: *Herrschaftsstruktur und Ständebildung* (Vienna: Verlag für Geschichte und Politik, 1973); Michael Mitterauer, 'Ständegliederung und Ländertypen', in *Herrschaftsstruktur und Ständebildung*, Vol. 3: *Beiträge zur Typology der österreichischen Länder aus ihren mittelalterlichen Grundlagen* (Vienna: Verlag für Geschichte und Politik, 1973), 115–203; Ernst Bruckmüller, *Sozialgeschichte Österreichs* (Vienna/Munich: Herold

Verlag, 1985); Herbert Knittler, *Nutzen, Renten Erträge. Struktur und Entwicklung frühneuzeitlicher Feudaleinkommen in Niederösterreich* (Vienna: Verlag für Geschichte und Politik, 1989); *Adel im Wandel. Politik, Kultur, Konfession, 1500–1700. Katalog der Niederösterreichischen Landesausstellung, Rosenburg 1990* (Vienna: NÖ. Landesregieirung, 1990); and Beatrix Bastl, *Herrschaftsschätzungen. Materialien zur Einkommens- und Besitzstruktur niederösterreichischer Grundherrschaften 1550 bis 1750* (Vienna: Böhlau Verlag , 1992). The interest of Austrian historians in economic history and the legal aspects of noble land ownership is, of course, older; see in particular Helmut Feigl's contribution, *Die niederösterreichische Grundherrschaft vom ausgehenden Mittelalter bis zu den theresianisch- josephinischen Reformen* (Vienna: Verein f. Landeskunde von NÖ. und Wien, 1964); and H. Feigl and W. Rosner (eds) *Adel im Wandel. Vorträge und Diskussionen des elften Symposions des Niederösterreichischen Instituts für Landeskunde Horn, 2.–5.Juli 1990* (Vienna: NÖ. Institut für Landeskunde, 1991).

39. See, for instance, Pánek, 'The Religious Question'; and Válka, 'Moravia and the Crisis of the Estates' System'. Much of the literature provides summaries of older (including Marxist) research, and therefore does at times refer to social composition and the structure of property; as does, for example, Jaroslav Mezník, 'Der böhmische und mährische Adel im 14. und 15. Jahrhundert', *Bohemia*, 28 (1987), pp. 69–91.
40. Günter Barudio, *Der Teutsche Krieg, 1618–1648* (Frankfurt-am-/Main: Fischer Verlag, 1985); Heinz Duchhart, *Protestantisches Kaisertum und Altes Reich* (Wiesbaden: Steiner Verlag, 1977); Martin Heckel, *Deutschland im konfessionellen Zeitalter* (Göttingen: Vandenhoeck and Ruprecht, 1983); and Volker Press, *Kriege und Krisen. Deutschland 1600–1715* (Munich: Verlag C. H. Beck, 1991).
41. Ernst Walter Zeeden, *Die Enstehung der Konfessionen. Grundlagen und Formen der Konfessionsbildung im Zeitalter der Glaubenskämpfe* (Munich: R. Oldenbourg, 1965); Gerhard Oestreich, *Geist und Gestalt des frühmodernen Staates* (Berlin: Duncker Humblot, 1969); Wolfgang Reinhard, 'Zwang zur Konfessionalisierung? Prolegomena zu einer Theorie des konfessionellen Zeitalters', in *Zeitschrift für Historische Forschung,* 10 (1983), pp. 257–77; and Heinz Schilling, 'Die Konfessionalisierung im Reich. Religiöser und gesellschaftlicher Wandel in Deutschland zwischen 1555 und 1620', *Historische Zeitschrift*, 246 (1988), pp. 1–45. More recently, Heinrich Richard Schmidt, *Konfessionalisierung im 16. Jahrhundrert* (Munich: Oldenbourg, 1992); Wolfgang Reinhard and Heinz Schilling, *Die katholische Konfessionalisierung: Wissenschaftliches Symposium der Gesellschaft zur Herausgabe des Corpus Catholicorum und des Vereins für Reformationsgeschichte 1993* (Gütersloh: Gütersloher Verlagshaus, 1995); Eberhard, 'Voraussetzungen und strukturelle Grundlagen der Konfessionalisierung in Ostmitteleuropa', in Joachim Bahlcke and Arno Strohmeyer (eds), *Konfessionalisierung in Ostmitteleuropa. Wirkungen des religiösen Wandels im 16. und 17. Jahrhundert in Staat, Gesellschaft und Kultur* (Stuttgart: Steiner Verlag, 1999), pp. 89–103; R. Po-Chia Hsia, *Social Discipline in the Reformation. Central Europe, 1550–1750* (London: Routledge, 1989) provides an English synthesis of research on confessionalization.
42. Most Austrian historians apply confessionalization to the social disciplining of commoners; see Thomas Winkelbauer, 'Sozialdisziplinierung und Konfessionalisierung durch Grundherren in den österreichischen und böhmischen Ländern im 16. und 17. Jahrhundert', *Zeitschrift für historische Forschung*, 19 (1992), pp. 317–39; and Vocelka, 'Public Opinion and the Phenomenon of *Sozialdisziplinierung*'.

43. Robert Bireley, 'Confessional Absolutism in the Habsburg Lands in the Seventeenth Century', and Anton Schindling, 'Delayed Confessionalization. Retarding Factors and Religious Minorities in the Territories of the Holy Roman Empire, 1555–1648', in Charles W. Ingrao (ed.) *State and Society in Early Modern Austria* (West Lafayette, Ind.: Purdue University Press), pp. 36–70.
44. Ronald G. Asch, *The Thirty Years' War. The Holy Roman Empire and Europe, 1618–48* (New York: St. Martin's Press, 1997), chs 1 and 2. Georg Schmidt still believes that 'the Thirty Years' War as a fight over power and influence justified with confessional motives', and that the defenestration in Bohemia was caused by fear of the Estates to lose influence and religious freedom; *Der dreißigjährige Krieg*, 4th rev. ed. (Munich: Beck, 1999) p. 29; *Geschichte des alten Reiches: Staat und Nation in der frühen Neuzeit, 1495–1806* (Munich: Beck, 1999), p. 151. See also Joachim Bahlcke's *Regionalismus und Staatsintegration im Widerstreit. Die Länder der Böhmischen Krone im ersten Jahrhundert der Habsburgerherrschaft (1526–1619)* (Munich: R. Oldenbourg Verlag, 1994); and Klaus Gerteis's introduction to a source collection on the Bohemian revolt, *Monarchie oder Ständestaat. Der Böhmische Aufstand von 1618. Quellen und wissenschaftliche Diskussion* (Trier: Auenthal Verlag, 1983); Winfried Eberhard, *Monarchie und Widerstand. Zur ständischen Oppositionsbildung im Herrschaftssystem Ferdinands I in Böhmen* (Munich: R. Oldenbourg Verlag, 1985); and Winfried Becker, 'Ständestaat und Konfessionsbildung am Beispiel der böhmischen Konföderationsakte von 1619', in Dieter Albrecht *et al.* (eds.) *Politik und Konfession*, (Berlin: Duncker and Humblot, 1983), pp. 77–96. There are exceptions: Bůžek, 'Nižší šlechta v předbělohorských cecháh'; Eduard Maur, 'Der böhmische und mährische Adel vom 16. bis zum 18. Jahrhundert', in H. Feigl and W. Rosner (eds.), *Adel im Wandel*, pp. 17–37; and Thomas Winkelbauer, 'Krise der Aristokratie? Zum Strukturwandel des Adels in den böhmischen und niederösterreichischen Ländern im 16. und 18. Jahrhundert', *Mitteilungen des Instituts für Österreichische Geschichtsforschung* (*MIÖG*), 100 (1992), pp. 328–53, who draws heavily on my previous research on the Austrian nobility.
45. Norbert Elias, *The Court Society*, trans. Edmund Jephcott (New York: Pantheon Books, 1983).
46. Ellery Schalk has levelled the most famous challenge to this interpretation: 'The Court as Civilizer', in Ronald G. Asch and Adolf Birk (eds.), *Princes, Patronage, and the Nobility: The Court at the Beginning of the Modern Age, c. 1450–1650*, (Oxford University Press, 1991), pp. 256–64; see also Schalk's *From Valor to Pedigree: Ideas of Nobility in the Sixteenth and Seventeenth Centuries* (Princeton, NJ: Princeton University Press, 1986).
47. For a synthesis of research by social scientists on clientage systems, see S. N. Eisenstadt and L. Roniger, *Patrons, Clients and Friends. Interpersonal Relations and the Structure of Trust in Society* (Cambridge University Press, 1984). Sharon Kettering, *Patrons, Brokers, and Clients in Seventeenth-Century France* (Oxford University Press, 1986), has been particularly influential in showing how historians can use the conceptual tools of social scientists on clientage.
48. Kristen B. Neuschel, *Word of Honour. Interpreting Noble Culture in Sixteenth-Century France* (Ithaca, NY: Cornell University Press, 1989), pp. 16–19.
49. Victor Morgan, 'Some Types of Patronage, Mainly in Sixteenth- and Seventeenth-Century England', in Antoni Maczak (ed.) *Klientelsysteme im Europa der Frühen Neuzeit* (Munich: Oldenbourg, 1988), pp. 91–126; quote on p. 106. However, Morgan's comment (p. 111) that 'feudal patronage represented a

command economy, and patrimonial patronage a market economy in the exercise of influence' seems misplaced, since economists also define modern centralized systems as command economies.

50. Kettering, *Patrons, Brokers, and Clients,* p. 184.
51. Eisenstadt, *Patrons, Clients and Friends,* pp. 50–1.
52. Two important books providing a traditional social interpretation of the Civil War and English Revolution are Lawrence Stone, *The Causes of the English Revolution, 1529–1642* (New York: Harper & Row, 1972), and Christopher Hill, *The Century of Revolution, 1603–1714* (Edinburgh: T. Nelson, 1961). For summaries of the debates, see the review articles by John Kenyon, 'Revisionism and Post-Revisionism in Early Stuart History', *Journal of Modern History* (JMH), 64 (Dec. 1992), pp. 686–99, and Tim Harris, 'From Rage of Party to Age of Oligarchy? Rethinking the Later Stuart and Early Hanoverian Period', JMH, 64 (Dec. 1992), pp. 700–20. J. C. D. Clark, *Revolution and Rebellion: State and Society in England in the Seventeenth and Eighteenth Centuries* (Cambridge University Press, 1986) offers a lengthier exposition on the topic. Some early revisionist approaches were presented by R. C. Richardson, 'Puritanism and the Ecclesiastical Authorities in the Case of the Diocese of Chester', in B. Manning (ed.), *Politics, Religion, and the English Civil War* (New York: Arnold, 1973); C. Roberts, 'The Earl of Bedford and the Coming of the English Revolution', JMH, 49 (1977), pp. 600–16; and Kevin Sharpe, *Factions and Parliaments: Essays on Early Stuart History* (Oxford: Clarendon Press, 1978). The most famous representative of the new doxa is Conrad Russell, *The Causes of the English Civil War* (Oxford: Clarendon Press, 1990).
53. The orthodox social interpretation claimed that it was a revolution of the bourgeoisie, who asserted its own specific interests against a conservative, feudal aristocracy and monarchy. It is safe to say that this view is now widely discredited. Since French capitalism was still in its infancy, many nobles were relatively dynamic entrepreneurs, and the bourgeoisie was predominantly an elite of notables, the new orthodoxy maintains that state breakdown in France could not have been caused by long-run social factors, hinging on class conflict. Instead, revisionists see the revolution as being precipitated by accidents, such as severe weather, war, and other short-term crises, and by divisions within the bureaucracy of the absolute state. Much of current historiography on the political history of the Ancien Regime concentrates on the history of the fiscal crisis and administrative institutions, or follows Furet's call for a history of political culture that studies the network of signs that supposedly determine political conflict; an outstanding exception is William Beik's, *Absolutism and Society in Seventeent-Century France* (Cambridge University Press, 1985). William Doyle offers the best summary of the revisionist position in *The Origins of the French Revolution* (Oxford University Press, 1980); see also his *The Oxford History of the French Revolution* (Oxford University Press,1989). Jonathan Dewald, *Aristocratic Experience and the Origins of Modern Culture* (Berkeley, Calif.: University of California Press, 1993); and Lynne Hunt, *The Family Romance of the French Revolution* (Berkeley, Calif.: University of California Press, 1992) offer newer approaches to the study of political discourse. For summaries of the debates, see Colin Jones, 'Bourgeois Revolution Revivified: 1789 and Social Change', in *Rewriting the French Revolution,* pp. 69–118; and Louis Bergeron, 'The Revolution: Catastrophe or New Dawn for the French Economy?' in Colin Lucas (ed.), *Rewriting the French Revolution* (Oxford University Press , 1991), pp. 69–131.

54. Robert Brenner has stressed this in his *Merchants and Revolution. Commercial Change, Political Conflict, and London's Overseas Traders, 1550–1653* (Princeton, NJ: Princeton University Press, 1993), p. 644. Other social theorists and historians of Western Europe have pointed to the difficulties of dissociating early modern rebellions from long-term processes of social change; see Ann Hughes, *The Causes of the English Civil War* (London: Macmillan, 1991); M. S. Kimmel, *Absolutism and Its Discontents: State and Society in 17th century France and England* (New Brunswick, NJ: Transaction Books, 1988); and Jones, 'Bourgeois Revolution Revivified' in Colin Lucas (ed.) *Rewriting the French Revolution* (Oxford University Press, 1991), pp. 69–118.
55. The historical sociologist, Jack A. Goldstone, *Revolution and Rebellion in the Early Modern World* (Berkeley, Calif.: University of California Press, 1991) has made a brilliant and suggestive beginning in explaining the multiplicity of early modern revolts.
56. See S. N. Eisenstadt, and L. Roniger, 'Patron–Client as a Model of Structuring Social Exchange', *Comparative Study of Society and History*, 22 (1980) pp. 51–61, for a critique of this neglect.
57. See, for example, Robert R. Harding's discussion of noble fidelity, *Anatomy of a Power Elite: The Provincial Governors of Early Modern France* (New Haven, Conn.: Yale University Press, 1978), pp. 34–7. Richard van Dülmen supports the first assertion with a quote from a German noble, who prayed in 1583 to God to protect his honour, which he 'loves more than gold, silver or [his] estate Mertschütz', *Entstehung des frühneuzeitlichen Europa, 1550–1648* (Frankfurt-am-Main: Fischer Taschenbuch Verlag, 1982), pp. 137. See also Peter Moraw, 'The Court of the German King and of the Emperor at the end of the Middle Ages, 1440–1519', in Asch and Birke (eds), *Princes, Patronage, and the Nobility*, p. 126; and Elias, *The Court Society*, pp. 64–5, 85.
58. As Bourdieu himself explains: 'capital can present itself in three fundamental guises: as *economic capital*, which is immediately and directly convertible into money and may be institutionalized in the form of property rights; as *cultural capital*, which is convertible, on certain conditions, into economic capital and may be institutionalized in the form of educational qualifications; and as *social capital*, made up of social obligations ("connections"), which is convertible, in certain conditions, into economic capital and may be institutionalized in the form of a title of nobility'. For a more detailed description of his concepts, see Pierre Bourdieu's 'The Forms of Capital', in John G. Richardson (ed.), *Handbook of Theory and Research for the Sociology of Education* (New York: Greenwood Press, 1986), pp. 241–58. I base my concepts on ideas developed by Bourdieu in his *Outline of a Theory of Practice* (Cambridge University Press, 1977); *The Logic of Practice* (Stanford, Calif.: Stanford University Press, 1980); *Distinction: A Social Critique of the Judgement of Taste* (Cambridge, Mass.: Harvard University Press, 1984); 'Social Space and the Genesis of Groups', *Theory and Society*, 14(6) (Nov. 1985), pp. 723–44; 'Social Space and Symbolic Power', *Sociological Theory*, 7(1) (1989), pp. 14–26; *In Other Words: Essays Towards a Reflexive Sociology* (Stanford, Calif.: Stanford University Press, 1990); and, with Jean-Claude Passeron, *Reproduction in Education, Society and Culture* (London: Sage, 1977). Viewing capital as a resource that potentially yields power, and connecting immaterial to economic forms, differs from Marx's conception of capital and capital accumulation, as well as from the ideas of orthodox economics. See Craig Calhoun for an accessible treatment of Bourdieu's work in 'Habitus, Field and Capital: The

Question of Historical Specificity', in Craig Calhoun *et al.* (eds), *Bourdieu: Critical Perspectives* (Chicago: University of Chicago Press, 1993), pp. 61–88.

59. I disagree with those mainstream sociologists and economists who view all human behaviour in terms of rational choice, or rational action theory. J. Elster (ed.), *Rational Choice* (Oxford: Basil Blackwell, 1986), pp. 1–33, outlines the problems they encounter. Nobles (as most other people) could not be fully informed maximizers, with knowledge of all the choices available to them, or the true probability distribution of contingencies. While I believe that human action is motivated, I do not view motivation as coincident with material interest and *a fortiori* with material interest conceived in universalistic, utilitarian terms. 'Interest' is not eternal, but a historical variant that needs to be studied through historical analysis. I agree with Bourdieu that '*practices form an economy,* that is, follow an immanent reason that cannot be restricted to economic reason [but] may be defined by reference to a wide range of functions and ends'. If we reduce action to mechanical reactions we cannot understand practices that 'are reasonable without being the product of a reasoned purpose, even less, of conscious computation'. See Pierre Bourdieu and Loïc J. D. Wacquant, *An Invitation to Reflexive Sociology* (Chicago: Chicago University Press, 1992), pp. 119–20.
60. Pierre Bourdieu defines the concentration of different forms of power, or capital, that leads to the private monopolization of public authority by the ruler as statist capital: 'The concentration of these different species of capital – economic (thanks to taxation), military, cultural, juridical and, more generally, symbolic – goes hand in hand with the rise and consolidation of the various corresponding fields. The result of this process is the emergence of a specific capital, *properly statist capital,* born of their cumulation, which allows the state to wield a power over the different fields and over the various forms of capital that circulate in them'. See Bourdieu and Wacquant, *An Invitation to Reflexive Sociology*, p. 114.

1 Political Culture, Political Space

1. Evans, *The Making of the Habsburg Monarchy*, pp. vii, xxiii; Evans, *Crown, Church and Estates*, p. xxix.
2. Sutter-Fichtner, 'Habsburg State-Building', p. 141.
3. Otto Hintze, for example, stressed that the outcome of state-building depended to a large extent on the influence of Estates, or parliaments, and on infrastructural development, and that it was essential to analyse how state institutions worked in connection with local elites and organizations. See the collection of essays by Otto Hintze in *Staat und Verfassung* Gerhard Oestreich (ed.) (Göttingen: Vandenhoeck and Ruprecht, 1970).
4. I define 'power' as a capacity or resource that enables actors to pursue and attain goals through mastering a particular environment. Following Max Weber and Michael Mann, I view the 'state' essentially as a delimited territory with a set of differentiated institutions whose reach radiates from the centre outward. The higher levels of the institutions are controlled by a state elite, which can include a monarch, with some binding rule-making power, backed up by a degree of organized force. State power is based on a resource-supported military and administrative organization. Next to this state elite is, for lack of a better term, 'civil society', defined as overlapping and intersecting power networks with specific spatial contours. See Michael Mann, *States, War and Capitalism* (Oxford:

Basil Blackwell, 1992), and his *The Sources of Social Power,* Vol. I: *A History of Power from the Beginning to A.D. 1760*; and Vol. II: *The Rise of Classes and Nation-States, 1760–1914* (Cambridge University Press, 1993).

5. Mann defines this power of actor A over B as 'despotic' power of the elite; *States, War and Capitalism,* p. 5. I changed this term (but not the meaning) because it is related too closely to another highly ambiguous term, namely 'enlightened despotism'.
6. See Mann, *States, War and Capitalism,* pp. 9–11, for a detailed explanation of these characteristics.
7. Tilly, *Coercion, Capital and European States*, p. 19.
8. Mann, *The Rise of Classes,* p. *61.*
9. Wayne TeBrake, *Shaping History: Ordinary People in European Politics, 1500–1700* (Berkeley, Calif.: University of California Press, 1998), p. 184.
10. Ertman, *Birth of the Leviathan,* p. 3.
11. Ingrao, *The Habsburg Monarchy*, 1618–1815 (Cambridge University Press, 1994), pp. 10–14.
12. H. G. Koenigsberger, '*Dominium Regale* or *Dominium Politicum et Regale*', in his *Politicians and Virtuosi: Essays in Early Modern History* (London: Hambledon Press, 1986).
13. Niccolò Machiavelli, Quentin Skinner and Russell Price (eds), *The Prince* (Cambridge, 1990), p. 8, quoted in J. H. Elliott, 'A Europe of Composite Monarchies', *Past & Present*, 137 (Nov. 1992), p. 52.
14. Herman Wiesflecker, *Maximilian I. Die Fundamente des habsburgischen Weltreiches* (Vienna: Verlag für Geschichte und Politik, 1991), pp. 189–92, 300–2.
15. I use the term 'crown' to avoid repetition. It is not identical with the state, but refers to the Habsburgs as rulers, either in their capacity as emperors or as archdukes.
16. Mann, *The Sources of Social Power I,* ch. 14.
17. Mann, *The Sources of Social Power I,* pp. *455.*
18. But, as we shall see, the distinction between *Kammergut* and *Landesunmittel- barkeit* was not delineated clearly. Otto Brunner, *Land und Herrschaft: Grundfragen der territorialen Verfassungsgeschichte Südostdeutschlands im Mittelalter* (3rd edn) (Brünn: R. M. Rohrer Verlag, 1943), pp. 472–3. Persons without *Landesunmittel-barkeit* were guests, subjects of others, or belonged to the royal domain (*Kammergut*).
19. At the end of the century, the position of the knights was still very inferior to the lords, and often indistinguishable from that of burghers. However, by the fifteenth century, the legal status of the two noble Estates had become more equal. For example, the distinction between their landed possessions, that is, between the *Güter* of the knights and the *Herrschaften* of the lords, became blurred. Although knights continued to be unable to invest fiefs, this distinction became meaningless with the breakdown of the feudal order. Consequently, intermarriage without loss of status and social mobility of knights into the *Herrenstand* became possible and more frequent during the fifteenth century. Nevertheless, social status and the ability to hold high offices continued to distinguish lords from knights, and they remained two distinct Estates. As will be shown in a subsequent chapter, the size of the two Estates fluctuated considerably over time, mainly because of the extinction of families and social mobility. But until the early seventeenth century, the *Ritterstand* was always larger than the Estate of Lords. For the diverse origins and complicated evolution of the *Herren-* and *Ritterstand* in the Austrian lands during the Middle Ages, see Feldbauer, *Herren und Ritter,* and Mitterauer, 'Ständegliederung und Ländertypen'. Mitterauer

has also studied patterns of marriage in his 'Zur Frage des Heiratsverhaltens im österreichischen Adel', in H. Fichtenau and E. Zöllner (eds), *Beiträge zur neueren Geschichte Österreichs,* (Vienna: Böhlaus, 1974), pp. 176–94.

20. Part of the clergy already acted sporadically as advisers and guarantors of royal contracts during the thirteenth century, but consolidated its power as an Estate only during the early fifteenth century. Up to the year 1500, the rulers invited any prelate who belonged to the *ordo ecclesiastics* and who possessed taxable landed property to attend assemblies. Since new orders rarely gained access to the First Estate, its composition changed only insignificantly after the fifteenth century. The 22 to 26 prelates who belonged to the *Prälatenstand* of Lower Austria during the late sixteenth and early seventeenth centuries were by no means all the heads of existing monasteries, chapters and dioceses, but included most of the older orders, which were under the special protection of the ruler (*Schirmvogtei*). A list dated 1583 names 24 prelates, but in 1619 only 22 paid homage to Ferdinand II; Niederösterreichisches Landesarchiv, Ständisches Archiv AI/5 (1583), fol. 118–9, and AIII/20 (1619), fol. 138. On the development of the First Estate, see Helmut Stradal, 'Die Prälaten', *Herrschaftsstruktur und Ständebildung,* Vol. 3: *Beiträge zur Typologie der österreichischen Länder aus ihren mittelalterlichen Grundlagen* (Vienna: Verlag für Geschichte und Politik, 1973), pp. 73–5; Herbert Hassinger, 'Die Landstände der österreichischen Länder. Zusammensetzung, Organization und Leistung im 16–18. Jahrhundert', *Jahrbuch für Landeskunde von Niederösterreich* (JbLkNÖ), NF 34 (1964), pp. 998.
21. Some towns began to participate in the political affairs of the territory during the late thirteenth century, when the Austrian rulers acknowledged their autonomy and granted them extensive privileges, but they joined the assemblies of the nobility and clergy only in the late fourteenth and early fifteenth centuries. The formation of the Fourth Estate was complete by the sixteenth century, ironically just as the economic and political power of towns began to wane. Mortgaging sovereign towns usually led to their exclusion from the Estates, but sometimes they continued to be invited to assemblies, thereby confusing the distinction between *Unmittelbarkeit* and *Mittelbarkeit.* In 1500, only 30 out of 251 *landesfürstliche* towns and markets of Lower Austria were assembled at the *Landtag,* and soon after the year 1500 the members of the Fourth Estate were reduced to 18, who together with the city of Vienna still constituted the entire curia in the early seventeenth century. In 1619, the cities of Vienna, Krems, Stein, Klosterneuburg, Eggenburg, Korneuburg, Bruck/Leitha, Tulln, Retz, Zwettl, Waidhofen/Thaya, Baden, Hainburg, Ybbs, Laa and the markets of Langenlois, Perchtoldsdorf, Mödling and Gumpoldskirchen belonged to the Fourth Estate of Lower Austria. Niederösterreichisches Landesarchiv (Vienna), Ständisches Archiv, Ständische Akten III/2 (9 Oct. 1619), fols. 140–4. Brunner, *Land und Herrschaft,* pp. 468, 428–30; Stradal, 'Die Prälaten', pp. 53–114; Herbert Knittler, *Städte und Märkte,* pp. 11–12, 40–4, 60–2.
22. Karl Gutkas, *Geschichte des Landes Niederösterreich* (5th edn) (St. Pölten: N. Ö Pressehaus, 1973), pp. 109–14, 117.
23. W. v. Janko, *Lazarus Freiherr von Schwendi, oberster Feldhauptmann und Rat Kaiser Maximilians II* (Vienna, 1871), p. 147, quoted in M. C. Mandlmayr and K. G. Vocelka, 'Vom Adelsaufgebot zum stehenden Heer. Bemerkungen zum Funktionswandel des Adels im Kriegswesen der frühen Neuzeit', *Wiener Beiträge zur Geschichte der Neuzeit,* 8 (1980), p. 121.
24. The continued summoning of their vassals to military service were but threats by the Habsburgs to extort larger monetary contributions; Mandlmayr and

Vocelka, 'Vom Adelsaufgebot zum stehenden Heer', pp. 113–15. Nevertheless, it was still customary for nobles to supply one fully equipped horse (*Gültpferd*) for every 100 lbs of tax units. Considering the small size of landholdings, it is not surprising that the crown tried to lower the required tax unit and gradually replaced the *Gültpferd* contributions with payments. During the war with the Ottomans of the later sixteenth century, the Estates frequently assumed the maintenance of cavalrymen. In Styria, many nobles preferred financial contributions (*Wart- und Rüstgeld*) for which the Estates hired horsemen; Winfried Schulze, *Landesdefension und Staatsbildung. Studien zum Kriegswesen des innerösterreichischen Territorialstaates, 1546–1619* (Vienna: Böhlaus, 1973), pp. 113–23; Gottfried Stangler, 'Die Niederösterreichischen Landtage von 1593-1607', (Ph.D. dissertation, University of Vienna, 1972), p. 91.

25. An exception is the rise of the military enterpriser during the Thirty Years' War, who could raise and recruit single or multiple regiments, and finance them initially. Such regiments and squadrons could be disposed of at the will of the proprietor, and commanding positions in such regiments were even available for sale. However, as we shall see in a subsequent chapter, regimental proprietorship was not very common among the Lower Austrian nobility. Thomas M. Barker, *Army, Aristocracy, Monarchy: Essays on War, Society and Government in Austria, 1618–1780 (*New York: Columbia University Press, 1982), pp. 15–18.
26. Wiesflecker, *Maximilian I*, p. 249.
27. Ingrao, *The Habsburg Monarchy*, pp. 32, 59. Other books provide slightly different figures on the Habsburg and the Bohemian Confederate army; see, for example, Jeremy Black, *A Military Revolution? Military Change and European Society, 1550–1800* (Atlantic Highlands, NJ: Humanities Press International, 1991), p. 12.
28. The military affairs of the Tyrol were, since the territorial division after Ferdinand I's death, outside of its jurisdiction, and after 1578 the Inner Austrian lands were also headed by a separate regional War Council. A section of the Imperial War Council remained in Vienna after Rudolf moved his court to Prague, but during the later years of Rudolf's reign, the entire central War Council appears to have resumed its seat in Vienna. Thomas Fellner and Heinrich Kretschmayr, *Die Österreichische Zentralverwaltung*, Vol. I: *Von Maximilian I. bis zur Vereinigung der österreichischen und böhmischen Hofkanzlei (1749)*, (Vienna: Adolf Holzhausen, 1907), pp. 237–9, 243–4; Henry F. Schwarz, *The Imperial Privy Council in the Seventeenth Century* (Cambridge: Harvard University Press, 1943), p. 44.
29. Schulze, *Landesdefension und Staatsbildung*, pp. 78–93.
30. Fellner and Kretschmayr, *Die Österreichische Zentralverwaltung* I, pp. 38, Schwarz, *Imperial Privy Council*, pp. 64–5 and appendix C.
31. Arnold Luschin von Ebengreuth, *Geschichte des älteren Gerichtswesens in Österreich ob und unter der Enns* (Weimar: Böhlaus, 1879), pp. 208.
32. For the taxation system, see Silvia Petrin and Max Weltin, 'Zum System der Gültbesteuerung in Niederösterreich', *Unsere Heimat*, 43 (1972), pp. 172–81. The authorities could not verify the accuracy of the reported income; arrears were always high and the Estates proved unwilling to impose strict preventive measures upon their peers. The crown suspected, and the Estates admitted, that taxes higher than those proclaimed were collected from the peasantry by the landowners, who filled their own pockets with the difference; see Hannelore Herold, 'Die Hauptprobleme der Landtagshandlungen des Herzogtums Österreich unter der Enns zur Zeit der Regierung Kaiser Maximilians II (1564–76)', (Ph.D.

dissertation, University of Vienna, 1970), pp. 185–6; Günther Ortner, 'Die niederösterreichischen Landtage von 1635–1648', (Ph.D. dissertation, University of Vienna, 1974), pp. 77–8; Stangler, 'Die niederösterreichischen Landtage', pp. 100–2.

33. Helmut Feigl, *Die niederösterreichische Grundherrschaft vom ausgehenden Mittelalter bis zu den theresianisch-josephinischen Reformen* (Vienna: Verein f. Landeskunde von NÖ, 1964), pp. 30–2, 238, 245; Angelika Hametner, 'Die niederösterreichischen Landtage von 1530–1564', (Ph.D. dissertation, University of Vienna, 1970), pp. 132–5. E. Kiebel, 'Ungeld und Landgericht in Niederösterreich', *Mitteilungen des Instituts für Österreichische Geschichtsforschung* (MIÖG) 52 (1938), pp. 269–87; Hassinger, 'Die Landstände der österreichschen Länder', pp. 1028–29; Roman Sandgruber, *Ökonomie und Politik. Österreichische Wirtschaftsgeschichte vom Mittelalter bis zur Gegenwart* (Vienna: Ueberreuter, 1995), pp. 47–102; Putschögl, *Die landständische Behördenorganization in Österreich ob der Enns vom Anfang des 16. bis zur Mitte des 18. Jahrhundert* (Linz: OÖ. Landesarchiv, 1978), pp. 333–9.
34. The Estates met more frequently if required, but it was customary that only the ruler called for their assembly. For the beginnings of the Estates' administration, see Max Vansca, 'Die Anfänge des ständischen Beamtentums in Österreich unter der Enns', *Merkblatt des Vereins für Landeskunde von Niederösterreich,* IX (1918), pp. 130–8, and for Upper Austria, Putschögl, *Die landständische Behördenorganization,* pp.15–62.
35. He was assisted by several assessors (*Beisitzer*) who were always nobles. Although the *Landmarschall* had lost many of his important medieval executive and police powers within the province, he still yielded much prestige and influence; NÖLA, StA, Hs 362. Ernst C. Hellbling, *Österreichische Verfassungs- und Verwaltungsgeschichte* (Vienna: Springer Verlag, 1956), pp. 232.
36. Schulze, *Landesdefension und Staatsbildung,* pp. 113–23; Stangler, 'Die niederösterreichischen Landtage', p. 91.
37. In Lower Austria, the actual fieldwork was performed by four district commanders (*Viertelhauptmänner*) and their five subordinate officers; Stangler, 'Die niederösterreichischen Landtage', pp. 62, 85, 90.
38. Most important were the comptrollers (*Raitherren*), who were responsible for auditing the accounts of the *Einnehmer*. In Lower Austria, two, and sometimes three, *Raitherren* were elected from among the three upper Estates. NÖLA, StA, Hs 362, fols. 18, 20; Schimka, 'Die Zusammensetzung des niederösterreichischen Herrenstandes', p. 40; for the financial administration of the Upper Austrian Estates, see Putschögl, *Die landständische Behördenorganisation,* chs 6 and 10.
39. Oskar Regele, *Der österreichische Hofkriegsrat 1556–1898.* Ergänzungsband 1 (Vienna: Mitteilungen des österreichischen Staatsarchivs, 1949), pp. 15–17; Hellbling, *Österreichische Verfassungs- und Verwaltungsgeschichte,* p. 230.
40. Karl Haselbach, 'Die volkswirtschaftlichen Verhältnisse Niederösterreichs im XVI. und XVII. Jahrundert', *Blätter des Vereins für Landeskunde von Niederösterreich* V, Neue Folge (1871), pp. 78–9; Fritz Weber, 'Die Finanz- und Zollpolitik im 16. Jahrhundert und der Rückgang des niederösterr. Weinhandels', JbLkNÖ, 31 (1953/4), pp. 133–48.
41. The figures provided by various authors seem to focus on different sources and are probably not very reliable, although they indicate a similar trend. Wiesflecker, *Maximilian I,* pp. 298, 386; Karl Oberleitner, *Österreichs Finanzen und Kriegswesen unter Ferdinand I. vom Jahre 1522 bis 1564* (Vienna: K.K. Hof und Staatsdruckerei, 1859), pp. 53–101; Alfons Huber, 'Studien über die finanziellen Verhältnisse Österreichs unter Ferdinand I', MIÖG, Erg. Bd. 4 (1893),

pp. 181–247; Andreas Schneider, 'Die Mitwirkung der niederösterreichischen Landstände bei der Türkenabwehr unter Ferdinand I und Maximilian II' (Ph.D. dissertation, University of Vienna, 1939). That the price inflation created financial difficulties for the Habsburgs is also evident from the tripling of the cost for the upkeep of the court in just four decades between the reigns of Ferdinand I and Maximilian II; Hubert Ch. Ehalt, *Ausdrucksformen absolutistischer Herrschaft. Der Wiener Hof im 17. und 18. Jahrhundert* (Vienna: Verlag für Geschichte und Politik, 1980), p. 57. However, comparisons in expenses for the court must be treated with great caution because its size fluctuated, as did the territories over which each emperor ruled.

42. For a succinct overview of population trends, see Jan de Vries, 'Population', in Thomas A. Brady, et al. (eds) *Handbook of European History, 1400–1600: Late Middle Ages, Renaissance and Reformation,* Vol I: *Structures and Assertions* (Leiden.: Brille, 1994), pp. 1–49; Massimo Livi Bacci provides a more extended treatment of *The Population of Europe, A History,* trans. C. DeNardi Ipsen and C. Ipsen (Oxford/Malden: Blackwell, 2000), chs 1–5; for the hereditary lands, see Kurt Klein, 'Die Bevölkerung Österreichs vom Beginn des 16. bis zur Mitte des 18. Jahrhunderts', in Heimhold Helczmanovsky (ed.) *Beiträge zur Bevölkerungs- und Sozialgeschichte Österreichs,* (Munich: Oldenburg, 1973), pp. 64–9. The figures on the population increase are derived from tax registers (*Gültbücher),* which do provide information about the number of peasant households, but not the number of children per household. Since this information is also based on reports from landholders who derived financial gain from not announcing increases in the number of peasant households, it is likely that the tax registers hide actual population increases; Roman Sandgruber, 'Zur Wirtschaftsentwicklung Niederösterreichs im 16. und 17. Jahrhundert', *Unsere Heimat,* XLV (1975), pp. 210–1; Sandgruber, *Ökonomie und Politik,* pp. 99–100, 105–9; see also Alfred F. Pribram, *Materialien zur Geschichte der Preise und Löhne in Österreich* (Vienna: Ueberreuter, 1938), p. 570.
43. Karl Haselbach, 'Die volkswirtschaftlichen Verhältnisse Niederösterreichs', pp. 78–9; Fritz Weber, 'Die Finanz- und Zollpolitik', 133–48.
44. Bruckmüller, *Sozialgeschichte Österreichs,* pp. 166–7; Herbert Hassinger, *Geschichte des Zollwesens, Handels und Verkehrs in den östlichen Alpenländern* (Stuttgart: Steiner Verlag, 1987), pp. 12–29.
45. MacHardy, 'The Rise of Absolutism', p. 438; Putschlögl, *Die landständische Behördenorganisation,* pp. 57–9; Gutkas, *Geschichte des Landes Niederöstereich,* pp. 325–30.
46. Julian H. Franklin, 'Sovereignty and the Mixed Constitution: Bodin and his Critics', in J. H. Burns (ed.), with the assistance of Mark Goldie, *The Cambridge History of Political Thought, 1450–1700,* (Cambridge University Press, 1994), pp. 307–9. On the controversies over definitions of premodern and modern sovereignty, see John Hoffman, *Sovereignty* (Minneapolis, Minn.: University of Minnesota Press, 1998), pp. 1–42.
47. Winfried Eberhard, 'The Political System and the Intellectual Traditions of the Bohemian Ständestaat from the Thirteenth to the Sixteenth Century', in R. J. W. Evans et al. (eds), *Crown, Church and Estates* p. 41.
48. Eberhard, 'The Political System and the Intellectual Traditions', p. 31.
49. This form of case law found through judicial decisions appears similar to English common law. Brunner, *Land and Lordship,* p. 321, believes that 'in the medieval period *lex,* the sphere of positive law, was held to be identical with *ius,* the "law

of nature" or justice'. However, modern scholars of medieval political theory believe that, at least since the twelfth century, continental jurists distinguished clearly between positive and natural law. See Kenneth Pennington, *The Prince and the Law, 1200–1600, Sovereignty and Rights in the Western Legal Tradition* (Berkeley, Calif.: University of California Press, 1993), ch. 4.

50. This desire to be 'emperor in his own territory' was the meaning behind the forgery of Rudolf IV's *Privilegium maius,* which asserted the duke's independence from the emperor in his own domain. Brunner, *Land and Lordship,* pp. 319–24.
51. Pennington, *The Prince and the Law,* pp. 213, 236.
52. Quoted in Brunner, *Land and Lordship,* p. 322, citing no original but Alfons Huber, *Geschichte des Herzogs Rudolf IV. von Österreich* (Innsbruck: Wagner, 1865), p. 31.
53. Eberhard, 'The Political System and the Intellectual Traditions', p. 40; and Eberhard, *Monarchie und Widerstand,* pp. 196–7.
54. Pennington, *The Prince and the Law,* pp. 269–90.
55. The meaning of *Ehrbarkeit* and *gute Sitten,* which in modern translation means honour and decency (the latter could also mean good customs) is not entirely certain, but it seems to refer to common medieval legal precepts against making dishonest, wicked and immoral laws, i.e., contrary to divine law. Pennington, 'Prince and the Law', pp. 69, 115, 204.
56. 'Zeiger in das Landrechtsbuch', ('Lib. P. Zaiger in das Land Rechts Buech oder Institutum Kayßers Ferdinandi I[mi]. Die N.Ö. Land Rechten Und Gerichtspersohnen betr.', 1721); N.Ö. Landesarchiv, Hs.178., fol 1a–10b ('Vorred'); see also Ursula Floßman, *Landrechte als Verfassung* (Vienna: Springer Verlag, 1976), pp. 20–1.
57. Both *utilitas publica* and *bonum publicum* are amorphous terms that were sometimes conflated but did not always have the same meaning; Pennington, *Prince and the Law*, pp. 235–6, 278.
58. Brunner, *Land and Lordship,* p. 352.
59. See Chapter 3 for more detail on this, and Gerhard Oestreich, *Neostoicism and the Early Modern State* (Cambridge University Press, 1982); Paul Kléber Monod, *The Power of Kings. Monarchy and Religion in Europe, 1589–1715* (New Haven, Conn.: Yale University Press, 1999), ch. 3.
60 Sturmberger, *Kaiser Ferdinand II und das Problem des Absolutismus* (Munich: Verlag R. Oldenbourg), pp. 18–20. Monod overstates his case by interpreting this as a demand on Ferdinand's part for absolute power, and that the archduke accepted a comprise with the Estates that denied him sovereign rights over their consciences; Monod, *The Power of Kings,* p. 91.
61. Franklin, 'Sovereignty', pp. 306–9, discusses the notion of sovereignty as Bodin revised it in his *Republic.*
62. Rebel's *Peasant Classes* analyses, *inter alia,* Habsburg regulation of labour services in Upper Austria; Herman Rebel, *Peasant Classes. The Bureaucratization of Property and Family Relations under Early Habsburg Absolutism, 1511–1636* (Princeton, NJ: Princeton University Press, 1983). For Lower Austria, see Thomas Winkelbauer, *Robot und Steuer. Die Untertanen der Waldviertler Grundherrschaften Gföhl und Altpölla zwischen feudaler Herrschaft und absolutistischem Staat* (Vienna: Verein f. Landeskunde von Niederösterreich, 1986).
63. Roland Axtmann, '"Police" and the Formation of the Modern State. Legal and Ideological Assumptions on State Capacity in the Austrian Lands of the Habsburg Empire, 1500–1800', *German History,* 10 (1992), pp. 39–61; Wilhelm Brauneder, 'Der soziale und rechtliche Gehalt der österreichischen Polizeiordnungen des 16.

Jahrhunderts', *Zeitschrift für historische Forschung,* 3 (1976), pp. 205–19; Helmut Feigl, 'Die Oberösterreichischen Taidinge als Quellen zur Geschichte der Reformation und Gegenreformation', MOÖLA, 14 (Linz, 1984), pp. 149–75; Gertraud Hampel-Kallbrunner, 'Beiträge zur Geschichte der Kleiderordnungen mit besonderer Berücksichtigung Österreichs' (Ph.D. Dissertation, University of Vienna, 1962); Vocelka, 'Public Opinion and the Phenomenon of *Sozialdisziplinierung'*, pp. 122–6.

64. Helmuth Feigl, *Die niederösterreichische Grundherrschaft,* pp. 210, 218–19.
65. During the late Middle Ages the dynasty had, with some success, attempted to make the exercise of high justice dependent on royal writ. But during the fifteenth century they began to sell this right again, so that the *Blutbann* was largely returned to noble landowners. Helmut Feigl, *Die niederösterreichische Grundherrschaft,* p. 27.
66. Hellbling, *Österreichische Verfassungs – und Verwaltungsgeschichte,* p. 145.
67. Gutkas, *Geschichte des Landes Niederöstereich,* pp. 149–50.
68. Gutkas, *Geschichte des Landes Niederöstereich,* p. 198.
69. Fellner-Kretschmayr, *Die Österreichische Zentralverwaltung,* I; pp. 219–33.
70. Gutkas, *Geschichte des Landes Niederösterreich,* pp. 148–50; Wiesflecker, *Maximilian I,* pp. 387–8.
71. Brunner, *Land und Herrschaft,* p. 350.
72. This is closer to Bousset's position; see J. H. Burns, 'Absolutism', in J. H. Burns (ed.) *The Cambridge History of Political Thought, 1450–1700* pp. 30–4; Burns, *Lordship, Kingship and Empire. The Idea of Monarchy 1400–1525* (Oxford: Clarendon Press, 1992).
73. Eberhard, 'The Political System and the Intellectual Traditions', p. 39.
74. Eberhard, *Monarchie und Widerstand,* pp. 410–53. It is unclear from Eberhard's account whether the Bohemian *Stände* wanted to gain a 'souveräne Position', or whether the *Landtage* were indeed the organ of making law ('das Organ der Gesetzgebung'). To dispense the *Landrecht,* to propose and consent to changes in laws, and to participate in codification, is not the same as making laws independently of the king.
75. Jurists, such as Baldus de Ubaldis, did not differentiate between *ultilitas publica, res publica* and *bonum publicum*; Pennington, *Prince and the Law,* pp. 232–4.
76. Eberhard, *Monarchie und Widerstand,* pp. 481–5.
77. Following TeBrake, *Shaping History,* p. 184, one could define this form of composite state as consisting of 'layered sovereignties'.
78. This dovetails with TeBrake's views on political development and protest in Western Europe; *Shaping History,* p. 11.

2 Religious Reformation and Civil War

1. Heinz Schilling, 'The Reformation and the Rise of the Early Modern State', in James D. Tracy (ed.), *Luther and the Modern State in Germany,* Vol VII (Kirksville, Mo.: Sixteenth Century Essays and Studies, 1986), pp. 21–30; Wolfgang Reinhard, 'Reformation, Counter-Reformation, and the Early Modern State. A Reassessment', *Catholic Historical Review,* LXXV (3) (July 1989), pp. 383–404; Winfried Eberhard, 'Entwicklungsphasen und Probleme der Gegenreformation und katholischen Erneuerung in Böhmen', *Römische Quartalschrif,* 84 (1989), pp. 374–57; Winfried Eberhard 'Reformation und Counterreformation in East Central Europe', in Thomas A. Brady, Heiko A. Oberman and James D. Tracy (eds), *Handbook of European History, 1400–1600,* vol. II: *Visions, Programs and Outcomes* (Leiden: Brill,

1995), pp. 551–84; Arno Herzig, *Der Zwang zum Wahren Glauben: Rekatholisierung vom 16. bis zum 18. Jahrhundert* (Göttingen: Vandenhoeck & Ruprecht, 2000).

2. For a comprehensive treatment of events, see Horst Rabe, *Reich und Glaubensspaltung. Deutschland, 1500–1600* (Munich: Verlag C. H. Beck, 1989), pt II. For an older, still relevant English treatment of international affairs, see H. G. Koenigsberger, *The Habsburgs and Europe, 1516–1660* (Ithaca, NY: Cornell University Press, 1971), chs 1 and 2.
3. František Kavka, 'Bohemia', pp. 131–54, and Katalin Peter, 'Hungary', pp. 155–67, in Bob Scribner *et al* (eds), *The Reformation in National Context* (Cambridge University Press, 1994); Winfried Eberhard, *Konfessionsbildung und Stände in Böhmen 1478–1530* (Munich/Vienna: Oldenbourg, 1981); Evans, *Making of the Habsburg Monarchy*, pt I.
4. Karl von Otto, 'Die Anfänge der Reformation im Herzogthum Oesterreich (1552–1564)', JbGPrÖ, 1 (1880), pp. 11–27.
5. Horst Rabe, *Reich und Glaubensspaltung*, p. 319; Ziegler, 'Nieder- und Oberösterreich', pp. 125–6.
6. Von Otto, 'Die Anfänge der Reformation', p. 15; Letter of 25 Aug. 1585, in Bibl, 'Die Berichte des Reichshofrates Dr. Georg Eder an die Herzoge Albrecht und Wilhelm von Bayern über die Religionskrise in Niederösterreich, 1579–97', JbLkNÖ, NF, 8 (1900), p. 150; Ziegler, 'Nieder- und Oberösterreich', p. 125.
7. Joseph Schmidlin, *Die kirchlichen Zustände in Deutschland vor dem Dreißigjährigen Kriege nach den bischöflichen Diözesenberichten an den Heiligen Stuhl*, Vol. I: *Österreich* (Freiburg/Breisgau: Herdersche Verlagsbuchhandlung, 1908); Karl Amon, 'Innerösterreich', pp. 103–16; Heinz Notflatscher, 'Tirol, Brixen, Trient', pp. 87–101, and Walter Ziegler, 'Nieder- und Oberösterreich', pp. 119–33, in Anton Schindling and Walter Ziegler (eds), *Die Territorien des Reichs im Zeitalter der Reformation und Konfessionalisierung. Land und Konfession, 1500–1650*, Vol. 1: *Der Südosten* (Münster: Aschendorffsche Verlagsbuchhandlung, 1989); for an English treatment, see Evans, *The Making of the Habsburg Monarchy*, ch. 1.
8. Theodor Brückler, 'Zum Problem der katholischen Reform in Niederösterreich in der zweiten Hälfte des 16. Jahrhunderts', *Österreich in Geschichte und Literatur*, 21 (1977), pp. 151–63.
9. 'Dr. Georg Eder an Herzog Albrecht V', (29 Dec. 1577) in Karl Schrauf (ed.) *Der Reichshofrat Dr. Georg Eder. Eine Briefsammlung*, Vol. I: *1573–1578* (Vienna: Adolf Holzhausen), pp. 332–3; see also the Letter of 29 April 1580 in Bibl's collection, 'Die Berichte des Reichshofrates Dr. Georg Eder', p. 111.
10. Amon, 'Innerösterreich', pp. 104–5.
11. Brunner, *Land und Lordship*, pp. 255–62.
12. I use the term Catholic Reformation to refer to the internal, spiritual renewal of the Church to differentiate it from its struggle against Protestantism, the Counter-Reformation. However, it must be kept in mind that the differences between the two movements cannot be delineated clearly, since both developments required the help of the state, internal reorganization, and theological and moral strengthening. See Hubert Jedin, *Katholische Reformation oder Gegenreformation. Ein Versuch zur Klärung der Begriffe nebst einer Jubiläumsbetrachtung über das Trienter Konzil* (Lucerne: Verlag Josef Stocker, 1946).
13. Brunner, *Land and Lordship*, pp. 291; Feigl, *Die niederösterreichische Grundherrschaft*, pp. 108–21.

14. von Otto, 'Die Anfänge der Reformation', p. 14; Amon, 'Innerösterreich', pp. 107.
15. Quoted in Georg Loesche, *Geschichte des Protestantismus im vormaligen und im neuen Österreich*, 3rd edn, (Leipzig: Julius Klinkhardt, 1930), pp. 68, without reference. For the activities of the Jörger family, see Heinrich Wurm, *Die Jörger von Tollet* (Graz/Cologne: H. Böhlaus, 1955), pp. 127–64.
16. Hans Lehnert, *Kirchengut und Reformation. Eine kirchenrechtsgeschichtliche Studie* (Erlangen: Verlag von Palm & Enke, 1935), pp. 132–33.
17. For the religious composition of the nobles, see Table 4.6 , ch 4, in this volume; Loesche, *Geschichte des Protestantismus*, pp. 129–30; Franz Loidl, *Geschichte des Erzbistums Wien* (Munich: Oldenbourg, 1993), p. 58.
18. Wurm, *Die Jörger von Tollet*, ch. VI.
19. Heinz Duchhart, *Protestantisches Kaisertum und altes Reich. Die Diskussion über die Konfession des Kaisers in Politik, Publizistik und Staatsrecht* (Wiesbaden: Franz Steiner Verlag, 1977), esp. ch. 2 and 3.
20. Rabe, *Reich und Glaubensspaltung*, p. 305; see also the genealogies in Karl Vocelka and Lynne Heller, *Die Lebenswelt der Habsburger* (Graz: Styria Verlag, 1997), appendix.
21. Sturmberger, *Kaiser Ferdinand II*, p. 41.
22. Harald Zimmermann, 'Der Protestantismus in Österreich ob und unter der Enns im Spiegel landesherrlicher Erlässe (1520–1610)', JbGPÖ, 98 (1982), pp. 98–210; Amon, 'Innerösterreich', pp. 106–8; Ziegler, 'Nieder- und Oberösterreich', pp. 122–24; Franz Machilek, 'Böhmen', in Anton Schindling und Walter Ziegler (eds), *Die Territorien des Reichs im Zeitalter der Reformation und Konfessionalisierung. Land und Konfession 1500–1650.* Vol. I: *Der Südosten* (Münster: Aschendorf, 1989), pp. 135–45.
23. Rabe, *Reich und Glaubensspaltung*, pp. 299–301.
24. Howard Louthan, *Quest for Compromise: Peacemakers in Counter-Reformation Vienna* (Cambridge University Press, 1997), pt II.
25. Mecenseffy, *Geschichte des Protestantismus*, p. 53; Viktor Bibl, 'Die Vorgeschichte der Religionskonzession Kaiser Maximilian II', JbLkNÖ, NF, 13–14 (1914–15), pp. 400–31.
26. 'auf und in allen Schlössern, Häusern und Gütern ... für sich und ihr Gesinde und ihre Angehörigen; auf dem Lande aber und bei ihren zugehörigen Kirchen zugleich auch für ihre Untertanen'. Quoted in Gutkas, *Geschichte des Landes Niederösterreich*, p. 202.
27. Louthan, *Quest for Compromise*, p. 103.
28. Otto Pickl, 'Die wirtschaftlichen Bestimmungen der innerösterreichischen Religionspaziflkation von 1572 und 1578 und ihre Auswirkungen', in P. Urban and B. Sutter (eds), *Johannes Kepler 1571–1971*. Gedenkschrift der Universität Graz (Graz: Böhlaus, 1975), 563–86; Ziegler, 'Nieder- und Oberösterreich', p.126; Amon, 'Innerösterreich', p. 110.
29. Rudolf Keller, *Der Schlüssel zur Schrift. Die Lehre vom Wort Gottes bei Matthias Flacius Illyricus* (Hannover: Lutherisches Verlagshaus, 1984); Oliver K. Olson, 'Matthias Flacius Illyricus, 1520–1575', in Jill Raitt (ed.), *Shapers of Religious Traditions in Germany, Switzerland, and Poland, 1560–1600* (New Haven: Yale University Press, 1981), pp. 1–17.
30. Reingrabner, 'Zur Geschichte der flacianischen Bewegung', pp. 265–301.
31. Reingrabner, 'Zur Geschichte der flacianischen Bewegung', pp. 274–5, 291–4; the Concordia formula asserted that while human will is not autonomous, sinners do have the capacity to be free and act together with God through justification.

32. Thomas A. Brady, *The Politics of the Reformation in Germany: Jacob Sturm (1489–1553) of Strasburg* (Atlantic Highlands, NJ: Humanities Press, 1997), pp. 22–30.
33. Michael Hughes, *Early Modern Germany, 1477–1806* (Philadelphia, Pa.: University of Pennsylvania Press, 1992), p. 69.
34. Rabe, *Reichs- und Glaubensspaltung,* pp. 376–80.
35. Rabe, *Reichs- und Glaubensspaltung,* pp. 408–19.
36. Rabe, *Reichs- und Glaubensspaltung,* pp. 402–5; Volker Press, *Kriege und Krisen. Deutschland 1500–1715* (Munich: Verlag C.H. Beck, 1991), pp. 90–5.
37. Press, *Kriege und Krisen,* pp. 166–7.
38. Louthan, *Quest for Compromise,* p. 155.
39. 'Munich Conference, 2nd Day' (14 Oct. 1579), Bayrisches Hauptstaatsarchiv, Kurbayern, Äußeres Archiv 32: Religions- und Correspondenzacta, vol. 42/32, reprinted in Alfred Kohler, 'Bayern als Vorbild für die innerösterreichische Gegenreformation', in F. M. Dolinar *et al.* (eds), *Katholische Reform und Gegenreformation in Innerösterreich, 1564–1628* (Graz: Verlag Styria, 1994), pp. 391–400; quote p. 395. See also Gernot Heiss, 'Princes, Jesuits and the Origins of Counter-Reformation in the Habsburg Lands', in Evans and Thomas, *Crown, Church and Estates,* pp. 92–109.
40. Johann Loserth, *Die Reformation und Gegenreformation in den Innerösterreichischen Ländern im* XVI. *Jahrhundert* (Stuttgart: Cotta Verlag, 1898); Amon, 'Innerösterreich', pp. 111–14; for recent contributions and an extensive bibliography, see Dolinar, *Katholische Reform und Gegenreformation in Innerösterreich, 1564–1628.*
41. Mecenseffy, *Geschichte des Protestantismus,* pp. 83–8; Victor Bibl, 'Erzherzog Ernst und die Gegenreformation in Niederösterreich (1576–1590)', MIÖG, 6 (1901), p. 590.
42. Melchior Khlesl, 'Memorandum' (ca. 1590), HHStA, Österr. Akten, Niederösterreich, Fasc. IX, reprinted in Victor Bibl, 'Eine Denkschrift Melchior Khlesls über die Gegenreformation in Niederösterreich (c. 1590)', JbLkNÖ, NF, 8 (1909), pp. 164–71.
43. Bibl, 'Eine Denkschrift Melchior Khlesls', pp. 165, 168. Franz Schönfellner, *Krems zwischen Reformation und Gegenreformation* (Vienna: Verein f. LKNÖ, 1985), chs 5 and 6, provides a detailed study of the urban Counter-Reformation.
44. Victor Bibl, *Die Einführung der katholischen Gegenreformation in Niederösterreich durch Kaiser Rudolf* II *(1576–1580),* (Innsbruck: Verlag d. Wagner'schen Universitäts-Buchhandlung, 1900), p. 13.
45. See Letters of 30 May 1579, 2 Sept. 1579, 28 Sept. 1581, 15 May 1982, 31 Dec. 1584, in Viktor Bibl, 'Die Berichte des Reichshofrates Dr. Georg Eder', pp. 81–85, 95, 122, 129, 141.
46. Letters of 8 Jan. 1587 and 15 Jan. 1585, in Bibl, 'Die Berichte des Reichshofrates Dr. Georg Eder', p. 143.
47. Bibl, 'Eine Denkschrift Melchior Khlesls über die Gegenreformation', p. 165; H. G. Erdmann, 'Melchior Khlesl und die Niederösterreichischen Stände' (Ph.D. Dissertation, University of Vienna, 1948), p. 98.
48. Karl Oberleitner, *Die evangelischen Stände im Lande ob der Enns unter Maximilian* II *and Rudolf* II. *1564–1597* (Vienna: Adolf Holzhausen, 1862); Jean Berenger, 'La rêvolt paysanne de Basse-Autriche de 1598', *Revue d'histoire economique et sociale,* 53 (1975), pp. 465–92; Helmut Feigl, 'Der niederösterreichische Bauernaufstand 1596/97', *Militärhistorische Schriftenreihe,* 22 (1972), pp. 1–40.

49. Viktor Bibl, *Die Religionsreformation K. Rudolfs II. in Oberösterreich* (Vienna: Alfred Hölder, 1922), pp. 41–61.
50. Wurm, *Die Jörger von Tollet,* p. 151.
51. Pánek, 'The Religious Question and the Political System', p. 137, calculates that in 1603 the nobility held eight times more land in Bohemia than the crown, but in 1529 it had been eighty times more. Machilek, 'Böhmen', pp. 135–52; Evans, *The Making of the Habsburg Monarchy,* pp. 59–70.
52. Graeme Murdock, Calvinism on the Frontier, 1600–1660. *International Calvanism and the Reformed Church in Hungary and Transylvania* (Oxford: Clarendon Press, 2000), pp. 26–29.
53. Gottfried Schramm, 'Armed Conflict in East-Central Europe: Protestant Noble Opposition and Catholic Royalist Factions, 1604–20', in R. J. W. Evans and T. V. Thomas, *Crown, Church and Estates,* pp. 176–85; Evans, *The Making of the Habsburg Monarchy,* p. 52; Zöllner, *Geschichte Österreichs,* p. 205; K. Maag and A. Pettegree, 'The Reformation in Eastern and Central Europe,' and J. Bahlcke, 'Calvinism and Estate Liberation Movement in Bohemia and Hungary (1570–1620)', in Karin Maag (ed.), *The Reformation in Eastern and Central Europe* (Aldershot: Scolar Press, 1997), pp. 1–18, 72–92.
54. Victor Bibl, 'Die katholischen und protestantischen Stände Niederösterreichs im XVII. Jahrhundert. Ein Beitrag zur Geschichte der ständischen Verfassung', JbLkNÖ, NF, 2 (1903), p. 212.
55. Bibl, 'Die katholischen und protestantischen Stände, pp. 201–19.
56. Bibl, 'Die katholischen und protestantischen Stände', pp. 213, 220, 202, 219; Ziegler, 'Nieder- und Oberösterreich', p. 129.
57. 'Böhmische Majestätsbrief' (9 July 1609), *Acta publica und schriftliche Handlungen ... der Römischen Kayserlichen Majestät und des Heiligen Römischen Reichs Geistlicher und Weltlicher Stände, Michael Kaspar Lundorp,* Vol. 1 (Frankfurt–Main, 1668), pp. 460–2; reprinted in Klaus Gerteis (ed.) *Monarchie oder Ständestaat. Der Böhmische Aufstand von 1618. Quellen und wissenschaftiche Diskussion* (Trier: Auenthal Verlag, 1983), pp. 10–14; Bahlke, *Regionalismus und Staatsintegration,* pp. 309–60; Pánek, 'The Religious Question and the Political System of Bohemia', p. 140.
58. Bibl, 'Die katholischen und protestantischen Stände', pp. 235–7, 238–51, 314.
59. Bibl, 'Die katholischen und protestantischen Stände', pp. 243–9.
60. 'daß Sy sich resolvirt, ehe dem Türggen Siebenbürgen lassen, als Ihr Mayest. zum Krig was verwilligen'; 'Letter of Cardinal Khlesl to Archduke Ferdinand' (May 1617) in J. Hammer-Purgstall, *Khlesl's, des Cardinals, Directores des geheimen Cabinetes Kaisers Matthias, Leben* [henceforth *Khlesl's Leben*] 4 vols; Vol. III (Vienna: Verlag Carl Gerold, 1850), No. 708, p. 518.
61. Gutkas, *Geschichte Niederösterreichs,* p. 238.
62. Bibl, 'Die katholischen und protestantischen Stände', pp. 252–6.
63. Duke Heinrich Julius von Braunschweig-Wolfenbüttel coined this term, quoted in Bahlcke, *Regionalismus und Staatsintegration,* p. 384.
64. Bahlcke, *Regionalismus und Staatsintegration,* pp. 285–7.
65. Bahlcke, *Regionalismus und Staatsintegration,* pp. 372–403.
66. Sturmberger, *Aufstand in Böhmen,* pp. 10–11; Gindely, *History of the Thirty Years' War,* ch. 1, still provides the most vivid description of events.
67. A contemporary broadsheet reports that they fell on much refuse and soft earth ('viel Kericht und weich Erdreich'); 'Warhafftige Zeitung, Aus Praag' (28 May 1619), in Friedel Pick (ed.) *Pragensia,* Vol. I: *Der Prager Fenstersturz i. J. 1619.*

Flugblätter und Abbildungen (Prague: A. Haase, 1918), p. iii; pp. 24–6 for stories on how the Virgin Mary or angels had saved the victims.

68. Press, *Kriege und Krisen*, pp. 186–91; Hammer-Purgstall, *Khlesl's Leben* III, pp. 45–111.
69. 'daß hierin den Ständen dieses Königreichs unerträgliche und gefährliche Mittel und Conditiones vorgeschlagen wereden'; 'Kf. Johann Georg von Sachsen an die böhmischen Direktoren' (31 Oct. 1618) and 'Schreiben der böhmischen Direktoren an den Kaiser' (29 Nov 1618) in Gottfried Lorenz (ed.) *Quellen zur Vorgeschichte und zu den Anfängen des dreißigjährigen Krieges* (Darmstadt: Wissenschaftliche Buchgesellschaft, 1991), pp. 303–12; quote p. 307.
70. Gindely, *Geschichte des dreissigjährigen Krieges*, pp. 93–5.
71. Bahlcke, *Regionalismus und Staatsintegration*, pp. 411–19; Gindely, *Geschichte des dreissigjährigen Krieges*, pp. 110–17.
72. Wolf of Hofkirchen's characterization of Ferdinand, quoted in Bibl, 'Die katholischen und protestantischen Stände', p. 275; Sturmberger, *Aufstand in Böhmen*, pp. 10–44.
73. Bibl, 'Die katholischen und protestantischen Stände', pp. 205, 289–93.
74. Sturmberger, *Aufstand in Böhmen*, pp. 46–52.
75. Bibl, 'Die katholischen und protestantischen Stände', pp. 293–4, 277–88.
76. Gindely, *Geschichte des dreissigjährigen Krieges*, p. 180.
77. Gindely, *Geschichte des dreissigjährigen Krieges*, ch. v; Polišenský, *War and Society*, pp. 61–5; Polišenský, *The Thirty Years War*, ch. 4.
78. The figures differ in various accounts; Khevenhiller believed that 32 lords and 38 knights paid homage, but Bibl prefers the figures provided by Londorp, who cited 47 knights and 39 lords as loyalists which appear to be too high; Bibl 'Die katholischen und protestantischen Stände', p. 301; see Table 2.1 in this chapter.
79. Press, *Kriege und Krisen*, p. 190.
80. Karl Richter, 'Die böhmischen Länder von 1471–1740', in Karl Bosl (ed.) *Handbuch der Geschichte der böhmischen Länder*. Vol. II: *Die böhmischen Länder von der Hochblüte der Ständeherrschaft bis zum Erwachen eines modernen Nationalbewusstseins* (Stuttgart: Aton Hiersemann, 1974), pp. 283–9; R. J. W. Evans, 'The Habsburg Monarchy and Bohemia, 1526–1848', in Mark Greengrass (ed.) *Conquest and Coalescence. The Shaping of the State in Early Modern Europe* (London: Edward Arnold, 1991), pp. 142–5.
81. The figures on the number of remaining nobles vary. Loesche mentions at one point 249 persons of 78 families, but on the same page he asserts that only 75 families with over 200 members were Protestants in 1647, a figure that Bibl confirms. Gutkas insists that of 450 members, 170 were still Protestant in 1647, which seems to contradict his later statement that 230 nobles belonging to 72 families were Protestant in 1657; *Geschichte Niederösterreichs*, pp. 238, 252; Loesche, *Geschichte des Protestantismus*, pp. 120; Bibl, 'Die katholischen und protestantischen Stände', p. 323. Mecenseffy, *Geschichte des Protestantismus*, pp. 157–8, 181.
82. Ziegler, 'Nieder- und Oberösterreich', p. 131.
83. It appears that a number of Protestant nobles – especially the heads of households – paid homage on behalf of other first degree relatives. In cases where this could be assumed with some certainty, the relatives were included among the Loyalists. Khevenhiller made several mistakes when copying the list of nobles who paid homage. For example, Hans Wolf Ruels is really Hans Wolf Kneissl, Rudolf von Ehrenbach is Rudolf von Teuffenbach, and Wolf Tauber is

identical to Wolf Rauber. In addition, some nobles (such as Sigmund Adam Traun and Ferdinand Herbertstein) appear on his list, but are also named in another document as having refused to give homage; Franz Christoph Khevenhiller, *Annales Ferdinandei oder wahrhaftige Beschreibung Kaysers Ferdinandi des Andern,* (12 vols.), Vol. IX (Leipzig: Weidmann, 1724), fols. 1065–9. Reingrabner failed to recognize these mistakes and counted these nobles both groups; *Adel und Reformation,* pp. 17–18. Christoph Carl Fernberger and Ferdinand Pongratz Gienger did not pay homage, but since they were landless and their fathers and landholding brothers *did,* it is likely that the former were neutral or loyal Protestants. Some of Hans Christoph Geyer's brothers paid homage to Ferdinand. But since another brother, Otto Friedrich, was a rebel, and Hans Christoph himself was head of a household, it was considered necessary to exclude the latter from all groups. For similar reasons I did not count Georg Katzler, Franz Adam Neudegg, Sigmund Mallenthein, Andreas Kainach and Gotthard Scharfenberg among any group.

84. While more lords than knights joined the opposition, the differences in the proportional and numerical distribution of lords and knights among the three groups are insignificant. The names of nobles are derived from the following: Haus-Hof- und Staatsarchiv (HHStA), Codes Diplomaticus Austriacus, Tom., IV (or Cod. Bohm, 99), fols 203–4, 205–6, 207–9; NÖLA, StA AIII/20, fols 137–42; Khevenhiller, *Annales Ferdinandei* IX, fols 1065–9; Handschrift der Österreichischen Nationalbiblilothek, Cod., 10.100d (Retzer Jurament); and Ignaz Hübel, 'Die Ächtungen von Evangelischen und die Konfiskationen protestantischen Besitzes im Jahre 1620 in Nieder- und Oberösterreich', JbGPÖ, 58, (1937), pp. 17–62; Hübel, "Die 1620 in Nieder- und Oberösterreich politisch kompromittierten Protestanten', JbGPÖ, 59 (1938), pp. 45–62, and JbGPÖ, 60 (1939), pp. 105–125. The statistical analysis of the socioeconomic background of the nobles is based on the sources cited in Ch. 4, nt 14. One of these documents (Cod. Bohm, 99/IV, fols 203–4) lists 114 nobles who refused homage on 13 July 1620. It includes 63 nobles who were proscribed and thus belonged to the active opposition. An additional 25 nobles who stood on the sidelines during the conflict could be identified, although 16 of them are also listed on another document (Cod. Bohm, 99/IV, fols 207–9). Both lists include nobles who had died (such as Augustin Khevenhiller, Hans Leysser, Adam Polani, Dietrich Welzer), while a few could not be identified and had to be excluded. A small number of others were Upper Austrians and had no property or membership in the Lower Austrian Estates. Some also appear on a list of nobles who had paid homage (such as Ferdinand Herbertstein, Wilhelm Zelking and Georg Bernhard Kirchberger).

85. Two conscription lists were issued, one on 12 September the other on 14 October 1620; copies in HHStA, Cod.Bohm, 99/IV, fols 205–6. They do not comprise all the rebels, as many were proscribed after the Battle of the White Mountain. The former document includes some members of the Fourth Estate, and a few names were copied incorrectly: Hans Bernhard von Thurn is identical to Franz Berhard Thurn, while Hans Scharfenberg could be Hugo Scharfenberg, to name but two of the errors. Hübel also lists non-members of the Estates and seven nobles who resided only in Upper Austria. Although I included most of the proscribed Protestants who were members of the Lower Austrian Estates among the opposition party, it was necessary to exclude those from the statistical analysis who were fully pardoned if their involvement was altogether doubtful. It is evident in a few instances that the court erroneously

declared as rebels some nobles who had been passive during the conflict, or had even been dead for some time. For example, Hans Wenzel Peuger, who insisted in several petitions that he had not been involved in any actions against the crown was finally fully pardoned. Others, such as Adam Polani, were proscribed, despite being dead; Hübel, 'Die 1620 in Nieder- und Oberösterreich politisch kompromittierten Protestanten', JbGPÖ, 60 (1939); p. 106. Other dubious cases excluded from all groups were Hans Dislaw Heissenstein, Johann Babtist Althan, Georg Woppinger and Hans Wilhelm Rächwein. Mentioned only by Wißgrill as proscribed rebels were Günther Herbertstein, Johann Ludwig Krackwitz, Hans Wilhelm Puchheim, Achaz Engelshofer, Hans Wilhelm Puchheim, and Christoph (II) Leisser.

86. A number of nobles who joined the Confederates or the Retzer opposition escaped prosecution, perhaps because other family members had paid homage to Ferdinand, or because they had died or emigrated before they could be proscribed. Such unproscribed nobles were included among the opposition: Georg Achaz Enekel, Lorenz and Rudolf Hofkirchen, Hans Albrecht Artstetter, Simon Schröttl, Halmeran Velderndorf, Wolf Sigmund Herbertstein, Maximilian Teufel (I), Maximilian Teufel (II), Rudolf Teufel, Johann Christoph Wolzogen, Johann Christoph and Otto Max Traun. Hans Wolzogen paid homage in July, a month after he signed the Retzer Jurament. No genealogical data could be found for some of the Retzer participants, such as Hans Ernst Neudegg and Georg Ludwig Lasperg; others were Upper Austrians (for example, Heinrich Wilhelm Scharfenberg, Wolf Christoph Schallenberg and Georg Erasmus Tschernembl). In some cases it appears that fathers were proscribed – either deliberately or by mistake – instead of their sons. For example, Georg Christoph Mühlwanger, who appears not to have participated actively in the the revolt, was proscribed instead of his sons Hans Georg and Karl Ludwig; Georg Woppinger was also proscribed instead of his son Johann Sebastian.
87. In earlier articles I defined this group as a 'neutral' party, but looking more closely at their backgrounds I have become convinced that 'passive opposition' is a more appropriate designation.
88. Wenzel Peuger, for instance, claimed that it was impossible for him to travel to Vienna; Hübel, 'Die 1620 in Nieder- und Oberösterreich politisch kompromittierten Protestanten', JbGPÖ, 60 (1939), p. 106. Christoph Leisser claimed he was prevented by the rebels from paying homage; Khevenhiller, *Annales Ferdinandei*, IX, p. 1068. To be certain, most of these nobles were excluded from all three groups.
89. MacHardy, 'Nobility in Crisis: The Case of Lower Austria', table VI.2.
90. See Ch. 6 for a detailed definitions of these categories. Landless nobles and property owners from all categories were well distributed among the other two 'parties' as well; MacHardy, 'Nobility in Crisis: The Case of Lower Austria', Table VI.3.
91. MacHardy, 'Nobility in Crisis: The Case of Lower Austria', Tables VI.4–6.
92. Georg Ehrenreich Rogendorf held an honourary hereditary sinecure. It is uncertain whether Sebastian Günther Hager (*Platzobrist*) still held a military charge, and whether it was with the Estates or the crown; it is also unclear whether Simon Schröttl (*Hofkanzleiexpediteur*) still occupied his position in 1620.
93. For the Kollonitsch family, see Franz Carl Wißgrill, *Schauplatz des landsäßigen Nieder-Oesterreichischen Adels vom Herrn- und Ritterstande von dem 11. Jahrhundert an bis auf unsere Zeiten,* 5 vols. (Vienna: Seizer, 1794–1824), V, p. 183.

94. Wißgrill, *Schauplatz des landsäßigen Nieder-Oesterreichsichen Adels,* III, pp. 318–26.
95. For genealogies of the Althan family, see Wißgrill, *Schauplatz des landsäßigen Nieder-Oesterreichsichen Adels*, I, pp. 73–103; W. Hauser, 'Das Geschlecht der von Althan' (Ph.D. Dissertation, University of Vienna, 1949).
96. NÖLA, StA, Besitzerbögen, VOWW, 69.
97. Hans Sturmberger, *Georg Erasmus Tschernembl. Religion, Libertät und Widerstand. Ein Beitrag zur Geschichte der Gegenreformation und des Landes ob der Enns* (Graz: Böhlaus, 1953).
98. For the barons von Hofkirchen, see Wißgrill, *Schauplatz des landsäßigen Nieder-Oesterreichischen Adels*, IV, pp. 359–62.
99. Hübel, 'Die 1620 in Nieder- und Oberösterreich politisch kompromittierten Protestanten', JbGPÖ, 59 (1938), p. 54; Hübel, 'Die Ächtungen von Evangelischen', JbGPÖ, 58 (1937), p. 2.
100. Reingrabner, *Adel und Reformation*, pp. 42–3, 109; Kielmansegg, *Geschichte der niederösterreichischen Statthalterei*, pp. 201–4.
101. Wilhelm was pardoned but only his wife's property was returned. He eventually converted to Catholicism. It seems that Ulrich may have died or emigrated before proscription. Hübel, 'Die 1620 in Nieder- und Oberösterreich politisch kompromittierten Protestanten', JbGPÖ, 59 (1938), p. 55; Kielmansegg, *Geschichte der niederösterreichischen Statthalterei*, p. 437; Wißgrill, *Schauplatz des landsäßigen Nieder-Oesterreichischen Adels*, IV, p. 362.
102. Liechtenstein and Mödling were sold in 1612 to Bartholomae Khevenhiller and Vösendorf to the baron of Krausenegg. NÖLA, StA, Besitzerbögen, VUWW 99, ad99, 42; Hübel, 'Die 1620 in Nieder- und Oberösterreich politisch kompromittierten Protestanten', JbGPÖ, 59 (1938), pp. 54–5.
103. Hübel, 'Die Ächtungen von Evangelischen', JbGPÖ, 58 (1937), pp. 18–19; Retzer Jurament, ÖNB, Cod.10.100d. It is uncertain why Hans Rudolf was not proscribed. He might also have left the country, but he appears again as a landowner in 1642. Wißgrill, *Schauplatz des landsäßigen Nieder-Oesterreichischen Adels*, IV, p. 360.
104. This has been pointed out by Reingrabner, *Adel und Reformation*, p. 109, nt 314.
105. On the Puchheim family see *Jahrbuch Adler*, Vol. XIV (1887), pp. 130–60, Vols XVI–XVII (1889–90), pp. 153–204, and Gustav Reingrabner, 'Die Herren Puchheim auf Horn und Wildberg', *Das Waldviertel*, 14 (1965), pp. 4–47.
106. Johann Christoph Puchheim died in 1619 and left a minor as his heir.
107. Four more family members were involved in the rebellion; they were small landholders or landless, and three of them were indebted. These were Andreas the Younger, Gottfried and Hartmann Puchheim. Only Sigmund Niklas seems to have been free of debts; Hübel, 'Die 1620 in Nieder- und Oberösterreich politisch kompromittierten Protestanten', JbGPÖ, 60 (1939), pp. 108–11. Another relative, Hans Wilhelm, was also proscribed, but he insisted that he had not been involved in any activities against the crown; he was eventually pardoned; *Jahrbuch Adler*, XVI–XVII (1889–90), 198–9.
108. It was rare for the Estates to confiscate property in order to collect tax arrears. It seems that taxes collected from the peasants but not delivered to the Estates' treasury were a popular form of interest-free loans and, if the *Stände* were unable to collect, a substantial source of income.
109. Wißgrill, *Schauplatz des landsäßigen Nieder-Oesterreichischen Adels*, V, p. 426, NÖLA, Besitzerbögen, VOMB, 49.
110. Hübel, 'Die 1620 in Nieder- und Oberösterreich politisch kompromittierten Protestanten', JbGPÖ, 59 (1938), pp. 59–60.

111. Wißgrill, *Schauplatz des landsäßigen Nieder-Oesterreichischen Adels*, V, p. 424.
112. Hübel, 'Die 1620 in Nieder- und Oberösterreich politisch kompromittierten Protestanten', JbGPÖ, 60 (1939), p. 119.
113. Hübel, 'Die 1620 in Nieder- und Oberösterreich politisch kompromittierten Protestanten', JbGPÖ, 60 (1939), pp. 106–7.
114. Wißgrill, *Schauplatz des landsäßigen Nieder-Oesterreichischen Adels* IV, P. 330; Hübel, 'Die 1620 in Nieder- und Oberösterreich politisch kompromittierten Protestanten', JbGPÖ, 59 (1938), p. 53.
115. Hübel, 'Die 1620 in Nieder- und Oberösterreich politisch kompromittierten Protestanten', JbGPÖ, 59 (1938), p. 38; Schwarz, *Imperial Privy Council*, p. 270; Kielmansegg, *Niederösterreichische Statthalterei*, p. 219.
116. Siebmacher, *Der Niederösterreichische Adel*, II, p. 217; Hübel, 'Die 1620 in Nieder- und Oberösterreich politisch kompromittierten Protestanten', JbGPÖ, 60 (1939), pp. 111–13.

3 Discourse of Division, 1618–20

1. Konrad Repgen, *Der dreißigjährige Krieg und Westfälischer Frieden. Studien und Quellen* (Paderborn: Ferdinand Schöningh, 1998), pp. 13–14. The protection of trade and commerce was argued most forcefully by Sweden in later periods. On conceptions of interest, see Albert Hirschman, *The Passions and the Interests. Political Arguments for Capitalism before its Triumph* (Princeton University Press, 1977), Part 1; Kelly Rogers (ed.), *Self-Interest: an anthology of philosophical perspectives* (New York: Routledge, 1997).
2. James D. Fearon, 'Rationalist explanations for war', *International Organization* 49/3 (September 1994), p. 389. He provides references to the literature in political science and international relations theory and an explanation of 'what prevents leaders from reaching *ex ante* (prewar) bargains that would avoid the costs and risks of fighting.' Although Fearon has many important conclusions, he erroneously argues on the basis that issues are always divisible. On rational choice theory and its critics see Jon Elster, 'Rationality, economy, and society', in Stephen Turner (ed.), *The Cambridge Companion to Weber* (Cambridge University Press, 2000), pp. 21–41; Elster, *Rational Choice* (Oxford: Basil Blackwell, 1986); and Elster, 'The Nature and Scope of Rational-Choice Explanation', in Ernest Le Pore and Brian P. McLaughin (eds), *Actions and Events: Perspectives on the Philosophy of Donald Davidson* (Oxford: Basil Blackwell, 1985), pp. 311–22; and particularly the important contribution to the issue of divisibility by Michael C. Howard and Ramish C. Kumar, 'Classical Liberalism in an Environment of Rational Choice involving Commitment and Security as well as Greed', in Sheila C. Dow and John Hillard (eds), *Keynes, Uncertainty and the Global Economy*, vol. 2 (Cheltenham: Edward Elgar, 2002), pp. 128–47. For the most famous debates over rational choice theory, see Donald P. Green and Ian Shapiro, *Pathologies of Rational Choice Theory: A Critique of Applications in Political Science* (New Haven, NT: Yale University Press, 1994) and Jeffrey Friedman (ed.), *The Rational Choice Controversy: Economic Models of Politics Reconsidered* (New Haven, CT: Yale University·Press, 1996). For a succinct review of the historiography on early modern war and the state, see Johannes Burkhardt, *Der dreißigjährige Krieg* (Frankfurt/Main: Suhrkamp Verlag), Ch. I.

3. Nearly three decades ago, Perez Zagorin defined the split within the English governing elite preceding the Civil War in the 1640s as a division between the court and the country. The country, an embryonic political opposition party, identified with parliament, local government, and radical Protestant reform. It set the moral and natural purity of pastoral life against the corruption and wickedness of the cosmopolitan court, which it thought was undermined by authoritarian popery and greedy favourites. The thesis initially found strong support, but the 'court and country school' placed too much emphasis on the pastoral idealization of rural life and court critique in political discourse. Perez Zagorin, *The Court and the Country* (London: Macmillan 1969), pp. 28–39; see also Lawrence Stone, *The Causes of the English Revolution* (New York: Harper & Row, 1972), pp. 105–8. Other historians of England soon found evidence of courtiers who were critical of the court and glorified country values, while country gentlemen held royal offices and were exponents of policies associated with the court; see Conrad Russell, *Parliament and English Politics, 1621–1629* (Oxford University Press, 1979), p. 6; Russell, *The Causes of the English Civil War* (Oxford: Clarendon Press, 1990), pp. 4–5; and Derek Hirst, 'Court, Country and Politics before 1629', in Kevin Sharpe (ed.), *Factions and Parliament* (Oxford: Clarendon Press, 1978), pp. 105–37. For historiographical treatment of the 'court and country' controversies, see J. C. D. Clark, *Revolution and Rebellion. State and Society in England in the Seventeenth and Eighteenth Centuries* (Cambridge University Press, 1986), pp. 136–44; and Ann Hughes, *The Causes of the English Civil War* (London: Macmillan, 1991), 84-9.
4. Helmhard von Hohberg, like many other Protestants before and after him, consistently criticized the court as the centre of 'pettiness, deceit, and envy', and contrasted this 'sinful and treacherous' life of court nobles with the simplicity and virtues of the lives of country nobles. Helmhard von Hohberg, *Gregorica curiosa oder Adeliges Land- und Feldleben* (Nuremberg, 1701), quoted in Brunner, *Adeliges Landleben,* p. 222. Wolfgang Neuber analyses this Protestant ethic, which emphasized the paternal rule of the whole household, and centred marital and family relations around a productive agrarian family economy, in the literary work of some twenty nobles in his 'Adeliges Landleben in Österreich und die Literatur im 16. und 17. Jahrhundert', *Adel im Wandel. Politik-Kultur-Konfession, 1500–1700* (Vienna: NÖ. Landesmuseum, 1990), pp. 543–53. On the continuity of critique, see Kiesel, *Bei Hof, bei Höll,* pp. 1–176. However, more research is needed in the evaluation of the influence of this literary discourse on the political propaganda in the Habsburg lands and how it relates to confessional differences in terms of actual cultural practices, such as rituals, art and tastes.
5. Besides the literature of humanists and Protestant writers, one can find occasional references in correspondence about the corruption and greed at court; see, for example, a letter by Hans von Tschernembl (the father of the future leader of the Austrian opposition) to Heinrich von Starhemberg (10 July 1572), quoted in Sturmberger, *Tschernembl*, p. 29.
6. The term *Partei* was used frequently in contemporary political discourse in relation to confessional communities of interest; see, for example, 'Böhmischer Majestätsbrief des Kaisers Rudolf II' (9 July 1609), and the instructions of the English King to Lord Doncaster, 'Instruktionen des englischen Königs für Doncaster' (14/24 April 1619) in Gottfried Lorenz (ed.), *Ausgewählte Quellen zur Deutschen Geschichte der Neuzeit. Freiherr von Stein-Gedächtnisausgabe*, Vol. XIX:

Quellen zur Vorgeschichte und zu den Anfängen des dreißigjährigen Krieges (Darmstadt: Wissenschaftliche Buchgesellschaft, 1991), pp. 95, 325 (subsequently *Quellen*).

7. *Landleute*, translated literally as 'the people of the land', had no democratic connotations. Brunner, *Land and Lordship*, pp. 341–9, was most famous for the phrase that the Estates were the *Land*, although others before him, such as G. von Below, made the same observation.
8. See, for example, the declaration of the Estates of the Duchy of Austria concerning their rights and liberties, where they differentiate constantly between the 'Landtsfürsten als Regenten, und dann dem landt'; see 'Historische Ausführungen', in *Historische Aktenstücke über das Ständewesen in Oesterreich*, 6 vols, Vol. I (Leipzig: Wilhelm Jurany, 1847–8), pp. 20–1.
9. Evans, *Rudolf II*, p. 86
10. There is no evidence, however, to support Schwarz' contention that either the 'Apologia' or the 'Manifest' of the Austrian Estates was supported by the Catholics; Schwarz, *Privy Council*, p. 84.
11. Thus, in May 1618, the Bohemian Protestant Estates claimed that the Emperor's officials, whom they had recently thrown out of the window 'according to ancient tradition', were 'evil' (*böse*) men, who had destroyed the law and the general peace (*'zustörern des Rechtens und allgemeinen Friedens'*); 'Apologie der böhmischen Stände sub utraque' (25 May 1618), subsequently quoted as 'Apologie', in *Quellen*, 249; 'Barbarische Tyranney' refers to Slawata and Smetziansky; in 'Die Andere Apologia der Stände des Königreichs Beheimb' (1619), in *Historische Aktenstücke*, IV, pp. 82, 106–7 (subsequently 'Andere Apologia'); for similar rhetoric, see also 'Begleitschreiben zur Apologie der böhmisichen Stände an den Kaiser' (26 May 1618), in *Quellen*, p. 252; and 'Schreiben der böhmischen Stände sub utraque an Ks. Matthias' (19 July 1618), in *Quellen*, pp. 92–8.
12. 'Der gesamten Oesterreichischen Stände offenes Manifest, an alle Europäischen Mächte über Kaiser Ferdinands II. Widerrechtlichen und gewaltthätigen Regierungsanritt und verübte grausame Verheerung der Erbländer 1619', in *Historische Aktenstücke*, I pp. 103 (subsequently quoted as 'Manifest'): 'ein Mann, aus Verschmitztheit, Betrug, Unverschämtheit, Geiz und Anmassung ganz zusammengesetzt'.
13. 'Andere Apologia' (1619), in *Historische Aktenstücke*, IV, p. 76–7. Khlesl's father was a baker.
14. 'Andere Apologia' (1619), *Historische Aktenstücke*, IV, p. 107: 'die schädlichen Giefftigen Räthe und ertz Feinde der Evangelischen Religion, Kleselius und seine Rottgesellen'.
15. See, for example, 'Andere Apologia', *Historische Aktenstücke*, IV, pp. 77–9, 99.
16. 'Manifest', *Historische Aktenstücke*, I, pp. 102–4. Tschernembl also makes a clear distinction between court and Estates; Sturmberger, *Tschernembl*, pp. 226–9.
17. 'Schreiben der böhmischen Stände sub utraque an Ks. Matthias' (19 July 1918), in *Quellen*, p. 297.
18. 'Andere Apologia' (1619), in *Historische Aktenstücke*, IV, pp. 60, 64, 68–9.
19. 'Andere Apologia', in *Historische Aktenstücke*, IV, p. 107: 'die schädlichen Giefftigen Räthe'; see also the 'Artickel Welche in aller Dreyer Herren Stände des Königreichs Böheimb aufm Präger Schloss gehaltenen Zusammenkunft, so sich den Dinstag nach Maria Magdalena angefangen und den Sambstag nach Johannis Enthauptung dieses 1619, Jahrs geendet, Verathschlaget, und geschlossen worden seynd, in *Historische Aktenstücke*, V, p. 5.

20. 'Andere Apologia', in *Historische Aktenstücke*, IV, pp. 60, 75, 104.
21. 'Andere Apologia', *Historische Aktenstücke*, IV, pp. 68–9; see also 'Artickel', in *Historische Aktenstücke*, V, p. 6, esp. the section on Cardinal von Dietrichstein, V, pp. 127–8.
22. 'Andere Apologia', *Historische Aktenstücke*, IV, pp. 57–8: 'in erwegung ... ihres ... fürnehmen, so zu entlicher ausztilgung und untergang der Stände Sub Utraq:, angestellet gewesen'.
23. 'Andere Apologia', *Historische Aktenstücke*, IV, pp. 66–9.
24. 'Andere Apologia', *Historische Aktenstücke*, IV, pp. 5, 68–9.
25. Bahlcke, *Regionalismus*, pp. 272–3.
26. Bahlcke, *Regionalismus*, p. 327. By imposing the Imperial ban (*Acht*) for breaking the peace (*Landfrieden*) the Habsburgs could remove all legal protection from a person.
27. 'Andere Apologia', *Historische Aktenstücke*, IV, pp. 90–5, provides a long list of grievances against the Jesuits.
28. 'Ein Jesuitischer Retzel/Von Teutschlandt und einer Dreiyfachen N.U.S. welche im selbigen ligt' (1620), in Maria Pfeffer, *Flugschriften zum Dreissigjährigen Krieg. Aus der Häberlin-Sammlung der Thurn- und Taxisschen Hofbibliothek* (henceforth *Flugschriften*), (Frankfurt-am-Main: Peter Lang, 1993), no. 4, C10/1 (Alte No. 1), pp. 124–5. Another pamphlet concerning their expulsion from Transylvania even accused them of sexual excesses; 'Siebenbürgischer in Ungern aus gelegter Mess kramm/welchen der Furst in Siebenbürgen unter den Jesuitern/München und aufrürischen Pfaffen mit grosser Verwunderung im Königreich Ungern ausgelegt unnd haufenweis verpartirt hat' (1619), in *Flugschriften*, no. 3, C1/23c (Alte No. 2), pp. 122–3.
29. 'Discurs von dem jetzigen Zustandt in Böhmen/In einem Gespräch ordentlich verfasset und beschrieben' (1618) in Pfeffer, *Flugschriften*, no. 1, C3/13 (Alte No. 19), pp. 118–19 (henceforth 'Discurs'); it consists of a debate held largely between Khlesl, the pope, the Jesuits and Catholics, while the Bohemian Estates, royal officials and officers provide a commentary. It is Khlesl who first fears a great blood bath ('ein gross Blut Badt'), but later, spurred on by the pope and Catholics, he wants to get on with it. The pope makes it clear to Khlesl that it is an old custom that popes thirst after Lutheran blood, which he was able quench with the help of the Jesuits: 'Päbpsten allzeit nach Lutherischen Blut gedürstet, welches wir auch/durch der Jesuiter Beystandt ... erstillet haben.'
30. 'Die Lande, ja das gantze Reich wird aufstehen'; quoted (without reference) in Sturmberger, *Tschernembl*, p. 289.
31. See 'Gutachten für Kg. Matthias zur Böhmen-Problematik' (ca. 1610), in *Quellen*, no. 18, p. 138;
32. 'Gravamina der korrespondierenden evangelischen Reichsstände' (17 August 1613), in *Quellen*, no. 23, pp. 162–5, 169.
33. 'Manifest', *Historische Aktenstücke*, I, pp. 100, 104.
34. 'Confoederations Artickel des Königreichs Böheimb und der Unirten Länder eines theils, dann des Erzthertzogthums Oesterreich Unter der Ens anderst theils" and "Confoederations Artickel des Königreichs Böheimb, und der Unirten Länder eines theils, dann des Ertzhertzogthumbs Oesterreich Ob der Ens anders theils', in *Historische Aktenstücke*, V, pp. 29, 33
35. 'Daß Ihre kaisl. Majestät den Aufstand in Böhmen nicht *per arma*, sondern durch gütigen Weg stillen solle' (1618), in Hammer-Purgstall, IV, no. 874, p. 96.

36. 'Apologie der böhmischen Stände sub utraque' (25 May 1618), in *Quellen,* no. 33, pp. 240, 248; Andere Apologia', in *Historische Aktenstücke,* IV, pp. 102–3. They further stipulated parity with Protestants in inferior urban offices; 'Artickel Welche in aller Dreyer Herren Stände des Königreichs Böheimb aufm Präger Schloß gehaltenen Zusammenkunft' (23–27 July 1619), *Historische Aktenstücke,* V, pp. 11–13, 29; this part of the document is identical with 'Böhmische Konföderationsakte' (31 July 1619), in *Quellen,* no. 55. However, the former document also includes the union with the Austrian Estates.
37. *Historische Aktenstücke,* I, p. 104.
38. As observed earlier, medieval and Renaissance jurists considered the prince's authority to be limited by natural law which obliged him or her to observe the *ordo iudicarius,* an ambiguous concept related to fundamental laws of the realm, such as rules of succession and the alienation of territory; see Pennington, *The Prince and the Law,* pp. 155, 278.
39. Stanka, *Konföderationsakte,* p. 144. The reasons for deposing Ferdinand were also added to the Articles of Confederation; see 'Auszug aus dem Landesartikel über die Absetzung Kg. Ferdinands' (19 Aug. 1619), in *Quellen,* no. 57, p. 368.
40. 'Manifest', in *Historische Aktenstücke,* I, 103–4: 'Kleiner und größere Städte in ganz Oesterreich wurden mit Soldaten angefüllt, aller Güter beraubt, der Beutesucht, Wollust und Grausamkeit der Kaiserlichen preisgegeben; göttliche wie menschliche Rechte wurden verletzt ... So hat Kaiser Ferdinand, ohne rechtmässiger Nachfolger zu sein, ohne gerechte Vollmacht, ohne rechtmässige Ueberytragung der Gewalt ... ohne Befragung der Stände ... die anmutigste ... Landschaft verwüsted'.
41. 'Andere Apologia', *Historische Aktenstücke,* IV, pp. 68–9; see also 'Artickel', in *Historische Aktenstücke,* V, p. 6; see especially the section on Cardinal von Dietrichstein, 127–8.
42. Brunner, *Land and Lordship,* pp. 118–225, 319–24, 350–1.
43. Pennington, *The Prince and the Law,* p. 282; see also Helmut G. Walther, *Imperiales Königtum, Konziliarismus und Volkssouveränität: Studien zu den Grenzen des Mittelalterlichen Souveränitätsgedankens* (Munich: Fink, 1976), pp. 115–20.
44. See Sturmberger's account of the Latin text of Tschernembl's 'Resistentia', in *Tschernembl,* p. 90–139.
45. *'Imperium principum absolutum'* in Latin, and 'absolute Herrschaft der Fürsten' in the German version of the 'Manifest' in *Historische Aktenstücke,* I, pp. 91–105. Like the 'Declaration', this document was probably composed by the Protestant noble Estate and the Fourth Estate of Lower and Upper Austria, rather than by all of the Austrian Estates.
46. 'Manifest', *Historische Aktenstücke,* I, p. 99: 'Erst die Regierung Ferdinands machte ... den Anfang, den von den Vorfahren betretenen Weg zu verlassen und die Freiheit der Oesterreicher durch spanische Härte zu schwächen und willkürlicher anzutasten.'
47. 'Manifest', in *Historische Aktenstücke,* I, p. 100.
48. 'Manifest', in *Historische Aktenstücke,* I, pp. 93, 100: 'durch falsche Auslegung und ohne Rechtsgrund verletzte'.
49. 'Manifest', in *Historische Aktenstücke,* I, p. 101: 'daß der Erzherzog Matthias selbst den traurigen Zustand der Verwaltung nach dem Rathe der Stände aufrichtete'.
50. For Tschernembl's view, see Sturmberger, *Tschernembl,* pp. 296–7. On 11 August 1601, Archduke Ferdinand reported to Archduke Matthias these remarks by Wolf Wilhelm von Hofkirchen; quoted in Sturmberger, *Tschernembl,* p. 278.

51. 'Andere Apologia', *Historische Aktenstücke*, IV, pp. 4–29, 34, 51–9, 76–9, 109, 125.
52. 'Andere Apologia', *Historische Aktenstücke*, IV, pp. 68–9, 82; see also 'Artickel', in *Historische Aktenstücke*, V, pp. 6, 127–8.
53. My interpretation here is based on Sturmberger's account of the Latin text of Tschernembl's 'Resistentia', in his *Tschernembl*, pp. 90–139.
54. Sturmberger, *Tschernembl*, pp. *90–107*, traces the influence of European resistance theory on Tschernembl, discusses why he thinks the 'Resistentia' was authored by Tschernembl, and analyses the content of the document.
55. Hotman claimed that the Estates General, or public council, shared with the king in decision-making concerning secular and religious policy, and, as the custodian of fundamental rights, had the right to depose a ruler. While *Vindiciae* makes Beza's basic division between tyrant by usurpation and legitimate ruler turned tyrant (tyrant by exercise), it differs from the Resistentia by giving permission to all members of the community to resist a tyrant by usurpation. Sturmberger makes the comparison between Tschernembl's tract and the *Vindicae* in *Tschernembl*, pp. 90–139. For an accessible treatment of Calvinist resistance theories, see Robert M. Kingdon, 'Calvinism and Resistance Theory, 1550–1580', in J. H. Burns (ed) with Mark Goldie *The Cambridge History of Political Thought, 1450–1700*, (Cambridge University Press, 1991), pp. 193–218; J. Dennert (ed.), *Beza, Brutus, Hotman: Calvinistische Monarchomachen*, trans. H. Klingelhofer (Cologne: Westdeutscher Verlag, 1968) provides primary sources on Beza and Hotman.
56. Sturmberger, *Tschernembl*, p. 101, thinks that Tschernembl had previous connections with Althusius through the circle around Jakob Grynäus. See also Bahlcke, *Regionalismus*, pp. 279, 289, and Chlumecký, *Carl von Zierotin*, pp. 256–86. On Althusius's thought, see Howell A. Lloyd, 'Constitutionalism', in *The Cambridge History of Political Thought*, pp. 254–97, and O. von Gierke, *Johannes Althusius und die Entwicklung der naturrechtlichen Staatstheorien* (Breslau: Marcus, 1929); trans. B. Freyd as *The Development of Political Theory* (New York: H. Fertig, 1966). A most accessible recent treatment of Althusius is Thomas O. Hueglin's *Early Modern Concepts for a Later Modern World. Althusius on Community and Federalism* (Waterloo: Wilfrid Laurier University Press), 1999.
57. 'Historische Ausführungen', in *Historische Aktenstücke*, I, p. 21: 'dadurch er Hertzog solcher Freihaiten von dem Landt, und nicht dz [*sic*] Land durch Ihne theilhaftig worden'.
58. 'Historische Ausführungen', in *Historische Aktenstücke*, I, p. 20: 'so erhelts sichs doch in der wahrheit, daß das Löbl. Erzhertzogthumb Oesterreich mit diesen [*Jus Majestatis*] und anderen *Regalien* ... also versehen, daß es solche zum Thail für sich selbsten hat, zum Thail mit dem Landsfürsten und *reciprocè*, zum Thail hat der Landtsfürst seine *Regalia* für sich selbsten, zum Thail *communia*, mit dem Landt: Also daß ein Thail von dem andern (doch unverletzt seines distinguirten Standts) *participirt:* und sich deselbigen zu gelegenen Zeiten, und *data occasione* gebrauchen thuet.
59. The term *Souveränität*, or *Souverän* is more modern and was not used in the German documents of the Estates or by the Habsburgs.
60. Franklin, 'Sovereignty', pp. 298–313, 307–9. Even Brunner seems to have had problems in conceiving of shared sovereignty when he denied a relationship between the medieval ideal of limited rule and conceptions of sovereignty; *Land und Herrschaft*, pp. 318, 322–3.

61. 'in the body as a whole complete and supreme sovereignty results from the union of the fragment of sovereignty coming together in one'; Henning Arnisaeus, *Doctrina political governum methodum quae est Aristotelis reducta* (Frankfurt, 1606), quoted in Franklin, 'Sovereignty', p. 326.
62. Majesty remained supreme 'in the whole body, or corporation, of those who rule (*archonton*), but in such a way that it was not distributed equally among the parts. The prince will be conceded some large degree of eminence ... or else it will be an aristocracy'; quoted in Franklin, 'Sovereignty', p. 325. Besold's *De statu republic mixto* probably appeared in the first decade of the seventeenth century, but the final version is only available in a collection of his writings of 1626.
63. 'Historische Ausführungen', in *Historische Aktenstücke*, I, pp. 39, 24–6, 32: 'So es aber dazue komen, das die Land ganz Erbloß worden, oder der herr seine Vogtbare 16 Jahr nicht erreicht, oder abwesent gewest, hat gemeine Landtschafft die verwaltung des Landts Regierung nicht sovil Ihr selbsten, alss dem Landtsfürsten zu guetten jederzeit auf sich benomen.'
64. 'Historische Ausführungen', in *Historische Aktenstücke*, I, p. 32: 'Es hat verner dieses Erzherzogthum, das Jus und Alte herkomen, wan es von seinem regierenden Landsfürsten, wider billigkeit beschwert, kein wendung und linderung erlangen und erbitten khan, das es seine zuflucht, zu einem Churfürsten des heilige Römischen Reichs nemen, und sich in desselben schuz und schirm absque omni nota rebellionis begeben kan.'
65. For example, in 1606, the Lower Austrian Estates had given a kind of ratification of the peace with the Ottomans, which Matthias had needed in his struggle against his brother, the Emperor Rudolf. See *Historische Aktenstücke*, IV, pp. 49–50.
66. 'Historische Ausführungen', in *Historische Aktenstücke*, I, p. 32; 'Andere Apologia', in *Historische Aktenstücke*, IV,p. 79: 'Was es doch wol mit Obrigkeit und Unterthanen auff dieser Welt, vor eine gelegenheit habe, Ob die Obrigkeiten keinen Legibus unterworffen, sondern nur alles vor sich *absolute* gegen den Unterthanen vornehmen känne?'
67. 'Andere Apologia', *Historische Aktenstücke*, IV, p. 80.
68. 'Andere Apologia', *Historische Aktenstücke*, IV, p. 57–8.
69. 'Andere Apologia', *Historische Aktenstücke*, IV, pp. 5, 66–9.
70. 'Andere Apologia', *Historische Aktenstücke*, IV, pp. 60, 104, 75.
71. 'Andere Apologia,'*Historische Aktenstücke*, IV, pp. 4–5, quote on p. 62: 'Die verbindnussen, so die Stände unter einander in offentlicher zusamenkunfft uffm Prager Schloß auffgerichted, sind niemands zu schaden, sondern Irer May: und dem Lande zum besten geschehen.' The Estates seem to refer to the alliance between the three Bohemian Estates rather than the Confederation, which had not been concluded at this point.
72. Rudolf Stanka, *Die böhmischen Conföderationsakte von 1619* (Berlin: Emil Ebering, 1932), pp. 143.
73. The phrase used is '*participation aliquot jurium Majestatis*', in 'Deduction, das ist notwendige Ausführung, Bericht und Erzehlung deren Ursachen und Motiven, darumb Kayser Ferdinandus II nach tödlichem Abgang weyland Kaysers Mathiae dess Regiments im Königreiche Böheim und desselben incorporierten Ländern verlustig' (henceforth 'Deduction'), in *Konföderationsakte*, pp. 136–51.
74. 'Artickel Oesterreich Under der Ens', *Historische Aktenstücke*, V, pp. 28–9: 'Dritten, Zur *Conservation,* aufnem- und erhaltung eines jeden benambten Königreichs und Lande, Königs und Landesfürsten Authoritet und Hoheit,

demselbigen als getrewe underthanen, in allen nöthen und zuständen, da nichts wider die Religion und Politische Privilegien, Mayestätsbrieff, *Concessiones,* Recht, Gerechtigkeit, Freyheit, alte löbliche Gewonheit, *attentirt,* gesucht, gehandelt und fürgenommen wird.'

75. 'Artickel Oesterreich Under der Ens', *Historische Aktenstücke,* v, pp. 28–9: 'Vierten, die *confederation* soll *Devensivè und Offensivè* seyn, wider alle diejenigen, die in den Confoederirten Landen, Brief und Sigel, als die Religions und Politischen Privilegien, Mayestätbrieff, *Concessiones, Capitulationes, Resolutionen, Confoederationen,* und alle dergleichen gefertigte *Instrumenta,* dispuirlich machen, zu uneinigkeit, mißtrauen, krieg, und blutvergießen, rath und that geben, sich darzu gebrauchen oder darbey befinden lassen.'
76. Evans, *The Making of the Habsburg Monarchy,* p. 56.
77. Seyfried Hoyer, 'Bemerkungen zu Luthers Auffassung über das Widerstandsrecht der Stände gegen den Kaiser (1539), 2nd edn, in Günter Vogler (ed.) *Martin Luther. Leben, Werk, Wirkung,* with Siegfried Hoyer and Adolf Laube (Berlin: Akademie-Verlag, 1986), pp. 255–63.
78. Irmtraud Lindeck-Pozza, 'Der Einfluss der staatsrechtlichen und bekenntnismäßigen Anschauungen auf die Auseinandersetzung zwischen Landesfürstentum und Ständen in Österreich während der Gegenreformation,' JbGPÖ, 20 (1939), pp. 81–96; and JbGPÖ, 60 (1940), pp. 15–24; and Hans Sturmberger, 'Jakob Andraea und Achaz von Hohenfeld. Eine Diskussion über das Gehorsam-Problem zur Zeit der Rudolfinischen Gegenreformation in Österreich', in Mezier-Andelberg (ed.) *Festschrift für Karl Eder* (Innsbruck, 1959), pp. 381–94, make this assertion. For a succinct summary of resistance theory, see also Winfried Schulze, 'Estates and the Problem of Resistance in Theory and Practice in the Sixteenth and Seventeenth Centuries', Evans and Thomas (eds), in *Crown, Church and Estates,* pp. 263–79.
79. 'Artickel Oesterreich Ob der Ens', *Historische Aktenstücke,* v, p. 33.
80. 'Böhmische Konföderationsakte' (31 July 1619), in *Quellen,* no. 55; Articles XXX, XXXV, XLIV.
81. Winfried Becker, 'Ständestaat und Konfessionsbildung am Beispiel der böhmischen Konföderationsakte von 1619', in Dieter Albrecht *et. al.* (eds), *Politik und Konfession. Festschrift für Konrad Repgen zum 60. Geburtstag* (Berlin: Duncker & Humblot, 1983), pp. 77–97, also concludes that the king was not a contractual partner of the Confederation.
82. Stanka, *Confederationsakte,* p. 153; Bahlcke, *Regionalismus,* p. 441.
83. The king was also prohibited to consult with or have Jesuits or foreigners as advisers at court and in urban offices. 'Böhmische Konföderationsakte', in *Quellen,* Articles XXXIII and XCV.
84. Stanka, *Konföderationsakte,* p. 93, asserts that the defensors appointed the commander-in-chief, but I found no evidence for this. Only Article LXXXI (81) determines that the confederated territories should elect such a commander: 'Hierauf haben sich die Unirte Lande entschlossen, einen General zu erwehlen.' Article LXXXV stipulates that the country which is endangered shall have command over the army until the commander-in-chief arrives. The Upper Austrians also repeated the content of these clauses, and state that the commander-in-chief should be elected in common council ('aus gesambtem Rath, ein general Haubt erwehlen'); see 'Artickel', *Historische Aktenstücke,* v, pp. 23–4. Since such a decision-making process had to include the Austrian lands, an election could not be in the hands of the defensors of the Bohemian lands,

whose powers were defined only in Articles LX to LXX. The Articles that follow pertain to measures concerning a general defence.

85. Bahlcke interprets the Articles of the Confederation to mean that only the Estates had the right to call an Estate General; *Regionalismus und Staatsintegration,* p. 434. Only after they decided that the Confederation had to be protected militarily, did the general defensors come in possession of the *'Jus convocandi reliquos'*, that is the right to call all subsequent meetings (Article LXVII).
86. In 1609, the Bohemian Estates had already been permitted to install defensors, but only in order to supervise the academy and the consistory, and the Letter of Majesty had left the king the right to issue instructions to them. Stanka, *Conföderationsakte,* pp. 104–8.
87. If the king or his representative could not resolve the matter within six weeks, the defensors would submit the grievance first to the assembly of the local Estates, and after that to a common assembly of the confederate territories' defensors, who would then decide on defensive action.
88. 'Böhmische Artickel, welche auff dem neulichstem General Landtag ... beschlossen worden', in *Historische Aktenstücke,* V, p. 103. It is possible that this article for the 'Abtretung des Regiments Ihrer Königlichen Mayestät über das Kriegsvolk, so hiebevor von den Ständen dieses Königreichs geworben worden', could refer to the Bohemian armada only.
89. Thus, the chancellery was prevented from establishing commissions in legal matters concerning the other regions and could not issue decrees that conflicted with their customary rights, laws and liberties (Articles XXXV and XLIII). Moreover, complaints from each region had to be made to the local defensors rather than the chancellery (XLI). All of this meant that much power was returned to regional organs of government, which came again under the control of the local Estates. Even in financial matters the Bohemian treasury asserted its independence from the central court treasury. 'Absonderliche Artickel, welche das Königreich Böheimb allein betreffen,' in *Historische Aktenstücke,* V.
90. Bahlcke, *Regionalismus und Staatsintegration,* pp. 439–41.
91. Stanka interprets the term *'Verfassung'* (constitution), which (according to Article LXXI) each confederate territory was to decide upon within six months, to refer to the making of new constitutional arrangements by the local Estates; *Conföderationsakte,* p. 95. However, I interpret this to refer to the military arrangements each country was to set up individually since Article LXXI is clearly wedged between points concerning general defence arrangements. The territorial Estates had traditionally co-operated with the crown and decided over such military matters as the raising of troops and defence of the borders.
92. In 1753, a memorandum to Empress Maria Theresa included the advice that a common law code and legal order was essential to unify her subjects for their own benefit 'unter einem Gott, einem Landsfürsten und einerlei Gesetz', quoted in Floßman, *Landrechte als Verfassung,* p. 47. I think this also reflected the aims of many of her predecessors, especially Ferdinand II.
93. For example, in 1614 the French cleric, Jean Barivac, in a refutation of the Huguenot *Vindiciae contra tyrannos,* claimed that the idea of resistance to the ruler was a Protestant invention, and that Calvinists intended to introduce republicanism modelled after the Swiss and the United Provinces; see J. P. Sommerville, 'Absolutism and royalism', in J. H. Burns (ed.), *The Cambridge History of Political Thought 1450–1700* (Cambridge University Press, 1994),

p. 356; Sturmberger, *Kaiser Ferdinand II*, p. 18; H. von Zwiedineck-Südenhorst (ed.), *Venetianische Gesandtschafts-Berichte über die Böhmische Rebellion (1618–1620)*, (Graz: Verlag von Leuschner & Lubensky, 1880), p. 18 and nt 10: 'di formar una confederatione et unione fra di esse, et ridursi à forma di governo libero, simile à quella di Svizzeri é stati Olandesi, col sottrarsi dal dominio di casa d'Austria, ò limitarlo, che non gli resta altro, che il nome'.

94. 'Böhemischer mit Niderländischem Hirn gefüllter Wunder: und Streitkopff', cited in Bahlcke, *Regionalismus und Staatsintegration*, p. 430; see also Bahlcke, 'Durch "starke Konföderation wohl stabiliert". Ständische Defension und politisches Denken in der habsburgischen Ländergruppe am Anfang des 17. Jahrhunderts', in Thomas Winkelbauer, (ed.), *Kontakte und Konflikte. Böhmen, Mähren und Österreich: Aspekte eines Jahrtausends gemeinsamer Geschichte*, (Horn/ Waidhofen: Waldviertler Heimatbund, 1993), p. 174.
95. Bahlcke, *Regionalismus und Staatsintegration*, p. 254.
96. 'Eder an Hg. Albrecht V. von Bayern' (30 May 1579), in *Quellen*, pp. 31–3.
97. 'Denkschrift Khlesls betr. die böhmischen Unruhen' (ca. mid-June 1618), in *Quellen*, p. 253.
98. 'Schreiben Cardinal Khlesl's an den Grafen Khevenhiller' (9 June 1618), in Hammer-Purgstall, *Khlesl's Leben*, IV, no. 864, pp. 76–7; and 'Schreiben Cardinal Khlesl's an Khuen' (30 May 1618), quoted in Hammer-Purgstall, *Khlesl's Leben*, IV, p. 128.
99. Mark Morford, *Stoics and Neostoics: Rubens and the Circle of Lipsius* (Princeton, NJ: Princeton University Press, 1991), p. 108; Sturmberger, *Kaiser Ferdinand II*, p. 41.
100. 'Testament Kaiser Ferdinands II (10 May 1621)', in Gustav Turba (ed.), *Die Grundlagen der pragmatischen Sanktion*, Vol. II: *Die Hausgesetze*, (Vienna: Wr. Staatswissenschaftliche Studien, 1913), pp. 335–51.
101. Sturmberger, *Kaiser Ferdinand II*, pp. 20–1, 43; see also J. H. Elliot, 'A Europe of Composite Monarchies', *Past & Present*, 137 (Nov. 1992), pp. 62–4.
102. This 'Schreiben Cardinal Khlesl's an Khuen' (30 May 1618) was part of the evidence used against him; Hammer-Purgstall, *Khlesl's Leben*, IV; p.128.
103. 'Schreiben Khlesl an den Grafen Khevenhiller' (9 June 1618), in Hammer-Purgstall, *Khlesl's Leben*, IV, no. 864, p. 76.
104. 'Denkschrift Khlesls betr. Die böhmischen Unruhen' (ca. mid-June 1618), in *Quellen*, p. 255.
105. Sturmberger, *Aufstand in Böhmen*, p. 38, and Bahlcke, *Regionalismus und Staatsintegration*, p. 406, insist that Khlesl urged compromise with the Bohemians, citing his letter to Khevenhiller of 26 June, 1618. However, I could find no evidence of such a recommendation in this letter; see Hammer-Purgstall, *Khlesl's Leben*, IV, no. 873, pp. 92–3. It seems that Karl and Gundacker von Liechtenstein, and Seyfried Christoph von Breuner, resented Khlesl's influence and dominance of the Privy Council, while the archdukes Maximilian and Ferdinand disliked his influence over Matthias and in particular his appeasement policy towards the Reich; Schwarz, *The Imperial Privy Council, p.* 77. It is curious that the strongest of non-Catholic protests against the crown's 'evil councillors' was levelled one day before Khlesl's fall; 'Schreiben der böhmisichen Stände sub utraque an Ks. Matthias' (19 July 1618), in *Quellen*, pp. 92–8. Certainly, Protestants exerted pressure on Matthias to dismiss Khlesl; see Matthias' complaint to archduchess Margaret (6 July 1618), that his non-Catholic subjects were forcing him not to use ecclesiastics as councillors; Hammer-Purgstall, *Khlesl's Leben*, IV, no. 876, pp. 106–7.

Sturmberger's interpretation that Khlesl's compromising attitude was the cause of his fall also seems to be unacceptable in light of the fact that only a month later the elector of Saxony and the English king were asked to mediate between the Bohemian Estates and the Habsburgs; see *Quellen,* pp. 298–332; and Sturmberger, *Aufstand in Böhmen,* p. 38. In October, Matthias himself approached the duke of Saxony to negotiate with the Bohemians; see 'Schreiben des Kaisers Matthias an den Kf. von Sachsen' (7 Oct. 1618), in *Quellen,* pp. 364–6. Even more surprising is Khlesl's critique of the Habsburg tradition to negotiate and compromise after he was reinstated, earning three times his previous salary; 'Schreiben Cardinal Khlesl's an den Churfürsten von Baiern vom Jahre 1624', Hammer-Purgstall, *Khlesl's Leben,* IV, no. 988, pp. 264–5. It is also difficult to see why Hammer-Purgstall considers a 'dangerous game' Khlesl's recommendation of quelling rebellion, while negotiating with the Bohemians. Considering the lack of resources the Habsburgs had available at the time, it seems the only rational policy to follow until Spain guaranteed financial support; Hammer-Purgstall, *Khlesl's Leben,* IV, p. 50. Clearly, his role in escalating the Bohemian conflict deserves a re-evaluation. Perhaps contemporary pamphlet rumours, which suggested that Khlesl was imprisoned in order to protect him, were not absurd, considering that Ferdinand II reinstalled him in his bishoprics and fortune after the rebels had been defeated and punished; see 'Discurs' (1618), in *Flugschriften,* no. 1, p. 119.

106. 'Denkschrift Khlesls' (mid-June 1618), in *Quellen,* pp. 253–5.
107. 'Auszüge aus 48 Aufsätzen Khlesl's und einiger an ihn geschriebenen Briefe, die nach seinem Verhaft in seinem Archiv gefunden wurden', in Hammer-Purgstall, *Khlesl's Leben,* IV, no. 926, Sub. No. 41: 'qui potestati resistit, Deo resistit.'
108. 'Schreiben des Kaisers and die Erzherzogin Margareth' (6 July 1618), no. 876, in Hammer-Purgstall, *Khlesl's Leben,* IV, p. 106.
109. 'Offener Brief Ks. Ferdinand II' (19 January 1620), in *Quellen,* 441: ordentlichen natürlichen Obrigkeit'.
110. On the medieval roots of divine right theory and its relationship to absolutism, see Glen Burgess, 'The Divine Right of Kings Reconsidered', *The English Historical Review,* CCCCXXV (Oct. 1992), pp. 837–61
111. On Neostoicism, see Gerhard Oestreich, *Neostoicism and the Early Modern State* (Cambridge University Press, 1982).
112. Sommerville, 'Absolutism', pp. 358–61; John Miller, 'Introduction', in John Miller (ed.), *Absolutism in Seventeenth-Century Europe* (London: Macmillan, 1990), pp. 1–41.
113. 'Kaiserliches Patent für Böhmen' (18 June 1618); 'Mandat des Kaisers Matthias and die böhmischen Stände'; 'Offener Brief des Kaisers Matthias aus Anlass der böhmischen Unruhen' (30 June 1618); and 'Ks. Matthias an die böhmischen Stände sub utraque' (31 Dec. 1618), in *Quellen,* pp. 257–65, 313–16.
114. 'Schreiben des Kaisers Matthias and den Kf. von Sachsen' (7 Oct. 1618), in *Quellen,* pp. 264–5: 'unserer hochbelaidigten und angegriffenen Kays. undt Königl. Hoheit und würden'.
115. 'Offener Brief des Kaisers Matthias aus Anlass der böhmischen Unruhen' (30 June 1618), in *Quellen,* pp. 260–4.
116. Sturmberger, *Tschernembl,* p. 285.
117. 'Offener Brief Ks. Ferdinand II' (19 Jan. 1620), in *Quellen,* pp. 447: 'so unter dem Mantel der Religion Ihre abschewliche Rebellion bedekket'.
118. 'Offener Brief Ks. Ferdinands II' (19 Jan 1620), in *Quellen,* pp. 439–43.

119. 'Offener Brief Ks. Ferdinand II' (19 Jan. 1620), in *Quellen*, pp. 444–8; see also 'Schreiben Ks. Ferdinands II. an die böhmischen Stände' (6 June 1620), in *Quellen*, pp. 462–3.
120. For an interesting analysis of this 'Theatre of Royal Power', see Monod, *The Power of Kings*, ch. 3.
121. Sturmberger, *Kaiser Ferdinand II*, pp. 39–45.
122. 'Offener Brief Ks. Ferdinand II' (19 Jan. 1620), in *Quellen*, p. 444: 'die fundamentalsatzungen des Königreichs ... das gantze Herkommen und achthundert jährige Observantz ... über einen Hauffen niederwerfen'.
123. Floßman, *Landrechte als Verfassung*, pp. 20–3: 'in allem aber zuforderst die Ehre Gottes, die natürliche Billigkeit und das gemeine Wesen in acht [nehmen]'.
124. 'Offener Brief Ks. Ferdinand II' (19 Jan. 1620), in *Quellen*, pp. 440–5: 'und eine gantz newe Form der Regierung/ ... vor sich selbsten angestellet/ .... welche [Stände] aber zu Verenderung des Königlichen guberno so wenig Macht haben'.
125. Sturmberger, *Kaiser Ferdinand II*, pp. 20, 26; see also his *Adam Graf Herberstorff. Herrschaft und Freiheit im konfessionellen Zeitalter* (Vienna: Verlag für Geschichte und Politik, 1976).

Conclusion to Part I

1. Recall that the changing composition of the *Reichskammergericht*, the high court of the Empire, and the Imperial deputation, the committee of the full diet, had brought a changed balance of power between the confessions in the Reich and in the hereditary lands, and this had led to stalemate over decisions concerning confessional and other disputes. The main institutions for religious conciliation in the Empire had thus became paralyzed and this strengthened the jurisdiction of the Aulic council, which was controlled by the Habsburgs and Catholics. Press, *Kriege und Krisen*, pp. 161–7.
2. See, for example, Stanka, *Conföderationsakte*, pp. 126–8, who treated the articles of Confederation concerning the appointment of only Lutherans to the most important offices under the topic of 'The Confessional Character of the Act of Confederation'.
3. Eisenstadt and Roniger, 'Patron Client Relations', pp. 50–1.

4 Social Capital, Symbolic Power and Religious Conflict

1. On the various concepts of strategy, see Graham Crow, 'The Use of the Concept of "Strategy" in Recent Sociological Literature', *Sociology*, 23/(1) (Feb. 1989), pp. 1–24. Biological reproduction for patrimonial transmission as an integral part of social reproduction strategies, but they are not the focal point of this study. Where necessary, I shall distinguish biological reproductive capital from other forms of family maintenance.
2. I have borrowed, but slightly modified G. A. Cohen's concepts as elaborated in *Karl Marx's Theory of History. A Defense* (Princeton NJ,: Princeton University Press, 1978), p. 85.
3. Goldstone, *Revolution and Rebellion*, pp. 227–8.

4. Winfried Becker, 'Ständestaat und Konfessionsbildung am Beispiel der böhmischen Konföderationsakte von 1619', in Dieter Albrecht *et al.* (eds), *Politik und Konfession. Festschrift für Konrad Repgen zum 60. Geburtstag,* (Berlin: Duncker & Humblot, 1983), pp. 77–97, views the Confederation as a progressive development.
5. In Lower Austria, for example, admissions to the noble Estates reached an unprecedentedly high level during the first two decades of the Thirty Years' War. However, such rapid upward mobility may also reflect the practice of new rulers, at the time of their accession, or shortly thereafter, to replace key officials with their own favourites, which frequently necessitated an improvement in status. Although the fiscal needs of rulers were another important factor behind intensified social mobility in sixteenth- and seventeenth-century Europe, the Habsburgs did not resort to the outright sale of titles, as did French and English rulers, although they imposed a fee, or tax, for issuing the decree. Nevertheless, for the Habsburgs, status promotion was also the cheapest form of distributing rewards during times of financial difficulty. On many occasions they repaid money-lenders with the grant of titles. For example, Lazarus Henkel, a wealthy merchant and purveyor to the crown, was raised to baron in 1608 after providing Emperor Rudolf II with a substantial loan, in the amount of 222 000 Gulden. Henkel, who claimed to be of old Hungarian nobility, was also repaid with landed property for this loan. Wißgrill, *Schauplatz des landsäßigen Nieder-Oesterreichischen Adels,* Vol. iv, p. 238.
6. Otto Brunner, 'Bürgertum und Adel in Nieder- und Oberösterreich', in *Neue Wege der Verfassung- und Sozialgeschichte* (Göttingen: Vandenhoeck and Rupprecht 1968), pp. 266-80.
7. Caspar Anfang, Georg Christoph Rosenberg and Georg Stettner were overseers of royal domains; see NÖLA, Ritterstandsarchiv (RStA), Aufnahmeakten C II. Georg Stettner's father had been chief forester on the royal domain in Styria, and Georg himself rose from the position of *Pfleger* of the monastery at Göttweig to secretary of the court treasury; see Johann Siebmacher, *Grosses und Allgemeines Wappenbuch*: *Der Niederösterreichische Adel,* 2 vols, Vol. II, (Nuremberg, 1919), pp. 228–9, 348. The statistical analysis of the following is based on sources provided in note 14 of this chapter.
8. The overwhelming majority were, or had been, councillors in the Imperial Aulic council (*Reichshofrat*), the functions of which were primarily judicial. While the Imperial court at Prague was separated from the archducal court at Vienna (1576–1612), a number of new knights were councillors to the archdukes; others held the position of councillor in the Lower Austrian *Regiment* or the court treasury.
9. The majority of these knights (15) held the title of *kaiserliche Hofdiener* (Imperial court servant) and were responsible for the judicial administration of the royal household (*Hofmarschallgericht*). The remainder – less than a fifth – served in the army.
10. Wißgrill, *Schauplatz des landsäßigen Nieder-Oesterreichischen Adels,* Vol. III, p. 388; Arnold Luschin v. Ebengreuth, 'Österreicher an italienischen Universitäten zur Zeit der Reception des römischen Rechts', *Sonderabdruck aus den Blättern für Landeskunde von Niederösterreich,* 1 (Vienna: Friedrich Jasper, 1886), pp. 49–50.
11. Wißgrill, *Schauplatz des landsäßigen Nieder-Oesterreichischen Adels,* Vol. v, p. 276; NÖLA, RStA, Aufnahmeakten CI. The rise of Christoph Pirkhaimer, the son of a town councillor, was also rapid. He studied jurisprudence in Bologna and Paris (1573), received a doctorate, became Imperial Aulic councillor, and was ennobled in 1589. In 1592, at the age of 37, he was installed as Chancellor of the Lower Austrian government (*Niederösterreichischer Kanzler*), and in 1596 was

admitted to the new *Ritterstand;* see *Jahrbuch des Heraldisch-Genealogischen Vereins Adler* (henceforth *Jahrbuch Adler*), Vol. III (Vienna, 1876), pp. 92; and Luschin v. Ebengreuth, 'Österreicher an italienischen Universitäten', p. 59.

12. For social mobility in seventeenth-century England, see Lawrence Stone's classic, *The Crisis of the Aristocracy, 1558–1641,* abridged edn. (Oxford: Clarendon Press, 1967); and Robert Brenner, *Merchants and Revolution. Commercial Change, Political Conflict, and London's Overseas Traders, 1550–1653* (Princeton, NJ: Princeton University Press, 1993.)
13. The Ottoman invasions, the redirection of trade routes, such as the neglect of the Danube, and the subsequent shift of trade and finance to South German cities, weakened the mercantile economy of Lower Austria. The towns were unable to recover their economic position during the period of urban growth in the sixteenth century, and this left them vulnerable during the commercial contraction that probably began about 1600; Sandgruber, *Ökonomie und Politik,* pp. 103–23; Evans, *The Making of the Habsburg Monarchy,* pp. 80–1; Bruckmüller, *Sozialgeschichte Österreichs*, chs. IV and V.3.
14. The statistical analyses of this chapter are based on data derived from a variety of sources: (NÖLA), RStA, Aufnahmeakten CI-XXXVIII, D1; Herrenstandsarchiv (hereafter: HStA), Aufnahmeakten (A–Z), Lade IV/5, fol. 10, Lade V, Varia; Ständisches Archiv (StA), Ständische Akten AI/3-4, AI/5, AIII/5, AIII/18, AIII/20; Codes Diplomaticus Austriacus, Tom. IV, Haus- Hof- und Staatsarchiv, Vienna, fols 203–309; Khevenhiller, *Annales Ferdinandei*, IX, fols 1065–60; Handschrift der österreichischen Nationalbibliothek, Cod. 10.100d (Retzer Jurament). This data was supplemented with information from genealogical works: Wißgrill, *Schauplatz des landsäßigen Nieder-Oesterreichischen Adels,* 5 vols; *Jahrbuch des Heraldisch-Genealogischen Vereins Adler* (Vienna: Verein Adler, 1872–90); Siebmacher, *Grosses und Allgemeines Wappenbuch*: *Der Niederösterreichische Adel*, 2 vols; Karl Friedrich von Frank, *Standeserhebungen und Gnadenakte für das Deutsche Reich und die Österreichischen Erblande bis 1806,* 5 vols (Senftenegg: Selbstverlag 1972); Ignaz Hübel, 'Die Ächtungen von Evangelischen und die Konfiskationen protestantischen Besitzes im Jahre 1620 in Nieder-und Oberösterreich, JbGPÖ, 59–60 (1938–9), pp. 42–62, 105–25; Kielmansegg, *Beiträge zur Geschichte der niederösterreichischen Statthalterei*; Schwarz, *The Imperial Privy Council.*
15. Another example is Johann Strasser the Younger, who succeeded his grandfather and father as mayor of Steyr, and held this position before he was admitted to the Estate of Knights in 1601; see *Jahrbuch Adler*, III (1876), p. 93. Wißgrill, *Schauplatz des landsäßigen Nieder-Oesterreichischen Adels,* IV, pp. 84–97, 471; Kielmansegg, *Beiträge zur Geschichte der niederösterreichischen Statthalterei*, p. 427; and Siebmacher, *Der Nieder-Österreichische Adel*, II, pp. 244–245.
16. The Estates considered anyone from outside of Lower Austria as 'foreign', although at times they included the Upper Austrians. In this study, all nobles who had settled in Lower Austria for more than three generations will be defined as natives.
17. Another third were first- and second-generation emigrants from the other hereditary lands, especially from Inner Austria, while about a fifth had recently migrated from the Reich. The majority of this last group had come from the Habsburg territories in Swabia, but a number were natives of Franconia, Saxony, Bavaria, Brandenburg and the Rhineland. For example, Igelshofer, Kleindienst, Rindsmaul, Lembsitz and Mierzer were first-generation immigrants from Styria. Heisperg had come to Lower Austria from Hessen; Kätzler, Kremmer and Hoe

from Franconia; Grünberg from Saxony; Hirschberg had emigrated from Brandenburg; and Reiffenberg from the Rhineland. Only a few knights had moved to Lower Austria from non-German-speaking countries, mainly from Bohemia and Italy. Some of these men already held noble titles at the time of immigration.

18. Another family, the Becks, had risen to power, wealth and noble status during the early sixteenth century through judicial functions, as military enterprisers and money-lenders to the Habsburgs. Joachim and Markus Beck, who held positions in the military, were admitted to the Estate of Lords in 1597, but it appears that an outstanding loan to the emperor, rather than courage, was the primary motive behind these promotions. However, Joachim Beck did distinguish himself during a military campaign in Hungary a year later; see Wißgrill, *Schauplatz des landsäßigen Nieder-Oesterreichischen Adels*, I, pp. 325–35; III, pp. 109–10.
19. The sources are less clear on the age of the noble status of the new lords. Most claimed to be of ancient nobility, and only seven families living in 1620 appear to have obtained noble status during the sixteenth century. Most of the Lower Austrian lords were barons, and only a handful of families – about a tenth – held the rank of count. Only one, Karl von Liechtenstein, was made prince (*Fürst*) in 1608. The following families were of new noble origin: Beck, Kunriz, Greiffenberg (Linsmayr), Salburg, Henkel, and probably also the Unverzagt and Wolzogen. Since the number of old families hardly changed, the addition of new members caused a relative decline of the old lords (from 35 per cent to 22 per cent). While social mobility was thus high, it must be noted that the proportion of families who had been elevated to barons during the previous four decades was as large in 1580 as in 1620 (about two-fifths).
20. Most of these lords served as royal or archducal chamberlains and belonged to the old nobility. Frequently, such honorary functions were combined with positions in the central administration. Thus, Christoph von Teuffenbach was war councillor as well as Imperial chamberlain; see Siebmacher, *Der Niederösterreichische Adel*, II, p. 315.
21. Hassinger, 'Die Landstände der österreichischen Länder', p. 1004.
22. NÖLA, StA, AI/5, fol. 24ff. Since some noble titles were granted only to the individual and not extended to their family and heirs, it is also possible that this affected the number of nobles who were recorded as having become extinct.
23. Rudolf Endres, *Adel in der frühen Neuzeit* (Munich: Oldenbourg Verlag, 1993), p. 50; Hellmuth Rössler (ed.), *Deutscher Adel, 1555–1740* (Darmstadt: Wissenschaftliche Buchgesellschaft, 1965) p. 179.
24. Jaroslav Honc, 'Populacni vyvoj sesti generaci 125 ceskych panskych rodu v letech 1522–1794', [Demographic trends among six generations of 125 families belonging to the Bohemian Lords, 1522–1794] in *Historická demografie*, 3 (1969), pp. 20–51, cited by E. Maur, 'Der böhmische und mährische Adel vom 16. bis zum 18. Jahrhundert', in H. Feigl and W. Rosner (eds), *Adel im Wandel*, p. 22.
25. Edouard Perroy, 'Social Mobility among the French Noblesse in the Later Middle Ages', *Past & Present*, 21 (1962), p. 31; Kenneth B. McFarlane, *The Noblity of Later Medieval England* (Oxford: Clarendon Press, 1973), pp. 173–4.
26. Between 1463–1666, the nobility of the French *election* Bayeux, for example, secured its survival by multiplying the number of children who belonged to the surviving lines. In other words, noble houses became extinct but, since the size of the surviving noble families multiplied, the nobility did not decline to the

extent that the extinction of lines would indicate; see James B. Wood, 'Demographic Pressure and Social Mobility among the Nobility of Early Modern France', *The Sixteenth Century Journal*, VIII(1) (April 1977), pp. 3–16; Wood, *The Nobility of the* Election *Bayeux, 1463–1666*. Continuity through Change (Princeton, NJ: Princeton University Press, 1980), ch. 2.

27. Thereafter, the proportion of individual members diminished slightly, or possibly remained steady, which is in line with the general population stagnation in Lower Austria from the Thirty Years' War to the late seventeenth century. Figures for 1415 and 1717 are derived from Hassinger, 'Die Landstände der österreichischen Länder', pp. 1003; for the *Herrenstand* in 1720 see NÖLA, StA, AI/5, fol. 183ff. The number of individuals listed in the latter document probably do not include landless nobles and could therefore have been higher. On demographic trends, see Klein, 'Die Bevölkerung Österreichs', pp. 67-8.
28. The actual disappearance of old lines was much more spectacular. Only about a third (75) of the families living in 1580 still belonged to the Estate of Knights in 1620, since thirty (15 per cent) rose to the Estate of Lords, and almost a half (92) seem to have become extinct in the male line. It must be stressed that these figures are tentative because it was difficult to determine the exact size of the *Ritterstand* from existing sources. For a number of families listed in some documents – such as the Hanauer, Haselbach, Hausmannstetter, Kirchhammer, Pfefferkorn, Pierbaum, Rosenhart – no evidence of immatriculation and membership in the Estates could be found. They were therefore excluded from the statistical analyses. Some, such as the Pfefferkorns, clearly did not belong to the Estates, but owned property belonging to the Estate of Knights. Others, such as the Hanauer, had become extinct in the male line but were listed as still living even in 1590. Some families had returned to the region of their origin (e.g., Schweinpeck and Kirchmayer). The evidence on a few families, such as the Mayer and Stubner, was so contradictory that they had to be excluded as well. For a list of nobles included in this study see MacHardy, 'Nobility in Crisis: The Case of Lower Austria', pp. 291–308.
29. While no estimates have been made for the size of the upper noble Estate for the late sixteenth century, a list drawn up by Baron Gundacker von Polheim in the early seventeenth century is considered to be the most reliable source for the year 1620; see, for example, Hassinger, 'Die Landstände der österreichischen Länder', p. 1003. However, the *Polheim'sche Libell* does not include most of the Protestants who were proscribed during 1620, and also excludes many landless nobles. It omits entire new families who owned property in Lower Austria, while including members of families who clearly belonged to the Estates of other provinces and countries, as well as nobles who had long been dead; see NÖLA, StA. AI/5, fol. 58ff. The *Polheim'sche Libell* was probably drawn up in 1621, and possibly later. The numerical differences between this list and my own estimates are not very great. I counted 24 more persons and 14 more families. However, our lists diverge greatly on the names of some 50 nobles who belonged to branches of families living in other provinces, notably in Upper Austria (for example, Bartholomäus Dietrichstein, Wolf and Erasmus Gera, and Gottfried Polheim), or others who had died before 1620 (such as Georg Christoph Concin, Marquard Christoph Urschenbeck, and Christian and Hans Wolfart Tschernembl). On the other hand, Polheim omitted the names of over 70 lords, most of whom had been proscribed or were landless, as well as a number of other nobles, for reasons not entirely clear (among them Wolfgang Georg

Althan, Georg Friedrich Herbertstein, Johann Eusebius Khuen and Georg Sigmund Lamberg).

30. The figures provided by various historians differ. For example, it is unclear how far the lesser Bohemian nobility declined in size; according to Richter, 'Die böhmischen Länder von 1471–1740', p. 243, it lost only about a tenth of its members, since most of the losses (311, or a third, disappeared between 1557 and 1615) were replaced with new admissions. However, according to Bůžek, 'Nižší šlechta v předbělohorských čecháh', p. 54, only 215 knights were admitted. In this case, the lesser nobility would have declined by 16 per cent. One of the problems seems to be that it is never clear which of the Bohemian territories have been included in the calculations, and whether the landless nobles, or only tax-paying nobles, have been counted. Compare also the figures provided by Winkelbauer, 'Krise der Aristokratie', pp. 328–53; Winkelbauer, 'Wandlungen des mährischen Adels um 1600', pp. 16–36; and Pánek, 'Das Ständewesen und die Gesellschaft', pp. 73–175.
31. This estimate is derived from the figures provided by Maur, 'Der böhmische und mährische Adel', p. 21. However, the statistics in Winkelbauer, 'Krise der Aristokratie?', pp. 332–3 suggest that the losses were lower.
32. Dewald, *The European Nobility*, pp. 16–27.
33. Bibl, 'Die Vorgeschichte der Religionskonzession Kaiser Maximilian II', pp. 400–31; Pickl, 'Die wirtschaftlichen Bestimmungen', pp. 563–86.
34. *Codex Austriacus ordine alphabetico compilatus d.i.: Eigentlicher Begriff und Inhalt aller unter deß Ertzhauses zu Oesterreich, fürnemblich aber der Regierung Leopoldi I. ausgegangenen in des Justitz- und Politzey–Wesen ... eingelauffenen Generalien etc.*, 6 vols; with *Appendix (Mit zahlreichen Handschriften), 1456–1718* (Vienna, 1704–77) Vol. I, p. 737 (henceforth *Codex Austriacus*)
35. The literature on social mobility in Western Europe is extensive. For an overview, see Dewald, *The European Nobility*. For the English nobility, see Stone, *The Crisis of the Aristocracy*; Stone, *An Open Elite? England, 1540–1880* (Oxford: Clarendon Press, 1984); see also Steven G. Ellis, *Tutor Frontiers and Noble Power: The Making of the British State* (Oxford: Clarendon Press, 1995); Helen Miller, *Henry VIII and the English Nobility* (Oxford: Basil Blackwell, 1986); Chris Given-Wilson, *The English Nobility in the Later Middle Ages* (London: Routledge, 1987). The historiography on social nobility in France before the Revolution is also rich; for a succinct summary of the debates, see Goldstone, *Revolution and Rebellion*, pp. 228–32. Social ascent into the nobility in sixteenth- and seventeenth-century France has been examined by James B. Wood, in *The Nobility of the* Election of *Bayeux*, and E. Schalk, 'Ennoblement in France from 1350 to 1660', *Journal of Social History*, 16 (1982), pp. 101–10. I. A. A. Thompson, 'The Purchase of Nobility in Castile, 1552–1700', *The Journal of European Economic History*, 8 (1979), pp. 313–60, and C. Jago, 'The Crisis of the Aristocracy in Seventeenth Century Castile', *Past & Present*, pp. 84 (1979), 60–90, review developments in Spain; see also Tommaso Astarita, *The Continuity of Feudal Power: The Carocciolo di Brienza in Spanish Naples* (Cambridge University, 1992), pp. 219–20; and John Lynch, *The Hispanic World in Crisis and Change, 1598–1700*, (New York: Basil Blackwell,1992), pp. 181–3. The nobilities of the Holy Roman Empire have received much attention in the past two decades; see Endres, *Adel in der frühen Neuzeit*, for an overview and bibliography; Wolfgang Zorn, 'Deutsche Führungsschichten des 17. und 18. Jahrhunderts. Forschungsergeb-nisse seit 1945', in Georg Jäger *et al.* (eds), *Internationales Archiv für*

Sozialgeschichte der deutschen Literatur, Vol. 6, (Tübingen, 1981), pp. 176–97; on social mobility, see also the articles in Winfried Schulze, (ed.), *Ständische Gesellschaft and soziale Mobilität* (Munich: Oldenbourg 1988).

36. For these developments in the German territories, see Ernst Böhme, *Das fränkische Reichsgrafenkollegium im 16. und 17. Jahrhundert* (Stuttgart: Franz Steiner Verlag, 1989), ch. 1; and Endres, *Adel in der frühen Neuzeit*, ch. 2; and for Bohemia, Richter, 'Die böhmischen Länder', p. 241.
37. Endres, *Adel in der frühen Neuzeit*, p. 78, misinterprets the conclusions I made in my article, 'Status, Konfession und Besitz', where I also stress this point and do not, as he assumes, assert that the nobility was closing its ranks.
38. Besides abstention from usury, nobles had to conduct themselves in an 'honourable fashion', which included peaceful relations with neighbours, refraining from adultery and marriage with commoners, or having illegitimate children. Any of these offences could lead to rescission of membership; see NÖLA, RstA AI, fol. 63ff.; NÖLA, RstA AI/4, fol. 2 (19 Feb. 1599). It should be noted that the establishment of a distinction between nobility and noble Estates created a situation in Lower Austria where engagement in bourgeois occupations theoretically became acceptable among nobility who did not belong to the *Herren-* and *Ritterstand*, whereas previously it had been prohibited to the entire nobility.
39. NÖLA, HStA, Lade xv, Varia (2 Apr. 1588).
40. For this voting procedure, see the minutes of the Estates' meetings in NÖLA, Ständische Bücher, pp. 55–87, 98–126.
41. A landed estate taxed at 10 lbs usually included some 5 to 25 peasant households, with a purchasing value between 5,000 and 10,000 Gulden, but the price could be higher. For example, in 1620, the estimated value of Hans Wilhelm Mayer's estate with 26 peasant households was 5,000 Gulden. Wolf Polani's property, with 34 peasant households, was worth 8,000 Gulden. See Hübel, 'Die 1620 in Nieder- und Oberösterreich politisch kompromittierten Protestanten', vol. 59 (1938), p. 59; vol. 60 (1939), p. 107.
42. E. G. Schimka, Die Zusammensetzung des niederösterreichischen Herrenstandes von 1520–1620 (Ph.D. Dissertation, University of Vienna, 1967), pp. 36–7.
43. Knittler, 'Adelige Grundherrschaft im Übergang', pp. 84–111, provides examples of income from landed estates. For salary levels of officials, see Fellner and Kretschmayr (eds), *Die Österreichische Zentralverwaltung*, Vol. II: *Aktenstücke 1491–1681*, pp. 202–6.
44. Some, such as Hans and Christoph Klee, and Johann Baptist Linsmayr, had been ennobled for only one year; NÖLA, RstA AI, fol. 86 (1612).
45. An attempt had already been made by the Estates in 1606 to exclude landless nobles from voting at the assemblies, but this rule could not easily be enforced ; see Dagmar Schopf, 'Die im Zeitraum von 1620–1740 erfolgten Neuaufnahmen in den niederösterreichischen Herrenstand', (Ph.D. Dissertation, University of Vienna, 1960), p. 5.
46. For example, before 1600, the Hüttendorfers, Facis, Isperers, Kneissls and Pirkhaimers, all waited for less than ten years after ennoblement to be incorporated. During the following two decades, Matthias von Bloenstein was admitted after being ennobled for only nine years, Ferdinand and Maximilian Hoe von Hoenegg for ten, and Zacharias Starzer for five.
47. *Codex Austriacus* I; pp. 736–8; quote on p. 737.
48. NÖLA, RStA AI/6–7, fol. 16–19.
49. Bibl, 'Die Berichte des Reichshofrates Dr. Georg Eder', p. 94.

50. For detailed statistical data on admissions, see MacHardy, 'Social Nobility and Noble Rebellion', pp. 132–3.
51. Georg Bernhard von Urschenbeck was *Landuntermarschall* from 1595 to 1608, followed by Christoph Greiss (until 1618). Spett, Grünberg, Hirschberg, Lembsitz, Mierzer, Golz, Kain and Pannicher were Protestants; only Reiffenberg was Catholic. The confession of the four remaining newcomers is uncertain.
52. After 1600, the number of Protestant knights from the Reich increased. These were the Heuberger, Wopping, Pannicher, Hoe, Grünberg, Hirschberg and Kain. Most were first- and second-generation émigrés from Saxony, Brandenburg, Bavaria and Swabia.
53. Since the religious affiliation of 82 families living in 1580 is unknown, it is highly unlikely that these were Catholic, as this would imply that the proportion of Catholic knights had been stagnant or decreasing until 1620. However, since all other evidence indicates that the Catholic nobility multiplied, and since the socioeconomic characteristics of the confessionally unknown knights resemble those of the Protestant nobility, it is more probable that, in 1580, the ratio between Catholic and Protestant knights was 10:90. If these unknown families are not counted, then 19 (16 per cent) of the lines and 28 (14 per cent) of their members were Catholic, while 166 (86 per cent) of the knights of 97 lines (84 per cent) were Protestant. One of these families, the Concin, had members belonging to both confessions. Such confessionally mixed families have been counted as separate branches and added to the total number of 'pure' families. By 1620, the proportion of Catholic families had increased to 29 (25 per cent), with 40 individuals (20 per cent), while the number of Protestants had declined to 161 knights (75 per cent), belonging to 87 lines (80 per cent); the confessionally mixed families had risen to 4. For the year 1620, the number of families with unknown confessional affiliation was 16, which provides for a fairly accurate distribution of the confessions, especially since a proportional number of these families seem to have belonged to the Catholic faith. If the percentage distribution is calculated on the above assumption, then the Catholic lines increased by about three-quarters from 19 to 33, and their members by almost two-thirds from 28 to 45, while the Protestant families had declined by about a half, from 179 to 99, and their members by almost a third, from 253 to 179.
54. Twenty-six of the new families were Protestant, while eighteen were Catholic. In actual numbers, then, incorporations of new Catholics were about the same in both noble Estates, but the proportion of new Catholics was higher in the Estate of Lords because of the smaller total number of admissions. Since the confession of eight new families is unknown, and two new families had members belonging to both confessions, the terminal number for calculating the percentage was 44 rather than 50. Two Catholic families, the Khevenhiller and Dietrichstein, re-emigrated to Lower Austria without being admitted formally.
55. The Rheingrafen were probably Catholics, while the confession of the Henkels at the time of admission is uncertain. The barons of Salburg and Krausenegg were also Catholic.
56. NÖLA, HStA, Aufnahmeakten S-22, fol. 2.
57. Overall, the proportion of immigrants from the other hereditary lands was very high in the Estate of Lords. Nearly half (28) of the new lords were first- and second-generation émigrés from these territories, especially from Styria. Only 16 per cent originated in the Reich, another 5 per cent came from Bohemia, and

3 per cent from Latin countries. It is peculiar why the emigration of Protestant lords from Inner Austria was so intense during this period. The Catholic influx might be explained by the successful Counter-reformatory activities of archduke Ferdinand in Inner Austria after 1595, and by the great demand for Catholic nobles at the Imperial Court. Ironically, the Counter-reformation also seems to have prompted Protestants to move to Lower Austria, where their religious persecution probably seemed comparatively mild.

58. Although the conversion to Catholicism of such prominent and old families as the Liechtenstein, or members of the barons of Puchheim and Althan, invigorated the Catholic opposition, it was hardly, as some historians assumed, the main force facilitating the formation of the Catholic Union in 1604. Reingrabner, *Adel und Reformation,* p. 14, has made this assertion. Only between six and eight branches of the Protestant knights, and ten of the lords, had converted to Catholicism by 1620. Since one of these (Salburg) had embraced Catholicism in 1608 before entering the Estate, and four others (the barons of Oedt, a branch of the Kollonitsch, Ehrenreich Gera, and Christoph Thonrädl) had converted before they advanced from the Estate of Knights, only five branches of the Protestant lords existing in 1580 had in fact converted by 1620. The Lampl and a branch of the Welzer also converted, but they remained in the *Ritterstand.* The confession of the Anfangs and the Grünbergs, both members of the Estate of Knights, is not known for 1580, but in 1620 they were Catholics. It is thus possible that they also were converts. Of the old lords, branches of the Puchheim, the Losenstein, Herbertstein and Althan, as well as the entire house of Liechtenstein, converted to Catholicism.

59. Reingrabner has asserted that 10 per cent of the nobles living in 1580–3 were Catholic, and that their proportion was higher in the *Ritterstand* than in the Estate of Lords. By 1620, about a quarter of the individual nobles were estimated to be Catholic, although by then, Reingrabner suspects, about a third of the nobles of the *Herrenstand* belonged to this confession. While the proportion of Catholics was already clearly larger in the Estate of Lords by 1580 – with or without the 'unknown' cases – it is nevertheless astonishing that Reingrabner's estimates of the percentage distribution, based on a few incomplete contemporary lists, is close to my own. However, the numerical distribution, the actual growth in the number of Catholics, and diminution of Protestant nobles, are not apparent from his study. He considered the uncertain cases to be small. In another study, Reingrabner provided a list of families which he determined as being Protestant, naming only 58 as belonging to the Estate of Knights in 1620; 'Der protestantische Adel in Niederösterreich – seine Zuzammensetzung und sein Beitrag zur Reformationsgeschichte des Landes' (Ph.D Dissertation, University of Vienna, 1973), pp. 266–7. This is much lower than the 87 knightly families I was able to identify as Protestants. He also lists members of the *Ritterstand,* such as Ulrich von Pranck, among the Estate of Lords, or includes nobles such as Georg Bernhard Kirchberger among those who paid homage in 1620, and among those who did not. Stephan Pathi is surely Stephan Palffy, and Weikhard von Polheim seems to be identical with Weikhard von Puchheim. We also differ on the number of families who had members belonging to both confessions (in 1620), such as the Althans, Geras, Khevenhillers and Oedts, as well as the barons of Eck (or Egg) whose Catholic line resided in Carnolia, and not in Lower Austria; see Reingrabner, *Adel und Reformation,* pp. 12–20; Reingrabner, 'Der protestantische Adel', pp. 266–7; and Wißgrill, *Schauplatz des landsässigen Nieder-Oesterreichischen Adels,* II, pp. 324–30.

60. Bireley, 'Ferdinand II: Founder of the Habsburg Monarchy', pp. 234–5.

5 Advancing at the Imperial Court

1. Evans, *Rudolf II*, pp. 139–45.
2. See MacHardy, 'Nobility in Crisis', ch. IV for a statistical analysis of the regional composition of nobles at Court.
3. Kettering, *Patrons, Brokers and Clients*, p. 141.
4. A 1574 list of the archducal court at Graz enumerates about 200 people belonging to the *Hofstaat;* the archduchess employed another 34, and her son another 20; Johann Andritsch, 'Landesfürstliche Berater am Grazer Hof (1564–1919)', in A. Novotny and B. Sutter (eds), *Innerösterreich, 1564–1619* (Graz: Böhlaus, 1968), p. 76. Hans Leo Mikoletzky, 'Der Haushalt des kaiserlichen Hofes zu Wien (vornehmlich im 18. Jahrhundert)', *Carinthia*, I (146) (1956), p. 668; Ehalt, *Ausdrucksformen absolutistischer Herrschaft*, p. 23; Paua S. Fichtner, 'To Rule is Not to Govern: The Diary of Maximilian II', in Solomon Wank *et al.* (ed.), *The Mirror of History. Essays in Honour of Fritz Fellner* (Santa Barbara, Calif. etc.: ABC-Clio, 1988), pp. 255–64; Žogler, *Der Hofstaat des Hauses Österreich*, pp. 53. It is beyond the scope of this book to deal with female patronage and the entourage of the empress and archduchesses. However, I intend to make this the subject of a future study.
5. Geoffrey Parker, *Europe in Crisis 1598–1648* (Ithaca, NY: Cornell University Press, 1980), p. 54; Kettering, *Patrons, Brokers and Clients*, p. 216; Kettering, *French Society, 1589–1715* (Harlow: Longman, 2001), p. 68; Henshall, *The Myth of Absolutism*, p. 91.
6. Until this time, the number of buildings within the walls of the city was around 1200. The garrison soldiers were particularly affected by the housing shortage, and forced to build their own sheds along the bastions; see Spielman, *The City & The Crown*, pp. 30, 65, 87.
7. These percentages are based on figures provided by Eva-Maria H. Götz's 'Lebenszyklus und soziale Prägung nachgeborener Söhne des österreichischen Adels' (Ph.D. Dissertation, University of Vienna, 1976), who analysed the careers of sons belonging to a sample of 25 families, mostly from the Estate of Lords.
8. For example, the incumbent of the *Erblandoberstkämmereramt* (master of the chambers) received the village and country court of Pottendorf as a fief from the crown. Wißgrill, *Schauplatz des landsäßigen Nieder-Oesterreichischen Adels*, I, p. 368. Most non-hereditary positions in the Imperial or archducal household terminated with the death of the incumbent, or of the ruler. In the latter case, his successor could replace the holders of the more important positions with members of his own entourage. A court position could also be terminated by the incumbent if the ruler agreed to it, and occasionally even dismissals occurred; Ehalt, *Ausdrucksformen absolutistischer Herrschaft*, pp. 33–4.
9. Spielman, *The City & The Crown*, pp. 56–8.
10. The *Obersthofmeister* also received foreign princes in the absence of the emperor. By the early seventeenth century, the *Oberstkämmerer* (master of the chambers), who had gained in prestige and functions, was put second in rank before the *Obersthofmarschall*. The *Oberstkämmerer* was aided by a large number of servants and attendants, the most important of whom were the chamberlains. The latter position was reserved for the old nobility, and was for many a stepping stone to more important careers at court. The marshal of the court was usually next in rank, and also in charge of visitors, and the reception of ambassadors and other dignitaries. His staff included a number of other officials with adminstrative and legal training. See Ferdinand Mencik, 'Beiträge zur Geschichte der kaiserlichen

Hofämter', *Archiv für österreichische Geschichte* (AÖG), 87 (2) (1988), pp. 534–1; 563; Žögler, *Der Hofstaat des Hauses Österreich*, pp. 66, 107, 139; Schwarz, *The Imperial Privy Council*, pp. 34–5; and Ehalt, *Ausdrucksformen absolutistischer Herrschaft*, pp. 48–52.

11. The statistical analysis of *Hofämter* is based on evidence provided by Mencik, 'Beiträge zur Geschichte der kaiserlichen Hofämter'; Schwarz, *The Imperial Privy Council;* Wißgrill, *Schauplatz des landsäßigen Nieder-Oesterreichischen Adels;* Siebmacher, *Der Niederösterreichische Adel* and *Der Oberösterreichische Adel.* However, it must be stressed that the thirty-two nobles do not represent all incumbents of the four highest offices. In particular, it was impossible to include the nobles serving Archduke Ernst.
12. Fellner and Kretschmayr, *Die Österreichische Zentralverwaltung,* I, pp. 145–8, 219–39; the names and backgrounds of privy councillors were derived from the *Hofstaatsverzeichnisse,* II: *Aktenstücke 1491–1681*, pp. 237–44; and Schwarz, *The Imperial Privy Council*, appendix C, which provides individual biographies for most privy councillors. It should be stressed that it was mainly the councillors who were installed at the beginning of a reign who were included in my statistics.
13. In 1576, about a third of the Aulic councillors belonged to the learned bourgeoisie, and another third each to the lesser and upper nobility. In 1629, a quarter belonged to the lower nobility and another quarter to the bourgeoisie. The number of Aulic councillors did not change significantly, as there were between 19 and 31 members serving each year.
14. In 1576, one of the five *Hofkammerräte* had belonged to the upper nobility, one was a commoner, while only three were knights. The president of the court treasury was usually chosen from among the upper nobility. A similar distribution of offices can be observed in the Lower Austrian *Regiment,* which was usually headed by members of the upper nobility. While four of the sixteen councillors *(Regimentsräte)* were learned commoners, the remaining positions were divided equally between the upper and lower noble Estates. The proportion of non-nobles among the councillors of the treasury, however, was much larger. The names of the *Regimentsräte* and *Kammerräte* were derived from J. Chmel, 'Die Regimentsräte des Nieder-Österr. Regiments. Von 1529 bis 1657. Die Kammerräte der Niederösterr. Kammer. Von 1539–1606. Aus den Friedensheimschen Wappen- und Regentenbuche zu Göttweig', *Notizblätter der Akademie,* 1 (1851), pp. 212–24, 228–51, 263–368.
15. Schwarz, *The Imperial Privy Council,* pp. 229–30, 249–52, 263, 277–9, 359–61, 370–6, 381–2, 407.
16. In 1576, the yearly income of a war councillor amounted to only 600 florins, but by 1615 some of them were receiving salaries commensurate with that of the *Hofkammerräte.* See 'Hofstaatsverzeichnisse (12 Dec. 1576 and 29 Mar. 1615)' in Fellner and Kretschmayr, *Die Österreichische Zentralverwaltung,* II; pp. 194, 204. However, some of the subordinate administrators, such as the dispatcher in the war chancery (*Hofkriegskanzleiexpediteur*) and the manager of military provisions (*Proviantamtsverweser*) belonged to the lesser nobility.
17. Hellbling, *Österreichische Verfassung- und Verwaltungsgeschichte,* pp. 230–32; Luschin von Ebengreuth, *Geschichte des älteren Gerichtswesens,* p. 275.
18. The warrior or his family had to pay ransoms in case of capture by the enemy, which could amount to over a year's salary, or the cost of a small estate; see Thomas M. Barker, *The Military Intellectual and Battle. Raimondo Montecuccoli and*

the Thirty Years War (Albany, NY: State University of New York Press, 1975), p. 16. The undesirability of war was stressed frequently by the Lower Austrian Estates; see G. Neugebauer, 'Die niederösterreichischen Landtage von 1577 bis 1592' (Ph.D. Dissertation, University of Vienna, 1979), p. 88. That the Estates made military service against the Ottomans a part of their admission requirements, the constant need for Imperial propaganda, and reminders to the nobility to observe their military duties, also testifies to the fact that nobles had become reluctant warriors; Mandlmayr and Vocelka, 'Vom Adelsaufgebot zum stehenden Heer', pp. 122–3. Single or multiple regiments were raised, recruited and financed initially by individuals and commanders, and officers stood in the service of the regimental proprietor rather than the ruler; for examples, see Barker, *Army, Aristocracy, Monarchy*, chs 4–6.

19. Of 57 regiments engaged in the Thirty Years' War, only 9 per cent belonged to nobles indigenous to Upper and Lower Austria, and the overwhelming majority (75 per cent) belonged to clans from outside the Habsburg hereditary lands. These percentages are calculated from the figures given by Barker in *Army, Aristocracy, Monarchy*, pp. 15–19. During the early seventeenth century only an estimated 5 per cent (fewer than 20 persons) of the upper nobility held positions in the Catholic Church. Götz, 'Lebenszyklus und soziale Prägung', pp. 117, 156. Unfortunately, Götz does not provide the base number for her statistic, which rests on a sample of 25 families from the upper nobility. See also Winner, 'Die niederösterreichischen Prälaten zwischen Reformation und Josephinismus', *Jahrbuch des Stiftes Klosterneuburg*, NF, 4 (1964), pp. 111–27.
20. One such exception was Cardinal Khlesl, who was appointed director of the Privy Council in 1612 even though he did not belong to old nobility. It appears, however, that it was for this reason that he did not hold the office of *Obersthofmeister*, which was customary for the director of the Privy Council.
21. An appointment to the *Regiment* was often a stepping stone to a seat in the court treasury, and sometimes to the Aulic council, but it could also happen that, after service as a *Hofkammerrat*, a knight resumed his position as a *Regimentsrat*, apparently without suffering any loss of prestige.
22. Thus, the Lower Austrian *Landmarschall*, the highest official of the Estates, was, with one exception (Georg Bernhard Urschenbeck, who received the baronage only one year before his instalment) always a member of the old lords, and his representative, the *Landuntermarschall*, belonged to the old knights. The important office of the deputies was nearly always given to the old baronage (exceptions were Sigmund Landau and Hans Christoph Urschenbeck), and in the Estate of Knights to the old lower nobility. Moreover, the *Raitherren* (comptrollers) of the *Ritterstand*, fairly influential officials, were with few exceptions old knights. It testifies to the low prestige of the financial administration that the Estate of Lords selected many of its comptrollers from the new baronage, and even from the Estate of Knights (Helmhard von Friedesheim, appointed in 1614, was from the *Ritterstand*). The inferior office of the *Obereinnehmer* (receiver general) was also given to new knights or commoners. This office was not, as Schimka has assumed, always a member of the *Ritterstand*. In fact, between 1578 and 1620, only one (Johann Khelhaimer) of the six *Obereinnehmer* belonged to the new Estate of Knights, the remainder being commomers, who possibly belonged to the Fourth Estate. Nevertheless, they advanced frequently to the *Ritterstand* at a later point. Functions in the military organization were distributed along similar lines – that is, the most prestigious offices and commands

went to the old nobility, while inferior fieldwork duties were performed by knights or commoners. Thus the Estates' military commander, the *Generallandobrist*, was always elected by the Estates from among the *Herrenstand*, while his deputy, the *Generalobristleutnant*, was a member of the *Ritterstand*. The majority of the four district commanders (*Viertelhauptmänner*), who performed the actual duties, were chosen from the Estate of Knights, while their five subordinate officers were frequently non-nobles. However, occasionally they were commoners (for example, Hans Wolf Kneissl), or members of the *Herrenstand*; see NÖLA, Hs. 362, fols 2, 4; 18, 20, 23; Schimka, 'Die Zusammensetzung des niederösterreichischen Herrenstandes', p. 40; Stangler, 'Die niederösterreichischen Landtage', p. 62.

23. The data for this statistic was derived from Schwarz, *The Imperial Privy Council*, appendix, pp. 198–391.
24. Councillors to the Austrian *Regiment* began their careers earlier, in their mid-thirties.
25. Only promotion to the less prestigious *Hofkammerrat* was speedier and occurred on average within five years.
26. Götz, 'Lebenszyklus und soziale Prägung', analysed the careers of sons belonging to a sample of 25 families, mainly from the Estate of Lords.
27. For income from landed estates, see the extensive data provided by Beatrix Bastl, *Herrschaftsschätzungen*, and. Knittler, 'Adelige Grundherrschaft', p. 96, although there are mistakes in the percentages she calculated. In 1621, the property of the Protestant rebel, Hans Wilhelm Mayer, was evaluated at 5000 Gulden; Hübel, 'Die 1620 in Nieder- und Oberösterreich politisch kompromittierten Protestanten', vol. 59 (1938), p. 61.
28. Fellner and Kretschmayr, *Die Österreichische Zentralverwaltung* II, pp. 191–2, 199, 203–4; Schwarz, *The Imperial Privy Council*, pp. 193, 278.
29. The noble Estates also provided competitive salaries for their top officials. For example, the important deputies had, besides free lodging, a yearly income of 800 florins, which was raised to 1200 florins after 1616, and the highest official, the *Landmarschall*, received about 2000 florins per year; NÖLA, StA, Hs 362, fols 9, 12; see also 'Hofstaatsverzeinisse (12 Dec. 1576 and 29 Mar. 1615)', in Fellner and Kretschmayr, *Die Österreichische Zentralverwaltung*, pp. 194, 204; Chmel, 'Die Regimentsräte des Nieder-Österr. Regiments', pp. 212–41, 263–68; and Hofkammer Archiv (HKA) Vienna, NiederÖsterreichische Herrschaftsakten, N 29/C/4, fol. 1551-4v.
30. Friedrich Edelmayer, 'Ehre, Geld, Karriere', in Friedrich Edelmayer and Alfred Kohler (ed.), *Kaiser Maximilian II. Kultur und Politik im 16. Jahrhundert* (Munich: Oldenbourg, 1992), pp. 126–34; H. Wertitsch, 'Die Kipperzeit in den österreichischen Ländern' (Ph.D. Dissertation, University of Graz, 1967); Schwarz, *The Imperial Privy Council*, pp. 194, 305; see also Robert D. Chesler, 'Crowns, Lords, and God: The Establishment of Secular Authority and the Pacification of Lower Austria, 1618–1648' (Ph.D. Dissertation, Princeton University, 1976), pp. 64–5.
31. For a discussion of seventeenth-century definitions of bribery at the Habsburg Court, see Spielman, *The City & The Crown*, pp. 72–4. However, by the mid-seventeenth century lists were established which fixed fees for certain services in a few offices.
32. Schwarz, *The Imperial Privy Council*, pp. 361, 371–72; Kielmansegg, *Beiträge zur Geschichte der niederösterreichischen Statthalterei*, pp. 210–17; Spielman, *The City & The Crown*, p. 72.

33. Graf Kufstein, *Studien zur Familiengeschichte,* Vol. III: *17. Jahrhundert* (Vienna/Leipzig, 1915), p. 9; for the sale of offices in France, England, Spain and Prussia, see K. Malettke (ed.), *Ämterkäuflichkeit: Aspekte sozialer Mobilität im europäischen Vergleich* (Berlin: Freie Universität, 1980).
34. Susanna Veronika Meggau was Trautson's third wife. Siebmacher insists she was Leonhard Helfried's daughter, but elsewhere he shows more clearly that it must have been his sister, Susanna; Siebmacher, *Oberösterreichische Adel II*, p. 490, and *NiederÖsterreichische Adel,* I, p. 378; Schwarz, *The Imperial Privy Council,* p. 301, 369–71; Kielmansegg, *Beiträge zur Geschichte der niederösterreichischen Statthalterei,* p. 210; *Jahrbuch Adler,* vol M, pp. 120–30.
35. For example, the marrriage alliance between the daughter of Karl von Liechtenstein and the nephew and heir of Franz von Dietrichstein was concluded after her father and his uncle had been appointed as privy councillors during the early seventeenth century; Schwarz, *The Imperial Privy Council,* pp. 370–7, 229–30, 406–7, 249–52, 277–9, 406.
36. Elisabeth Vavra, 'Adelige Lustbarkeiten', in *Adel im Wandel,* pp. 429–37, describes noble festivities at court and elsewhere; see also Beatrix Bastl, 'Feuerwerk und Schlittenfahrt. Ordnungen zwischen Ritual und Zeremoiell', *Wiener Geschichtsblätter,* 4 (1996), pp. 197–229; Hans Commenda, 'Adelige Lustbarkeiten in Linz vom 16. bis zum 18. Jahrhundert', *Historisches Jahrbuch der Stadt Linz* (1958), pp. 141–80; and Karl Vocelka, 'Manier-Groteske-Fest-Triumph. Zur Geistesgeschichte der frühen Neuzeit', *Österreich in Geschichte und Literatur,* 21 (1977), pp. 137–50.
37. See, for example, R. Alewyn, *Das große Welttheater. Die Epoche der höfischen Feste* (Munich: Beck Verlag, 1985) and the analyses of early modern European courts in Asch and Birke (eds.), *Princes, Patronage, and the Nobility.* For a detailed analysis of Habsburg piety, see Anna Coreth, *'Pietas Austriaca'. Österreichische Frömmigkeit im Barock,* 2nd rev. edn (Vienna: Verlag für Geschichte und Politik, 1982).
38. Quoted in Dewald, *The European Nobility,* p. 154.
39. J. H. Hexter's seminal essay, 'The Education of the Aristocracy in the Renaissance', in his *Reappraisals in History,* 2nd edn (Chicago: University of Chicago Press, 1979), pp. 45-70, still deserves attention. For the education of the German nobility, see Winfried Dotzauer, 'Deutsches Studium und deutsche Studenten an europäischen Hochschulen (Frankreich, Italien) und die nachfolgende Tätitgkeit in Stadt, Kirche und Territorium in Deutschland', in Erich Maschke and Jürgen Sydow (eds), *Stadt und Universität im Mittelalter und in der Frühen Neuzeit* (Sigmaringen: Jan Thorbecke Verlag, 1974); Notker Hammerstein, 'Universität und Reformation', *Historische Zeitschrift,* 258 (2) (April 1994), pp. 339–57; Reiner A. Müller, *Universität und Adel. Eine soziokulturelle Studie zur Geschichte der bayerischen Landesuniversität Ingoldstadt: 1472–1648* (Berlin: Dunker & Humblot, 1974); Müller, 'Aristokratisierung des Studiums? Bemerkungen zur Adelsfrequenz an süddeutschen Universitäten im 17. Jahrhundert', *Geschichte und Gesellschaft,* 10 (1984), pp. 31–46; Anton Schindling, *Humanistische Hochschule und freie Reichsstadt. – Gymnasium und Akademie in Strassburg: 1538 bis 1621* (Mainz: von Zabern, 1977); W. Zorn, 'Adel und Gelehrtes Beamtentum', in H. Aubin and W. Zorn (eds), *Handbuch der deutschen Wirtschafts- und Sozialgeschichte* (Stuttgart: Union Verlag, 1971). On French higher education, see L. W. B. Brockliss, *French Higher Education in the Seventeenth and Eighteenth Centuries* (Oxford: University Press, 1987), and on the French nobility, Mark Motley, *Becoming a French Aristocrat: The Education of the Court Nobility 1580–1715* (Princeton, NJ: Princeton University Press, 1990). Norbert Conrads, *Ritterakademien*

der Frühen Neuzeit: Bildung als Standesprivileg im 16. und 17. Jahrhundert (Göttingen: Vandenhoeck & Ruprecht, 1982), provides comparisons between noble academies in France and Germany, and R. Kagan, *Students and Society in Early Modern Spain* (Baltimore, Md; John Hopkins University Press, 1974), synthesizes research on education in Spain. R. J. W. Evans deals with higher education in the Habsburg lands, 'Die Universität im geistigen Milieu der Habsburgischen Länder, 17.–18. Jahrhundert', in Alexander Patschovsky and Horst Rabe (eds), *Die Universität in Alteuropa* (Vienna: Univ–Verlag, 1994), pp. 79–200; Bahlcke, *Regionalismus und Staatsintegration im Widerstreit,* ch. 4b, has a section on higher education in the Bohemian lands. See also references below on the Habsburg territories.

40. Charles Girard (ed.), *Oeuvres mêlées de Saint-Evremod*, 3 vols (Paris, 1867), vol II, p. 259; quoted in Jonathan Dewald, *Aristocratic Experience*, p. 81.
41. Richard Pace, *De Fructu* (Basle, 1571), quoted in Lawrence Stone, *The Crisis of the Aristocracy*, p. 305.
42. This does not mean that *habitus* is just a habit, or a mechanism, or a role and set of norms. It is an open system of disposition, that is durable but not immutable: 'The tendency toward self-reproduction of the structure is realized only when it enrolls the collaborations of agents who have internalized its specific necessity in the form of habitus and who are *active producers* even when they consciously or unconsciously contribute to reproduction. But what is necessary to reproduce the structure is still historical action ... agents are the product of this structure and continually make and remake this structure, which they may even radically tranform [*sic*] under definite structural conditions'; Bourdieu and Wacquant, *Reflexive Sociology,* p. 140; see also Bourdieu, *The Logic of Practice*, pp. 52–65. For similar conceptions of *habitus*, see James M. Ostrow, *Social Sensitivity: A Study of Habit and Experience* (Albany, NY: State University of New York Press, 1990), who also traces the concept of habitual sensitivity to Maurice Merleau-Ponti and John Dewey. On the various concepts of strategy, see Graham Crow, 'The Use of the Concept of "Strategy" in Recent Sociological Literature', *Sociology*, 23 (1) (February, 1989), pp. 1–24. Biological reproduction for patrimonial transmission formed an important part of social reproduction strategies, but they are not the focal point of this book. When necessary, I will distinguish biological reproductive capital from other forms of family maintenance.
43. Helmut Engelbrecht, *Geschichte des österreichischen Bildungswesens. Erziehung und Unterricht auf dem Boden Österreichs*. Vol. 2: *Das 16. und 17. Jahrhundert* (Vienna: Österreichischer Bundesverlag, 1983), ch. 4; Cyriacius Spangenberg, *Adels Spiegel. Historischer Ausfürlicher Bericht. Was Adel Sey und heisse/ Woher er kome,* Vol. I (Schmalkalden: Michel Schmück, 1591), pp. 138–9, insisted that children's education should begin at seven, as soon as they have acquired reason ('sobald bei Verstand').
44. Instructions of Karl Eusebius von Liechtenstein (1611–48) to his son , quoted in Heiss, *'Ihre keiserlichen Mayestät zu Diensten ... unserer ganzen fürstlichen Familie aber zur Glori.* Erziehung und Unterricht des Fürsten von Liechtenstein im Zeitalter des Absolutismus', in Evelin Oberhamer (ed.), *Der ganzen Welt ein Lob und Spiegel. Das Fürstenhaus Liechtenstein in der frühen Neuzeit* (Vienna: Verlag für Geschichte und Politik, 1990), pp. 155, 175.
45. 'da fast aller ampter voller Rechtshandel sindt, und ohne lateinische sprach nicht gefuert werden'; excerpt from the religious regulations concerning the school of the Estates in Horn, Kirchenordnung (3 January 1577), quoted in Heiss, 'Konfession, Politik und Erziehung', p. 50.

46. Engelbrecht, *Das 16. und 17. Jahrhundert*, pp. 57, 97–8.
47. Ulrike Knall-Brskovsky, 'Ethos und Bildwelt des Adels', in *Adel im Wandel*, p. 483. For a succint treatment of elementary education in the Austrian lands, and the impact of the religious Reformation, see Engelbrecht, *Geschichte des österreichischen Bildungswesens*, pp. 42–184. Heiss, 'Bildungsverhalten des niederösterreichischen Adels', pp. 152–62, covers the early education of noble sons. The rules of courtly behaviour for pages are particularly instructive; see Ferdinand Mencik, 'Beiträge zur Geschichte der kaiserlichen Hofämter', pp. 534–41; Žögler, *Der Hofstaat des Hauses Österreich*, p. 135; and Mandlmayr and Vocelka, 'Vom Adelsaufgebot zum Stehenden Heer', pp. 112–25.
48. For the various noble virtues, see Spangenberg, *Adels-Spiegel*, vol. II, pp. 161–73. The instructions of Karl Eusebius von Liechtenstein (1611–48) to his sons are quoted in Heiss, 'Erziehung und Unterricht', pp. 157–8. The 'Ordnung für die Schüler der Landschaftsschule in Linz (um 1578)', Oberösterreichisches Landesarchiv (Linz), Ständisches Archiv, Landschaftsschulsachen 1567–1601, Hs. 19, fols 219–25, is reprinted in Engelbrecht, *Das 16. und 17. Jahrhundert*, pp. 391–4. On bodily posture see ibid, pp. 157, 109; Peter Burke, *The Fortunes of the Courtier: The European Reception of Castiglione's Cortegiano* (University Park: Pennsylvania State University Press, 1995), pp. 7–18, 29; and Heiss, 'Bildungsverhalten des niederösterreichischen Adels', p. 150.
49. Heiss, 'Bildungsverhalten des niederösterreichischen Adels' and 'Erziehung und Unterricht', pp. 155–81, does not appreciate sufficiently the continuity in educational practices between the late Middle Ages and early modern times. Stone considers the late seventeenth century as the highpoint of the private tutor in *The Crisis of the Aristocracy*, p. 309.
50. 'damit man baide die Lernung nnd die Hofzucht bekhomen hat', Th. G. v. Karajan (ed.), *Sigmunds von Herbertstein Selbstbiographie* MCCCCLXXXVI *bis* MDLIII, (Vienna: K. K. Hof- und Staatsdruckerei, 1855), p. 70; see Dewald, *Aristocratic Experience*, ch. 3, for the tensions the separation of children from their families produced.
51. 'Hofstaatsverzeichnis Kaiser Rudolfs II. (12 Dec. 1576)', in Fellner and Kretschmayr, *Die Österreichische Zentralverwaltung* II, p. 197; Mencik, 'Beiträge zur Geschichte der kaiserlichen Hofämter', pp. 534–41.
52. H. J. Zeibig (ed.), 'Die Familien-Chronik der Beck von Leopoldsdorf', *Archiv für Österreichische Geschichte* 8 (1852), pp. 209–33; Wißgrill, *Schauplatz des landsäßigen Nieder-Oesterreichischen Adels*, II, pp. 328–31.
53. Bourdieu defines the concentration of different forms of power, or capital, that leads to the private monopolization of public authority by the ruler as statist capital: 'The concentration of these different species of capital – economic (thanks to taxation), military, cultural, juridical and, more generally, symbolic -– goes hand in hand with the rise and consolidation of the various corresponding fields. The result of this process is the emergence of a specific capital, *properly statist capital*, born of their cumulation, which allows the state to wield a power over the different fields and over the various forms of capital that circulate in them'; Bourdieu and Wacquant, *Reflexive Sociology*, p. 114.
54. Elias, *The Court Society*, pp. 64–5, 85.
55. Heiss, 'Standeserziehung und Schulunterricht. Zur Bildung des niederösterreichischen Adeligen in der frühen Neuzeit', in *Adel im Wandel*, p. 392; Otto Brunner, *Adeliges Landleben und Europäischer Geist. Leben und Werk Wolf Helmhards von Hohberg, 1612–1688* (Salzburg: Otto Müller, 1949), pp. 76–80.

56. Stone, *The Crisis of the Aristocracy*, pp. 309, 317; Endres, *Adel in der frühen Neuzeit*, p. 96. Some scholars have noted a decline in university attendance of nobles around the middle of the seventeenth century; see Houston, *Literacy in Early Modern Europe*, p. 88. While the disruptions of the Thirty Years' War probably had a restraining impact on the noble cavalier's tour on the Continent, declining enrolments at universities may have also been caused by the establishment of noble academies and Jesuit colleges.
57. Harry Kühnel, 'Die adelige Kavalierstour im 17. Jahrhundert', JbLkNÖ, NF XXVI (1964), and Gernot Heiss, 'Integration in die höfische Gesellschaft als Bildungsziel: Zur Kavalierstour des Grafen Johann Sigmund von Hardegg 1646/50', JbLkNÖ, 48–9 (1982–3), pp. 99–114, have made important contributions; see also MacHardy, 'Der Einfluss von Status, Konfession und Besitz', pp. 56–83; on Bohemia, see František Šmahel, 'L' université de Prague de 1433 à 1622: recrutement géographique, carrières et mobilité sociales de étudiants gradués," in Dominique Julia, Jacques Revel and Roger Chartier (eds), *Les Universités Européennes du XVIe au XVIIIe Siècle: Histoire sociale des populations étudiantes*, Vol. 1 (Paris: École des Hautes Études en Sciences Sociales, 1986), pp. 65–88; and Jiři Pešek and David Šaman, 'Les Étudiants de Bohême dans les Universités et les Académies d'Europe Centrale et Occidentale entre 1596 et 1620', in Julia, Revel and Chartier, *Les Universités européennes*, pp. 89–112.
58. Karajan, *Herbertstein Selbstbiographie*, p. 71.
59. The data for university attendance was taken largely from A. Luschin von Ebengreuth, 'Österreicher an italienischen Universitäten zur Zeit der Reception des römischen Rechts', in *Sonderabdruck aus den Blättern für Landeskunde von Niederösterreich*, 3 vols (Vienna: Friedrich Jasper, 1886). This was supplemented with genealogical information from Wißgrill, *Schauplatz des landessäßigen Nieder-Oesterreichischen Adels;* and Siebmacher, *Der Niederösterreichische Adel*. In addition to these sources, the evidence on social status is based on statistical analyses of data was derived from a variety of archival sources: NÖLA, StA, Ständische Akten AI/3-4; AI/5; AIII/5; AIII/18; AIII/20; Ritterstands Archiv, Aufnahmeakten CI–XXXVIII, DI; Herrenstands Archiv, Aufnahmeakten (A–Z); Lade IV/5, fol. 10; Lade V, Varia.
60. Hans von Jörger was seventeen when he went to Tübingen and Padua; Karel von Žerotín attended the Universities of Genf (Geneva) and Basel at the age of sixteen, while Hans Wilhelm von Stubenberg began his tour at seventeen. Wurm, *Die Jörger von Tollet*, p. 132; Gustav Korkisch, 'Karl von Zerotin', in Karl Bosl (ed.), *Lebensbilder zur Geschichte der Böhmischen Länder*, 3 vols, Vol. I (Munich/Vienna: Oldenbourg, 1974), p. 64; and Martin Bircher, *Johann Wilhelm von Stubenberg (1619—23): Studien zur Österreichischen Barockliteratur Protestantischer Edelleute* (Berlin: Walter de Gruyter, 1968). Some nobles travelled at an earlier age, usually with their older siblings. Thus, in 1590, Hans Jakob von Kufstein joined his brothers on a cavalier's tour at the age of thirteen, and Sigmund von Hardegg was only ten years old when he began his tour; see Karl Graf Kufstein, *Studien zur Familiengeschichte*, vol. III, p. 7, and Heiss, 'Bildungsverhalten des niederösterreichischen Adels', p. 153, ref. 71. Only a few *Akademien* existed at this time, but some Austrian nobles attended academies in the Reich for a few years before enrolling in universities. Thus, Georg Erasus Tschernembl was thirteen years old when he went to the German Protestant academy at Altdorf. After four years he began his cavalier's tour to Paris, England, Geneva, Strasbourg and Bologna. Most of these academies did not yet have university status; see Sturmberger, *Georg Erasmus Tschernembl*, pp. 33–4.

61. For example, during the late seventeenth century a Count Weissenwolf spent 12 000 Gulden for a cavalier's tour that lasted one year; Heiss, 'Erziehung und Unterricht', p. 172. The cavalier's tour of two sons of the count of Lamberg cost 18 000 florins; see Kühnel, 'Die adelige Kavalierstour', p. 378. However, if the son had stayed, as did Adam von Dietrichstein, with his tutor in just one city to attend an academy, the yearly cost would have amounted to only 1000 Gulden; see Friedrich Edelmayer, '"*Ignotum est ignoti nulla cupido*". Die Berichte des Elias Preuß über die Studien von Siegmund II. von Dietrichstein', in Kurt Mühlberger and Thomas Maisel (eds), *Aspekte der Bildungs und Universitätsgeschichte. 16. bis 19. Jahrhundert* (Vienna: Universitäts-Verlag, 1993), p. 245; and Ingrid Matschinegg, 'Studium und Alltag in der Fremde. Das Reiserechnungsbuch Innerösterreichischer Studenten in Padua (1548–1550)', in *Von Menschen und ihren Zeichen. Sozialhistorische Untersuchungen zum Spätmittelalter und zur Neuzeit* (Bielefeld: Verlag für Regionalgeschichte, 1990), pp. 90–121.
62. Bircher, *Johann Wilhelm von Stubenberg*, pp. 24–5; Sturmberger, *Georg Erasmus Tschernembl*, pp. 39–44. For a general description of the cavalier's tour, see E. M. Leobenstein, 'Die Adelige Kavalierstour im 17. Jahrhundert' (Ph.D. Dissertation, University of Vienna, 1966); Kühnel, 'Die adelige Kavalierstour', pp. 364–85; and Stone, *The Crisis of the Aristocracy*, pp. 314–16.
63. Only nobles admitted to the *Herren-* and *Ritterstand* were included in my statistics. Since membership brought tax privileges, most nobles eventually gained entrance into the Estates during this period.
64. Donna Bohanan, 'The Education of Nobles in Seventeenth-Century Aix-en-Provence', in *Journal of Social History*, 21 (1987), pp. 759. However, Bohanan does not indicate the total size of the old and the new nobility of Aix-en-Provence and what percentage of each group earned final degrees. Motley, *French Aristocrats*, p. 11, notes that the sword families distained the legal profession and for this reason preferred military training. Stone, *The Crisis of the Aristocracy*, p. 311, shows that very few of the English aristocracy obtained degrees, in contrast to sons of the gentry and the mercantile and professional classes.
65. 'ist ietz Lantmann worden, hat also den titel eines doctoris nicht gerne'; see 'Hofstaatsverzeichnis (N.d., ca. 1629)', in Fellner and Kretschmayr, *Die Österreichische Zentralverwaltung*, II, p. 211.
66. This is evident in many instructions and wills of noble fathers; see, for example, Bircher, *Johann Wilhelm von Stubenberg*, p. 23; and the evidence provided by Heiss, 'Erziehung und Unterricht', pp. 155–8; and his 'Standeserziehung und Schulunterricht', pp. 391–407.
67. Karajan, *Herbertsteins Selbstbiographie*, p. 72. The cultural capital he thus acquired proved to be a valuable investment. After attending university and serving a few years in the military, Sigmund soon advanced to become Ferdinand I's privy councillor, and Archduchess Elisabeth's master of the court, a career very much in contrast to those of his ancestors, including his father, who were overseers *(Pfleger)* of royal domains. His father, Leonhard, ensured that all his sons would acquire at court the cultural and social capital essential to rising in the social hierarchy. Sigmund and his brothers, Georg and Johann, who made careers as officers, obtained estates and fiefs from the Habsburgs and were raised to the baronage in 1537. Thus, all three of Leonhard's sons enhanced the fortune and honour of the family through cultural investments, and henceforth the barons of Herbertstein were counted among the most prominent families of the upper

nobility in the hereditary lands; see Wißgrill, *Schauplatz des landsäßigen Nieder-Oesterreichischen, Adels* II: pp. 249–310.

68. Bircher, *Johann Wilhelm von Stubenberg*, p. 24; Sturmberger, *Adam Graf Herbertstorff*, p. 40; Heiss, 'Integration in die höfische Gesellschaft', pp. 110–12; and Houston, *Literacy in Early Modern Europe*, pp. 77– 81.
69. There were twenty five *Truchsess* attending at Rudolf's court in 1576, seven *Fürschneider* and twelve *Mundschenken*. By 1588 Rudolf already employed twenty-three *Fuerschneider* but only eight *Mundschenken*, who each received a small yearly allowance of 480 florins; see 'Hofstaatsverzeichnis Kaiser Rudolfs II (1576)', in Fellner and Kretschmayr, *Die Österreichische Zentralverwaltung*, II; pp. 194–200; Ehalt, *Ausdrucksformen absolutistischer Herrschaft*, p. 42; and Schwarz, *The Imperial Privy Council*, pp. 210–12.
70. From the instructions of Hartmann von Liechtenstein for the cavalier's tour of his sons (1659, 1674, 1682), quoted in Heiss, 'Erziehung und Unterricht', p. 162.
71. Heiss, 'Erziehung und Unterricht', p. 152–68; Vavra, 'Adelige Lustbarkeiten', p. 436; Wilhelm Schlag, 'Die Jagd', in *Adel im Wandel*, pp. 343–56, describes changes in the hunt.
72. From the instructions of Karl Eusebius von Liechtenstein (1611–48) to his son, quoted in Heiss, 'Erziehung und Unterricht', p. 159.
73. Heiss, 'Standeserziehung und Schulunterricht', pp. 397–401. Beatrix Bastl, 'Feuerwerk und Schlittenfahrt. Ordnungen zwischen Ritual und Zeremoniell', *Wiener Geschichtsblätter*, 51 (4) (1996), pp. 197–229, provides an extensive description of some of these regulations concerning rank and court rituals. On noble dress, see Annemarie Bönsch, 'Adelige Bekleidungsformen zwischen 1500–1700', in *Adel im Wandel*, pp. 169–87; Engelbrecht, *Das 16. Und 17. Jahrhundert*, p. 213; and Harry Kühnel, 'Die österreichische Adelskultur des 16. und 18. Jahrhunderts im Spiegel der Kunst- und Wunderkammern', *Österreich in Geschichte und Literatur*, 13 (1969), pp. 433–45. Stone, *The Crisis of the Aristocracy*, p. 315, also noticed a shift in noble circles toward the teaching of an 'aesthetic, art-historical and antiquarian knowledge and understanding'.
74. Burke, *The Fortunes of the Courtier*, pp. 60, 115, 140, 164, 173–4, discusses the reception of Castiglione's work in the Holy Roman Empire and his influence on Guevara, pp. 83, 111, 115–16. On Guevara's reception in the Habsburg lands, see Brunner, *Adeliges Landleben*, pp. 113, 130; and Kiesel, *Bei Hof, Bei Höll*, ch. 8. For an overview on the humanist critique of court life see also Kiesel's '"Lang zu hofe, lang zu helle:" Literarische Hofkritik der Humanisten', in Peter Uwe Hohendahl and Paul Michael Lützeler (eds), *Legitimationskrisen des Deutschen Adels 1200–1900* (Stuttgart: J. B. Metzlersche Verlagsbuchhandlung, 1979), pp. 61–82.
75. 'to use in every thyng a certain Reckelesness [*sprezzatura*], to cover art withall, and seeme whatsoever he doth and sayeth to do it wythout pain ... Therefore that may be said to be a very art that appeereth not to be art, neyther ought a man to put more diligence in anything then in covering it: for in case it be open, it loseth credit', Count Baldassare Castiglione, *The Book of the Courtier*, Virginia Cox (ed.) (London, 1994), Book 1, XXVI, p. 53.
76. Burke, *The Fortunes of the Courtier*, p. 32.
77. Heiss, 'Erziehung und Unterricht', p. 174.
78. Bourdieu, *In Other Words*, p. 11.
79. The constantly repeated sumptuary legislation of the seventeenth century suggests that the dress codes by which nobles distinguished themselves from com-

moners were transgressed constantly by well-to-do commoners; see *Codex Austriacus*, I, pp. 736–39
80. Leobenstein, 'Die adelige Kavalierstour', p. 80; Heiss, 'Bildungsverhalten des niederösterreichischen Adels', pp. 153, 156.
81. Not only do my statistics reveal an increase in higher education, at least until 1620, but also in the eighteenth century two-thirds of the nobility in German universities were still inscribed in law faculties; see Houston, *Literacy in Early Modern Europe*, p. 87. For the lesson plans of the princes of Liechtenstein between 1661 and 1684, see Heiss, 'Erziehung und Unterricht', p. 168.
82. Klaus Bleeck and Jörn Garber, 'Nobilitas: Standes- und Privilegienlegitimation in deutschen Adelstheorien des 16. und 17. Jahrhunderts', in Elger Blühm, Jörn Garber, Klaus Garber (eds), *Hof, Staat und Gesellschaft in der Literatur des 17. Jahrhunderts* (Amsterdam: Radopi, 1982), pp. 75–9.
83. 'allein durch dis mitl der studien ... zu hoch ansehenlichen ämbtern, ehrlichen digniteten und würden [gekommen]'; from the school regulations of the Linzer *Landschaftsschule* (1 Sep. 1586), Oberösterreichisches Landesarchiv Linz, Ständisches Archiv, Hs. 19, fol. 247, quoted in Heiss, 'Standeserziehung und Schulunterricht', p. 392.
84. See the request of the Estate of Lords to Archduke Ernst (18 May 1587), NÖLA, StA, B1/1-2, fol. 608; RStA AI/6-7, fols 16–19; and *Codex Austriacus* I, p. 737.
85. Frischlin, who lost his teaching position in Tübingen, had helped the Inner Austrian Estates to reorganize their Protestant schools in 1582. He was imprisoned after his return to Wurtemberg for renewed attacks on princely ministers; see H. C. Erik Midelfort, 'Adeliges Landleben und die Legitimationskrise des deutschen Adels im 16. Jahrhundert', in Georg Schmidt (ed.), *Stände und Gesellschaft im Alten Reich* (Stuttgart: Steiner Verlag, 1989), pp. 251–2. It is not entirely clear why Frischlin resigned his position in Krain, but he seems to have provoked a quarrel with the Estates' deputies over the issue of where to publish school books; see Heiss, 'Konfession, Politik und Erziehung', pp. 30–1; and Brunner, *Adeliges Landleben*, pp. 159, 162–4.
86. For a discussion of this literature, see Bleeck and Garber, 'Standes- und Privilegienlegitimation', pp. 49–114.
87. '*Nicht von Geburt recht Adel kömpt /Sondern die Tugend macht berhümbt /Wer sich der Tugend stetz befleist /Derselb rechten Adel beweist /Wer liegt in Lastern wie ein Schwein /Der kan fürwar nicht Edel sein*', Spangenberg, *Adels-Spiegel*, II, p. 173.
88. Spangenberg, *Adels-Spiegel*, I, pp. 5, 31, 134, 218–19, 124, 212; and II, pp. 1, 12, 32, 124–25, 146.
89. See, for example, Spangenberg's painstaking proof of the existence of ennoblement by rulers since Hebraic times, in *Adels-Spiegel*, II, pp. 1–2, and his insistence that political authority had the right to ennoble, I, p. 124.
90. Heiss, 'Standeserziehung und Schulunterricht', p. 392; Brunner, *Adeliges Landleben*, pp. 76–80.
91. 'Das Familienbuch Sigmunds von Herbertstein', in J. Zahn, (ed.), *Archiv für Österreichische Geschichte*, 39 (1868), p. 306, quoted in Heiss, 'Bildungsverhalten des niederösterreichischen Adels', p. 144.
92. German theorists further fortified this conception of virtue with the idea that true nobility of birth had not been bestowed by the ruler, but was based on rights acquired autonomously in a far-removed past, and that any subsequent status advance of old nobles on part of the prince was merely a confirmation of their quality and ancient rights; see Bleeck and Garber, 'Standes- und Privilegienlegitimation', pp. 96–109.

93. Engelbrecht summarizes the basic similarities and differences in his *Geschichte des österreichischen Bildungswesens*, ch. 6.
94. In 1580, 15 out of 47 Catholic nobles attended universities, compared to only 41 of 259 of the combined Protestant nobility. The proportions change only slightly if we include and distribute the nobles whose confession could not be determined.
95. In 1580, 22 of 93 Protestant lords were university educated, while in 1620, 74 of 161 already had attended university. In 1620, the proportion of those with university education among the Protestant lords was in fact slightly higher than the proportion of Catholic lords who had attended universities. Among the Catholic lords, 7 out of 19 had higher education in 1580, a number that rose to 32 out of 76 in 1620. The proportions change only slightly if we include and distribute the nobles whose confessions could not be determined.
96. In 1580, 19 of the 166 knights whose confessions could be identified as Protestant had attended universities. In 1620, already 31 of 161 were university educated. Among the Catholics, 8 of 28 knights visited universities in 1580 and their number had risen to 16 out of 40 by 1620. The proportions change insignificantly if we include and distribute the nobles whose confession could not be determined.
97. The two servitors were Karl Ludwig Fernberger, who was councillor of the Lower Austrian government (*Regimentsrat),* and the Aulic councillor, Georg Bernhard Neuhaus. Six others were, or had been, serving in the estates administration.

6 Confessionalizing Count Patronage

1. R. J. W. Evans, 'The Austrian Habsburgs. The Dynasty as a Political Institution', in A. G. Dickens (ed.), *The Courts of Europe. Politics, Patronage and Royalty, 1400–1800* (London: Thames and Hudson, 1977), p. 137. Evans long ago pointed to the preferential treatment of Catholics at the Imperial court. However, the extent of this, and the effect it had on the Protestant nobility, remained uncertain.
2. 'Munich Conference, 2nd Day' (14 Oct. 1579), in Alfred Kohler, 'Bayern als Vorbild', pp. 391–400.
3. 'Letter of Dr. Eder to Duke Albrecht of Bavaria' (30 May 1579), in Bibl, 'Die Berichte des Reichshofrates', pp. 82–5.
4. Johann Andritsch, 'Landesfürstliche Berater am Grazer Hof (1564–1619)', pp. 93, 83, 85–8.
5. Viktor Bibl, 'Eine Denkschrift Melchior Khlesls über die Gegenreformation in Niederösterreich (c. 1590)', JbLkNÖ NF, 8 (1909), p. 165; H. Erdmann, 'Melchior Khlesl und die niederösterreichischen Stände' (Ph.D. Dissertation, University of Vienna, 1948), p. 98.
6. On the situation in Lower Austria, see his Letters of 20 April 1581, 15 March 1582, and 4 February 1587; for some of Eder's reports on appointments at the Imperial Court see the Letters of 29 April 1583, 31 December 1584 and 19 March 1585; in Bibl, 'Die Berichte des Reichshofrates', pp. 119–21, 129, 131, 141, 145, 153.
7. Eder's letters of 1 December 1579, 26 January 1584, and 8 January 1587 to Duke Wilhelm v of Bavaria, in Bibl, 'Die Berichte des Reichshofrates', pp. 99, 135, 152.
8. Bibl, 'Die katholishen und protestantischen Stände', pp. 175–82, 187–94, 202, 206, 214, 249, 282–3.
9. Bahlcke, *Regionalismus und Staatsintegration*, p. 392.

10. Inge Auerbach, 'The Bohemian Opposition, Poland-Lithuania, and the Outbreak of the Thirty Years' War', in Evans and Thomas (eds), *Crown, Church and Estates,* p. 205, insists that the Bohemian Confederates were concerned mainly with 'safeguarding ... the political rights of the Protestants and a redistribution of public offices in their favour'.
11. In addition to the data on the confessions of nobles cited in previous chapters (see Ch. 2, nt 84; Ch. 4, nt14, and Ch. 5, nts 11, 12 and 14), the data for the following analysis of the *Hofämter,* which includes nobles from the other Habsburg territories, has been derived from Fellner and Kretschmayr, *Die Österreichische Zentralverwaltung,* II: *Aktenstücke,* 'Hofstaatsverzeichnisse', 12 Dec. 1576, 29 Mar. 1615; N.d., ca. 1629, pp. 191–4, 209–11 (the last document, which Fellner–Kretschmayr believe is dated 1627 or 1628, was not written before 1629, since a 'Caspar Ters' was admitted to the Estates only that year); Mencik, 'Beiträge zur Geschichte der kaiserlichen Hofämter'; Schwarz, *The Privy Council;* Wißgrill, *Schauplatz des landsäßigen Nieder–Oesterreichischen Adels;* and Siebmacher, *Der Niederösterreichische Adel,* and *Oberösterreichischer Adel.*
12. Schwarz, *The Imperial Privy Council,* p. 372. Since this change occurred after the Battle of the White Mountain, the Rogendorfs rather than the Trautsons are included in the following tables.
13. Heinrich and Karl von Liechtenstein (until their conversion), Baron Streun von Schwarzenau, Johann Wilhelm and Wolf Sigmund von Losenstein were Protestant.
14. Schwarz, *The Imperial Privy Council,* pp. 229–30, 249–52, 263, 277–9, 307–12, 359–61, 374–6, 381–2, 407.
15. The names of these privy councillors are derived from the 'Hofstaatsverzeichnisse' of 12 Dec. 1576, 29 Mar. 1615; N.d., ca. 1629, in Fellner and Kretschmayr, *Die Österreichische Zentralverwaltung,* II: pp. 191–211; and Schwarz, *The Imperial Privy Council,* appendix C, who also provides collective biographies for most councillors. It should be stressed that mainly the councillors who were installed at the beginning of each reign are included in the statistic.
16. Schwarz, *The Imperial Privy Council,* pp. 204–48.
17. Schwarz, *The Imperial Privy Council,* pp. 292–4, believes incorrectly that Losenstein also retained his post as *Obersthofmarschall.* In fact, he was replaced by the Catholic Hans Bernhard von Herbertstein; see Mencik, 'Beiträge zur Geschichte der kaiserlichen Hofämter', p. 466.
18. Schwarz, *The Imperial Privy Council,* pp. 64–5.
19. Fellner and Kretschmayr, *Die Österreichische Zentralverwaltung,* I, p. 230; II, pp. 192–93, 209–11. By 1629 many of these 'foreigners' in the Aulic council were admitted to the Lower Austrian Estates, so that the previous proportion of the Lower Austrians was re-established. However, unless their major landholdings were also in the province, there was little assurance for old native nobles that these newcomers would protect local noble interests.
20. The proportion of Aulic councillors among Lower Austrian nobles declined from a half in 1576 to nearly a quarter in 1629; 'Hofstaatsverzeichnisse' of 12 Dec. 1576, and N.d., ca. 1629, in Fellner and Kretschmayr, *Die Österreichische Zentralverwaltung,* II, pp. 192–3, 209–15.
21. I shall use the terms 'crown servants' or 'princely servants' to include all officials and officers in the employ of the Habsburg emperors and the archdukes of Lower Austria. The term 'service nobility' also includes those nobles employed by the Lower Austrian Estates. The data for this section was collected from

various sources. Most important among them are: NÖLA, StA, Aufnahmeakten and HS 362; Chmel, 'Die Regimentsräte des Nieder-Österr. Regiments'; Fellner and Kretschmayr, *Die Österreichische Zentralverwaltung,* II: *Aktenstücke 1491–1681;* Mencik, 'Beiträge zur Geschichte der kaiserlichen Hofämter'; Schwarz, *The Imperial Privy Council;* Kielmansegg, *Beiträge zur Geschichte der niederösterreichischen Statthalterei;* Wißgrill, *Schauplatz des landsäßigen Nieder-Oesterreichischen Adels,* 5 vols; *Jahrbuch Adler,* vols. II, III, V, X, XIV, XVI–XVII; Siebmacher, *Der Niederösterreichische Adel,* 2 vols; and *Oberösterreichischer Adel.* For references on the religious background of nobles, see Ch. 2, nt 84; Ch. 4, nt 14. Although it is possible that the sources may not have revealed all the occupations of nobles, the percentage distributions are likely to be rather accurate since they are commensurate with the proportions derived from the much more selective data obtained by Götz, 'Lebenszyklus und soziale Prägung nachgeborener Söhne'.

22. The knights employed by the Estates did not change substantially in 1620 because these positions were the preserve of members of the *Stände;* the number (but not the proportion) of knights serving in the military remained stable as well. Another nineteen Protestant knights were in the service of the Confederate Army. Although a few of them had previously been officers of the crown, they now served the Estates. But since this was temporary employment, it was necessary to create a separate category for them. Moreover, the majority of the Confederates were in fact part of the *Landadel,* since they held no positions before the war began. If calculated in this manner, the proportion of knights who were simply landed gentlemen would have increased slightly before the Battle of the White Mountain. Note also that because the members of the *Ritterstand* had declined by 1620, the percentage distribution of knights installed in the various offices remained fairly constant in all but two categories, the household and 'other offices'.
23. Most common were the titles of *Hofkammerprokurator, Hofkammerdiener,* or secretary. The largest group of knights holding 'other positions' were managers (*Pfleger*) on crown lands. Some of these officials, such as the estate managers, fell under the jurisdiction of the master of the household, but it was more appropriate to list them under a separate category, since their position did not require a presence at the Imperial court. At times it was difficult to delineate the various categories neatly, since political and judicial functions were not strictly differentiated at court. Some of the household officials also held judicial functions, and some servants of the Estates had military as well as administrative duties. Moreover, some nobles held double positions. Since they were counted in both categories in Tables 6.1 to 6.6, it is important to remember that the base numbers that appear in these statistics are larger than the actual number of knights and lords. It is also worth noting that few knights were engaged in the military administration, perhaps because it was small in size. They usually held inferior positions related to military provisioning and finances. The proportion (5 per cent) of knights serving actively in the military in 1580 seems small, but it was peacetime and there was no standing army. Most of them were active on the Hungarian military border and only three had a commanding position. Since administrative positions within the Estates frequently were divided among the first three orders, a rather large number of knights – nearly a tenth – were employed by the *Stände* in important functions, particularly in military affairs.
24. Neugebauer, 'Die niederösterreichischen Landtage von 1577 bis 1592', p. 155.
25. In 1580, the number of lords employed by the crown was smaller than among the *Ritterstand,* but since the *Herrenstand* had fewer members, the proportion

of office-holders among the lords was in fact larger. Three-fifths (78) of the lords served the crown, and another 6 per cent were employed by the Estates, so that two-thirds of the Estate of lords belonged to the service nobility. Among the knights, the ratio between court nobility and country gentlemen was nearly the reverse. The distribution of lords in the various offices also differed from that among knights, largely because of status differences. A much higher proportion – over a quarter – of the *Herrenstand* had functions in the Imperial household in 1580. Thirteen of these – or a third – held *Erbämter*, which did not require a permanent presence at court. However, five of these also occupied other positions in the administration. Altogether, ten of the household officials held double positions, mainly in the courts of appeal and the Privy Council. The remaining lords in the household were chamberlains and/or high functionaries. While only a few more lords than knights held positions in the political/judicial administration, they constituted a high proportion – nearly a fifth – of the smaller *Herrenstand*. In the financial and 'other offices', the lords had fewer representatives than the knights, because these positions were inferior in status.

26. This proportion includes those serving in the Confederate army, but even without them the increase was still high (from 43 to 152). Overall, the *Herrenstand* improved its numerical presence slightly in less important administrative offices, and multiplied enormously in the officer corps, but it must be remembered that these careers yielded less influence than those in the household and the political/judicial administration.
27. This includes the nobles whose confession could not be determined with certainty, but not those who held double positions. If we exclude the unknown cases, then the change would be insignificant, since the Protestant officials in the administration would have declined from 92 to 27.
28. Although the noble status of about a fifth of the knights living in 1580 and 1620 could not be determined with certainty, a calculation by the date of ennoblement rather than by date of admission does not change my conclusions significantly. Moreover, even if one included and distributed the knights whose noble status could not be determined, among the new and old nobility belonging to the office holders, the old nobility would still have lost its pre-eminent position.
29. However, because the number of new members nearly doubled, the office-holders among them declined proportionally.
30. Results did not change significantly when I determined the figures and averages for newly-created barons, rather than consider the date of admission to the *Herrenstand*. Thus, in 1580, the old baronage (that is, those who had held their title for more than fifty years) occupied a higher number of offices in most categories, but, as in the Estate of Knights, a higher proportion – two thirds – of all the new barons served the crown. Nevertheless, almost three-fifths of the old baronage were also princely servants. Even if the lords who had received their baronage within the previous hundred years were considered as new barons, close to half of the old baronage would have been officials. By 1620, they had lost a significant number of positions in the political and judicial administration. The total number of princely servants from the old baronage increased slightly, only because more found employment as officers.
31. Their number would increase to 91 if the nobles in the Confederate Army were included.

32. The reduction of household officials from the Estate of Lords only affected the new baronage. But the gains in the military and in the Estates' organization, where they were now dominant numerically, led to the growth of the service nobility – by about a fifth – among the new baronage. The newcomers to the Estate of Lords did not improve their position as much as did the new knights, and the old baronage did not lose as many offices as did the old knights. It was more difficult to eliminate the old upper nobility from appointments than old knights, particularly because they were also more likely to hold hereditary positions in the household.
33. In 1580, the proportion (two-thirds) of the service nobility was already higher among Catholics than among Protestants (one-third), but we must keep in mind that the Catholic *Ritterstand* was still very small.
34. A numerical parity between the confessions was retained among Lower Austrian knights serving in the military administration, although in 1620 the Protestants improved their numerical position slightly vis-à-vis the Catholics in the officer corps. However, Protestant knights mainly held lower military ranks, such as *Rittmeister* and below. In any case, this was hardly an advantage, since it removed Protestants from the Imperial court. While the Protestants also retained control over the Estates' military organization, and remained dominant in its administration, the Catholics had gained access to the top position by 1620. Both confessions suffered from the preference for non-nobles as estate managers on crown lands ('other positions').
35. The knights whose confessions could not be determined were included in these calculations. However, the proportions do not change significantly if they are excluded. Those fighting for the Confederate army were included among the country nobility.
36. Although in 1620 the native nobility among the Estate of Knights held more positions than non-natives, they suffered significant losses, especially in the political/judicial administration. Altogether, the service nobility among the natives declined by more than a third (from 33 to 20), so that less than a fifth of them were in the employ of the crown; in 1580 it had been a quarter. Moreover, they were no longer dominant among the officer class. For the data on the geographic origin of Lower Austrian knights, see MacHardy, 'Nobility in Crisis', Tables IV.4 and IV.5.
37. In 1620, the native lords were outnumbered by servants from the other hereditary lands, and the proportion of servants among them was reduced from two thirds to less than a third. For the data on the geographic origin of Lower Austrian lords, see MacHardy, 'Nobility in Crisis', Tables IV.9 and IV.10.
38. Since the number of lords whose confession is unknown is small, the proportion for both Protestants and Catholics hardly alters when the 'unknown' are included in the statistics.
39. This analysis is based on lists of knights living in 1580 and 1620, and therefore does not necessarily present the total of appointments made during the intervening forty years. It should also be noted that the promotion of knights to the war council declined and came to a standstill after 1609, because the *Hofkriegsrat* – as mentioned earlier – became dominated by the upper nobility. The withdrawal of the latter from the *Hofkammerrat* may partially explain the higher frequency of appointments of knights to that council.
40. These calculations are based on a sample of 41 Lower Austrian lords living in 1580 and 1620, and include appointments to the *Reichshofrat*, the *Hofkammerrat*, and the *Hofkriegsrat*.

41. Only two of a sample of nine knights installed as *Regimentsräte* between 1600 and 1620 belonged to the Protestant faith. The figures for these statistics are derived from the lists of knights living in 1620 and 1580, and do not necessarily present the total of appointments during the intervening forty years.
42. In 1620, 14 out of 74 Lower Austrian Protestant lords with higher education were employed, compared to 23 of the 32 university-educated Catholics.
43. The two servitors were Karl Ludwig Fernberger, who was Lower Austrian *Regimentsrat,* and the Aulic councillor Georg Bernhard Neuhaus. Six others were, or had been, serving in the Estates' administration.
44. *Jahrbuch Adler,* III (1873), pp. 108–9; Luschin v. Ebengreuth, *Österreicher an italienischen Universitäten,* I, p. 56, II, p. 27.
45. Siebmacher, *Der Niederösterreichische Adel,* II, p. 526; Schwarz, *The Imperial Privy Council,* pp. 381–2; Luschin v. Ebengreuth, *Österreicher an italienischen Universitäten,* I, p. 85, II, p. 43.
46. Wißgrill, *Schauplatz des landessäßigen Nieder-Oesterreichischen Adels* II, p. 390; Schwarz, *The Imperial Privy Council,* p. 210.
47. Siebmacher, *Oberösterreichischer Adel,* p. 359.
48. Schwarz, *The Imperial Privy Council,* pp. 300–3; Starzer, *Beiträge zur Geschichte der niederösterreichischen Statthalterei,* p. 218, Wißgrill, *Schauplatz des landessäßigen Nieder-Oesterreichischen Adels,* IV (5), p. 201.
49. Schwarz, *The Imperial Privy Council,* pp. 281–8; Evelin Oberhammer, 'Viel ansehnliche Stuck und Güeter. Die Entwicklung des fürstlichen Herrschaftsbesitzes', and Herbert Haupt, 'Die Namen und Stammen der Herren von Liechtenstein. Biographische Skizzen', both in Evelin Oberhammer (ed.), *Der ganzen Welt ein Lob und Spiegel,* pp. 33–45, 204–12. Herbert Haupt, *Fürst Karl I. von Liechtenstein, Obersthofmeister Kaiser Rudolfs II. und Vizekönig von Böhmen. Hofstaat und Sammeltätigkeit.* Textband (Vienna: Böhlaus, 1983), provides an overview of the career, court and cultural activities of Karl (1569–1627).
50. See esp., Polišenský and Snider, *War and Society in Europe.*
51. F. Tremel, *Wirtschafts- und Sozialgeschichte Österreichs* (Vienna: Deuticke, 1969), pp. 248–55; Evans, *The Making of the Habsburg Monarchy,* pp. 168.
52. Jonathan Dewald, *The European Nobility,* ch. 2, provides a succint overview of developments and literature of the subject; for economic trends generally, see Jan de Vries, *The Economy of Europe in an Age of Crisis, 1600–1750* (Cambridge, Mass.: Harvard University Press, 1976), and Robert S. Duplessis, *Transitions to Capitalism in Early Modern Europe* (Cambridge University Press, 1997).
53. Bastl's assertion, in *Herrschafts–Schätzungen,* that revenues from manorial farming for the district below the Vienna Woods made up more than two-thirds of noble income are apparently based on a mistaken calculation (on page 20). My re-calculation shows that the proportion was well below two-fifths. Bastl provides estimates of income from landed property for over 280 estates in Lower Austria. Only one fifth of these covered the period between 1560 and 1620 and I calculated the income from manorial farming of these 58 estates. However, the income from *Eigenwirtschaft* was higher in the district under the Manhartsberg, where it constituted nearly two fifths of the total estate revenue, and was lowest in the district above the Vienna Woods, where under one third of landed income was derived from the manorial economy. Moreover, it is important to note that income from forestry was not based on the actual sale of wood, but on estimates of the value of forests. As Bastl notes, this was usually calculated much higher than the revenue that could be derived from the sale.

54. Peter Stenitzer, 'Der Adelige als Unternehmer? Das Wirtschaften der gräflichen Familie Harrach in Oberösterreich im 16. und 17. Jahrundert', *Frühneuzeit-Info*, 2 (1991), pp. 41–60, deals with the relationship between rents and inflation. For a detailed treatment of the changing position of the peasantry, see Feigl, *Die niederösterreichische Grundherrschaft*, pp. 20–4, 92–105, 156–162. The conflicts between peasants and landowners has been well described by Thomas Winkelbauer, *Robot und Steuer*. The fullest treatment of the position of the peasantry during the sixteenth and early seventeenth centuries is Hermann Rebel's *Peasant Classes*, pp. 130–5, which provides particularly interesting evidence on feudal payments and the commutation of labour services into money payments in Upper Austria.
55. Herbert Knittler, 'Gewerblicher Eigenbetrieb und frühneuzeitliche Grundherrschaft am Beispiel des Waldviertels', *MIÖG*, 92 (1984), pp. 115–46. Average arable land in 1620 was 183.3 hectares in the district below the Manhartsberg, 89.2 hectares in the district below the Vienna Woods, and 84.5 hectares in the district above the Manhartsberg. Some landowners did establish fisheries and breweries and extend their trade in cattle and wood; see Knittler, 'Adelige Grundherrschaft im Übergang', pp. 84–7, 103–7; and Knittler, *Nutzen, Renten Erträge.*
56. I calculated these proportions of revenue from *Eigenwirtschaft* from the data printed in Bastl, *Herrschafts–Schätzungen.* Income from manorial farming increased in all districts, but in particular above the Manhartsberg (from a quarter to over two-thirds of total revenue). However, these figures must be treated with caution, as they are not based on changes in revenue from the same property, but on evidence from a total of fifty-six estates, of which only eighteen had income estimates for the period before 1620.
57. Pickl, 'Die wirtschaftlichen Bestimmungen der innerösterreichischen Religionspazifikation von 1572', pp. 580–2, provides a list of nobles who were moneylenders to the Habsburgs. See Rudolf Wolkan, 'Die Ächtung der Horner Konföderierten und die Konfiskation ihrer Güter. Ein Beitrag zur Geschichte der Gegenreformation und des Ständewesens in Niederösterreich' (Ph.D. Dissertation, University of Vienna), pp. 178–81 for the debt levels on the estates confiscated from the rebels.
58. This and the following statistical analyses of noble landed property are based on the lists of property and its various owners (*Besitzerbögen)* established between 1824 and 1874, as well as the tax registers (*Gültbücher*) of the four Lower Austrian districts: Gültbücher VUMB, VOMB, VUWW, VUMB, 1571 and 1637; NÖLA, StA. As these sources are by no means reliable, they were supplemented by a survey of peasant households per estate established in 1590–1 by the Lower Austrian Estates and analyzed in A. Eggendorfer, 'Das Viertel ober dem Manhartsberg im Spiegel des Bereitungsbuches von 1590/91' (Ph.D. Dissertation, University of Vienna, 1974); L. Hansen, 'Das Viertel ober dem Wienerwald im Spiegel des Bereitungsbuches von 1591' (Ph.D. Dissertation, University of Vienna, 1974); H. Nader, 'Das Viertel unter dem Wienerwald im Spiegel des Bereitungsbuches 1590/91' (Ph.D. Dissertation, University of Vienna, 1970); F. Graf, 'Das Viertel unter dem Manhartsberg im Spiegel des Bereitungsbuches von 1590' (Ph.D. Dissertation, University of Vienna, 1972); and Eva Maria Havlik, 'Strukturwandel des ständischen Besitzes im Viertel unter dem Manhartsberg. Untersuchungen zum Herren- und Ritterstand aufgrund der Gültbücher, 1571–1701' (Ph.D. Dissertation, University of Vienna, 1983).

59. I am indebted to Jack Goldstone, *Revolution and Rebellion*, pp. 58–67, for pointing out the non-linear aspects of population growth in early modern England and France.
60. Landless nobles multiplied from 72 to 183. Unfortunately, the number of landless were typed incorrectly as having risen from 35 to 96 in my article 'The Rise of Absolutism,' p. 414, nt 23; which only represents the increase for the Protestant nobility. However, the percentage calculations were correct.
61. It was impossible to account for forty-three estates (with some 4,000 peasant households) which had belonged to the knights in 1580. The Church or towns may have obtained these estates, and some of them could have been integrated into larger units, but this remains unclear. Even if we assume that these forty-three estates, which cannot be accounted for by sales or by other transfers, disappeared as a consequence of mistakes in the records, and reduce accordingly the number of nobles I have counted among the propertyless, the unlanded nobility would still have doubled by 1620.
62. I defined as small those estates that had 1–49 peasant households, as medium–sized those that had 50–399 households, and as large all those estates with over 400 housholds. I had previously made more divisions among the medium and large estates, but this did not yield any interesting differences.
63. They lost 45 of 153 medium-sized estates, and 11 of 41 large–sized estates. Altogether, the Protestants had owned 49,624 peasant households in 1580, which was reduced to 36,523 by 1620.
64. Together with the increase in landless members, this appears to be the major reason why the distribution of wealth among the Catholic lords was the most unequal in the entire noble estate. Thus, in 1620, the upper quartile of the Catholic lords, who had possessed nearly two–thirds of the households in 1580, owed nearly nine–tenths of the peasant households in the Catholic Estate of Lords.
65. In 1580 the Catholic nobles owned 5,182 peasant households, and by 1620 they had 13,914.

Conclusion to Part II

1. As I explained earlier, Bourdieu claims that the construction of perceptions of the social world takes place in practice, and that agents unconsciously internalize schemes of perception linking the objective structures of society (social space) with subjective individual and collective practices. While *habitus* can be flexible, a change in *habitus* usually lags behind changes in objective conditions. Consequently, individuals can find it difficult to quickly adapt to a fundamental transformation of circumstances, and the resulting mismatch between *habitus* and objective conditions explains why they become inclined to engage in political struggles. Bourdieu defines this dispositional lag as the 'hysteresis effect'; see *Outline of a Theory of Practice*, pp. 78–83, and *Distinction*, pp. 143.

Bibliography

Primary sources

Unpublished sources

Vienna, Niederösterreichisches Landesarchiv (NÖLA), Ständisches Archiv (StA):
Besitzerbögen (established 1825–74, for Lower Austria).

Gültbücher, 1571 and 1637:	Viertel unter dem Manhartsberg (VUMB). Viertel ober dem Manhartsberg (VOMB). Viertel unter dem Wienerwald (VUWW). Viertel ober dem Wienerwald (VOWW).
Herrenstands Archiv (HstA):	Aufnahmeakten (A–Z); Lade IV/5; Lade V, Varia; Lade XV, Varia.
Ritterstands Archiv (RstA):	A 1 (admission rules), Aufnahmeakten CI–XXXVIII, D1.
Ständische Akten	A I, nos. 3–7; A III, nos. 2, 5, 18, 20; B I, nos. 1–2; IV, no. 20.
Ständische Bücher	nos. 55–87, 98–126.
Sammlungen:	Handschriften (Hs), nos. 59, 178, 243, 339, 353, 362, 378, 338, 731.

Vienna, Haus- Hof- und Staatsarchiv (HHStA):
Codes Diplomaticus Austriacus, Tom. IV (or Cod. Bohm 99), fols 203–6.

Vienna, Hofkammerarchiv (HKA):
NiederÖsterreichische Herrschaftsakten, N 29/C/4, fols 1551–54v.

Vienna, Österreichische Nationalbibliotek (ÖNB):
Handschrift, Cod.10.100d (Retzer Jurament).

Printed sources

Bibl, Viktor, 'Die Berichte des Reichshofrates Dr. Georg Eder an die Herzoge Albrecht und Wilhelm von Bayern über die Religionskrise in Niederösterreich, 1579–87'; JbLkNÖ, NF, 8 (1900), pp. 67–154.

Bibl, Viktor, 'Die Vorgeschichte der Religionskonzession Kaiser Maximilian II' JbLkNÖ, NF, 13–14 (1914–15), pp. 400–31.

Bibl, Viktor, 'Eine Denkschrift Melchior Khlesls über die Gegenreformation in Niederösterreich (c. 1590)', JbLkNÖ *NF*, 8 (1909), 158–71.

Castiglione, Count Baldassare, *The Book of the Courtier*, Virginia Cox (ed.) (London 1994).

Codex Austriacus ordine alphabetico compilatus d.i.: eigentlicher Begriff und inhalt aller unter deß Ertzhauses zu Oesterreich, fürnembelich aber der Regierung Leopoldi I, ausgegangenen in des Justitz- und Politzey-Wesen ... eingelauffenen Generalien etc., 6 vols; with *Appendix (Mit zahlreichen Handschriften), 1456–1718* (Vienna, 1704–77).

Fellner, Thomas and Heinrich Kretschmayr (eds), *Die Österreichische Zentralverwaltung.* I. Abteilung: *Von Maximilian I. bis zur Vereinigung der österreichischen und böhmischen Hofkanzlei 1749*, II. Abteilung: *Aktenstücke 1491–1681* (Vienna: Adolf Holzhausen, 1907).

Frank, Karl Friedrich von, *Standeserhebungen und Gnadenakte für das deutsche Reich und die österreichischen Erblande bis 1806 sowie kaiserlich österreichische bis 1823.* 5 vols (Senftenegg: Selbstverlag, 1972).

Gerteis, Klaus, *Monarchie oder Ständestaat. Der Böhmische Aufstand von 1618. Quellen und wissenschaftliche Diskussion* (Trier: Auenthal Verlag, 1983).

Hammer-Purgstall, J., *Khlesl's, des Cardinals, Directores des geheimen Cabinetes Kaisers Matthias, Leben.* 4 vols (Vols I–II: Vienna: Kaulfuß, Prandel & Co., 1947; Vols. III–IV: Vienna: Verlag Carl Gerold, 1850–1).

Historische Aktenstücke über das Ständewesen in Oesterreich, 4 vols (Leipzig: Whilhelm Jurany, 1848).

Jahrbuch des Heraldisch-Genealogischen Vereins Adler (continuation of Wißgrill), vols II, III, V, X, XIV, XVI–XVII (Vienna: Verein Adler, 1872–90).

Karajan, Theodor G. von (ed.), *Sigmunds von Herbertstein Selbstbiographie MCCCCLXXXVI bis MDLIII* (Vienna: K. K. Hof- und Staatsdruckerei, 1855).

Khevenhiller zu Franckenburg, Franz Christoph Graf von, *Annales Ferdinandei das ist wahrhaftige Beschreibung Kaysers Ferdinandi des Andern ... Geburth Auferziehung und in Krieg und Friedens-Zeiten vollbrachten Thaten geführten Kriegen und vollzogenen Geschäften*, 12 vols, Vol. IX (Leipzig: Weidmann, 1724).

Lorenz, Gottfried (ed.), *Ausgewählte Quellen zur Deutschen Geschichte der Neuzeit. Freiherr von Stein-Gedächtnisausgabe, Vol. XIX: Quellen zur Vorgeschichte und zu den Anfängen des dreißigjährigen Krieges* (Darmstadt: Wissenschaftliche Buchgessellschaft, 1991).

Machiavelli, Niccolò, *The Prince*, (eds) Quentin Skinner and Russell Price, (Cambridge: Cambridge University Press, 1988).

Pfeffer, Maria (ed.), *Flugschriften zum Dreissigjährigen Krieg. Aus der Häberlin-Sammlung der Thurn- und Taxisschen Hofbibliothek* (Frankfurt-am-Main: Peter Lang, 1993).

Pick, Friedel (ed.), *Pragensia*, Vol. I: *Der Prager Fenstersturz i. J. 1619. Flugblätter und Abbildungen* (Prague: A. Haase, 1918).

Schrauf, Karl (ed.), *Der Reichshofrat Dr. Georg Eder. Eine Briefsammlung*, Vol I: *1573–1578* (Vienna: Adolf Holzhausen, 1904).

Siebmacher, Johann, *Grosses und allgemeines Wappenbuch*: *Oberoesterreichischer Adel*, (eds) Alois Freiherr von Starkenfels and Johann Kirnbauer von Erzstätt (Nuremberg, 1904.)

Siebmacher, Johann, *Grosses und allgemeines Wappenbuch*: *Der Niederösterreichische Landständische Adel*, (ed.) Johann-Baptist Witting (Nuremberg, 1918.)

Spangenberg, Cyriacius, *Adels-Spiegel. Historischer ausfürlicher Bericht: Was Adel sey und heisse, woher er komme (etc.)*, 2 vols (Schmalkalden: Michel Schmück, 1591–94).

Stanka, Rudolf (ed.), *Die böhmischen Conföderationsakte von 1619* (Berlin: Emil Ebering, 1932).

Turba, Gustav (ed.), *Die Grundlagen der pragmatischen Sanktion*, Vol. II: *Die Hausgesetze* (Vienna: Wr. Staatwissenschaftliche Studien, 1913).

Wißgrill, Franz Carl, *Schauplatz des landsäßigen Nieder-Oesterreichischen Adels vom Herrn- und Ritterstande von dem 11. Jahrhundert an bis auf unsere Zeiten*, 5 vols (Vienna: Seizer, 1794–1824).

Zeibig, Hartmann Joseph (ed.), 'Die Familien-Chronik der Beck von Leopoldsdorf', *Archiv für Österreichische Geschichte*, 8 (1852).

Zwiedineck-Südenhorst, Hans von (ed.), *Venetianische Gesandtschafts-Berichte über die böhmische Rebellion (1618–1620)* (Graz: Leuschner & Lubensky, 1880).

Secondary sources

Adel im Wandel. Politik, Kultur, Konfession, 1500–1700. Katalog der Niederösterreichischen Landesausstellung, Rosenburg 1990. Vienna: NÖ. Landesregierung, 1990.

Albrecht, Dieter (ed.), *Politik und Konfession. Festschrift für Konrad Repgen zum 60. Geburtstag* (Berlin: Duncker & Humblot, 1983).

Alewyn, Richard, *Das große Welttheater. Die Epoche der höfischen Feste* (Munich: Verlag C. H. Beck, 1985).

Amon, Karl, 'Innerösterreich', in Anton Schindling and Walter Ziegler (eds), *Die Territorien des Reichs im Zeitalter der Reformation und Konfessionalisierung. Land und Konfession, 1500–1650*, Vol. 1: *Der Südosten* (Münster: Aschendorffsche Verlagsbuchhandlung, 1989), pp. 103–16.

Anderson, Perry, *Lineages of the Absolutist State* (London: Verso, 1979).

Andritsch, Johann, 'Landesfürstliche Berater am Grazer Hof (1564–1919)', in A. Novotny and B. Sutter (eds.), *Innerösterreich, 1564–1619* (Graz: Böhlaus, 1968), pp. 76–103.

Asch, Ronald G., *The Thirty Years War. The Holy Roman Empire and Europe, 1618–48* (New York: St. Martin's Press, 1997).

Asch, Ronald G., and Adolf M. Birke (eds), *Princes, Patronage, and the Nobility. The Court at the Beginning of the Modern Age, c. 1450–1650* (New York: Oxford University Press, 1991).

Astarita, Tommaso. *The Continuity of Feudal Power: The Carocciolo di Brienza in Spanish Naples* (Cambridge University Press, 1992).

Aubin, Hermann and Wolfgang Zorn (eds), *Handbuch der deutschen Wirtschafts- und Sozialgeschichte* (Stuttgart: Union Verlag, 1971).

Auerbach, Inge, 'The Bohemian Opposition, Poland–Lithuania, and the Outbreak of the Thirty Years' War', in R. J. W. Evans and T. V. Thomas (eds), *Crown, Church and Estates. Central European Politics in the Sixteenth and Seventeenth Centuries* (New York: St. Martin's Press, 1991), pp. 196–225.

Axtmann, Roland, '"Police" and the Formation of the Modern State. Legal and Ideological Assumptions on State Capacity in the Austrian Lands of the Habsburg Empire, 1500–1800', *German History*, 10 (1992), pp. 39–61.

Bahlcke, Joachim. '"Durch starke Konföderation wohl stabiliert". Ständische Defension und politisches Denken in der habsburgischen Ländergruppe am Anfang des 17. Jahrhunderts', in Thomas Winkelbauer (ed.), *Kontakte und Konflikte. Böhmen, Mähren und Österreich: Aspekte eines Jahrtausends gemeinsamer Geschichte* (Horn/Waidhofen: Waldviertler Heimatbund, 1993), pp. 165–84.

Bahlcke, Joachim, *Regionalismus und Staatsintegration im Widerstreit. Die Länder der Böhmischen Krone im ersten Jahrhundert der Habsburgerherrschaft (1526–1619)* (Munich: Oldenbourg Verlag, 1994).

Bahlcke, Joachim, 'Calvinism and Estate Liberation Movements in Bohemia and Hungary (1570–1620)', in Karin Maag (ed.), *The Reformation in Eastern and Central Europe* (Aldershot: Scholar Press, 1997), pp. 72–92.

Bahlcke, Joachim and Arno Strohmeyer (eds), *Konfessionalisierung in Ostmitteleuropa. Wirkungen des religiösen Wandels im 16. und 17. Jahrhundert in Staat, Gesellschaft und Kultur* (Stuttgart: Steiner Verlag, 1999).

Barker, Thomas M., *The Military Intellectual and Battle. Raimondo Montecuccoli and the Thirty Years War* (Albany, NY: State University of New York Press, 1975).

Barker, Thomas M., *Army, Aristocracy, Monarchy: Essays on War, Society and Government in Austria, 1618–1780* (New York: Columbia University Press, 1982).

Barudio, Günter, *Der Teutsche Krieg, 1618–1648* (Frankfurt-am-Main: Fischer Verlag, 1985).

Bastl, Beatrix, *Herrschaftschätzungen. Materialien zur Einkommens- und Besitzstruktur niederösterreichischer Grundherrschaften 1550 bis 1750* (Vienna: Böhlau Verlag, 1992).

Bastl, Beatrix, 'Feuerwerk und Schlittenfahrt. Ordnungen zwischen Ritual und Zeremoniell', *Wiener Geschichtsblätter*, 4 (1996), pp. 197–229.

Becker, Winfried, 'Ständestaat und Konfessionsbildung am Beispiel der böhmischen Konföderationsakte von 1619', in Dieter Albrecht, *et. al.* (eds), *Politik und Konfession. Festschrift für Konrad Repgen zum 60. Geburstag* (Berlin: Duncker & Humblot, 1983), pp. 77–97.

Beik, William, *Absolutism and Society in Seventeenth-Century France. State Power and Provincial Aristocracy in Languedoc* (Cambridge University Press, 1985).

Bérenger, Jean, 'La rêvolt paysanne de Basse-Autriche de 1598', *Revue d'histoire economique et sociale*, 53 (1975), pp. 465–92.

Bergeron, Louis, 'The Revolution: Catastrophe or New Dawn for the French Economy?', in Colin Lucas (ed.), *Rewriting the French Revolution* (Oxford: Oxford University Press, 1991), pp. 69–118.

Bibl, Victor, *Die Einführung der katholischen Gegenreformation in Niederösterreich durch Kaiser Rudolf II (1576–1580)* (Innsbruck: Verlag d. Wagner'schen Universitäts-Buchhandlung, 1900).

Bibl, Victor, 'Erzherzog Ernst und die Gegenreformation in Niederösterreich (1576–1590)', MIÖG, 6, Ergbd. (1901), pp. 573–95.

Bibl, Viktor, 'Die katholischen und protestantischen Stände Niederösterreichs im XVII. Jahrhundert. Ein Beitrag zur Geschichte der ständischen Verfassung', *Jahrbuch für Landeskunde von Niederösterreich* (JbLkNÖ), NF II (1903), pp. 167–325.

Bibl, Victor, 'Eine Denkschrift Melchior Khlesls über die Gegenreformation in Niederösterreich (c. 1590)', JbLkNÖ, NF (1909), 8, pp. 158–71.

Bibl, Viktor, *Die Religionsreformation K. Rudolfs II. in Oberösterreich* (Vienna: Alfred Hölder, 1922).

Bircher, Martin, *Johann Wilhelm von Stubenberg (1619–23): Studien zur österreichischen Barockliteratur Protestantischer Edelleute* (Berlin: Walter de Gruyter, 1968).

Bireley, S. J. Robert, 'Ferdinand II: Founder of the Habsburg Monarchy', in R. J .W. Evans and T. V. Thomas (eds), *Crown, Church and Estates. Central European Politics in the Sixteenth and Seventeenth Centuries* (New York: St. Martin's Press, 1991), pp. 226–44.

Bireley, S. J. Robert, 'Confessional Absolutism in the Habsburg Lands in the Seventeenth Century', in Charles W. Ingrao (ed.), *State and Society in Early Modern Austria* (West Lafayette, Indiana: Purdue University Press, 1994), pp. 36–53.

Black, Jeremy, 'Recent Work on European Absolutism', *Teaching History* (January 1988), pp. 39–40.

Black, Jeremy, *A Military Revolution? Military Change and European Society, 1550–1800* (Atlantic Highlands, NJ: Humanities Press International, 1991).

Bleeck, Klaus and Jörn Garber, 'Nobilitas: Standes- und Privilegienlegitimation in deutschen Adelstheorien des 16. und 17. Jahrhunderts', in Elger Blühm, Jörn Garber, Klaus Garber (eds), *Hof, Staat und Gesellschaft in der Literatur des 17. Jahrhunderts* (Amsterdam: Radopi, 1982), pp. 75–9.

Blickle, Peter, Andreas Lindt and Alfred Schindler (eds), *Zwingli und Europa: Referate und Protokoll des Internationalen Kongresses aus Anlass des 500. Geburtstages von Huldrych Zwingli vom 26. bis 30. März 1984* (Zurich: Vandenhoeck & Ruprecht, 1985), pp. 199–216.

Bohanan, Donna, 'The Education of Nobles in Seventeenth-Century Aix-en-Provence', *Journal of Social History*, 21 (1987), pp. 757–63.

Böhme, Ernst, *Das fränkische Reichsgrafenkollegium im 16. und 17. Jahrhundert* (Stuttgart: Franz Steiner Verlag, 1989).

Bonney, Richard, 'Absolutism: What's in a Name?', *French History*, 1(1) (1987), pp. 93–117.

Bönsch, Annemarie, 'Adelige Bekleidungsformen zwischen 1500–1700', in *Adel im Wandel. Politik, Kultur, Konfession, 1500–1700* (Vienna: NÖ. Landesregierung, 1990), pp. 169–87.

Bourdieu, Pierre, *Outline of a Theory of Practice* (Cambridge University Press, 1977).

Bourdieu, Pierre, *The Logic of Practice* (Stanford, Calif.: Standford University Press, 1980).

Bourdieu, Pierre, *Distinction: A Social Critique of the Judgement of Taste* (Cambridge, Mass.: Harvard University Press, 1984).

Bourdieu, Pierre, 'Social Space and the Genesis of Groups', *Theory and Society*, 14(6) (November 1985), pp. 723–44.

Bourdieu, Pierre, 'The Forms of Capital', in John G. Richardson (ed.), *Handbook of Theory and Research for the Sociology of Education* (New York: Greenwood Press, 1986).

Bourdieu, Pierre, 'Social Space and Symbolic Power', *Sociological Theory*, 7(1) (1989), pp. 14–26.

Bourdieu, Pierre, *In Other Words: Essays Towards a Reflexive Sociology* (Stanford, Calif.: Stanford University Press, 1990).

Bourdieu, Pierre and Jean-Claude Passeron, *Reproduction in Education, Society and Culture* (London: Sage, 1977).

Bourdieu, Pierre and Loïc J. D. Wacquant, *An Invitation to Reflexive Sociology* (Chicago: University of Chicago, 1992).

Braddick, Michael, *State Formation in Early Modern England, c. 1550–1700* (Cambridge University Press, 2000).

Brady, Thomas A., Jr., Heiko Oberman, James D. Tracy (eds), *Handbook of European History, 1400–1600: Late Middle Ages, Renaissance and Reformation,* Vol I: *Structures and Assertions* (Leiden: E. J. Brill, 1994).

Brady, Thomas A., *The Politics of the Reformation in Germany: Jacob Sturm (1489–1553) of Strasburg* (Atlantic Highlands, NJ: Humanities Press, 1997).

Brauneder, Wilhelm, 'Der soziale und rechtliche Gehalt der österreichischen Polizeiordnungen des 16. Jahrhunderts', *Zeitschrift für historische Forschung*, 3 (1976), pp. 205–19.

Brenner, Robert, *Merchants and Revolution. Commercial Change, Political Conflict, and London's Overseas Traders, 1550–1653* (Princeton, NJ: Princeton University Press, 1993).

Bretholz, Berthold, *Neuere Geschichte Böhmens* (Gotha: F. A. Perthes, 1920).

Brockliss, L. W. B., *French Higher Education in the Seventeenth and Eighteenth Centuries* (Oxford University Press, 1987).

Brückler, Theodor, 'Zum Problem der katholischen Reform in Niederösterreich in der zweiten Hälfte des 16. Jahrhunderts', *Österreich in Geschichte und Literatur*, 21 (1977), pp. 151–62.

Bruckmüller, Ernst, *Sozialgeschichte Österreichs* (Vienna/Munich: Herold Verlag, 1985).

Brunner, Otto, *Land und Herrschaft: Grundfragen der territorialen Verfassungsgeschicte Südostdeutschlands im Mittelalter*, 1st edn. (Baden bei Wien: Rohrer 1939); 3rd edn. (Brünn: Rohrer, 1943).

Brunner, Otto, *Adeliges Landleben und Europäischer Geist. Leben und Werk Wolf Helmhards von Hohberg, 1612–1688* (Salzburg: Otto Müller, 1949).

Brunner, Otto, 'Bürgertum und Adel in Nieder- und Oberösterreich', in *Neue Wege der Verfassung- und Sozialgeschichte*, 2nd edn (Göttingen: Vandenhoeck & Rupprecht, 1968), pp. 24–48.

Brunner, Otto, *Land and Lordship. Structures of Governance in Medieval Austria*, transl. from 4th rev. edn by Howard Kaminsky and James Van Horn Melton (Philadelphia, Pa.: University of Pennsylvania Press, 1992).

Burgess, Glen, 'The Divine Right of Kings Reconsidered', *The English Historical Review*, CCCCXXV (October 1992), pp. 837–61.

Burke, Peter, *The Fortunes of the Courtier: The European Reception of Castigliones Cortegiano* (University Park: Pennsylvania State University Press, 1995).

Burns, James H., *Lordship, Kingship and Empire. The Idea of Monarchy 1400–1525* (Oxford: Clarendon Press, 1992).

Burns, James. H. (ed.), *The Cambridge History of Political Thought, 1450–1700* (Cambridge University Press, 1994).

Bůžek, Václav, 'Nižší šlechta v předbélohorských čecháh (Prameny, metody, stav a perspektivy bádání) [The Lower Nobility of Bohemia at the time before the Battle of the White Mountain (Sources, Methods, State and Perspectives of Research)], *Český časopis historický* 1 (1993), pp. 37–53.

Calhoun, Craig, 'Habitus, Field and Capital: The Question of Historical Specificity', in Craig Calhoun, *et al.* (eds), *Bourdieu: Critical Perspectives* (Chicago: University of Chicago Press, 1993), pp. 61–88.

Carsten, Francis L, *Princes and Parliaments in Germany from the Fifteenth to the Eighteenth Century* (Oxford: Clarendon Press, 1959).

Chesler, Robert D., 'Crowns, Lords, and God: The Establishment of Secular Authority and the Pacification of Lower Austria, 1618–1648' (Ph.D. Dissertation, Princeton University, 1976).

Chlumecký, Petr, *Carl von Zierotin und seine Zeit, 1564–1615* (Brünn: A. Ritsch, 1862).

Chmel, J., 'Die Regimentsräte des Nieder-Österr. Regiments. Von 1529 bis 1657. Die Kammerräte der Niederösterr. Kammer. Von 1539–1606. Aus dem Friedensheimschen Wappen- und Regentenbuche zu Göttweig', *Notizblätter der Akademie*, 1 (1851), pp. 212–24, 228–51, 263–368.

Clark, J. C. D., *Revolution and Rebellion: State and Society in England in the Seventeenth and Eighteenth Centuries* (Cambridge University Press, 1986).

Cohen, G. A., *Karl Marx's Theory of History. A Defence* (Princeton, NJ: Princeton University Press, 1978).

Collins, James B., *The State in Early Modern France* (Cambridge University Press, 1995).

Commenda, Hans, 'Adelige Lustbarkeiten in Linz vom 16. bis zum 18. Jahrhundert', *Historisches Jahrbuch der Stadt Linz* (1958), pp. 141–80.

Conrads, Norbert, *Ritterakademien der Frühen Neuzeit: Bildung als Standesprivileg im 16. und 17. Jahrhundert* (Göttingen: Vandenhoeck & Ruprecht, 1982).

Coreth, Anna, *'Pietas Austriaca'. Österreichische Frömmigkeit im Barock*, 2nd rev. edn. (Vienna: Verlag für Geschichte und Politik, 1982).

Crow, Graham, 'The Use of the Concept of 'Strategy' in Recent Sociological Literature', *Sociology* 23/1 (February 1989), pp. 1–24.

Dennert, Jürgen (ed.), *Beza, Brutus, Hotman: Calvinistische Monarchomachen*, trans. H. Klingelhofer (Cologne: Westdeutscher Verlag, 1968).

Deppermann, Klaus, 'Der preussische Absolutismus und der Adel. Eine Auseinandersetzung mit der marxistischen Absolutismustheorie', *Geschichte und Gesellschaft* 8 (1982), pp. 538–53.

Dewald, Jonathan, *The Formation of a Provincial Nobility. The Magistrates of the Parlement of Rouen, 1499–1610* (Princeton, NJ: Princeton University Press, 1980).
Dewald, Jonathan, *Aristocratic Experience and the Origins of Modern Culture* (Berkeley, Calif.: University of California Press, 1993).
Dewald, Jonathan, *The European Nobility, 1400–1800* (Cambridge University Press, 1996).
Dolinar, France M., Maximilian Liebmann, Helmut Rumpler and Luigi Tavano (eds), *Katholische Reform und Gegenreformation in Innerösterreich, 1564–1628* (Graz: Verlag Styria, 1994).
Dotzauer, Winfried, 'Deutsches Studium und deutsche Studenten an europäischen Hochschulen (Frankreich, Italien) und die nachfolgende Tätitgkeit in Stadt, Kirche und Territorium in Deutschland', in Erich Maschke and Jürgen Sydow (eds), *Stadt und Universität im Mittelalter und in der Frühen Neuzeit* (Sigmaringen: Jan Thorbecke Verlag, 1974).
Dow, Sheila C., and John Hillard (eds), *Keynes, Uncertainty and the Global Economy*, 2 vols (Cheltenham: Edward Elgar, 2002).
Doyle, William, *The Origins of the French Revolution* (Oxford University Press, 1980).
Doyle, William, *The Oxford History of the French Revolution* (Oxford University Press, 1989).
Duchhardt, Heinz, *Protestantisches Kaisertum und Altes Reich* (Wiesbaden: Steiner Verlag, 1977).
Duchhardt, Heinz, 'Absolutismus – Abschied von einem Epochenbegriff?', *Historische Zeitschrift*, 258 (1994), pp. 113–22.
Dülmen, Richard van, *Entstehung des frühneuzeitlichen Europa, 1550–1648*. Frankfurt-am-Main: Fischer Taschenbuch Verlag, 1982.
DuPlessis, Robert. S., *Transitions to Capitalism in Early Modern Europe* (Cambridge University Press, 1997).
Eberhard, Winfried, *Konfessionsbildung und Stände in Böhmen 1478–1530* (Munich/Vienna: Oldenbourg, 1981).
Eberhard, Winfried, *Monarchie und Widerstand. Zur ständischen Oppositionsbildung im Herrschaftssystem Ferdinands I. in Böhmen* (Munich/Vienna: Oldenbourg, 1985).
Eberhard, Winfried, 'Entwicklungsphasen und Probleme der Gegenreformation und katholischen Erneuerung in Böhmen', *Römische Quartalschrift*, 84 (1989), pp. 374–57.
Eberhard, Winfried, 'The Political System and the Intellectual Traditions of the Bohemian Ständestaat from the Thirteenth to the Sixteenth Century', in R. J. W. Evans, *et al.* (eds), *Crown, Church and Estates* (New York: St. Martin's Press, 1991), pp. 23–47.
Eberhard, Winfried, 'Reformation und Counterreformation in East Central Europe', in Thomas A. Brady, Heiko A. Oberman and James D. Tracy (eds), *Handbook of European History, 1400–1600*, Vol. II: *Visions, Programs and Outcomes* (Leiden: Brill, 1995), pp. 551–84.
Eberhard, Winfried, 'Voraussetzungen und strukturelle Grundlagen der Konfessionalisierung in Ostmitteleuropa', in Joachim Bahlcke and Arno Strohmeyer (eds), *Konfessionalisierung in Ostmitteleuropa. Wirkungen des religiösen Wandels im 16. und 17. Jahrhundert in Staat, Gesselschaft und Kultur* (Stuttgart: Steiner Verlag, 1999), pp. 89–103.
Edelmayer, Friedrich, 'Ehre, Geld, Karriere', in Friedrich Edelmayer and Alfred Kohler (eds), *Kaiser Maximilian II. Kultur und Politik im 16. Jahrhundert* (Vienna: Oldenbourg, 1992), pp. 109–42.
Edelmayer, Friedrich, '"*Ignotum est ignoti nulla cupido*". Die Berichte des Elias Preuß über die Studien von Siegmund II. von Dietrichstein', in Kurt Mühlberger and Thomas Maisel (eds), *Aspekte der Bildungs- und Universitätsgeschichte. 16. bis 19. Jahrhundert* (Vienna: Universitäts-Verlag, 1993), pp. 235–55.

Eggendorfer, A., 'Das Viertel ober dem Manhartsberg im Spiegel des Bereitungsbuches von 1590/91' (Ph.D. Dissertation, University of Vienna, 1974).
Ehalt, Hubert, *Ausdrucksformen absolutistischer Herrschaft. Der Wiener Hof im 17. und 18. Jahrhundert* (Vienna: Verlag für Geschichte und Politik, 1980).
Eickels, Christine van, *Schlesien im böhmischen Ständestaat. Voraussetzung und Verlauf der böhmischen Revolution von 1618, in Schlesien* (Cologne: Böhlau Verlag, 1994).
Eisenstadt, S. N. and L. Roniger, 'Patrons–Clients Relations as a Model of Structuring Social Exchange', *Comparative Study of Society and History*, 22 (1980), pp. 51–61.
Eisenstadt, S. N. and L. Roniger, *Patrons, Clients and Friends: Interpersonal Relations and the Structure of Trust in Society* (Cambridge University Press, 1984).
Elias, Norbert, *The Court Society*, trans. Edmund Jephcott (New York: Pantheon Books, 1983).
Elliott, J. H., 'A Europe of Composite Monarchies', *Past & Present*, 137 (November 1992), pp. 48–71.
Ellis, Steven G., *Tutor Frontiers and Noble Power: The Making of the British State* (Oxford: Clarendon Press, 1995).
Elster, Jon, 'The Nature and Scope of Rational-Choice Explanation', in Ernest Le Pore and Brian P. McLaughlin (eds), *Actions and Events: Perspectives on the Philosophy of Donald Davidson* (Oxford: Basil Blackwell, 1985), pp. 311–22.
Elster, Jon (ed.), *Rational Choice* (Oxford: Basil Blackwell, 1986).
Elster, Jon, 'Rationality, economy, and society', in Stephen Turner (ed.), *The Cambridge Companion to Weber*, (Cambridge University Press, 2000), pp. 21–41.
Endres, Rudolf, *Adel in der frühen Neuzeit* (Munich: Oldenbourg Verlag, 1993).
Engelbrecht, Helmut, *Geschichte des österreichischen Bildungswesens. Erziehung und Unterricht auf dem Boden Österreichs*, Vol. 2: *Das 16. und 17. Jahrhundert* (Vienna: Österreichischer Bundesverlag, 1983).
Erdmann, H. G., 'Melchior Khlesl und die niederösterreichischen Stände' (Ph.D. Dissertation, University of Vienna, 1948).
Ertman, Thomas, *Birth of the Leviathan. Building States and Regimes in Medieval and Early Modern Europe* (Cambridge University Press, 1997).
Evans, R. J. W., *Rudolf II* (Oxford, Clarendon Press, 1973).
Evans, R. J. W., 'The Austrian Habsburgs. The Dynasty as a Political Institution', in A. G. Dickens (ed.), *The Courts of Europe. Politics, Patronage and Royalty, 1400–1800* (London: Thames and Hudson, 1977), pp. 121–45.
Evans, R. J. W., *The Making of the Habsburg Monarchy, 1550–1700* (Oxford: Clarendon Press, 1979).
Evans, R. J. W., 'The Court: A Protean Institution and an Elusive Subject', in Ronald G. Asch and Adolf M. Birke (eds), *Princes, Patronage, and the Nobility* (Oxford: Oxford University Press, 1991a) pp. 481–93.
Evans, R. J. W., 'The Habsburg Monarchy and Bohemia, 1526–1848', in Mark Greengrass (ed.), *Conquest and Coalescence. The Shaping of the State in Early Modern Europe* (London: Edward Arnold, 1991b) pp. 134–54.
Evans, R. J. W., 'Die Universität im geistigen Milieu der Habsburgischen Länder, 17.–18. Jahrhundert', in Alexander Patschovsky and Peter Baumgart (eds), *Die Universität in Alteuropa* (Vienna: Univ.-Verlag, 1994), pp. 79–200.
Evans, R. J. W. and T. V. Thomas (eds), *Crown, Church and Estates. Central European Politics in the Sixteenth and Seventeenth Centuries* (New York: St. Martin's Press, 1991).
Fearon, James D., 'Rationalist explanations for war', *International Organization* 49(3) (September 1994), pp. 379–414.

Feigl, Helmut, *Die niederösterreichische Grundherrschaft vom ausgehenden Mittelalter bis zu den theresianisch-josephinischen Reformen* (Vienna: Verein für Landeskunde von NÖ. und Wien, 1964).

Feigl, Helmut. 'Der niederösterreichische Bauernaufstand 1596/97', *Militärhistorische Schriftenreihe*, 22 (1972), pp. 1–40.

Feigl, Helmut. 'Die oberösterreichischen Taidinge als Quellen zur Geschichte der Reformation und Gegenreformation', MOÖLA, 14 (1984), pp. 149–75.

Feigl, Helmut and W. Rosner (eds), *Adel im Wandel. Vorträge und Diskussionen des elften Symposions des niederösterreichischen Instituts für Landeskunde Horn, 2.–5. Juli 1990* (Vienna: NÖ. Institut für Landeskunde, 1991).

Feldbauer, Peter, *Der Herrenstand in Oberösterreich. Ursprünge, Anfänge, Frühformen* (Vienna: Verlag für Geschichte und Politik, 1971).

Feldbauer, Peter, *Herren und Ritter,* vol 1: *Herrschaftsstruktur und Ständebildung* (Vienna: Verlag für Geschichte und Politik, 1973).

Fichtner, Paula Sutter, 'To Rule is Not to Govern: The Diary of Maximilian II', in Solomon Wank, *et. al.* (eds), *The Mirror of History. Essays in Honor of Fritz Fellner* (Santa Barbara, Calif.: ABC-Clio, 1988), pp. 255–64.

Fichtner, Paula Sutter, 'Habsburg State-Building in the Early Modern Era: The Incomplete Sixteenth Century', *Austrian History Yearbook,* xxv (1994), pp. 139–57.

Fichtner, Paula Sutter, *Emperor Maximilian II* (New Haven: Yale University Press, 2001).

Floßman, Ursula, *Landrechte als Verfassung* (Vienna: Springer Verlag, 1976), pp. 20–1.

Franklin, Julian H., 'Sovereignty and the Mixed Constitution: Bodin and his Critics', in J. H. Burns with Mark Goldie (eds), *The Cambridge History of Political Thought, 1450–1700* (Cambridge University Press, 1994), pp. 298–328.

Freyd, B., *The Development of Political Theory* (New York: H. Fertig, 1966).

Friedman, Jeffrey (ed.), *The Rational Choice Controversy: Economic Models of Politics Reconsidered* (New Haven, CT: Yale University Press, 1996).

Gerhard, Dietrich, 'Ständische Vertretungen und Land', in *Festschrift für Hermann Heimpl zum 70. Geburtstag am 19. September 1971* (Göttingen: Max Planck-Institut für Geschichte, 1971), pp. 447–72.

Gierke, Otto von, *Das deutsche Genossenschaftsrecht,* Vol. I: *Rechtsgeschichte der deutschen Genossenschaft,* (Berlin: Weidmann, 1868).

Gierke, Otto von, *Johannes Althusius und die Entwicklung der naturrechtlichen Staatstheorien* (Breslau: Marcus, 1929).

Gindely, Anton, *Geschichte des dreissigjährigen Krieges*, 3 vols., Vol. 1: *Geschichte des böhmischen Aufstandes von 1618* (Prague: Tempsky, 1869).

Gindely, Anton, *History of the Thirty Years' War*, 2 vols, trans. Andrew Ten Brook (Freeport: Books for Libraries Press, 1972).

Given-Wilson, Chris, *The English Nobility in the Later Middle Ages* (London: Routledge, 1987).

Goldstone, Jack A., *Revolution and Rebellion in the Early Modern World* (Berkeley, Calif.: University of California Press, 1991).

Goodare, Julian, *State and Society in Early Modern Scotland* (Oxford University Press, 1999).

Götz, Eva-Maria H., 'Lebenszyklus und soziale Prägung nachgeborener Söhne des österreichischen Adels' (Ph.D. Dissertation, University of Vienna, 1976).

Graf, F., 'Das Viertel unter dem Manhartsberg im Spiegel des Bereitungsbuches von 1590' (Ph.D. Dissertation, University of Vienna, 1972)

Green, Donald P., and Ian Shapiro, *Pathologies of Rational Choice Theory: A Critique of Applications in Political Science* (New Haven, NT: Yale University Press, 1994).

Gutkas, Karl, *Geschichte des Landes Niederösterreich*, 5th edn (St. Pölten: NÖ. Pressehaus, 1973).
Gutmann, Myron P., 'The Origins of the Thirty Years' War', *Journal of Interdisciplinary History*, XVIII (Spring 1988), pp. 751–2.
Hahn, Peter-Michael, 'Absolutistische Polizeigesetzgebung und ländliche Sozialverfassung', *Jahrbuch für die Geschichte Mittel- und Ostdeutschlands*, 29 (1980), pp. 13–29.
Hametner, Angelika, 'Die niederösterreichischen Landtage von 1530–1564' (Ph.D. Dissertation, University of Vienna, 1970).
Hammerstein, Notker, 'Universität und Reformation', *Historische Zeitschrift*, 258 (2) (April 1994), pp. 339–57.
Hampel-Kallbrunner, Gertraud, 'Beiträge zur Geschichte der Kleiderordnungen mit besonderer Berücksichtigung Österreichs' (Ph.D. Dissertation, University of Vienna, 1962).
Hansen, L., 'Das Viertel ober dem Wienerwald im Spiegel des Bereitungsbuches von 1591' (Ph.D. Dissertation, University of Vienna, 1974).
Harding, Robert R., *Anatomy of a Power Elite: The Provincial Governors of Early Modern France* (New Haven, Ct: Yale University Press, 1978).
Harris, Tim, 'From Rage of Party to Age of Oligarchy? Rethinking the Later Stuart and Early Hanoverian Period', *Journal of Modern History*, 64 (December 1992), pp. 700–20.
Hartung, Fritz, *Deutsche Verfassungsgeschichte vom 15. Jahrhundert bis zur Gegenwart*, 5th edn (Stuttgart: Koehler, 1950).
Haselbach, Karl, 'Die volkswirtschaftlichen Verhältnisse Niederösterreichs im XVI. Und XVII. Jahrunder', *Blätter des Vereins für Landeskunde von Niederösterreich V, Neue Folge* (1871), pp. 78–9.
Hassenpflug-Elzholz, Eila, *Böhmen und die böhmischen Stände in der Zeit des beginnenden Zentralismus. Eine Strukturanalyse der böhmischen Adelsnation um die Mitte des 18. Jahrhunderts* (Munich: R. Oldenbourg, 1982).
Hassinger, Herbert, 'Die Landstände der österreichischen Länder. Zusammensetzung, Organisation und Leistung im 16–18. Jahrhunder', *Jahrbuch für Landeskunde von Niederösterreich*, NF, 34 (1964), pp. 989–1035.
Hassinger, Herbert, *Geschichte des Zollwesens, Handels und Verkehrs in den östlichen Alpenländern* (Stuttgart: Steiner Verlag, 1987).
Haupt, Herbert, 'Die Namen und Stammen der Herren von Liechtenstein. Biographische Skizzen', in Evelin Oberhammer (ed.), *Der ganzen Welt ein Lob und Spiegel. Das Fürstenhaus Liechtenstein in der frühen Neuzeit* (Vienna/Munich: Böhlaus, 1983).
Haupt, Herbert, *Fürst Karl I. von Liechtenstein, Obersthofmeister Kaiser Rudolfs II. und Vizekönig von Böhmen. Hofstaat und Sammeltätigkeit.* Textband (Vienna: Böhlaus, 1983).
Hauser, W., 'Das Geschlecht der von Althan' (Ph.D. Dissertation, University of Vienna, 1949).
Havlik, Eva Maria, 'Strukturwandel des ständischen Besitzes im Viertel unter dem Manhartsberg. Untersuchungen zum Herren- und Ritterstand aufgrund der Gütbücher, 1571–1701' (Ph.D. Dissertation, University of Vienna, 1983).
Heckel, Martin, *Deutschland im konfessionallen Zeitalter* (Göttingen: Vandenhoeck & Ruprecht, 1983).
Heiss, Gernot, 'Konfession, Politik und Erziehung: Die Landschaftsschulen in den nieder- und innerösterreichischen Ländern vor dem dreissigjähringen Krieg', *Wiener Beiträge zur Geschichte der Neuzeit*, 5 (1978), pp. 13–63.
Heiss, Gernot, 'Bildungsverhalten des niederösterreichischen Adels im gesellschaftlichen Wandel. Zum Bildungsgang im 16. und 17. Jahrhundert', *Wiener Beiträge zur Geschichte der Neuzeit*, 8 (1981), pp. 138–58.

Heiss, Gernot, 'Integration in die höfische Gesellschaft als Bildungsziel: Zur Kavalierstour des Grafen Johann Sigmund von Hardegg 1646/50', *Jahrbuch für Landeskunde von Niederösterreich*, 48–9 (1982–3), pp. 99–114.

Heiss, Gernot, '*Ihro keiserlichen Mayestät zu Diensten ... unserer ganzen fürstlichen Familie aber zur Glori*. Erziehung und Unterricht des Fürsten von Liechtenstein im Zeitalter des Absolutismus', in Evelin Oberhamer (ed.), *Der ganzen Welt ein Lob und Spiegel. Das Fürstenhaus Liechtenstein in der frühen Neuzeit* (Vienna: Verlag für Geschichte und Politik, 1990), pp. 150–86.

Heiss, Gernot, 'Princes, Jesuits and the Origins of Counter-Reformation in the Habsburg Lands', in R. J. W. Evans and T. V. Thomas (eds), *Crown, Church and Estates* (New York: St. Martin's Press), pp. 92–109.

Heiss, Gernot, 'Standeserziehung und Schulunterricht. Zur Bildung der niederösterreichischen Adeligen in der frühen Neuzeit', in *Adel im Wandel. Politik, Kultur, Konfession, 1500–1700* (NÖ. Landesregierung, 1990), pp. 391–407.

Hellbling, Ernst C., *Österreichische Verfassungs- und Verwaltungsgeschichte* (Vienna: Springer Verlag, 1956).

Henshall, Nicholas, *The Myth of Absolutism: Change and Continuity in Early Modern European Monarchy* (London: Longman, 1992).

Herold, Hannelore, 'Die Hauptprobleme der Landtagshandlungen der Herzogtums Österreich unter der Enns zur Zeit der Regierung Kaiser Maximilians II (1564–76)' (Ph.D. Dissertation, University of Vienna, 1970).

Herzig, Arno, *Der Zwang zum wahren Glauben: Rekatholisierung vom 16. bis zum 18. Jahrhundert* (Göttingen: Vandenhoeck & Ruprecht, 2000).

Hexter, J. H., 'The Education of the Aristocracy in the Renaissance', in J. H. Hexter (ed.), *Reappraisals in History*, 2nd edn (Chicago: University of Chicaco Press, 1979), pp. 45–70.

Hill, Christopher, *The Century of Revolution, 1603–1714* (Edinburgh: T. Nelson, 1961).

Hintze, Otto, 'Weltgeschichtliche Bedingungen der Repräsentivverfassung', *Historische Zeitschrift*, 143 (1931), pp. 1–47.

Hintze, Otto, 'Typology der ständischen Verfassung des Abendlandes', in *Abhandlugen zur allgemeinen Verfassungsgeschichte*, 2nd edn (Göttingen: Vandenhoeck & Ruprecht, 1962).

Hintze, Otto, *Staat und Verfassung*, (ed.) Gerhard Oestreich. (Göttingen: Vandenhoeck & Ruprecht, 1970).

Hirschman, Albert, *The Passions and the Interests. Political Arguments for Capitalism before Its Triumph* (Princeton University Press, 1997).

Hirst, Derek, 'Court, Country and Politics before 1629', in Kevin Sharpe (ed.), *Faction and Parliament* (Oxford University Press, 1978), pp. 105–37.

Hoffman, John, *Sovereignty* (Minn.: University of Minnesota Press, 1998).

Houston R. A., *Literacy in Early Modern Europe* (White Plains, NY: Longman, 1988).

Howard, Michael C. and J. E. King, *A History of Marxian Economics*. Vol. I: *1883–1929* (Princeton, NJ: Princeton University Press, 1989.

Howard, Michael C. and Ramish C. Kumar, 'Classical Liberalism in an Environment of Rational Choice involving Commitment and Security as well as Greed', Sheila C. Dow and John Hillard (eds.), *Keynes, Uncertainty and the Global Economy*, Vol. 2 (Cheltenham: Edward Elgar, 2002), pp. 128–147.

Hoyer, Seyfried, 'Bemerkungen zu Luthers Auffassung über das Widerstandsrecht der Stände gegen den Kaiser (1539)', in Günter Vogler, with Siegfried Hoyer and Adolf Laube (ed.), *Martin Luther. Leben, Werk, Wirkung*, 2nd edn (Berlin: Akademie-Verlag, 1986), pp. 255–63.

Hroch, Miroslav and Josef Petráň, *Das 17. Jahrhundert. Krise der Feudalgesellschaft?*, Trans. Elíska and Ralph Melville (Hamburg: Hoffmann and Campe, 1981).

Hsia, R. Po-Chia, *Social Discipline in the Reformation. Central Europe, 1550–1750* (London: Routledge, 1989).

Hübel, Ignaz, 'Die Ächtungen von Evangelischen und die Konfiskationen protestantischen Besitzes im Jahre 1620 in Nieder- und Oberösterreich', *Jahrbuch der Gesellschaft für Geschichte des Protestantismus in Österreich,* Vol. 58 (1937), pp. 17–62; Vol. 59 (1938), pp. 42–62; Vol. 60 (1939), pp. 105–25.

Hübel, Ignaz, 'Die 1620 in Nieder- und Oberösterreich politisch kompromittierten Protestanten'. *Jahrbuch für die Geschichte des Protestantismus in Österreich,* Vol. 59 (1938), pp. 42–62, Vol. 60 (1939), pp. 105–25.

Huber, Alfons, *Geschichte des Herzogs Rudolf* IV. *von Österreich* (Innsbruck: Wagner, 1865).

Huber, Alfons, 'Studien über die finanziellen Verhältnisse Österreichs unter Ferdinand I', *Mitteilungen des Instituts für Österreichische Geschichtsforschung,* Erg. Bd. 4 (1893), pp. 181–247.

Hueglin, Thomas O., *Early Modern Concepts for a Later Modern World. Althusius on Community and Federalism* (Waterloo: Wilfrid Laurier University Press, 1999).

Hughes, Ann, *The Causes of the English Civil War* (London: Macmillan, 1991).

Hughes, Michael, *Early Modern Germany, 1477–1806* (Philadelphia, Pa: University of Pennsylvania Press, 1992).

Hunt, Lynne, *The Family Romance of the French Revolution* (Berkeley, Calif.: University of California Press, 1992).

Ingrao, Charles, *The Habsburg Monarchy, 1618–1815* (Cambridge University Press, 1994).

Jago, C., 'The Crisis of the Aristocracy in Seventeenth Century Castile', *Past & Present,* 84 (1979), pp. 60–90.

Jedin, Hubert, *Katholische Reformation oder Gegenreformation. Ein Versuch zur Klärung der Begriffe nebst einer Jubiläumsbetrachtung über das Trienter Konzil* (Luzern: Verlag Josef Stocker, 1946).

Jones, Colin, 'Bourgeois Revolution Revivified: 1789 and Social Change', in Colin Lucas (ed.), *Rewriting the French Revolution* (New York: Oxford University Press, 1991).

Kagan, R., *Students and Society in Early Modern Spain* (Baltimore, Md: Johns Hopkins University Press, 1974).

Kavka, František, 'Bohemia', in Bob Scribner, Roy Porter and Mikulas Teich (eds), *The Reformation in National Context* (Cambridge University Press, 1994) pp. 131–54.

Keller, Rudolf, *Der Schlüssel zur Schrift. Die Lehre vom Wort Gottes bei Matthias Flacius Illyricus* (Hannover: Lutherisches Verlagshaus, 1984).

Kenyon, John, 'Revisionism and Post-Revisionism in Early Stuart History', *Journal of Modern History,* 64 (December. 1992), pp. 686–99.

Kettering, Sharon, *Patrons, Brokers, and Clients in Seventeenth-Century France* (New York: Oxford University Press, 1986).

Kettering, Sharon, *French Society, 1589–1715* (Harlow: Longman, 2001).

Kiebel, Ernst, 'Ungeld und Landgericht in Niederösterreich', *Mitteilungen des Instituts für Österreichische Geschichtsforschung,* 52 (1938), p. 32.

Kielmansegg, Erich von, *Beiträge zur Geschichte der niederösterreichischen Statthalterei. Die Landeschefs und Räthe dieser Behörde 1501–1896* (Vienna: Selbstverlag, 1897).

Kiesel, Helmut, *Bei Hof, Bei Höll. Untersuchungen zur literarischen Hofkritik von Sebastian Brant bis Friedrich Schiller* (Tübingen: Niemeyer, 1979a).

Kiesel, Helmut, 'Lang zu hofe, lang zu helle', Literarische Hofkritik der Humanisten', in Peter Uwe Hohendahl and Paul Michael Lützeler (eds), *Legitimationskrisen des Deutschen Adels 1200–1900* (Stuttgart: J. B. Metzlersche Verlagsbuchhandlung, 1979b) pp. 61–82.

Kimmel, M. S., *Absolutism and Its Discontents: State and Society in 17th Century France and England* (New Brunswick, NJ: Transaction Books, 1988).

Kingdon, Robert M., 'Calvinism and Resistance Theory, 1550–1580', in J. H. Burns (ed.) with Mark Goldie, *The Cambridge History of Political Thought, 1450–1700* (Cambridge University Press, 1991), pp. 193–218.

Kiser, Edgar, 'The Formation of State Policy in Western European Absolutism: A Comparison of England and France', *Politics and Society,* 15 (1986–7), pp. 259–96.

Klein, Kurt, 'Die Bevölkerung Österreichs vom Beginn des 16. bis zur Mitte des 18. Jahrhunderts', in Heimhold Helczmanovsky (ed.), *Beiträge zur Bevölkerungs- und Sozialgeschichte Österreichs* (Munich: Oldenbourg 1973), pp. 64–9.

Knall-Brskovsky, Ulrike, 'Ethos und Bildwelt des Adels', *Adel im Wandel. Politik, Kultur, Konfession, 1500–1700,* p. 483.

Knittler, Herbert, *Städte und Märkte,* Vol. 2: *Herrschaftsstruktur und Ständebildung* (Vienna: Verlag für Geschichte und Politik, 1973).

Knittler, Herbert, 'Adelige Grundherrschaft im Übergang', *Wiener Beiträge zur Geschichte der Neuzeit,* 8 (1981), pp. 84–111.

Knittler, Herbert, 'Gewerblicher Eigenbetrieb und frühneuzeitliche Grundherrschaft am Beispiel des Waldviertels', *Mitteilungen des Instituts für Österreichische Geschichtsforschung,* 92 (1984), pp. 115–46.

Knittler, Herbert, *Nutzen, Renten Erträge. Struktur und Entwicklung frühneuzeitlicher Feudaleinkommen in Niederösterreich* (Vienna: Verlag für Geschichte und Politik, 1989).

Koenigsberger, Helmut G., *The Habsburgs and Europe, 1516–1660* (Ithaca, NY: Cornell University Press, 1971).

Koenigsberger, H. G., *Politicians and Virtuosi: Essays in Early Modern History* (London: Hambledon Press, 1986).

Kohler, Alfred, 'Bayern als Vorbild für die innerösterreichische Gegenreformation', in F. M. Dolinar (eds), *Katholische Reform und Gegenreformation in Innerösterreich, 1564–1628* (Graz: Verlag Styria, 1994).

Korkisch, Gustav, 'Karl von Zerotin', in Karl Bosl (ed.), *Lebensbilder zur Geschichte der Böhmischen Länder,* 3 vols (Munich/Vienna: Oldenbourg, 1974), pp. 60–74.

Kühnel, Harry, 'Die adelige Kavalierstour im 17. Jahrhundert', *Jahrbuch für Landeskunde von Niederösterreich,* NF, XXVI(1) (1964), pp. 364–95.

Kühnel, Harry, 'Die österreichische Adelskultur des 16. and 18. Jahrhunderts im Spiegel der Kunst- und Wunderkammern,' *Österreich in Geschichte und Literatur,* 13 (1969), pp. 433–45.

Kufstein, Karl Graf, *Studien zur Familiengeschichte.* Vol. III: *17. Jahrhundert* (Vienna/ Leipzig: Braumüller, 1915).

Lee, Stephen J., *The Thirty Years War* (London: Routledge, 1991).

Leffler, Phyllis K., 'French Historians and the Challenge to Louis XIV's Absolutism', *French Historical Studies,* 14(1) (1985), pp. 1–22.

LeGates, Marlene, 'Princes, Parliaments and Privilege: German Research in European Context', *European Studies Review* 10 (1980), pp. 151–76.

Lehnert, Hans, *Kirchengut und Reformation. Eine kirchenrechtsgeschichtliche Studie.* (Erlangen: Verlag von Palm & Enke, 1935).

Leobenstein, E. M., 'Die adelige Kavalierstour im 17. Jahrhundert' (Ph.D. Dissertation, University of Vienna, 1966).
Le Pore, Ernest and Brian P. McLaughlin (eds), *Actions and Events: Perspectives on the Philosophy of Donald Davidson* (Oxford: Basil Blackwell, 1985).
Lindeck-Pozza, Irmtraud, 'Der Einfluss der staatsrechtlichen und bekenntnismäßigen Anschauungen auf die Auseinandersetzung zwischen Landesfürstentum und Ständen in Österreich während der Gegenreformation', *JbGPÖ*, 20 (1939), pp. 81–96; and *JbGPÖ*, 60 (1940), pp. 15–24.
Livi-Bacci, Massimo, *The Population of Europe. A History*, trans. C. DeNardi Ipsen and C. Ipsen (Oxford/Malden: Basil Blackwell, 2000).
Lloyd, Howell A., 'Constitutionalism', in J. H. Burns (ed.), *The Cambridge History of Political Thought 1450–1700* (Cambridge University Press, 1994), pp. 254–97.
Loesche, Georg, *Geschichte des Protestantismus im vormaligen und im neuen Österreich*, 3rd edn (Leipzig: Julius Klinkhardt, 1930).
Loidl, Franz, *Geschichte des Erzbistums Wien* (Munich: Oldenbourg, 1993).
Loserth, Johann, *Die Reformation und Gegenreformation in den innerösterreichischen Ländern im XVI. Jahrhundert* (Stuttgart: Cotta Verlag, 1898).
Louthan, Howard, *The Quest for Compromise: Peacemakers in Counter-Reformation Vienna* (Cambridge: Cambridge University Press, 1997).
Luschin von Ebengreuth, Arnold, *Geschichte des älteren Gerichtswesens in Österreich ob und unter der Enns* (Weimar: Böhlaus, 1879).
Luschin von Ebengreuth, Arnold, 'Österreicher an italienischen Universitäten zur Zeit der Reception des römischen Rechts', in *Sonderabdruck aus den Blättern für Landeskunde von Niederösterreich*, 1 (Vienna: Friedrich Jasper, 1886).
Lynch, John, *The Hispanic World in Crisis and Change, 1598–1700* (New York: Basil Blackwell, 1992).
Maag, Karin (ed), *The Reformation in Eastern and Central Europe* (Aldershot: Scolar Press, 1997).
Maag, Karin and A. Pettegree, 'The Reformation in Eastern and Central Europe', in Karin Maag (ed), *The Reformation in Eastern and Central Europe* (Aldershot: Scolar Press, 1997), pp. 1–18.
MacHardy, Karin J., 'Der Einfluss von Status, Besitz und Konfession auf das politische Verhalten des niederösterreichischen Ritterstandes 1580–1620', *Spezialforschung und Gesamtgeschichte*, 8 (1981), pp. 56–83.
MacHardy, Karin J., 'Crisis in History: Or Hermes Unbounded', *Storia della Storiografia*, 17 (1990), pp. 5–27.
MacHardy, Karin J., 'The Rise of Absolutism and Noble Rebellion in Early Modern Habsburg Austria, 1570 to 1620', *Comparative Studies in Society and History*, 34 (1992), pp. 407–38.
MacHardy, Karin J., 'Geschichtsschreibung im Brennpunkt postmoderner Kritik', *Österreichische Zeitschrift für Geschichtswissenschaften*, 4(3) (1993), pp. 337–69.
MacHardy, Karin J., 'Social Nobility and Noble Rebellion in Early Modern Habsburg Austria', *History and Society in Central Europe*, 2 (1994), pp. 97–139.
MacHardy, Karin J., 'Cultural Capital, Family Strategies and Noble Identity in Early Modern Habsburg Austria 1579–1620)', *Past & Present*, 163 (May 1999), pp. 36–75.
MacHardy, Karin J. and Gisela Brude-Firnau, *Fact and Fiction: German History and Literature, 1848–1924*, (Tübingen: Francke Verlag, 1990).
Machilek, Franz, 'Böhmen', in Anton Schindling and Walter Ziegler (eds.), *Die Territorien des Reichs im Zeitalter der Reformation und Konfessionalisierung. Land und*

Konfession 1500–1650, Vol. I: *Der Südosten*, (Münster: Aschendorffsche Buchhandlung, 1989), pp. 135–45.

Mączak, Antoni and Wolfgang E. J. Weber (eds), *Der frühmoderne Staat in Ostzentraleuropa* (Augsburg: Wissner, 1995).

Mączak, Antoni (ed.), *Klientelsysteme im Europa der Frühen Neuzeit* (Munich: Oldenbourg, 1988)

Makkai, Laszlo, 'Die Entstehung der gesellschaftlichen Basis des Absolutismus in den Ländern der österreichischen Habsburger', *Études Historiques*, 1 (1960), pp. 630–67.

Malettke, Klaus (ed.), *Ämterkäuflichkeit: Aspekte sozialer Mobilität im europäischen Vergleich* (Berlin: Freie Universität, 1980).

Mamatey, Victor S., 'The Battle of the White Mountain as Myth in Czech History', *East European Quarterly*, xv(3) (September 1981), pp. 335–45.

Mandlmayr, M. C. and K. G. Vocelka, 'Vom Adelsaufgebot zum stehenden Heer. Bemerkungen zum Funktionswandel des Adels im Kriegswesen der frühen Neuzeit', *Wiener Beiträge zur Geschichte der Neuzeit*, 8 (1980), pp. 112–25.

Mann, Michael, *The Sources of Social Power*, Vol. I: *A History of Power from the Beginning to A.D. 1760* (Cambridge University Press, 1986).

Mann, Michael, *States, War and Capitalism* (Oxford: Basil Blackwell, 1992).

Mann, Michael, *The Sources of Social Power*, Vol. II: *The Rise of Classes and Nation-States, 1760–1914* (Cambridge University Press, 1993).

Matschinegg, Ingrid, 'Studium und Alltag in der Fremde. Das Reiserechnungsbuch innerösterreichischer Studenten in Padua (1548–1550)', in I. Matschinegg (ed.), *Von Menschen und ihren Zeichen. Sozialhistorische Untersuchungen zum Spätmittelalter und zur Neuzeit* (Bielefeld: Verlag für Regionalgeschichte, 1990), pp. 90–121.

Maur, Eduard Helmut, 'Der böhmische und mährische Adel vom 16. bis zum 18. Jahrhundert', in Helmut Feigl and W. Rosner (eds), *Adel im Wandel* (Vienna: NÖ. Institut für Landeskunde,1991), pp. 17–37.

McFarlane, Kenneth B., *The Nobility of Later Medieval England* (Oxford: Clarendon Press, 1973).

Mecenseffy, Grete, *Geschichte des Protestantismus in Österreich* (Graz: Böhlaus, 1956).

Melton, James Van Horn, 'Continuities in German Historical Scholarship, 1933–1960', in Hartmut Lehmann and James van Horn Melton (eds), *Path of Continuity: Central European Historiography from the 1930s to the 1950s* (Cambridge University Press, 1994), pp. 1–18.

Mencik, Ferdinand, 'Beiträge zur Geschichte der kaiserlichen Hofämter', *Archiv für österreichische Geschichte*, 87(2) (1988), pp. 447–563.

Mezník, Jaroslav, 'Der böhmische und mährische Adel im 14. und 15. Jahrhundert', *Bohemia*, 28 (1987), pp. 69–91.

Midelfort, H. C. Erik, 'Adeliges Landleben und die Legitimationskrise des deutschen Adels im 16. Jahrhundert', in Georg Schmidt (ed.), *Stände und Gesellschaft im Alten Reich* (Stuttgart: Steiner Verlag, 1989), pp. 251–2.

Mikoletzky, Hans Leo, 'Der Haushalt des kaiserlichen Hofes zu Wien (vornehmlich im 18. Jahrhundert)', *Carinthia* I (146) (1956), pp. 652–74.

Miller, Helen, *Henry VIII and the English Nobility* (Oxford: Basil Blackwell, 1986).

Miller, John (ed.), *Absolutism in Seventeenth-Century Europe* (London: Macmillan Press, 1990).

Mitterauer, Michael, 'Ständegliederung und Ländertypen', in *Herrschaftsstruktur und Ständebildung*, Vol. 3: *Beiträge zur Typology der österreichischen Länder aus ihren mitte-*

lalterlichen Grundlagen (Vienna: Verlag für Geschichte und Politik, 1973), pp. 115–203.

Mitterauer, Michael, 'Zur Frage des Heiratsverhaltens im österreichischen Adel', in H. Fichtenau and E. Zöllner (eds.), *Beiträge zur neueren Geschichte Österreichs* (Vienna: Böhlaus, 1974), pp. 176–94.

Monod, Paul Kléber, *The Power of Kings. Monarchy and Religion in Europe, 1589–1715* (New Haven, Ct: Yale University Press, 1999).

Moraw, Peter, 'The Court of the German King and of the Emperor at the end of the Middle Ages, 1440–1519', in Ronald G. Asch and Adolf M. Birke (eds.), *Princes, Patronage, and the Nobility: The Court at the Beginning of the Modern Age, c. 1450–1650* (New York: Oxford University Press, 1991).

Morford, Mark, *Stoics and Neostoics: Rubens and the Circle of Lipsius* (Princeton, NJ: University of Princeton Press, 1991).

Morgan, Victor, 'Some Types of Patronage, Mainly in Sixteenth- and Seventeenth-Century England', in Antoni Maczak (ed.), *Klientelsysteme im Europa der Frühen Neuzeit* (Munich: Oldenbourg, 1988), pp. 91–126.

Motley, Mark, *Becoming a French Aristocrat: The Education of the Court Nobility 1580–1715* (Princeton, NJ: Princeton University Press, 1990).

Müller, Reiner A., *Universität und Adel. Eine soziokulturelle Studie zur Geschichte der bayerischen Landesuniversität Ingoldstadt: 1472–1648* (Berlin: Duncker & Humblot, 1974).

Müller, Reiner A., 'Aristokratisierung des Studiums? Bemerkungen zur Adelsfrequenz an süddeutschen Universitäten im 17. Jahrhundert', *Geschichte und Gesellschaft* 10 (1984), pp. 31–46.

Murdock, Graeme, *Calvinism on the Frontier, 1600–1660. International Calvinism and the Reformed Church in Hungary and Transylvania* (Oxford: Clarendon Press, 2000).

Nader, Helmut, 'Das Viertel unter dem Wienerwald im Spiegel des Bereitungsbuches 1590/91' (Ph.D. Dissertation, University of Vienna, 1970).

Neuber, Wolfgang, 'Adeliges Landleben in Österreich und die Literatur im 16. und 17. Jahrhundert', in *Adel im Wandel. Politik, Kultur, Konfession, 1500–1700* (Vienna: NÖ. Landesregierung, 1990), pp. 543–53.

Neugebauer, G., 'Die niederösterreichischen Landtage von 1577 bis 1592' (Ph.D. Dissertation, University of Vienna, 1979).

Neuschel, Kristen B., *Word of Honor. Interpreting Noble Culture in Sixteenth Century France*. Ithaca, NY: Cornell University Press, 1989).

Notflatscher, Heinz, 'Tirol, Bixen, Trient', in Anton Schindling and Walter Ziegler (eds), *Die Territorien des Reichs im Zeitalter der Reformation und Konfessionalisierung. Land und Konfession, 1500–1650*, Vol. 1: *Der Südosten* (Münster: Aschendorffsche Verlagsbuchhandlung, 1989), pp. 87–101.

Oberhammer, Evelin, 'Viel ansehnliche Stuck und Güeter. Die Entwicklung des fürstlichen Herrschaftsbesitzes', in Evelin Oberhammer (ed.), *Der ganzen Welt ein Lob und Spiegel. Das Fürstenhaus Liechtenstein in der frühen Neuzeit* (Vienna/Munich: Verlag für Geschichte und Politik, 1990).

Oberleitner, Karl, *Österreichs Finanzen und Kriegswesen unter Ferdinand I. vom Jahre 1522 bis 1564* (Vienna: K. K. Hof und Staatsdruckerei, 1859).

Oberleitner, Karl, *Die evangelischen Stände im Lande ob der Enns unter Maximilian II and Rudolf II. 1564–1597* (Vienna: Adolf Holzhausen, 1862).

Oestreich, Gerhard, *Geist und Gestalt des frühmodernen Staates* (Berlin: Duncker Humblot, 1969).

Oestreich, Gerhard, *Neostoicism and the Early Modern State* (Cambridge University Press, 1982).

Olson, Oliver K., 'Matthias Flacius Illyricus, 1520–1575', in Jill Raitt (ed.), *Shapers of Religious Traditions in Germany, Switzerland, and Poland, 1560–1600* (New Haven, Ct: Yale University Press, 1981), pp. 1–17.

Ortner, Günther, 'Die niederösterreichischen Landtage von 1635–1648' (Ph.D. Dissertation, University of Vienna, 1974).

Ostrow, James M., *Social Sensitivity: A Study of Habit and Experience* (Albany, NY: State University of New York Press, 1990).

Otto, Karl von, 'Die Anfänge der Reformation im Herzogthum Oesterreich (1552–1564)', *Jahrbuch der Gesellschaft für die Geschichte des Protestantismus in Oesterreich* 1 (1880), pp. 11–27.

Pánek, Jaroslav, 'Das Ständewesen und die Gesellschaft in den böhmischen Ländern in der Zeit vor der Schlacht auf dem Weissen Berg (1526–1620)', *Historica*, XXV (1985), pp. 90–129.

Pánek, Jaroslav, 'The Religious Question and the Political System of Bohemia before and after the Battle of the White Mountain', in R. J. W. Evans and T. V. Thomas (eds), *Crown, Church and Estates* (New York: St Martin's Press, 1991), pp. 129–48.

Parker, Geoffrey, *Europe in Crisis 1598–1648* (Ithaca, NY: Cornell University Press, 1980.

Parker, Geoffrey (ed.), *The Thirty Years' War* (London: Routledge, 1984).

Patschovsky, Alexander and Horst Rabe (eds), *Die Universität in Alteuropa* (Vienna: Univ-Verlag, 1994).

Pennington, Kenneth, *The Prince and the Law, 1200–1600, Sovereignty and Rights in the Western Legal Tradition* (Berkeley, Calif.: University of California Press, 1993).

Perroy, Edouard, 'Social Mobility among the French Noblesse in the Later Middle Ages', *Past & Present*, 21 (1962), pp. 25–37.

Pések, Jiři and David Šaman 'Les Étudiants de Bohême dans les Universités et les Académies d'Europe Centrale et Occidentale entre 1596 et 1620', in Dominique Julia, Jacques Revel and Roger Chartier (eds.), *Les Universités Européennes du XVIe au XVIIIe Siècle: Histoire sociale des populations étudiantes*, Vol. 1 (Paris: École des Hautes Études en Sciences Sociales, 1986), pp. 89–112.

Peter, Katalin, 'Hungary', in Bob Scribner, Roy Porter and Nikulas Teich (eds), *The Reformation in National Context* (Cambridge University Press, 1994), pp. 155–67.

Petrin, Silvia and Max Weltin, 'Zum System der Gültbesteuerung in Niederösterreich', *Unsere Heimat*, 43 (1972), pp. 172–81.

Pickl, Otto, 'Die wirtschaftlichen Bestimmungen der Innerösterreichischen Religionspazifikation von 1572 und 1578 und ihre Auswirkungen', in P. Urban and B. Sutter (eds), *Johannes Kepler 1571–1971. Gedenkschrift der Universität Graz* (Graz: Böhlaus, 1975), pp. 562–86.

Polišenský, J. V., *The Thirty Years War*, trans. Robert Evans (London: B. T. Batsford, 1971).

Polišenský, J. V. and Frederic Snider, *War and Society in Europe, 1618–1648*. (Cambridge University Press, 1978).

Press, Volker, *Kriege und Krisen. Deutschland 1600–1715* (Munich: Verlag C. H. Beck, 1991).

Pribram, Alfred F., *Materialien zur Geschichte der Preise und Löhne in Österreich* (Vienna: Ueberreuter, 1938).

Putschögl, Gerhard, *Die landständische Behördenorganisation in Österreich ob der Enns vom Anfang des 16. bis zur Mitte des 18. Jahrhunderts* (Linz: Oberösterreichisches Landesarchiv, 1978).

Rabe, Horst, *Reich und Glaubensspaltung. Deutschland, 1500–1600* (Munich: Verlag C. H. Beck, 1989).

Raeff, Marc, *The Well-Ordered Police State. Social and Institutional Change through Law in the Germanies and Russia, 1600–1800*, New Haven, Conn.: Yale University Press, 1983).

Raitt, Jill (ed.), *Shapers of Religious Traditions in Germany, Switzerland, and Poland, 1560–1600* (New Haven, Conn.: Yale University Press, 1981).

Rebel, Hermann, *Peasant Classes. The Bureaucratization of Property and Family Relations under Early Habsburg Absolutism, 1511–1636* (Princeton, NJ: Princeton University Press, 1983).

Regele, Oskar, *Der österreichische Hofkriegsrat 1556–1898*. Ergänzungsband, 1 (Vienna: Mitteilungen des österreichischen Staatsarchivs, 1949).

Reingrabner, Gustav, 'Die Herren Puchheim auf Horn und Wildberg', *Das Waldviertel*, 14 (1965), pp. 4–47.

Reingrabner, Gustav, 'Der protestantische Adel in Niederösterreich – seine Zuzammensetzung und sein Beitrag zur Reformationsgeschichte des Landes' (Ph.D. Dissertation, University of Vienna, 1973).

Reingrabner, Gustav, *Adel und Reformation. Beiträge zur Geschichte des Protestantischen Adels im Lande unter der Enns während des 16. und 17. Jahrhunderts* (Vienna: Verein für Landeskunde von Niederösterreich, 1976).

Reingrabner, Gustav, 'Zur Geschichte der flacianischen Bewegung im Lande unter der Enns', *Jahrbuch für Landeskunde von Niederösterreich*, 54/55 (1988-9), pp. 265–301.

Reinhard, Wolfgang, 'Zwang zur Konfessionalisierung? Prolegomena zu einer Theorie des konfessionellen Zeitalters', *Zeitschrift für Historische Forschung* 10 (1983), pp. 257–77.

Reinhard, Wolfgang, 'Reformation, Counter-Reformation, and the Early Modern State. A Reassessment', *Catholic Historical Review*, LXXXV(3) (July 1989), pp. 383–404.

Reinhard, Wolfgang, and Heinz Schilling, *Die katholische Konfessionalisierung: Wissenschaftliches Symposium der Gesellschaft zur Herausgabe des Corpus Catholicorum und des Vereins für Reformationsgeschichte 1993* (Gütersloh: Gütersloher Verlagshaus, 1995).

Repgen, Konrad, *Der dreißigjährige Krieg und Westfälischer Frieden. Studien und Quellen* (Paderborn: Ferdinand Schöningh, 1998).

Richardson, R. C., 'Puritanism and the Ecclesiastical Authorities in the Case of the Diocese of Chester', in B. Manning (ed.), *Politics, Religion, and the English Civil War* (New York: Edward Arnold, 1973), pp. 3–37.

Richter, Karl, 'Die böhmischen Länder von 1471–1740', in Karl Bosl (ed.), *Handbuch der Geschichte der böhmischen Länder*, Vol. II: *Die böhmischen Länder von der Hochblüte der Ständeherrschaft bis zum Erwachen eines mondernen Nationalbewusstseins* (Stuttgart: Anton Hiesemann, 1974).

Roberts, C., 'The Earl of Bedford and the Coming of the English Revolution', *Journal of Modern History*, 49 (1977), pp. 600–16.

Rogers, Kelly (ed.), *Self-interest: an anthology of philosophical perspectives* (New York: Routledge, 1997).

Rössler, Hellmuth (ed.), *Deutscher Adel, 1555–1740* (Darmstadt: Wissenschaftliche Buchgesellschaft, 1965).

Russell, Conrad, *Parliament and English Politics, 1621–1629* (Oxford University Press, 1979).

Russell, Conrad, *The Causes of the English Civil War* (Oxford: Clarendon Press, 1990).

Sampson, Edward E., *Celebrating the Other. A Dialogic Account of Human Nature* (Boulder, Col.: Westview Press, 1993).

Sandgruber, Roman, 'Zur Wirtschaftsentwicklung Niederösterreichs im 16. und 17. Jahrhundert', *Unsere Heimat,* XLV (1975), pp. 210–21.

Sandgruber, Roman, *Ökonomie und Politik. Österreichische Wirtschaftsgeschichte vom Mittelalter bis zur Gegenwart* (Vienna: Ueberreuter, 1995).

Schalk, Ellery, 'Ennoblement in France from 1350 to 1660', *Journal of Social History,* 16 (1982), pp. 101–10.

Schalk, Ellery, *From Valor to Pedigree: Ideas of Nobility in the Sixteenth and Seventeenth Centuries* (Princeton, NJ: Princeton University Press, 1986).

Schilling, Heinz, *Konfessionskonflikt und Staatsbildung: Eine Fallstudie über das Verhältnis von religiösem und sozialem Wandel in der Frühneuzeit am Beispiel der Grafschaft Lippe* (Gütersloh: Gerd Mohn, 1981).

Schilling, Heinz, 'The Reformation and the Rise of the Early Modern State', in James D. Tracy (ed.), *Luther and the Modern State in Germany*, Vol. VII, Kirksville, Miss: Sixteenth Century Essays & Studies, 1986), pp. 21–30.

Schilling, Heinz, 'Die Konfessionalisierung im Reich. Religiöser und gesellschaftlicher Wandel in Deutschland zwischen 1555 und 1620', *Historische Zeitschrift,* 246 (1988), pp. 1–45.

Schimka, E. G., 'Die Zusammensetzung des niederösterreichischen Herrenstandes von 1520–1620' (Ph.D. Dissertation, University of Vienna, 1967).

Schindling, Anton, *Humanistische Hochschule und freie Reichsstadt-Gymnasium und Akademie in Strassburg: 1538 bis 1621* (Mainz: von Zabern, 1977).

Schindling, Anton and Walter Ziegler (eds), *Die Territorien des Reichs im Zeitalter der Reformation und Konfessionalisierung. Land und Konfession, 1500–1650,* Vol. 1: *Der Südosten* (Münster: Aschendorffsche Verlagsbuchhandlung, 1989).

Schindling, Anton, 'Delayed Confessionalization. Retarding Factors and Religious Minorities in the Territories of the Holy Roman Empire, 1555–1648', in Charles W. Ingrao (ed.), *State and Society in Early Modern Austria,* (West Lafayette, Ind.: Purdue University Press, 1994), pp. 54–70.

Schlag, Wilhelm, 'Die Jagd', in *Adel im Wandel, Politik, Kultur, Konfession 1500–1700* (Vienna: NÖ. Landesregierung, 1990), pp. 343–56.

Schmidlin, Joseph, *Die kirchlichen Zustände in Deutschland von dem dreißigjährigen Kriege nach den bischöflichen Diözesanberichten and den Heiligen Stuhl,* Vol. I: *Österreich* (Freiburg/Breisgau: Herdersche Verlagsbuchhandlung, 1908).

Schmidt, Georg, *Der dreißigjährige Krieg,* 4th rev. ed. (Munich: Verlag C. H. Beck, 1999), p. 29.

Schmidt, Georg, *Geschichte des alten Reiches: Staat und Nation in der frühen Neuzeit, 1495–1806* (Munich: Verlag C. H. 1999).

Schmidt, Heinrich Richard, *Konfessionalisierung im 16. Jahrhundert* (Munich: Oldenbourg, 1992).

Schmiedt R. F., 'Vorgeschichte, Verlauf und Wirkungen des dreissigjährigen Krieges', in Max Steinmetz (ed.), *Deutschland von 1476 bis 1648: von der frühbürgerlichen Revolution bis zum Westfälischen Frieden* (Berlin: Deutscher Verlag der Wissenschaffen, 1967), pp. 271–383.

Schneider, Andreas, 'Die Mitwirkung der niederösterreichischen Landstände bei der Türkenabwehr unter Ferdinand I und Maximilian II' (Ph.D. Dissertation, University of Vienna, 1939).

Schönfellner, Franz, *Krems zwischen Reformation und Gegenreformation* (Vienna: Verein für Landeskunde von Niederösterreich, 1985).

Schopf, Dagmar, 'Die im Zeitraum von 1620–1740 erfolgten Neuaufnahmen in den niederösterreichischen Herrenstand' (Ph.D. Dissertation, University of Vienna, 1960).

Schulze, Winfried, *Landesdefension und Staatsbildung. Studien zum Kriegswesen des innerösterreichischen Territorialstaates, 1546–1619* (Vienna: Böhlaus, 1973).

Schulze, Winfried, 'Zwingli, lutherisches Widerstandsdenken, monarchomachischer Widerstand', in Peter Blickle *et al.* (eds), *Zwingli und Europa* (Göttingen: Vandenhoeck & Ruprecht, 1985), pp. 199–216.

Schulze, Winfried (ed.), *Ständische Gesellschaft and soziale Mobilität* (Munich: Oldenbourg, 1988).

Schulze, Winfried, 'Estates and the Problem of Resistance in Theory and Practice in the Sixteenth and Seventeenth Centuries', in R. J. W. Evans and T. V. Thomas (eds), *Crown, Church and Estates* (New York: St Martin's Press, 1991), pp. 263–79.

Schulze, Winfried, 'German Historiography from the 1930s to the 1950s', in Hartmut Lehmann and James Van Horn Melton (eds), *Path of Continuity. Central European Historiography from the 1930s to the 1950s* (Cambridge University Press, 1994), pp. 19–47.

Schulze, Hagen, *States, Nations and Nationalism. From the Middle Ages to the Present*, trans. W. E. Yuill (Cambridge, Mass.: Blackwell, 1996).

Schwarz, Henry F., *The Imperial Privy Council in the Seventeenth Century* (Cambridge, Mass.: Harvard University Press, 1943).

Scribner, R. W., 'Police and the Territorial State in Sixteenth-century Würtemberg', in E. I. Kouri and Tom Scott (eds), *Politics and Society in Reformation Europe* (London: Macmillan, 1987), pp. 103–20.

Sharpe, Kevin, *Factions and Parliaments: Essays on Early Stuart History* (Oxford: Clarendon Press, 1978).

Shephard, Robert, 'Court Factions in Early Modern England', *The Journal of Modern History*, 64(4) (December 1992), pp. 721–45.

Skocpol, Theda, *States and Social Revolutions: A Comparative Analysis of France, Russia, and China* (Cambridge, Mass.: Cambridge University Press, 1979.

Šmahel, František, 'L'université de Prague de 1433 à 1622: recrutement géographique, carrières et mobilité sociales de étudiants gradués', in Dominique Julia, Jacques Revel and Roger Chartier (eds), *Les Unuversitiés Européennes du* XVI *au* XVIII *Siècle. Histoire sociale des populations étudiantes.* Tom. I: *Bohême, Espagne, État italiens, Pays germaniques, Pologne, Provinces-Unies* (Paris: École des Hautes Études en Sciences Sociales, 1986), pp. 65–88.

Sommerville, J. P., 'Absolutism and royalism', in J. H. Burns (ed.), *The Cambridge History of Political Thought 1450–1700* (Cambridge University Press, 1994), pp. 356–71.

Spangenberg, Hans, *Vom Lehnstaat zum Ständestaat. Ein Beitrag zur Entstehung der landständischen Verfassung* (Munich/Berlin: Oldenbourg, 1912).

Spielman, John P., *The City and the Crown. Vienna and the Imperial Court, 1600–1740* (West Lafayette, Ind.: Purdue University Press, 1993).

Stangler, Gottfried, 'Die niederösterreichischen Landtage von 1593–1607' (Ph.D. Dissertation, University of Vienna, 1972).

Starkey, David, 'Introduction: Court History in Perspective', in David Starkey, *et al.* (eds),*The English Court from the Wars of the Roses to the Civil War* (New York: Longman, 1987), pp. 1–24.

Stenitzer, Peter, 'Der Adelige als Unternehmer? Das Wirtschaften der gräflichen Familie Harrach in Oberösterreich im 16.und 17. Jahrundert', *Frühneuzeit-Info*, 2 (1991), pp. 41–60.

Stone, Lawrence, *The Crisis of the Aristocracy, 1558–1641,* abridged edn (Oxford: Clarendon Press, 1967).

Stone, Lawrence, *The Causes of the English Revolution, 1529–1642* (New York: Harper & Row, 1972).

Stone, Lawrence, *An Open Elite? England, 1540–1880* (Oxford: Clarendon Press, 1984).

Stradal, Helmut, 'Die Prälaten', in *Herrschaftsstruktur und Ständebildung,* Vol. 3: *Beiträge zur Typologie der österreichischen Länder aus ihren mittelalterlichen Grundlagen* (Vienna: Verlag für Geschichte und Politik, 1973), pp. 53–114.

Sturmberger, Hans, *Georg Ersasmus Tschernembl. Religion Libertät und Widerstand. Ein Beitrag zur Geschichte der Gegenreformation und des Landes ob der Enns* (Graz: Böhlaus, 1953).

Sturmberger, Hans, *Kaiser Ferdinand II und das Problem des Absolutismus* (Munich: Oldenbourg, 1957).

Sturmberger, Hans, *Aufstand in Böhmen. Der Beginn des dreißigjährigen Krieges* (Munich/Vienna: Oldenbourg, 1959a).

Sturmberger, Hans, 'Jakob Andraea und Achaz von Hohenfeld. Eine Diskussion über das Gehorsamproblem zur Zeit der Rudolfinischen Gegenreformation in Österreich', in Helmut J. Mezler-Andelberg (ed.), *Festschrift Karl Eder zum siebzigsten Geburtstag* (Innsbruck: Universitätsverlag Wagner, 1959b), pp. 67–105.

Sturmberger, Hans, *Adam Graf Herberstorff. Herrschaft und Freiheit im konfessionellen Zeitalter* (Vienna: Verlag für Geschichte und Politik, 1976).

Sutherland, N. M., 'The Origins of the Thirty Years' War and the Structure of European Politics', *English Historical Review,* 107 (July 1992), pp. 587–625.

TeBrake, Wayne, Shaping History: *Ordinary People in European Politics, 1500–1700* (Berkeley, Calif.: University of California Press, 1998).

Thompson, I. A. A., 'The Purchase of Nobility in Castile, 1552–1700', *The Journal of European Economic History,* 8 (1979), pp. 313–60.

Tilly, Charles, (ed.), *The Formation of National States in Western Europe* (Princeton, NJ: Princeton University Press, 1975).

Tilly, Charles, *Coercion, Capital and European States, AD 990–1992* (Cambridge, Mass.: Blackwell, 1992).

Tremel, Ferdinand, *Wirtschafts– und Sozialgeschichte Österreichs* (Vienna: Deuticke, 1969).

Urban, Paul and B. Sutter (eds), *Johannes Kepler 1571–1971. Gedenkschrift der Universität Graz* (Graz: Leykan, 1975).

Válka, Josef, 'Moravia and the Crisis of the Estates System in the Lands of the Bohemian Crown', in R. J. W. Evans and T. V. Thomas (eds), *Crown, Church and Estates* (New York: St Martin's Press, 1991), pp. 149–157.

Vansca, Max, 'Die Anfänge des ständischen Beamtentums in Österreich unter der Enns', *Merkblatt des Vereins für Landeskunde von Niederösterreich,* IX (1918), pp. 130–38.

Vavra, Elisabeth, 'Adelige Lustbarkeiten', in *Adel im Wandel. Politik, Kultur, Konfession, 1500–1700* (Vienna: NÖ. Landesregierung, 1990), pp. 429–37.

Vierhaus, Rudolf, *Germany in the Age of Absolutism,* trans. Jonathan B. Knudsen (Cambridge University Press, 1988).

Vocelka, Karl, 'Manier-Groteske-Fest-Triumph. Zur Geistesgeschichte der frühen Neuzeit', *Österreich in Geschichte und Literatur,* 21 (1977), pp. 137–50.

Vocelka, Karl, 'Public Opinion and the Phenomenon of *Sozialdisziplinierung* in the Habsburg Monarchy', in Charles Ingrao (ed.), *State and Society in Early Modern Austria* (Cambridge University Press, 1994), pp. 119–40.

Vocelka, Karl and Lynne Heller, *Die Lebenswelt der Habsburger* (Graz: Styria Verlag, 1997).

Vries, Jan de, *The Economy of Europe in an Age of Crisis, 1600–1750* (Cambridge, Mass.: Harvard University Press, 1976).

Vries, Jan de, 'Population', in Thomas A. Brady Jr., et. al. (eds), *Handbook of European History, 1400–1600: Late Middle Ages, Renaissance and Reformation*, Vol I: *Structures and Assertions* (Leiden: Brill, 1994), pp. 1–49.

Walther, Helmut G., *Imperiales Königtum, Konziliarismus und Volkssouveränität: Studien zu den Grenzen des mittelalterlichen Souveränitätsgedankens* (Munich: Fink, 1976).

Wertitsch, H., 'Die Kipperzeit in den österreichischen Ländern' (Ph.D. Dissertation, University of Graz, 1967).

Weber, Fritz, 'Die Finanz- und Zollpolitik im 16. Jahrhundert und der Rückgang des niederösterr. Weinhandels', *JbLkNÖ*, 31 (1953/54), pp. 133–48.

Wiesflecker, Herman, *Maximilian I. Die Fundamente des habsburgischen Weltreiches* (Vienna: Verlag für Geschichte und Politik, 1991).

Wilson, Peter H, *Absolutism in Central Europe* (London/NewYork: Routledge, 2000).

Winkelbauer, Thomas, *Robot und Steuer. Die Untertanen der Waldviertler Grundherrschaften Gföhl und Altpölla zwischen feudaler Herrschaft und absolutistischem Staat* (Vienna: Verein für Landeskunde von Niederösterreich, 1986).

Winkelbauer, Thomas, 'Sozialdisziplinierung und Konfessionalisierung durch Grundherren in den österreichischen und böhmischen Ländern im 16. Und 17. Jahrhundert', *Zeitschrift für historische Forschung*, 19 (1992a), pp. 317–39.

Winkelbauer, Thomas, 'Wandlungen des mährischen Adels um 1600', in Karlheinz Mack (ed.), *Jan Amos Comenius und die Politik seiner Zeit* (Munich: Verlag für Geschichte und Politik, 1992b), pp. 17–35.

Winkelbauer, Thomas, 'Krise der Aristokratie? Zum Strukturwandel des Adels in den böhmischen und niederösterreichischen Ländern im 16. und 18. Jahrhundert', *Mitteilungen des Instituts für Österreichische Geschichtsforschung*,100 (1992c), pp. 328–53.

Winkelbauer, Thomas (ed.), *Kontakte und Konflikte. Böhmen, Mähren und Österreich: Aspekte eines Jahrtausends gemeinsamer Geschichte* (Horn/ Waidhofen: Waldviertler Heimatbund, 1993).

Winner, Gerhard, 'Die niederösterreichischen Prälaten zwischen Reformation und Josephinismus', *Jahrbuch des Stiftes Klosterneuburg*, NF, 4 (1964), pp. 111–27.

Wolkan, Rudolf, 'Die Ächtung der Horner Konföderierten und die Konfiskation ihrer Güter. Ein Beitrag zur Geschichte der Gegenreformation und des Ständewesens in Niederösterreich' (Ph.D. Dissertation, University of Vienna).

Wood, James B., 'Demographic Pressure and Social Mobility among the Nobility of Early Modern France', *The Sixteenth Century Journal*, VIII(1) (April 1977), pp. 3–16.

Wood, James B., *The Nobility of the Election Bayeux, 1463–1666. Continuity through Change* (Princeton, NJ: Princeton University Press, 1980).

Wurm, Heinrich, *Die Jörger von Tollet* (Graz-Cologne: Böhlaus, 1955).

Zagorin, Perez, *The Court and the Country* (London: Macmillan, 1969).

Zeeden, Ernst Walter, *Die Enstehung der Konfessionen. Grundlagen und Formen der Konfessionsbildung im Zeitalter der Glaubenskämpfe* (Munich: Oldenbourg, 1965).

Ziegler, Walter, 'Nieder- und Oberösterreich,' in Anton Schindling & Walter Ziegler (eds), *Die Territorien des Reichs im Zeitalter der Reformation und Konfessionalisierung. Land und Konfession, 1500–1650*, Vol. 1: *Der Südosten* (Münster: Aschendorffsche Verlagsbuchhandlung, 1989), pp. 87–101.

Zimmermann, Harald, 'Der Protestantismus in Österreich ob und unter der Enns im Spiegel landesherrlicher Erlässe (1520–1610)', *Jahrbuch der Gesellschaft für Geschichte des Protestantismus in Österreich*, 98 (1982), pp. 98– 210.

Žögler, Ivan Ritter von, *Der Hofstaat des Hauses Österreich,* Wiener Staatswissenschaftliche Studien, vol. 14 (Vienna: Deuticke, 1917).

Zorn, Wolfgang, 'Adel und Gelehrtes Beamtentum', in H. Aubin and W. Zorn (eds), *Handbuch der deutschen Wirtschafts- und Sozialgeschichte* (Stuttgart: Union-Verlag, 1971).

Zorn, Wolfgang, 'Deutsche Führungsschichten des 17. und 18. Jahrhunderts. Forschungsergebnisse seit 1945', *Internationales Archiv für Sozialgeschichte der deutschen Literatur,* 6 (1981), pp. 176–97.

Author Index

Subject Index